THE COLLECTED COURSES OF
THE ACADEMY OF EUROPEAN LAW

Series Editors

PROFESSOR NEHA JAIN
PROFESSOR CLAIRE KILPATRICK
PROFESSOR SARAH NOUWEN
PROFESSOR JOANNE SCOTT
European University Institute, Florence

Assistant Editor
JOYCE DAVIES
European University Institute, Florence

VOLUME XXVI/1

Human Rights in Transition

THE COLLECTED COURSES OF THE ACADEMY OF EUROPEAN LAW

The Academy of European Law is housed at the European University Institute in Florence, Italy. The Academy holds annual advanced-level summer courses focusing on topical, cutting-edge issues in Human Rights Law and The Law of the European Union. The courses are taught by highly qualified scholars and practitioners in a highly interactive environment. General courses involve the examination of the field as a whole through a particular thematic, conceptual, or philosophical lens or look at a theme in the context of the overall body of law. Specialized courses bring together a number of speakers exploring a specific theme in depth. Together, they are published as monographs and edited volumes in the Collected Courses of the Academy of European Law series. The Collected Courses series has been published by Oxford University Press since 2000. The series contains publications on both foundational and pressing issues in human rights law and the law of the European Union.

OTHER TITLES IN THE SERIES INCLUDE:

Revisiting the Fundamentals of the Free Movement of Persons in EU Law
Edited by Niamh Nic Shuibhne

Data at the Boundaries of European Law
Edited by Deirdre Curtin and Mariavittoria Catanzariti

Legal Mobilization for Human Rights
Edited by Gráinne de Búrca

The UK's Withdrawal from the EU
A Legal Analysis
Michael Dougan

Justifying Contract in Europe
Political Philosophies of European Contract Law
Martijn W. Hesselink

Contemporary Challenges to EU Legality
Edited by Claire Kilpatrick and Joanne Scott

Reframing Human Rights in a Turbulent Era
Gráinne de Búrca

New Legal Approaches to Studying the Court of Justice
Revisiting Law in Context
Edited by Claire Kilpatrick and Joanne Scott

Human Rights in Transition

Edited by

NEHAL BHUTA

OXFORD
UNIVERSITY PRESS

OXFORD
UNIVERSITY PRESS

Great Clarendon Street, Oxford, OX2 6DP,
United Kingdom

Oxford University Press is a department of the University of Oxford. It furthers the University's objective of excellence in research, scholarship, and education by publishing worldwide. Oxford is a registered trade mark of Oxford University Press in the UK and in certain other countries

Published in the United States of America by Oxford University Press
198 Madison Avenue, New York, NY 10016, United States of America

British Library Cataloguing in Publication Data
Data available

Library of Congress Control Number: 2023951393

ISBN 978–0–19–890192–1

DOI: 10.1093/oso/9780198901921.001.0001

Printed and bound by
CPI Group (UK) Ltd, Croydon, CR0 4YY

Foreword

Nehal Bhuta, editor

This edited volume brings together leading scholars in international law and international human rights to reflect upon the future of human rights, but with a firm grounding in an assessment of the present and the (recent and distant) past. It is neither uniformly critical nor uniformly celebratory of the possible futures for human rights law and politics. It thus eschews the polarized and one-sided approach which can too easily dominate either side of the debate. Instead, drawing on deep learning and a range of engagements with human rights institutions, the authors develop a *prognosis* for the contours of human rights law and politics, and its impacts, in the current conjuncture.

The results are a very rich set of essays which delve deeply into specific topics in human rights law and practice, and work outwards from a rigorous analysis of the past and present, to an argument about *how to think* about the future. No author is overtly concerned with saving or damning the human rights enterprise. Instead, each combines critical analysis with sober reflection to provide a fertile point of view on the present from which *intimations of the future* can be discerned. Despite the fact that at every moment the future rapidly becomes the present and then the past, the concreteness of these essays, and their great care in unpicking the challenges of the present, will remain valuable to anyone interested in understanding, diagnosing, and ultimately acting to help bring about, the possible futures of human rights.

Chapter 1 by Nehal Bhuta ('Recovering Social Rights') begins by rehearsing the range of criticisms levelled at contemporary human rights law, and unpacking the sense of uncertainty and crisis that seems to be gathering around it. As such, it sets up many of the critical arguments which will be the starting point for other chapters. But the first chapter is also an original piece of research into the past of the concept of social right, with a view to grasping how these past concepts might provide a better foundation for a response to the challenge of inequality than contemporary legalism. Along the way, the chapter establishes, for the first time, the connection between certain nineteenth century rights ideas, and the twentieth century idea of the social state.

Chapter 2 by Florian F. Hoffmann ('The Future of Social and Economic Rights') follows directly from the first one, by conducting a sweeping and detailed analysis of the ways in which social and economic rights have evolved as legal concepts and legal practices over the last three decades. The grounding analysis is not only synthetic but contains much original insight and reflection from a seasoned scholar and brings the reader quickly to the frontier of contemporary thinking on this issue. It then looks for intimations of the future of these approaches through a reflection of contemporary innovations at national and international levels.

Chapter 3 by Christina Eckes ('Mutual Trust and the Future of Fundamental Rights Protection in the EU's Compound Legal Order') provides a rigorous and careful analysis of the place of human rights in the EU legal order, with attention to the special complexities posed by the jurisprudence of the Court of Justice of the European Union and its relationship with the European Convention on Human Rights. It starts with a valuable and comprehensive synthesis of the fundamental questions and issues, before developing a concrete normative proposal for what the future of this relationship should be and how it should evolve. This chapter adds an important European dimension to the collection, making developments in the European legal order more accessible, but will also provoke interest among scholars focused on the future of human rights within the European *espace juridique*.

Chapter 4 ('Human Rights Connectivity and the Future of the Treaty Body System') by Sarah H. Cleveland, a notable human rights scholar who has played important institutional roles in the international human rights system, brings a nuanced, practice-informed and institution-based analysis of current challenges to human rights law. The chapter examines developments in the practice and approach of one of the most influential human rights treaty bodies, the Human Rights Committee, and uses this examination as a springboard to propose normative and legal reforms for the future.

Chapter 5 ('Feminist Futures in Human Rights') by Hilary Charlesworth—pioneering scholar of feminist international law and now a sitting judge of the International Court of Justice (ICJ)—examines the interplay between feminist theory and international human rights law through a retrospective on the feminist invocations of human rights and a synoptic reflection of critiques of those engagements. Written in an elegant and magisterial style, the chapter forecasts the future possibilities of feminism in and through human rights law.

In the final chapter ('Climate Pathways and the Future of Human Rights'), Stephen Humphreys addresses one of the most urgent contemporary challenges to human rights law and its future—climate change. It is a theoretically sophisticated and empirically nuanced argument which critically interrogates the idea of the future and places this interrogation into the service of an examination of what human rights law might achieve in the transforming of the current landscape of policy. The chapter is in many ways a grounded theoretical reflection, rich in legal and factual analysis, but ultimately discerning a range of challenges and problems which must be overcome if human rights is to be able to contribute to addressing climate change. This chapter should be read as an important intervention into the *prospects* for human rights as a means of addressing climate change, not limited to a reaction to a specific human rights decision or litigation strategy.

Table of Contents

Table of Cases

UNITED KINGDOM TABLE OF CASES

EUROPEAN COURT OF JUSTICE TABLE OF CASES

INTERNATIONAL TABLE OF CASES

European Committee for Social Cohesion

European Court of Human Rights

Inter-American Court of Human Rights

NATIONAL TABLE OF CASES BY JURISDICTION

Germany

Netherlands

Notes on Contributors

Nehal Bhuta holds the Chair of Public International Law at the University of Edinburgh and is Co-Director of the Edinburgh Centre for International and Global Law. He previously held the Chair of Public International Law at the European University Institute (EUI) in Florence, where he was also Co-Director of the Institute's Academy of European Law. He is a member of the editorial boards of the *European Journal of International Law*, **the** *Journal of International Criminal Justice*, *Constellations*, and he was a founding editor of the interdisciplinary journal *Humanity*. He is also a series editor of the Oxford University Press series in The History and Theory of International Law. Prior to the EUI, he was on the faculty at the New School for Social Research, and at the University of Toronto Faculty of Law. Before entering academia, he worked with Human Rights Watch and the International Center for Transitional Justice.

Hilary Charlesworth is a Melbourne Laureate Professor at Melbourne Law School and a Distinguished Professor at the Australian National University. Her research includes the structure of the international legal system, human rights law and international humanitarian law, international legal theory, particularly feminist approaches to international law, and the art of international law. She is an associate member of the Institut de Droit International and served as Judge ad hoc in the International Court of Justice in the *Whaling in the Antarctic* case (*Australia v. Japan*) (2011–2014) and in the *Arbitral Award of 3 October 1899* case (*Guyana v. Venezuela*). She was elected to the International Court of Justice in November 2021.

Sarah H. Cleveland holds the Louis Henkin Chair in Human and Constitutional Rights at Columbia University Law School. She previously served as Vice Chair and Member of the UN Human Rights Committee (2015–2018), and Member of the Venice Commission of the Council of Europe (2010–2019). From 2009 to 2011, she served as the Counselor on International Law to the Legal Adviser at the US Department of State. A former Rhodes Scholar and law clerk to US Supreme Court Justice Harry Blackmun, she is a graduate of Brown University (AB), Oxford University (MSt) and Yale Law School (JD). Cleveland has taught and written widely on issues of international law, human rights and national security, including *The Restatement and Beyond: The Past, Present, and Future of U.S. Foreign Relations Law* (2020) (co-edited); and Henkin et al., *Human Rights* (2009). In 2023, she was elected to serve as a judge on the International Court of Justice.

Christina Eckes is Professor of European Law at the University of Amsterdam and director of the Amsterdam Centre for European Law and Governance (ACELG). Her current research interests are the separation of powers in 21st century Europe, strategic climate litigation in Europe, and EU external relations. Since 2020, she leads the NORFACE project *Separation of powers for 21st century Europe* (*SepaRope*). Previously, she focused on human rights protection in the EU's multilayered constitutional landscape, EU external relations, and EU counter-terrorism policies. Her publications include *EU Powers under External Pressure – How the EU's External Actions Alter its Internal Structures* (OUP, 2019) and *EU Counter-Terrorist Policies and Fundamental Rights – The Case of Individual Sanctions* (OUP, 2009).

Florian F. Hoffmann is a Professor of Law at the Pontifícia Universidade Católica do Rio de Janeiro (PUC-Rio), Brazil, a co-speaker of the UNHCR Cátedra Sérgio Vieira de Mello in Refugee Studies at PUC-Rio, and an associate researcher at the Human Rights Center of the Law Department (Núcleo de Direitos Humanos). Prior to this he was the Franz Haniel Chair of Public Policy (2010–2016) and the Director of the Willy Brandt School of Public Policy (2012–2015) at the University of Erfurt (Germany). Before this he taught at the London School of Economics and Political Science (2008–2010) and the PUC-Rio (2003–2008). His work has focused on the interface between law and politics, and his main research interests are international law, human rights, and (international) legal theory.

Stephen Humphreys is a Professor of International Law at the London School of Economics. He is a Commissioner on the IUCN World Commission on Environmental Law. He was a Lead Author on the Intergovernmental Panel on Climate Change's 2018 *Special Report on Global Warming of 1.5 °C* and on the 2014 Report of the International Bar Association's Task Force on Climate Justice and Human Rights. Before joining LSE, he was Research Director at the International Council on Human Rights Policy in Geneva, where his research on climate change fed directly into the UN's initial consideration of human rights in the context of climate change. Stephen first began working on climate change in the late 1990s with ENDA Tiers Monde in Dakar, and on human rights as a Senior Officer at the Open Society Institute, in Budapest and later New York. He holds a PhD from Cambridge and a Master's from SOAS, as well as a BA in English Literature from Trinity College Dublin. He is the author of *Human Rights and Climate Change* (CUP, 2009) and *Theatre of the Rule of Law* (CUP, 2010).

1

Recovering Social Rights

*Nehal Bhuta**

But there is an alternative way of thinking about the relations between past and present. This stems from the fact that, in the case of some of our most important normative concepts, the way in which they used to be understood differs greatly from our current way of thinking about them . . . We need to explore the possibility that some of the ways in which we used to think about our moral and political concepts may be more fruitful, and more helpful to our current purposes, than the way we are currently thinking about them.[1]

1. Introduction

This chapter responds to a fundamental challenge made against social rights: that they are an inadequate legal and political language to address widening income and wealth inequality. In the opening sections of this chapter, I set out the terms of this challenge and situate it within wider critiques of the law and practice of human rights. These critiques, which have intensified and accelerated over the last fifteen years, collocate several different streams of remonstration against human rights: that they are beholden to a neo-liberal political economy; that they are excessively legalist and thus inadequate for deeper, transformative, social change; and that, in any event, social rights in particular were never more than *emanations* of changing socio-economic dynamics driven by other social forces—and therefore inapt to drive such changes in their own right. Growing economic inequality within states, even as the juridification and constitutionalization of social rights has flourished since 1990, appears to provide a summative example of the validity of these criticisms.

* I thank the following for their feedback on a first draft of this chapter: Dan Edelstein, Benjamin Straumann, Anthony Pagden, Gráinne de Búrca, Philip Alston, Samuel Moyn, Doreen Lustig, Julian Sempill, Colm O'Cinneide, Joseph Weiler, Benedict Kingsbury, the Florence Reading Group, Jan Klabbers, and Philipp Dann. Thanks also to Francesca Iurlaro for stellar editorial work.

[1] Quentin Skinner, in Bialy, 'Freedom, Silent Power and the Role of an Historian in the Digital Age – Interview with Quentin Skinner', 48/7 *History of European Ideas* (2022) 871.

Nehal Bhuta, *Recovering Social Rights*. In: *Human Rights in Transition*. First Edition. Edited by Nehal Bhuta, Oxford University Press. © Nehal Bhuta 2024. DOI: 10.1093/oso/9780198901921.003.0001

I argue that these claims reflect a great deal of truth about the present of social rights, but do not accurately characterize their past. In the latter sections of the chapter, I recover a different register of social rights thinking that has faded from our collective memories—a register which infused the discussions of social rights in the drafting of the Universal Declaration of Human Rights. I call these 'natural social rights' or 'collective natural rights', and trace their lineages through English Radical thought, French Physiocratic thought, Jacobin and Neo-Jacobin thinking, to early twentieth century state theories and constitutional social rights. The essential insight gained from recovering these repertoires of social rights is the surprising extent to which social rights ideas laid the conceptual foundations for the social state. Rather than understanding social rights as nothing more than the weak offspring of a social welfare state brought into being by class conflict, we can see them as a historically powerful political-ethical discourse that helped *articulate and motivate* the concept of the state as a public power that must *organize* the economy in order to ensure a 'society of equals'.[2] At the heart of nineteenth century ideas of social right was the demand for the creation of equal social citizens and the construction of social democracy, through the creation of a social democratic state. Recovering these ideas helps us better understand the ways that social rights *could be* a germane response to the challenge of inequality in the present.

2. The Challenge of Inequality

Contemporary human rights law, and the specific modalities and repertoires of political thought and action which have formed around it over the last 40 years,[3] have never been free of critics or controversy. From early repudiations of the claim to universality which have dogged human rights ideas since their twentieth century formulation in international declarations and treaties,[4] to the consistent complaint that such legal norms are mere ciphers for power politics and hegemonic (liberal, neo-liberal, imperial) agendas, criticism readily paints those who embrace the demands of international human rights law as either useful innocents in the service of more powerful economic, social and political forces, or marginal professionalized cadres of specialists whose stirring legal formulae cannot challenge the deep structures of power, privilege, and inequality that striate global society. At

[2] See the rich history of the concept of political and economic equality recounted in P. Rosanvallon, *The Society of Equals* (2013, trans. Goldhammer).

[3] De Búrca's 2021 book provides a sympathetic and accurate snapshot of the modes of political action and languages of legal politics which are presently articulated to international human rights legal norms (G. de Búrca, *Reframing Human Rights in a Turbulent Era* (2021). Sally Merry's *Human Rights and Gender Violence* (2008) remains an essential study for understanding the complex world-making and knowledge-making entailed in the practices of human rights as a global legal politics.

[4] The well-known 'cultural relativism' controversy initiated by the 1947 statement of the American Anthropological Association.

best, palliative and modestly ameliorative,[5] at worst, distracting from and counter-productive to real social change,[6] the bill of particulars against human rights has waxed and waned over several decades, but seems to have gathered momentum in the years since the 2008 global financial crisis—the latter often indexed as the apogee and nadir of post-Cold War liberal politics and neo-liberal economics.[7] Novelist and critic Pankaj Mishra rehearsed familiar claims of human rights as a naïve *and* cynical 'anti-politics', irremediably hitched to a neo-liberal political economy, when he wrote that, 'framed as indivisible from the spread of free markets and other good things necessary to the design of Pax Americana … It also helped that human rights at the end of history offered a seductive "anti-politics", which … misled a generation of young activists into believing that … they should forsake political organisation for single-issue, non-governmental groups unsullied by compromise.'[8] He looked forward to the prospect that 'the days when young people transposed their political idealism into the vernacular of liberal internationalism seem to be behind us'.

The association of the flourishing of human rights law—its 'breakthrough'[9] as a lingua franca of global political contestation and vernacular for ideas for social and political change—with the 1980s and 1990s ascendancy of liberal internationalism and neo-liberal economics led many to grasp contemporary human rights law and politics as inextricably bound up with both: either as direct instruments of a 'morality of markets'[10] or as fellow travellers and all-too-willing companions to fateful projects of Western democracy promotion, trade and capital liberalization, constraint of non-Western developmental states' economic policies, and the galloping concentration of wealth and income since 1989.[11] Indeed, the post-Cold War rise of a concept of Civil Society as the locus of associational issue-based mobilization, and as a vector of an effervescent critical political morality of state action in the name of universal values and international expertise,[12] provided an influential model—and funding source—for the proliferation of non-government

[5] Most trenchantly argued by S. Moyn, *Not Enough: Human Rights in an Unequal World* (2018).

[6] Koskenniemi, 'Rocking the Human Rights Boat: Reflections by a Fellow Passenger', in N. Bhuta et al. (eds), *The Struggle for Human Rights: Essays in Honour of Philip Alston* (2021) 51.

[7] A. J. Bacevich, *The Age of Illusion: How America Squandered its Cold War Victory* (2020); A. Tooze, *Crashed: How a Decade of Financial Crisis Changed the World* (2018).

[8] Mishra, 'The Mask It Wears: The Wrong Human Rights', 40/12 *London Review of Books* (2018), citing in part T. Judt, *Ill Fares the Land* (2010), quotation marks omitted.

[9] J. Eckel and S. Moyn (eds), *The Breakthrough: Human Rights in the 1970s* (2014), for a collection of valuable essays. For one of the earlier histories of the place of human rights law and argumentation in international politics between 1945 and 1960, see A. W. B. Simpson, *Human Rights and the End of Empire: Britain and the Genesis of the European Convention* (2001).

[10] J. Whyte, *The Morals of the Market: Human Rights and the Rise of Neoliberalism* (2019).

[11] See for example Marks, 'Human Rights and Root Causes', 74/1 *Modern Law Review* (2011) 57.

[12] The theoretical origins of this reinvention of the concept of civil society are unclear but one locus classicus—influenced both by critical theory and engagement with Communist bloc dissident movements, was A. Arato and J. Cohen, *Civil Society and Political Theory* (2nd ed., 1994) 29–82.

organizations in human rights, development and beyond.[13] Human rights law and politics, and its ever-expanding 'mainstreaming' in international organizations and development agencies,[14] seemed bound up with the 20 years in which 'liberalism fell in love with itself and lost its way ... [and in which] ... The expectation that others should adopt Western-style liberal democratic institutions and norms seemed as natural as the sun.'[15] For those sceptical of this arc of progress, and critical of its consequences (and the professional cadre of human rights lawyers and human rights activists were very rarely among such critics),[16] the response was discouraging: 'To reject globalized neoliberalism was to be labelled either a socialist or an economic Neanderthal.'[17]

[13] Carothers, with characteristically acerbic insight, observed in 1999 that 'at the core of much of the current enthusiasm about civil society is a fascination with nongovernmental organizations, especially advocacy groups devoted to public interest causes – the environment, human rights, women's issues, election monitoring, anticorruption, and other "good things" ... In many countries, however, NGOs are outweighed by more traditional parts of civil society. Religious organizations, labour unions, and other groups often have a genuine base in the population and secure domestic sources of funding, features that advocacy groups usually lack, especially the scores of new NGOs in democratizing countries. The burgeoning NGO sectors in such countries are often dominated by elite-run groups that have only tenuous ties to the citizens on whose behalf they claim to act, and they depend on international funders for budgets they cannot nourish from domestic sources.' T. Carothers, 'Civil Society', 117 *Foreign Policy* (1999–2000) 18–24. Among many critical anthropological inquiries into the nature of such 'civil society' politics in the developing world, see: H. Englund, *Prisoners of Freedom: Human Rights and the African Poor* (2006) and J. Elyachar, *Markets of Dispossession: NGOs, Economic Development and the State in Cairo* (2005). On the role of US-based foundations in exporting the NGO model of 'public interest advocacy' in relation to various kinds of causes, see B. Garth and Y. Dezalay, *The Internationalization of Palace Wars: Lawyers, Economists, and the Contest to Transform Latin American States* (2002).

[14] Koskenniemi, 'Human Rights Mainstreaming as a Strategy for Institutional Power', 1 *Humanity Journal* (2010) 47–58.

[15] S. Holmes and I. Krastev, *The Light that Failed: A Reckoning* (2019) 204.

[16] See Alston's (himself one of the rare exceptions) wider reflection on international lawyers as handmaidens of globalization: Alston, 'The Myopia of the Handmaidens: International Lawyers and Globalization', 3 *European Journal of International Law* (1997) 435. Perhaps the most notable concentration of critics of *one* face of liberal internationalism and economic liberalization in the form of austerity and structural adjustment, was found among development economists who infused a language of economic and social rights into their advocacy for a global economic policy which rejected capital account liberalization, structural adjustment, and public sector retrenchment, in favour of an approach emphasizing the realization of human capabilities and fulfilment of human needs as the true benchmark of economic development: Amartya Sen, Mahbub Ul Haq, Jean Dreze, Sakiko Fukuda Parr, Frances Stewart. This circle influentially pioneered the United Nations Development Programme's annual human development reports, which in the 1990s became a focal point for critique of the so-called 'Washington Consensus' in economic development policy. Alston campaigned persistently to have key Bretton Woods Institutions such as the World Bank adopt human rights law as a legal and policy framework for their programming and decision making.

During the high tide of the 'NGOization' of human rights law and practice in the 1990s, two entrants notably focused on the advocacy of economic and social rights, leading them into more or less direct confrontation with the consequences of various kinds of economic liberalization: The Centre for Economic and Social Rights (founded 1995) and the Centre on Housing Rights and Evictions (founded 1991 and ceased operations, 2014). In states where economic and social rights had been constitutionalized as part of a regime transition, domestic NGOs also began using economic and social rights as means of contesting the consequences of specific government policies (some, but not all, deriving from austerity plans): most visibly, South Africa in the 1990s, but also Colombia, India, and Brazil.

[17] Bacevich (n. 7) 198.

The 2008 global financial crisis, and the waves of recession and austerity that swept the advanced capitalist world for almost a decade, punctuated this optimistic vision of globalized economic and political progress. It also exposed the extent to which it had never been a shared experience of progress, but rested instead on a thirty-year unwinding of an earlier political and economic settlement in the industrialized world.[18] The 'golden age' of capitalist expansion, the so-called *trente glorieuses* of 1945 to 1975, had multiple sources,[19] but rested on four pillars: 'strong trade unions, mass education, high taxes, and large government transfers'.[20] The post-war varieties of social democracy in the industrialized world were several,[21] and all succeeded in diminishing intra-societal wealth and income inequality and increasing social mobility to an unprecedented degree[22] (even as advanced capitalist states remained 'highly hierarchical ... in economic and monetary terms').[23] But the unravelling of this political and economic settlement from the 1970s, accelerating rapidly during the 1990s, is now understood as closely associated with the return to late nineteenth century levels of wealth and income inequality, stagnating or declining real incomes for all but the top decile of income earners, and declining measures of social mobility.[24] Summarizing the American context, economic historian Adam Tooze concludes that since 1976, the average American 'shared only to a small degree in national economic growth as measured by GDP ... Almost all the benefits of growth were being monopolized by the highest paid and those wealthy enough to own significant portfolios of financial assets. The financial crisis revealed how in extremis national economic policy was subordinated to the needs of a cluster of giant transnational banks ... Between 1977 and 2014 the share of national income going to the top 1 percent before taxes and benefits had risen by 88.8 percent ... Nor did the tax and welfare state prevent the share of the bottom 50% from declining from 25.6% to 19.4%.'[25]

[18] A. Glyn, *Capitalism Unleashed: Finance, Globalization and Welfare* (2007).

[19] S. A. Marglin and J. B. Schor (eds), *The Golden Age of Capitalism: Reinterpreting the Postwar Experience* (1992); T. Piketty, *Capital and Ideology* (2020) chapters 10 and 11.

[20] B. Milanovic, *Capitalism, Alone: The Future of the System That Rules the World* (2019) 42; broadly consistent with this is Piketty (n. 19) chapters 11 and 13.

[21] See Piketty (n. 19) chapter 11; E. N. Wolff, *A Century of Wealth in America* (2017); T. Piketty, *Capital in the Twenty First Century* (2014).

[22] See Milanovic (n. 20) 1–34; R. D. Putnam, *The Upswing: How America Came Together A Century Ago and How We Can Do It Again* (2021).

[23] Piketty (n. 19) 493.

[24] See two alarmed reports from the OECD: OECD, *A Broken Social Elevator? How to Promote Social Mobility*, 15 June 2018 and OECD, *Under Pressure: The Squeezed Middle Class*, 1 May 2019.

[25] Tooze (n. 7) 458.

The declining power of organized labour,[26] increased financialization[27] (in the sense of the growing importance of financial markets as a source of profits in the economy and in driving economic policy-making)[28] and transformations of corporate governance models through strident demands for shareholder value and lean production,[29] have all contributed to the widespread sense that rising inequality is a 'core concern across the industrialized world'[30] and is undermining social cohesion, trust in governance, and perceptions of declining opportunity.[31] The normative and social consequences of rising inequality are 'trickling up' and reshaping all dimensions of 'normal politics'.[32] Social segregation is rigidifying such that the rich are 'unlikely to sit in the same doctors' waiting rooms, have their children attend the same schools, or travel in the same train compartments as the bottom quintile of society. The current levels of inequality in many countries mean that the rich and poor live in different worlds.'[33] Entrenched and deepening *material* inequality consolidates and raises the salience of *status* inequality: that sense of societally-conferred value and esteem which pervades social life, and which deeply shapes 'people's expectations for themselves and others and their

[26] Stansbury and Summers, 'The Declining Worker Power Hypothesis: An Explanation of the Recent Evolution of the American Economy', *Brookings Papers on Economic Activity* (Spring 2020), 1–96, https://www.brookings.edu/wp-content/uploads/2020/12/StansburySummers-Final-web.pdf (last visited 22 February 2023). The paper observes that 'Since the early 1980s in the United States, the shares of income going to labor have fallen, measures of corporate valuations like Tobin's q have risen, average profitability has risen even as interest rates have declined, and measured markups have risen.' (at 1). The authors argue that this fall in the labour share of income (ergo, income not derived from capital ownership) is best explained by a decline in worker power in the sense of the ability of workers to extract a share of profits generated by companies operating in imperfectly competitive markets (which the authors term 'labour rents') through unionization or the threat of unionization (at 3). They conclude that the evidence in their paper 'suggests that the American economy has become more ruthless, as declining unionization, increasingly demanding and empowered shareholders, decreasing real minimum wages, reduced worker protections, and the increases in outsourcing domestically and abroad have disempowered workers ...' (at 63).

[27] B. Nolan et al., *Inequality and Prosperity in the Industrialized World: A Growing Challenge*, Citi GPS and Oxford Martin School Report, September 2017 https://www.oxfordmartin.ox.ac.uk/downloads/Citi_GPS_Inequality.pdf (last visited 13 March 2023), 18, 93; Huber, Petrova, and Stephens, 'Financialization, Labor Market Institutions and Inequality', 29/2 *Review of International Political Economy* (2020) 425; Greenwald, Lettau, and Ludvigson, 'How the Wealth was Won: Factors Shares as Market Fundamentals', *NBER Working Paper* 25769 (2019) https://www.nber.org/system/files/working_papers/w25769/w25769.pdf (last visited 22 February 2023).

[28] G. Krippner, *Capitalizing on Crisis: The Political Origins of the Rise of Finance* (2012) 27; G. F. Davis, *Managed by the Market: How Finance Re-Shaped America* (2009); G. Dumenil and D. Levy, *Capital Resurgent: Roots of the Neoliberal Revolution* (2004).

[29] See the compelling story told by N. Lemann, *Transaction Man: The Rise of The Deal and the Decline of the American Dream* (2019). See also Benkler, 'A Political Economy of Oligarchy: Winner-Take-all Ideology, Superstar Norms and the Rise of the 1%', Working Paper (2017). http://www.benkler.org/Political%20economy%20of%20oligarchy%2001.pdf (last visited 22 February 2023).

[30] Nolan et al. (n. 27) 122.

[31] Ibid. 21.

[32] J. Hopkins, *Anti-System Politics: The Crisis of Market Liberalism in Rich Democracies* (2020), chapters 1 and 2; W. Davies, *This is Not Normal: The Collapse of Liberal Britain* (2020) 216–230.

[33] Satz and White, 'What is Wrong with Inequality?' *Institute for Fiscal Studies* (2022) 1–29 https://ifs.org.uk/inequality/wp-content/uploads/2021/09/What-is-wrong-with-inequality.pdf (last visited 22 February 2023).

consequent actions in social contexts'.[34] Unsurprisingly, for those experiencing stagnant or steadily diminishing incomes and reduced expectations of acquiring even modest amounts of wealth, the sense of having 'fallen backwards' or 'slipped downwards' in status relative to previous comparable generations (that of their parents or grandparents) creates bewilderment, resentment, anxiety, and anger:

> For those at the bottom of the pile, none of this was news. Opinion polls, especially those commissioned by the right wing, had for a long time been recording the profound resentment among the American population at the way that both the economy and the political system seemed to be engineered to their disadvantage ... But if one stepped back from the poisonous language and crude logic, the assumptions that inequality was 'systemic' and that 'the system' was rigged against ordinary working class Americans were not paranoid but simply realistic.... In many ways, the liberal centrists were the last to know.[35]

Inequality not only creates conflict between those at the top and those at the bottom; it also 'creates conflict at every step of the societal ladder' by elongating the social distance between the poles of the hierarchy and increasing status competition for all.[36] Status anxiety—the sense that one's *previously recognized* social value and esteem is being driven down before one's eyes due to de-industrialization, capital flight, economic austerity, stagnant or declining life possibilities[37]—has been both theoretically[38] and empirically[39] linked with support for radical 'anti-system' political movements. Cohen summarizes these connections when she writes:

> The sources of social honour and social security ... [in society] ... the forms of life, associational connections, organizations, modes of cooperation, and social capital that emerge around labour, occupation, neighbourhood and region – are as important to social identity and self-respect as material income. Indeed, anxiety

[34] Ridgeway, 'Why Status Matters for Inequality', 79 *American Sociological Review* (2014) 1–16, at 3.

[35] Tooze (n. 7) 459. In an interview in 2020, former US President Barack Obama reflected on the strength of the liberal centrist consensus through the 1990s and 2000s: 'And what's a fair criticism is the fact that through Clinton and even through how I thought about these issues when I first came into office, I think there was a residual willingness to accept the political constraints we'd inherited from the post-Reagan era – that you had to be careful about being too bold on some of these issues. And probably there was an embrace of market solutions to a whole host of problems that wasn't entirely justified.' Chait, 'In Conversation with Barack Obama', *New York Magazine*, 9 December 2020.

[36] Bang Petersen, Osmundsen, and Bor, 'Beyond Populism: The Psychology of Status-Seeking and Extreme Political Discontent', in J. Forgas, B. Crano, and K. Fiedler (eds), *The Psychology of Populism: The Tribal Challenge to Liberal Democracy* (2021) 62.

[37] See for example, F. Stockman, *American Made: What Happens to People When Work Disappears* (2021).

[38] Gidron and Hall, 'Populism as a Problem of Social Integration', 53 *Comparative Political Studies* (2020) 1027.

[39] Antonucci et al., 'The Malaise of the Squeezed Middle: Challenging the Narrative of The "Left Behind" Brexiter', 21 *Competition and Change* (2017) 211.

about declining social status in economic society and disrespected sociocultural forms of life in civil society that once gathered social honour is intimately related to doubts about society-wide social solidarity and about the representativeness, receptivity, and responsiveness of political (and other) elites to the needs and concerns of ordinary people.[40]

3. Human Rights, Legalism, and the Problem of Social Justice

When Philip Alston lamented in 2015 that extreme inequality and its consequences 'should ... be seen as a cause for shame' on the part of the international human rights movement, and that 'questions of resources and redistribution can no longer be ignored as part of human rights advocacy',[41] he was sounding a canary-like alarm that the atmosphere in which the close filiation between human rights advocacy and various strands of liberal centrism, liberal progressivism, and liberal internationalism had thrived, was deoxygenating rapidly. The 'class cluelessness' of much human rights talk had long been a source of castigation by Marxist and Socialist writers.[42] South African anti-apartheid activist and former Communist Party member Mark Heywood reminisces that 'Movements [in the 1970s] that were mobilizing mass anger against racism, notably the Anti-Apartheid movement in England, did not particularly do so on the basis of human rights ... We stigmatized campaigns for human rights as liberal "reformism" ... Call for reform was also seen as legitimizing the capitalist state and thus postponing its final crisis.'[43] Heywood notes with chagrin, however, that the hoped-for final crisis of capitalism and liberal democracy did not take place, and the predicted agents of systemic change did not deliver either:

> Strikes and uprisings were regarded as the only legitimate forms of struggle along the pathway to 'revolutionary consciousness.' In this schema Marxists saw systems of law as intrinsically biased against the poor and working class and part of the superstructure of 'capital' – not an effective instrument in the quest for equality ... I adopted these beliefs and, whilst in England, spent my student and post student years supporting great but ultimately unsuccessful struggles such as those of the British mine workers, car workers and printers.[44]

[40] Cohen, 'Populism and the Politics of Resentment', 1 *Jus Cogens* (2019) 5, at 9.

[41] Alston, 'Extreme Inequality as the Antithesis of Human Rights', *Open Democracy*, 27 October 2015, https://www.opendemocracy.net/en/openglobalrights-openpage/extreme-inequality-as-antithesis-of-human-rights/ (last visited 2 March 2023).

[42] Fudge and Glasbeek, 'The Politics of Rights: A Politics of Little Class', 1/1 *Social and Legal Studies* (1992) 45. See Kolakowski, 'Marxism and Human Rights', 112/4 *Daedalus* (1983) 81, for a reflection which rehearses the longstanding Marxist critiques of rights.

[43] Heywood, 'South Africa's Journey from Socialism to Human Rights', 11/2 *Journal of Human Rights Practice* (2019) 305.

[44] Ibid. 308.

Human rights ideas carried with them no such sociological, economic- or political-theoretical baggage. Precisely because of their apparent compatibility with a range of economic and political systems from the vantage-point of a late-Cold War battle of ideological attrition, among their most visible advocates and proponents from the 1970s were a range of social movements in the West and East that deliberately sought to bend the limits of institutionalized politics in both the 'empire of liberty' and the 'empire of justice',[45] and their many proxy regimes. In a story which has now been told in many variations,[46] human rights law and activism became a compelling oppositional language precisely by placing itself *beyond* ideological and system-theoretic accounts of law, politics, and economics[47]—including, inevitably, a language of class that was strongly tethered to repertoires of scientific socialism, critiques of bourgeois society, and claims about the likely course of historical change.[48] Human rights were, in Samuel Moyn's evocative phrase, a last utopia because they articulated ideals which seemed compatible with the desiderata of most utopian end-states, but could frame normative responses to concrete political injustices in the present: torture, arbitrary imprisonment, political repression and authoritarianism, and even severe deprivation. Any number of nascent social movements defined by opposition to racial, sexual, religious, and political oppression, could make common cause with human rights ideas and rhetorics,[49] gaining an Esperanto of denunciation without much commitment to common social, political, and economic diagnoses of 'root causes' or necessary tactics and methods. The politics and practices that assembled under the banner of human rights from the 1970s onwards were always diverse—some explicitly neo-liberal,[50] and others

[45] To borrow Odd Arne Westad's stylization of the ideological claims of West and East in his Global Cold War: Third World Interventions and The Making of Our Time (2005).

[46] S. Hopgood, *Keepers of the Flame: Understanding Amnesty International* (2006); S. Moyn, *The Last Utopia: Human Rights in History* (2010); Slezkine, 'From Helsinki to Human Rights Watch: How an American Cold War Monitoring Group Became an International Human Rights Institution', 5/3 *Humanity Journal* (2014) 345; N. Richardson Little, *The Human Rights Dictatorship: Socialism, Global Solidarity and Revolution in East Germany* (2020); essays collected in Eckel and Moyn (n. 9).

[47] At some point, this argument was also used by the Carter administration: see Guilhot, 'Limiting Sovereignty or Producing Governmentality? Two Human Rights Regimes in US Political Discourse', 15/4 *Constellations* (2008) 502.

[48] See T. Judt, *Post War: A History of Europe Since 1945* (2005) 560.

[49] See the helpful survey by Eckel, 'The Rebirth of Politics from the Spirit of Morality: Explaining the Human Rights Revolution of the 1970s', in Eckel and Moyn (n. 9) 226.

[50] Whyte (n. 10); Q. Slobodian, *The Globalists: The End of Empire and the Birth of Neoliberalism* (2018); the French 'new philosophers', discussed in Judt (n. 48) 562–563, were part of a wider critique of the state as at once inadequate to the emancipatory ideals of the Left, and irremediably captured by established political power players and organized interests, whether from the Left or Right. The declension of this sceptical ethos was a disillusionment with the state as an instrument of *both* welfare *and* freedom, and the rise of a critical political morality preoccupied with the limits of what the state could achieve, or the pathologies arising from attempts to exceed those limits. The claims themselves were hardly new (as Judt put it, 'in condemning the distortions of radical utopianism, the young Parisian "new philosophers" of the mid-Seventies like André Glucksmann or Bernard-Henri Lévy were in most respects unoriginal', 562). But, 'timing was all ... In light of twentieth century history the state was beginning to look less like the solution than the problem, and not only or even primarily for economic reasons.' (560). Luhmann slyly observed as early as 1981 that the disenchantment of the 68ers led directly to a new individualism: N. Luhmann, *Political Theory in the Welfare State* (1981) 219.

merely sceptical of the institutional and economic sclerosis besetting advanced capitalist governments and business.[51] For still others, particular human rights treaty norms could be invoked in newly activated international expert bodies to form a tissue of condemnation and criticism of government violence in the Southern Cone and elsewhere.[52] Around the same period, the momentum of a global vision of a post-colonial, state-led developmentalism, buttressed and coordinated by a New International Economic Order orchestrated through international institutions, had been effectively slowed by Western diplomatic and economic resistance (and armed intervention, in some cases).[53] It would soon be further eviscerated by petro-dollar-fuelled debt expansion and Volker-shock induced interest rate rises. But in the face of a severe crisis of the theory and practice of state-led development itself, economic and social rights seemed to offer a vocabulary for maintaining the priority of certain human-welfare-related *goals* for development.[54] Exactly how such rights were to be made real was hotly contested, and the debates tracked radically different agendas of what a just global settlement between the advanced capitalist (colonial) and developing (post-colonial) states might possibly mean.[55] For the most part, the invocation of economic and social rights was paired with a (real or feigned) agnosticism in relation to grand programmes of social and economic change—even as one such programme, neo-liberalism, was sweeping the globe from Chile to Christchurch in more or less radical variations.[56]

[51] Sabin's account of Ralph Nader's assault on big government and big business as a complicitous cartel of special interests acting against the basic interests of ordinary people and their consumer well-being, shows well the *anti-establishment* flavour of political mobilization which was common to the New Left and the New Right, and spawned an influential model of 'public interest' political activism which was highly congenial to the emerging human rights profession. P. Sabin, *Public Citizen: The Attack on Big Government and the Remaking of American Liberalism* (2021). See also Hamilton, 'The Populist Appeal of Deregulation: Independent Truckers and the Politics of Free Enterprise, 1935–1980', 10/1 *Enterprise and Society* (2009) 137; E. Popp Berman, *Thinking like an Economist: How Efficiency Replaced Equality in U.S. Public Policy* (2022) chapters 6–8.

[52] Kelly, '"Magic Words": The Advent of Transnational Human Rights Activism in Latin America's Southern Cone in the Long 1970s', in Eckel and Moyn (n. 9) 88.

[53] See essays in *Humanity* special issue on NIEO, 6/1 *Humanity* (2015); see also, on SUNFED, D. van den Meerssche, *The World Bank's Lawyers: The Life of International Law as Institutional Practice* (2022); C. R. W. Dietrich, *Oil Revolution: Anticolonial Elites, Sovereign Rights, and the Economic Culture of Decolonization* (2017); J. Friedmann, *Ripe for Revolution: Building Socialism in the Third World* (2022).

[54] Dehm, 'Highlighting Inequalities in the Histories of Human Rights: Contestations over Justice, Needs and Rights in the 1970s', 31/4 *Leiden Journal of International Law* (2018) 871; Dehm, 'Righting Inequality: Human Rights Responses to Economic Inequality in the United Nations', 10/3 *Humanity Journal* (2019) 443.

[55] D. Bell (ed.), *Empire, Race and Global Justice* (2019); Moyn (n. 5), chapters on Shue and Beitz.

[56] The coherence of neo-liberalism as a theory, ideology, and practice, should not be overstated. See for example the bitter divide between Milton Friedman and Henry Hazlitt over the merits of guaranteed minimum income from the state (which Friedman advocated and Hazlitt opposed): Coleman, 'Getting Tough or Rolling Back the State? Why Neoliberals Disagreed on a Guaranteed Minimum Income', *Modern Intellectual History* (2022) 1. See also S. L. Collier, *Post-Soviet Social: Neoliberalism, Social Modernity, Biopolitics* (2011); Collier, 'Neoliberalism as Big Leviathan, or . . . ? A Response to Wacquant and Hilgers', 20/2 *Social Anthropology* (2012) 186; Mudge, 'What is Neoliberalism?', 6/4 *Socio-economic Review* (2008) 703. Nonetheless, a 2016 note from International Monetary Fund (IMF) staff economists helpfully synthesizes what the family of neo-liberal economic policies have in common: 'The first is increased competition – achieved through the opening up of domestic markets, including financial

While much has been written recently about the rise of human rights *politics* after 1970, much less attention has been paid to the distinctively legalistic complexion it developed. The absence of a comprehensive political and economic vision—or indeed a common philosophical foundation—for human rights belies somewhat the extent to which late twentieth century human rights practice became united through their *juristic* qualities. Despite the diverse movements and actors that enrolled the language of human rights in their cause, a distinctive characteristic of human rights as a repertoire of claim-making, criticism, and increasingly professionalized activism was its reliance upon international legal norms. Like much of international law, these norms were only ever partially judicialized in regional arrangements (such as the European Court of Human Rights or the Inter-American Court of Human Rights) and some domestic constitutions, but court-driven enforcement was far from the whole story:[57] human rights law's 'theory of change' was profoundly *juridical* and in the last instance, *statist*. Taking the state, its laws and institutions as the object of reform, human rights activism combined various kinds of fact-finding and critical exposé ('naming and shaming') with demands for the revision of the state's legal and political order to enable the realization of the claimed rights (or, at the very least, desist from their violation).[58] At the heart of the enterprise was the cautious refinement and elaboration of the juridical concepts embedded in human rights legal instruments (mostly treaties), by a network of expert bodies to which interpretive authority was loosely delegated, and the international lawyers that were appointed to these bodies or interacted with them.

Thus, essential to the unruly constellation of agents and actors assembled under the banner of an 'international human rights movement'[59] was the politics of law

markets, to foreign competition. The second is a smaller role for the state, achieved through privatization and limits on the ability of governments to run fiscal deficits and accumulate debt ...' Ostry, Loungani, and Furceri, 'Neoliberalism: Oversold?', *Finance and Development* (June 2016) 38.

[57] See most insightfully, Merry (n. 3), and de Búrca, 'Human Rights Experimentalism', 111/2 *American Journal of International Law* (2017) 277. In an increasingly condescending mode, but still perceptive, see Kennedy, 'Spring Break', 63/8 *Texas Law Review* (1985) 1377; Kennedy, 'Autumn Weekends: An Essay on Law and Everyday Life', in A. Sarat and T. R. Kearns (eds), *Law in Everyday Life* (1993) 191, and Kennedy, 'The International Human Rights Movement: Part of the Problem?', 15 *Harvard Human Rights Journal* (2002) 101.

[58] See A. Buchanan, *The Heart of Human Rights* (2013), for the clearest attempt to articulate the fundamentally statist presuppositions of international human rights law.

[59] A 'movement,' notably with no secretariat, no published platform, no stable membership criteria, and no electoral agenda. Compare Simmons, 'The Future of the Human Rights Movement', 28/2 *Ethics and International Affairs* (2014) 183. Simmons works assiduously to show some of the empirical regularities in the contours of who or what claims to be a human rights organization, and rightly criticizes those who limit this term to a handful of Northern-based NGOs. But she is unable to identify much concrete evidence that we had and used the idea of a human rights organization—let alone a human rights movement—before the mid-1960s. Most of her non-Western examples (which are very vaguely specified) track the rise of the concerted efforts to export and reproduce the civil society/NGO model of issue-centric political activism, from West/North to East/South, from the 1990s. See, for example, Moyn's persuasive argument that decolonization was not a 'human rights movement' in the contemporary sense: Moyn (n. 46).

and legal expertise, sitting alongside and articulated (in varying degrees) to diverse social movement politics. Some members of the cadre of self-professed human rights lawyers came to increasingly believe in the autonomous power of the relevant legal concepts to become a focal point for political and social change[60]—a belief often notable for its unawareness of the many puzzles, problems and paradoxes of seeking social change through law (studied ad infinitum in law and society scholarship, but also in law and economics).[61] This inclination towards legalism was reinforced by the increasing judicialization of human rights norms,[62] and also by some notable judicial victories in the late 1990s and early 2002.[63] But this evolution joined forces with another one: the triumphant liberal vision of political and legal isomorphism (including, for example, the constitutional entrenchment of rights guarantees) which was promoted through 20 years of rule of law reform,[64] economic restructuring,[65] post-conflict state-building and constitution-making[66]

[60] This belief was not a fantasy. Developments in the early and mid-1990s in established liberal democracies did show that the right combination of a politically-persuadable government and energetic human rights advocacy by NGOs, could, together with a decision or view of a human rights expert-body finding a human rights law violation, engender important legislative reforms ending discriminatory legal regimes. This dynamic was often associated with successful mobilization of public opinion around the specific issue, with the framing of human rights (in conjunction with the other abovementioned factors) helping to shift perceptions about the legitimacy of discriminatory or abusive treatment. See for example the discussion of the change to Hong Kong inheritance laws in Merry (n. 3) and the case study of torture norms in B. Simmons, *Mobilizing for Human Rights: International Law in Domestic Politics* (2009). These developments occasionally promoted more ambitious efforts to theorize the impact of the normative mobilization of human rights 'scripts' on the perceived legitimacy of the state: see for example, R. Goodman and D. Jinks, *Socializing States: Promoting Human Rights through International Law* (2013).

Ultimately the question of the empirical *efficacy* of human rights law in bringing about human rights-realizing states of affairs in politics and economics, became an academic cottage industry which generated more heat than light: see, with diverse degrees of polemicism and empiricism for and against: E. Posner, *The Twilight of Human Rights Law* (2014); E. Hafner-Burton, *Making Human Rights a Reality* (2015); K. Tsutsui, *Rights Make Might: Global Human Rights and Minority Social Movements in Japan* (2018); K. Sikkink, *Evidence for Hope: Making Human Rights Work in the 21st Century* (2017); B. A. Simmons, *Mobilizing for Human Rights*: International Law in Domestic Politics (2009).

[61] An example of this naivety is J. Kozma, M. Nowak, and M. Scheinin, *A World Court of Human Rights: Consolidated Statute and Commentary* (2010).

[62] Notable uptick in activity by the European Court of Human Rights and the Inter-American Court of Human Rights (discussed in K. Alter, *The New Terrain of International Law: Courts, Politics, Rights* (2014)), which ought to be placed in a wider context of the proliferation and increased ambition of international organizations' governance and adjudication functions—whether as courts and tribunals, or as administrative bodies. As Zürn points out, this trend towards the delegation of certain competences to international bodies is a secular one, but accelerates from the late 1980s and becomes the subject of various express theorizations after 2000: M. Zürn, *A Theory of Global Governance* (2018).

[63] *Minister of Health and Others v. Treatment Action Campaign and Others (No 2)* (2002) (10) BCLR 1033 (CC) (5 July 2002).

[64] S. Pahuja, *Development, Economic Growth and the Politics of Universality* (2011); S. Humphreys, *Theatre of the Rule of Law: Transnational Legal Intervention in Theory and Practice* (2010); Bhuta, 'Against State Building', 15/4 *Constellations* (2009) 517. Rajah, 'Rule of Law as Transnational Legal Order', in T. C. Halliday and G. Shaffer (eds), *Transnational Legal Orders* (2015) 340.

[65] See G. Shaffer (ed), *Transnational Legal Ordering and State Change* (2012) and Halliday and Shaffer (n. 64); T. C. Halliday and B. G. Carruthers, *Bankrupt: Global Lawmaking and Systemic Financial Crisis* (2009).

[66] See the recent V. Sripati, *Constitution-Making under UN Auspices* (2020).

and, indeed, 'rights-based' development programming.[67] The powerful legacy of this strong gravitational attraction between the contemporary politics of human rights and a politics of legalism is reflected in the strenuous difficulty of giving *any* common concrete content to a human rights concept or claim, *except by recourse* to juridical concepts (refined, elaborated upon, contested, explained, etc. by possessors of legal expertise and bodies endowed with legal authority).

In reflecting on the contemporary challenges posed to the practice of human rights politics, self-declared 'human rights practitioners' observe that this legalism and its associated repertoires have become a source of paralysis. Sharp laments that the 'legalistic referee model' of human rights activism 'remains fundamentally top-down and legal-institutional, with a core focus on the press and political elite'.[68] The 'limited idiom of the legalistic referee simply does not resonate very well outside of elite circles' and lacks a programmatic repertoire to do much more than condemn economic inequality and its consequences. In a sense, Human Rights Watch's Executive Director Ken Roth showed a sincere fidelity to this *modus operandi* when he argued that addressing distributive justice in the (contemporary legal) language of human rights would be mere 'sloganeering'.[69] A 'grass roots' human rights campaigner in the UK suggests that *avoiding* polarized national debates about specific legal decisions has been an effective means to shift attention to 'everyday concerns' such as education, health and social care, housing, an adequate standard of living—'especially socioeconomic rights . . . of particular importance in the current austerity-dominated context'.[70] Rodríguez-Garavito, in a wide ranging reflection, observes that among the 'blind spots and accumulated liabilities' of the politics of human rights practice is its reliance on legal language and an elite constituency in the Global North,[71] which 'have failed to engage with and appeal to large sectors of the population . . . '.[72]

This sense of anxiety about the adequacy of contemporary human rights practice and its legalism among committed, self-reflective human rights activists, refracts a wider sense that we are in the midst of an epochal transition: a conjuncture of multiple crises and upheavals, some with deep and slow-moving causes, and others evolving rapidly over relatively short timescales. Can the human rights enterprise adapt and survive?[73] *Should* they? Long-standing critiques of human

[67] See for example, OECD and World Bank, *Integrating Human Rights into Development: Donor Approaches, Experiences and Challenges*, 3rd ed. (2016).

[68] Sharp, 'Through a Glass, Darkly: Three Important Conversations for Human Rights Professionals', 11/2 *Journal of Human Rights Practice* (2019) 296, at 300–301.

[69] Roth, 'Defending Economic, Social and Cultural Rights: Practical Issues Faced by an International Human Rights Organization', 26/1 *Human Rights Quarterly* (2004) 63.

[70] Gready, 'Reflections on a Human Rights Decade, Near and Far', 11/2 *Journal of Human Rights Practice* (2019) 422–437, at 430.

[71] Rodríguez-Garavito, 'Human Rights 2030: Existential Challenges and a New Paradigm for the Human Rights Field', in Bhuta (n. 6) 334.

[72] Ibid. 334.

[73] Ibid.

rights practice, as well as more recent ones, seem to have gathered an immediacy and currency that has led some critics to hope that human rights are losing, and will continue to lose, 'their imaginative near monopoly as a framework for reform'.[74] But a careful anthropological scholar of human rights practice can equally conclude that human rights remain a pervasive language and thought-practice for articulating social justice demands, 'which occupies an important place among global social movements and has consequences for local people and their experiences of injustice around the world'.[75]

To paraphrase Gramsci's well-worn dictum, an old order is dying, but a new one has not yet taken shape; we look for intimations of the future in our present and near-past. Will human rights become, for the second time in one hundred years, an enterprise 'sponsored by marginal figures—by a few international jurists without political experience or professional philanthropists supported by the uncertain sentiments of professional idealists?'[76] Or, will they renew themselves as a political-ethical language which energizes and authorizes a vision and ideal for human society adequate to the present?[77] Stedman-Jones, reflecting on the rise and fall of a nineteenth century movement for political and social justice,[78] astutely observed '[the existence of a political movement] is distinguished by a shared conviction articulating a political solution to distress and a political solution to its causes. A particular political vocabulary must convey a practicable hope of a general alternative and a believable means of realizing it, such that potential recruits can think within its terms.'[79]

A diversity of proposals and ideas[80] have emerged, but the challenge of economic and social inequality remains persistent: can human rights articulate a political

[74] Moyn, 'Human Rights Have Lost Their Monopoly as a Framework for Reform,' *Global Open Rights*, 19 May 2021. See also S. Hopgood, *The Endtimes of Human Rights* (2015); Posner (n. 60); Mishra (n. 8); Koskenniemi (n. 6).

[75] Merry, 'The State of Human Rights Consciousness: Not Yet End Times', in Bhuta (n. 6) 62, at 69.

[76] H. Arendt, *The Origins of Totalitarianism* ([1951] 2017), 382.

[77] Sen's 2004 paper also embodies a dissatisfaction with human rights as legalism, when he sought to argue that the 'Human rights can be seen as primarily ethical demands. They are not principally "legal," "proto-legal" or "ideal-legal" commands.... The effectiveness of the human rights perspective does not rest on seeing them invariably as putative proposals for legislation ... [We should see human rights] as pronouncements in social ethics, sustainable by open public reasoning.' Sen, 'Elements of a Theory of Human Rights', 32/4 *Philosophy and Public Affairs* (2004) 315, at 319, 345, 355–356.

[78] Stedman Jones, 'The Language of Chartism', in J. Epstein and D. Thompson (eds), *The Chartist Experience: Studies in Working Class Radicalism and Culture, 1830–1860* (1982) 3, at 7.

[79] Ibid. Sassoon points out that the global success of Marxist socialism in becoming a political movement and political vocabulary attracting millions of committed adherents, reflected its ability to 'comprehend the most varied issues: short-term demands such as an improvement in working conditions; national reforms such as pension schemes; comprehensive schemes such as economic planning and a new legal system; major political changes such as the expansion of the suffrage; utopian projects such as the abolition of the state, etc.' In the end, all major movements for social change must 'be able to define the contending parties, name them and thus establish where the barricades should go up, or where the trenches should be dug ...'. D. Sassoon, *A Hundred Years of Socialism: The West European Left in the Twentieth Century* (1996) 7.

[80] Compare for example: De Búrca (n. 3), J. Snyder, *Human Rights for Pragmatists: Social Power in Modern Times* (2022), Rodríguez-Garavito (n. 71).

solution, and a believable means of realizing it? Human rights law and practice have excelled in labelling the harms of inequality as denials of guaranteed rights,[81] bringing with them at times powerful critiques of particular dimensions of contemporary economic and social policy. But this has led directly to the criticism that contemporary human-rights-based critiques of inequality focus on tangible harms and their impact on human dignity but are consistently unable to articulate a structural account of causes and solutions. Indeed, in light of human rights law and practice's *success* as a kind of legalism that bracketed any strong commitments to system-theoretic diagnoses (or even stable alliances with such diagnoses emerging from other domains of knowledge), this limitation appears baked in to a certain (dominant) modality of the politics of human rights. The result is a significant vulnerability to the criticism most sharply put by Moyn: that contemporary human rights law and its practice modalities are *unthreatening* to increasing levels of inequality because it *accommodates*, rather than directly challenges, the dominant political economy of the age.[82] Moyn's controversial criticism of economic and social human rights as having cashed out as a claim to 'sufficiency' of provision, rather than confronting the widening gap between rich and poor, has attracted much attention and ire. Some have sought to contest it empirically, although exactly what is being measured and what such data allows us to conclude about the distributive effects of strategies (usually litigious) to enforce economic and social rights, remains contradictory and unclear.[83]

4. The Post-1945 Welfare State and Human Rights

There is a deeper point and puzzle raised by Moyn's argument, however, which is historical and conceptual: Moyn's fundamental claim is not that economic and social rights claims are always and at all times demands for sufficiency. Rather, it is that social and economic rights are janus-faced and chameleon-like concepts, the concrete content of which depends on the wider political and economic ecology of

[81] See, much more trenchantly than most, Alston, Special Rapporteur Reports on: *Privatization* (2018), *Marginalization of Human Rights* (2016), *Universal Basic Income* (2017), *The Enjoyment of Civil and Political Rights by Persons Living in Poverty* (2017). https://www.ohchr.org/en/special-procedures/sr-poverty/annual-reports (last visited 3 March 2023).

[82] Moyn (n. 5). See also Ragnarsson, 'Humanising not Transformative? The UN Committee on Economic, Social and Cultural Rights and Economic Inequality in OECD countries 2008–19', 8/2 *London Review of International Law* (2020) 261; Ragnarsson, 'Conceptions of Equality and the Distribution of Wealth in Human Rights Adjudication', 68 *Scandinavian Studies in Law* (2022) 13.

[83] See for example Versteeg, 'Can Rights Combat Inequality?', 133 *Harvard Law Review* (2018) 2017; compare Versteeg and Chilton, 'Rights without Resources: The Impact of Constitutional Rights on Social Spending', 60/4 *Journal of Law and Economics* (2017) 713; Socal, Amon, and Biehl, 'Right to Medicines Litigation and Universal Health Coverage: Institutional Determinants of the Judicialization of Health in Brazil', 22/1 *Health and Human Rights* (2020) 221.

the given moment in history that surrounds them.[84] Thus, within a mid-century global embrace of the state as an interventionist agent of economic management, provider of public goods, and supplier of services from telecommunications to health care, economic, and social rights represented a kind of short-hand summary of the expected outcomes of an ambitious project of egalitarian national citizenship. This project rested on a theory of national states as robust and effective collective agents that not only mitigated the effects of national and global market capitalism, but re-made and contained it in order to create and maintain a stable political and economic order—one which aimed to manage, if not permanently resolve, the critical contradictions inherited from capitalism's 'anxious triumph'[85] in the nineteenth century:[86] between the rising tide of mass democracy and egalitarian demands, and social and political order in societies characterized by substantial continuing inequalities of property and income;[87] between decentralized market decision-making and price-setting, and the purposive public allocation of resources to provide social goods, raise living standards and prevent immiseration; between capital owners and wage-earners over income shares; and between the restraint of the oligopolistic and monopolistic tendencies of unconstrained competition and business cycles, and the corporatist coordination of 'big business, big government and big labour' to achieve planned outcomes.[88]

In this telling, the codification of economic and social rights in the Universal Declaration on Human Rights, and in the International Covenant on Economic

[84] Moyn's arguments can at times be hard to narrow down, as they are wide ranging. But I suggest that what I present here is an indispensable pillar of them, and a reading which gives them the greatest coherence. See Moyn (n. 5), especially chapters 1 and 2.

[85] D. Sassoon, *Anxious Triumph: A Global History of Capitalism, 1860–1914* (2019).

[86] As Conway points out, from the vantage point of 1945 Europe, liberal democracy had largely failed to resolve these contradictions, and thus if it were to be renewed after the fascist defeat, it required a re-founding that strengthened its capacity to broker political and economic compromises while enhancing a technical problem-solving ability within the state itself. See M. Conway, *Western Europe's Democratic Age: 1945–1968* (2020). The result was an expansion of state finances, state management, and state provision which was unprecedented. The strong presumption that national economies would be planned economies, even if private property and markets remained, is evident in G. Myrdal, *Beyond the Welfare State: Economic Planning and its International Implications* (1960). In his recent book, Wilkinson also re-reads European integration as a project to revive a liberal state backstopped by an elite-led, managerial, representative democracy: M. Wilkinson, *Authoritarian Liberalism and the Transformation of Modern Europe* (2021). This reading largely confirms the positive assessment given by Aron in 1961, when he drily remarked that 'it is the disappearance or scarcity of revolutionaries that sanctions the legitimacy of a democratic regime (or, as I prefer to it, constitutional-pluralistic regime) ... Partial planning and partial state ownership of property have strengthened rather than weakened democracy by helping to win the working class over to the regime.': Aron, 'The Situation of Democracy: Western Political Institutions in the Twentieth Century', 90/2 *Daedalus* (1961) 350; Steinmetz-Jenkins, 'Raymond Aron, Friedrich Hayek, and the "Third World": An Alternative History of the End of Ideology Debate', 12/3 *Humanity Journal* (2022) 241.

[87] See J. W. Müller, *Contesting Democracy: Political Ideas in Twentieth-Century Europe* (2013).

[88] The explicit corporatism of the *trente glorieuses* in various national approaches to prices, wages, competition, and finance has been extensively excavated. In many respects, the collective agency of the state rested on having other collective agents (such as concentrated, vertically integrated industrial conglomerates, and sector-wide labour unions) as interlocutors and collaborators in a national economic management.

and Social Rights, were *emanations* and *emendations* of a political-economic context, and this context provided the essential presuppositions for what we might expect the rights-concepts to denote and index. While the rights could be read alone as mere guarantees of sufficiency, they were in this context refractions of a moderately egalitarian enterprise in which achievement of these guarantees rested on the theory of a strong state with redistributive and 'levelling-up' ambitions and programmes. To use a contemporary term anachronistically, the historical state-concept presupposed by economic and social rights in the context of their codification, was a 'market-shaping'[89] state concerned with creating public values, such as 'deproletarianization' and expansive public education programmes.[90] The denouement of this story is that the juridification of economic and social rights is *symptomatic* of a political, economic, and social matrix of forces which lies elsewhere; the independent agency of the rights concepts and rights language as a framework of thought and action, is limited and marginal. Critically, in Moyn's argument, the concepts of rights are unable to bring into being the presuppositions of their egalitarian possibilities; as those presuppositions are eviscerated from the 1970s onwards—as our state theories and state concepts are reworked under a different constellation of economic forces, political agents, and social movements from left and right—social and economic rights lose their connection with the political economy upon which they leaned. Stripped of this concrete historical relationship, we are left with juridical concepts to which elaborate *juristic* content can be given, but where the *political-ethical* foundation of those concepts in a deeper, historically evanescent political and economic movement, recedes from public and private recollection. Instead, the juridical concepts are mobilized by those best equipped to articulate them and directed towards those institutions most adept at hearing them: lawyers and jurists, international expert committees, and courts. Once such

[89] See Mazzucato and Collins, 'Putting Value Creation Back into "Public Value": From Market-Fixing to Market-Shaping', 25/4 *Journal of Economic Policy Reform* (2022) 345.

[90] As is well-known, the strong state theory was common to several varieties of inter-war and post-Second World War schools of economic thought, from German historical school-inspired US institutional economists and New Deal planners, to Austrian Ordoliberals (sometimes called neo-liberals in early accounts). The theoretical divergences lay in the drawing of the boundaries and limits of the state's market-shaping role, the extent of bureaucratic power, and the relative priority given to the protection of property rights, to the function of the price-mechanism, and to the role of courts as policing (and constructing) the boundary between state and market, and between state and 'life world.' One might surmise the distinction as between 'strong state, planned economy' and 'strong state, free economy.' See, inter alia: Nedergaard, '"I Ain't Gonna Work on Maggie's Farm No More": The Five Ordoliberal Critiques of Capitalism', 43/4 *Policy Studies* (2020) 759; Jessop, 'Ordoliberalism and Neoliberalization: Governing through Order or Disorder', 45/7–8 *Critical Sociology* (2019) 967; Friedrich, 'The Political Thought of Neo-Liberalism', 49/2 *American Political Science Review* (1955) 509, discussing ordoliberals as 'neo-liberals,' as does Foucault, in his *Birth of Biopolitics* (1979), where he sharpens the distinction between the statism of the ordoliberals, and the statism of the planners. On the strong statism of the US 'social economists,' see: S. Fine, *Laissez-Faire and the General-Welfare State: A Study of Conflict in American Thought, 1865-1901* (1956) chapters 7–9; D. Rodgers, *Atlantic Crossings: Social Politics in a Progressive Age* (2000); Kirat and Marty, 'The Late Emerging Consensus Among American Economists on Antitrust Laws in the 2nd New Deal (1935–1941)', 29 *History of Economic Ideas* (2021) 11.

concepts become principally juristic in their mode of determination and activation, they can (like any positive juridical concept) be positioned as boundary concepts for the *legality* of this or that programme or policy, but appear largely untethered from a programmatic structural commitment which is inscribed in the *purpose* of the state as a juridical *and* material order.[91] Hence, Moyn ultimately dismisses the contemporary possibilities of economic and social rights as playing a 'defensive minor role in pushing back against the new political economy [of neoliberalism]'.[92]

As a claim about the possibility of juridical rights to *bring about* epochal and tectonic shifts in political and economic ordering, Moyn's claim seems realistic. It also sounds an echo of an earlier generation of socialist theorists' scepticism about the relationship between legal forms and social and economic substance. When invited in March 1947 by UNESCO to give their views about the proposal for an international bill of rights, leading communist sympathizers and socialists in Western Europe replied that 'expressing abstract ethical principles in a political and social vacuum' would be ineffective unless there was an underlying commitment to 'the physical and material conditions that may make the emergence of these rights in practice a real possibility'.[93] Communist organizer and British Communist Party founding member R. Palme Dutt hewed closely to the then-Party line when he responded with a lengthy exposition of a historical materialist theory of history, maintaining that civil and political rights reflected 'eighteenth and early nineteenth century conceptions of liberty and human rights ... [which] ... did not clearly see the new forms of class domination which were arising and paid less attention to the problems of economic and social inequality and domination.' By contrast, the 1936 Soviet Constitution, with its extensive enumeration of economic and social rights, reflects the reality that such rights can be achieved 'only through a socialist organization of society'.[94] Belgian socialist Luc Somerhausen was sceptical of rights declarations to the extent that they did not reflect a reality of a 'social organization which will make it possible for man to protect himself against exploitation'.[95] The common thread in this critique of rights is that the value and consequence of social and economic rights 'could not be considered independently from a wider theory of historical change and justice within which these rights might, or might not, play a role'.[96]

[91] A notable effort to explicate a logic of structural commitment in the purpose of the state is Alston's Recognition-Institutionalization-Accountability framework in his 2016 report on the marginalization of economic and social rights.

[92] Moyn (n. 5) 176.

[93] Hyman Levy, Dean of the Royal College of Science at Imperial College London, and Communist Party member since 1931, Letter in reply to the UNESCO Human Rights Survey, in M. Goodale (ed), *Letters to the Contrary: A Curated History of the UNESCO Human Rights Survey* (2018) 169.

[94] R. Palme Dutte, in Goodale (n. 93), 175, 176.

[95] L. Somerhausen, in Goodale (n. 93), 167, 168.

[96] Goodale, 'From Human Welfare to Human Rights: Considering Socio-economic Rights through the 1947–1948 UNESCO Human Rights Survey', in S. L. B. Jensen and C. Walton (eds), *Social Rights and the Politics of Obligation in History* (2022).

The sceptical attitude of socialists reflected the pervasive influence of the mid-nineteenth century critique of bourgeois right pioneered by Proudhon[97] and embraced by Marx,[98] in which the very language of natural right itself was powerfully depicted as consecrating the legal order of market society: the sacredness of property and contract *über alles*, regularizing and legitimating a regime of what would later (anachronistically) be labelled 'possessive individualism'.[99] And indeed, such a polemical understanding of natural right in 1840 was not entirely a straw person: the first half of the nineteenth century saw the flourishing of strong claims that found the purpose and limits of the state in the protection of property and contract, as the essence of the exercise of *libertas* and as the condition sine qua non of the progressive development of manners and civilization.[100] The regime of *propriétarisme*,[101] as Piketty has labelled it, had strong roots in *one lineage* of natural rights thinking that was active before[102] and during the French Revolution, and which was amplified by the Girondin constitution and the Napoleonic Code.[103] In this lineage, which was to form the core of nineteenth century economic liberalism,[104] the foundation of justice and economic progress was that right which a man had to his own: his own person and will, and his own property as a product of his labour.[105] To the European social democrats amongst whom the Marxian critique of natural right gained currency after 1860,[106] rights language seemed beholden to this individualist ideology, and were thus an unpromising vehicle through which to motivate the historical forces that would, in any event, create a just social, economic, and political order. Social and economic rights should await the transformation of social and economic relationships but could not be expected

[97] P. J. Proudhon, *What is Property?* (1840).

[98] K. Marx, *On the Jewish Question* (1843/1844). Marx claimed in 1844 that Proudhon's *What is Property?* had the same significance for modern political economy as Abbé Sieyes' 1789 text, *What is the Third Estate?* had for modern politics: Engels and Marx, 'The Holy Family or Critique of Critical Criticism' in *Marx and Engels Collected Works*, vol. 4 (1975) 31, cited in Stedman Jones, 'Rights and Socialism, 1750–1880' in D. Edelstein and J. Pitts (eds), *The Cambridge History of Rights*, vol. 4 (2023) forthcoming.

[99] C. B. MacPherson, *The Political Theory of Possessive Individualism: Hobbes to Locke* (1962).

[100] For a survey of the American discourse, see Fine (n. 90); for France and UK, see Todd, 'Economic Liberalism and Rights in the Nineteenth Century', in Edelstein and Pitts (n. 98). See also Sassoon (n. 85) chapter 5.

[101] Piketty (n. 19) chapters 3–5.

[102] See Bourke, 'Rights, Property and Politics: Hume to Hegel', in Edelstein and Pitts (n. 98).

[103] Piketty (n. 19) 122: 'More generally, reference to property rights in various declarations of rights and constitutions were often used in the nineteenth and twentieth centuries to impose drastic legal limits on any possibility of a peaceful, legal redefinition of the property regime, and that continues to be the case today.'

[104] G. de Ruggiero, *The History of European Liberalism*, trans. Collingwood (1927) 128–129.

[105] Pocock, 'Virtues, Rights and Manners: A Model for Historians of Political Thought', in J. G. A. Pocock (ed), *Virtue, Commerce, and History: Essays on Political Thought and History* (1985): 'Social first and political after, the civil and common law define individuals as possessors by investing them with right and property in things, and ultimately (as in Locke) in themselves.' (45).

[106] Spengler, 'The Right to Work: A Backward Glance', 28/2 *The Journal of Economic History* (1968) 171, at 189. For the official adoption of Marxist thought by European social democratic parties after 1860, see S. L. Mudge, *Leftism Reinvented: Western Parties from Socialism to Neoliberalism* (2018).

to play much of a role in bringing about such a transformation. Moyn's deflationary sketch of economic and social rights circa 1948, as adding little but an indirect justification for welfare states which were already *in statu nascendi*,[107] evinces a close kinship with this influential sceptical story, leading him to conclude that there is little need for a history of economic and social rights distinct from a history of the welfare state itself.[108] Economic and social rights are latecomers to the party, an effort to update 'a language forged in one age for the sake of another'[109] in a possibly quixotic attempt to save rights 'from their libertarian associations with nineteenth century political economy to serve the purposes of social reconstruction'.[110]

5. The Grammar of Social Rights—1945–1917

But it remains an open question whether social rights were ever, or could ever be, more than mere summations of what we expected an extant welfare state to do for us. The immediate drafting history of the Universal Declaration of Human Rights (UDHR) goes some way towards confirming Moyn's claims, but also points to deeper roots and longer histories behind the use of rights language to frame the nature of the state and its relationship with the economic order.

The final text of the UDHR's 'social rights' provisions was adopted with widespread support from drafting member states, and was indeed drawn from constitutions and social welfare legislation 'common in Latin America, socialist states, western Europe, Scandinavia, the UK, the US, Canada and Australia'.[111] The precise terminology of 'welfare state' is not readily found in discussions surrounding the UN Secretariat's draft of the Universal Declaration, nor in influential preparatory reports submitted by the American Law Institute[112] or the Latin American state-backed Inter-American Juridical Committee.[113] This should be no surprise, as a discreet concept of 'welfare state' was not much in use until after 1947, and even then its meanings were far from uniform.[114] Rather than a clearly articulated state concept and state theory, what formative discussions surrounding the social

[107] Moyn (n. 5) 45, 59.

[108] Ibid. 12–13.

[109] Ibid. 53

[110] Ibid. 62.

[111] Saul, 'Introduction: The Drafting of the International Covenant on Economic, Social and Cultural Rights, 1948–1966,' *Sydney Law School Legal Studies Research Paper No.15/79* (2015) 1, at 18, 20.

[112] Committee of Advisers on Essential Human Rights, American Law Institute, 'Statement of Essential Rights', 243 *The Annals of the American Academy of Political and Social Science* (1946) 18, Arts 11–15.

[113] Pan-American Union, Inter-American Juridical Committee, 'Draft Declaration of the International Rights and Duties of Man and Accompanying Report, 31 December 1945', 40/3 *American Journal of International Law* (1946) 93. The committee consisted of Francisco Campos, F. Nieto del Rio, Charles G. Fenwick, and A. Gómez Robledo.

[114] Garland, 'The Emergence of the Idea of "The Welfare State" in British Political Discourse', 35/1 *History of the Human Sciences* (2021) 1.

rights provisions of the UDHR show is an incompletely theoried common *topos* of ideas which coalesce around the broad notion of a positive state which *structures and shapes* national economies in order to bring about the enjoyment of social rights;[115] the social rights themselves did not express any singular vision of state and economy, but were a 'placeholder' for stronger and weaker versions of a positive state. In a March 1947 UN Economic and Social Council (ECOSOC) discussion of an early report from the Commission on Human Rights concerning a draft bill of rights, the US delegate (Stinebower) urged that the 'bill of rights should be as bold and as broad as possible and . . . it should embrace social rights such as those of employment, social security and equal opportunity as well as minimum standards of economic, cultural and social well-being'.[116] A few months later, in the Commission on Human Rights,[117] the US delegate (Roosevelt) clarified that a right to employment did not entail a duty on the state to provide work but rather the creation of conditions affording a 'fair and equal opportunity to work'. In the US's redraft suggestions of June 1947, the right to a fair and equal opportunity to work was nonetheless embedded within a general right to economic security of expansive scope, which proposed a right to 'a decent standard of living . . . to wages and hours and conditions of work calculated to insure *a just share of the benefits of progress to all*; . . . It is the duty of the state to undertake measures that will promote full employment and good working conditions . . . and assure adequate food, housing, and community services necessary to the well-being of the people'.[118]

The Chilean delegate to both ECOSOC and the Commission on Human Rights (Santa Cruz) observed in the March meeting that 'in the opinion of his government the State should intervene in guiding the internal economy of a country, supplying what private initiative was not able to give and ensuring that production and distribution of goods was adjusted to the general welfare of the population . . . [This was] a way of transforming the political democracy of the nineteenth century into an economic democracy'.[119] In June, the French delegate (Cassin) explained that 'in two wars, the State had demanded the maximum from millions of men and . . . had taken over the control of the entire economy . . . He admitted that unemployment

[115] The Polanyian concept of 'embeddedness' comes to mind, although the term had only been recently coined to capture the movement of thought from laissez faire state to positive state—a movement the arc of which can be traced to beginning of the 19th century.

[116] Economic and Social Council Summary Record, 14 March 1947, in W. J. Schabas, *The Universal Declaration of Human Rights: The Travaux Préparatoires* (2013) 332, at 246.

[117] Commission on Human Rights Summary Record, 23 June 1947, in Schabas, ibid, 873.

[118] US Suggestions for Redrafts of Certain Articles in the Draft Outline, 11 June 1947, Art. 38, in Schabas (n. 116) 716.

[119] Economic and Social Council Summary Record, in Schabas (n. 116) 246. In a similar vein, Walter Nash, future Prime Minister of New Zealand, stated that he 'felt that the right to live healthily for the maximum period of time with the availability of all essentials for cultural, spiritual and mental progress transcended all others . . . Individual rights could not be enjoyed unless the requisite materials and facilities were provided by collective organization and work' (Ibid. 248).

cannot be overcome immediately but he felt that the Declaration should establish fundamental rights, such as the right to work, for the future.'[120]

The American Law Institute Statement of Essential Human Rights, finalized in December 1945 and published with commentary in the Annals of the American Academy of Political and Social Science,[121] enumerated five social rights: work, fair labour conditions, social security, education, food and housing. One of the committee members, C. Wilfried Jenks—already prominent in the drafting of the ILO's 1944 Philadelphia Declaration—concisely summarized what he took to be the common expectations concerning state action underlying the right to work: 'its general acceptance by almost all shades of political and economic thought is attributable to a world depression sandwiched between periods of full employment resulting from two World Wars. It now *holds the central place among the social claims which the common man expects the social system to satisfy*.'[122] In order to meet this 'social claim' and the other social rights in the Statement, Jenks outlines an extensive programme of state coordination, state financing, state regulation, and state production: the right to work (as full employment) was a 'basic social objective in the light of which economic and financial policy must be determined'. The right to food anticipated not only food safety regulation, but price controls for essential foods, school meals, large scale crop planning; the right to housing implied large scale public investment in building housing, as well as 'control of the mortgage business'. Nothing less than 'a high degree of cooperation among private agencies under supervision of government and in the framework of a government plan can make adequate housing available to modern urban man'.[123] Ellingston, commenting on the Right to Work, explained at length why 'people living in an industrial society have discovered that without [economic] rights they can no longer be free'[124]:

> The people of the world, shaken by two world wars and ruinous depression within a short twenty-five years, have discovered that neither peace nor freedom is possible to man in an industrial society without economic security ... To leave social

[120] Cassin, Commission on Human Rights Summary Record, 23 June 1947, in Schabas (n. 116) 873. Cassin was repeating here a common sense of the politicians and policy makers deeply influenced by the Beveridge Report of 1942 and his book on Full Employment of 1944: see T. B. Smith, 'Renegotiating the Social Contract: Western Europe, Great Britain, Europe and North America" in M. Geyer and A. Tooze (eds) *The Cambridge History of the Second World War: Volume III, Total War: Economy, Society and Culture* (2015), 553–574.

[121] The Committee appointed by the Institute to draft the statement was composed of 25 men, including William Draper Lewis, Percy Corbett, Manley Hudson, Wilfred Jenks, and Karl Loewenstein.

[122] Jenks, 'The Five Economic and Social Rights', 243 *Annals of the American Academy of Political and Social Science* (1946) 40, at 41(emphasis added).

[123] Ibid. 44–45.

[124] Ellingston, 'The Right to Work', 243 *Annals of the American Academy of Political and Social Science* (1946) 27, at 27.

> and economic rights out of a modern bill of rights would be to stage Hamlet without the Dane.
>
> ... The modern individual has become the tooth on a gear of a gigantic economic machine. He depends for employment, shelter, and nearly all the other necessities and amenities of life no longer solely on his own efforts but on the efforts and good will of many other men, working through an intricate economic system.
>
> ... Our interdependent industrial economy simply cannot operate successfully unless every member of our society, the sharecropper and the street cleaner as well as the banker and the skilled tool maker, enjoys a high standard of living. The more we increase our productive capacity, as we have during the war, the higher we must raise the level of consumption and the standard of living for everybody. This is not a matter about which business—or government or labor—is any longer free to make a choice.
>
> ... A fully developed industrial economy introduces a new law to control the material relations among men—the law of compulsory abundance ... All this means that in a completely industrial economy, full employment with attendant full consumption is vital to everybody ... Protection of the right to work is a basic condition of the stability of our industrial society.[125]

Ellingston reflects pointedly on the function of rights language in relation to this expansive social economic vision, insisting that 'capacity for immediate enforcement is not the test of a right ... A bill of rights is ... a directive to the whole society and a guide to legislators and executives in the framing of laws and regulations that will gradually make rights effective.'[126] He takes as an exemplar of this the French Declaration of the Rights of Man in 1789, the exhortatory natural rights grammar of which served to 'raise the beacon around which public opinion can mobilize, by which the controlling ideas and values of society can be mobilized, and by which the acts of legislatures and executives can be guided and judged'.[127]

The relationship between state and economy imagined as the necessary implication of social rights is also found in the Inter-American Juridical Committee's explanation of its Draft Declaration. Drafted at the behest of the Inter-American Conference on War and Peace,[128] the Juridical Committee explained the inclusion of social rights (work, education, and social security) as reflecting both a new theory of the state and a new conception of democracy. The state was to be understood as 'a cooperative commonwealth' in which 'the resources of the community must be used to raise the standard of living and to provide a decent subsistence for all its members'.[129] Modern industrial society required not 'the earlier doctrines

[125] Ibid. 32.
[126] Ibid. 34.
[127] Ibid. 34.
[128] Composed of 19 Latin American States and the United States, meeting at Chapultepec between 21 February and 8 March, 1945.
[129] 'Inter-American Juridical Committee Draft Declaration and Accompanying Report' (n. 113) 102.

of extreme individualism' but 'the organization of the economic life of the state' in order to 'secure equality of opportunity for all and to *bring the rewards of labour more into conformity with the contribution of labour to the national welfare*'.[130] The new conception of democracy accompanying the new theory of the state emphasized the full development of the individual and 'his full moral stature' which cannot be realized 'under conditions of malnutrition, disease, bad housing and sanitation'.[131] The 'newer body of economic and social rights' was underlain by 'the broad principle of distributive justice':

> A generation or more ago states had but a limited understanding of the obligations of the community to promote the welfare of its individual citizens. The rights of the individual were rights against the interference of the state, not rights to the active assistance of the state. But within more recent years it has come to be understood that the individual can not always by his own efforts attain the standard of living adequate to the development of his human personality. The complicated economic life of modern states has made the old doctrine of *laissez faire* no longer adequate. *At the same time the concept of the democratic state as a cooperative commonwealth whose objective is the general welfare of its members has come to be more clearly understood.*[132]

These contemporary rationalizations of social rights go some way to confirming Moyn's observation that social rights circa 1945 depended upon 'a much larger consensus concerning the purposes of the state and even its role in planning the economy'.[133] But what they also show is that while these presuppositions were not *written in* to the UDHR, they were clearly articulated by those justifying the inclusion of social rights within that document and others. There was a striking consistency in explaining social rights in terms of their necessity *in light of the expected role of the state in a post-war economic order*, and with reference to the need to create a 'moral' or 'social' economy as the true medium for the realization of such rights. The grammar of rights in these discussions exceeds the function of an indirect justification for what would come to be called the welfare state; Ellingston's extrapolation of the value of a declaration intimates an affinity between revolutionary natural rights declarations and social rights language: the statement of rights *recalls us to an order of which they are an objective property and foundation*, even if we can understand certain dimensions of that order as simultaneously oriented towards subjective needs fulfilment ('the development of human personality').

130 Ibid.
131 Ibid.
132 Ibid. 108 (emphasis added).
133 Moyn (n. 5) 67.

The logic of social rights is that of an *ordo* not a *ius*. Rather than a positivistic commitment awaiting juristic refinement, social rights are the *dogmatic*[134] of a socio-economic order to be brought about through a decisive collective agent, the state, which does far more than set boundaries for private economic decision making or guarantee the conditions for virtuous competition. The strong state envisaged by social rights circa 1945 fundamentally shapes private economic activity by directing its purposes, replacing it altogether in some domains, or enveloping it within thinner or thicker layers of constraining and facilitative public administration—dynamics accelerated by two World Wars, which demanded extensive public control over national economies and made concrete the organization of economic planning.[135]

The logic of social rights in this iteration can perhaps be most accurately described as an *aide-memoire* for a *material or economic constitution*.[136] This was more than symbolism. The social rights declarations, whether international or constitutional, rehearsed the social and political objectives of the state's (extensive) economic agency. They redescribed an immanent *topos* of ideas and arguments about the telos of the state's relationship to the economic, and at the same time rearticulated the purpose and meaning of the state's agency in terms of the realization of social rights. The concept and theory of the state was reshaped in this image, to the extent that political and social forces continued to grasp the state as *the* principal means to these declared ends.[137]

In his recent reconstruction of the 'grammar of constitutionalism' in India's 1947 Constitution, Khosla unpacks the logic of its declaration of economic and social rights as unenforceable and non-justiciable 'directive principles': 'The codification of the constitutional text [on, inter alia, socioeconomic rights] was seen as crucial to the creation of a common meaning because the ambit of understanding that a people come to form shares a relationship to the language that people employ. The

[134] E. Christodoulios, *The Redress of Law: Globalisation, Constitutionalism and Market Capture* (2021), chapter 2.3. A dogma in this account is an axiom for the intelligibility of the nature and purpose of the legal order: 'The dogmatic is set in place pre-interpretatively, setting in place the conditions of interpretation. It is in that profound sense axiomatic and heteronomous ... The *non-negotiability* of the fundamental values of reciprocity, solidarity and community that underlie what it means to *belong* in a world are installed and enshrined at the level of the dogmatic as the mainsprings of human association.' (235).

[135] Engerman, 'The Rise and Fall of Central Planning,' in M. Geyer and A. Tooze (eds), *The Cambridge History of the Second World War: Volume III, Total War: Economy, Society and Culture* (2015) 575–598.

[136] For a synthesis of various accounts of a material constitution, see Wilkinson and Goldoni, 'The Material Constitution', 81/4 *Modern Law Review* (2018) 567.

[137] In this sense, social rights circa 1945—and the various historical and conceptual claims which are made to explain and authorize them—follow a similar dynamic to other kinds of state theory: 'The creation of the modern state in Europe was accompanied by a political theory that ... reflected its development, reacted to its problems and offered solutions of a legal and institutional kind. This kind of political reflection is quickly absorbed by politics itself and becomes an aspect of the object on which it reflects. It descends, so to say, from the heights of pure theory into the murky atmosphere of reality and in this way is deflected, exploited, reified and thus becomes an aspect of whatever a new theory tries to discover.' Luhmann (n. 50) 25.

vocabulary that is put into use has a constitutive relationship to the social reality that comes into being.... Codification was employed to give the exercise of state power a normative direction, making it clear that certain commitments and conditions were necessary for such power to hold legitimacy.'[138] Codifying socioeconomic rights in the Indian Constitution was not merely an outgrowth of a political common ground among drafters, reduced to a legalistic register; it was a means through which the agency of the state in relation to private economic ordering was sought to be asserted, authorized, and inscribed within the purposes of the new Indian state.[139]

Mexico's 1917 revolutionary constitution[140] inspired a wider trend across Latin America to constitutionalize social rights and the broader economic purposes of the state.[141] The 1917 Constitution codified labour's right to organize,[142] enumerated an extensive catalogue of labour, health, and welfare rights,[143] guaranteed universal secular education,[144] and firmly asserted the authority of the state over the Catholic Church. It also comprehensively asserted the state's authority to regulate, redistribute, curtail and expropriate private property, encoding the theory that all private property rights (including to the subsoil and territorial waters) were a privilege created by the Nation that could be governed for the common good.[145] The result was 'the world's first fully conceived social democratic charter'[146] and the principal model for the uniform inclusion of social rights in Latin American constitutions—a uniformity that would be influentially registered through the survey of national constitutions undertaken by the UN Secretariat as a preliminary guide to the drafting of the Universal Declaration on Human Rights.[147]

The demand to include social rights *and* the 'right of the nation' over public property in the 1917 constitution reflected a logic of constitutionalization that was not a straightforward positivistic encapsulation of an already-existing welfare state (which, in fact, did not exist in Mexico at that time), but was closer to that evinced in the drafting of the Indian constitution. The constitutional text aimed to firmly and clearly assert the function of the state in resolving 'the social question'—by integrating 'deep political and social reforms into the juridical structure

[138] M. Khosla, *India's Founding Moment: The Constitution of a Most Surprising Democracy* (2020) 29–30.
[139] Ibid. 44–55.
[140] Branch and Rowe, 'The Mexican Constitution of 1917 Compared with the Constitution of 1857', 71 *Annals of the American Academy of Political and Social Science* (1917) 1.
[141] Grandin, 'The Liberal Tradition in the Americas: Rights, Sovereignty, and the Origins of Liberal Multilateralism', 117/1 *American Historical Review* (2012) 68; Thornton, '"Our Balkan Peninsula:" The Mexican Question in the League of Nations Debate', 46/2 *Diplomatic History* (2022) 237; R. Gargarella, *Latin American Constitutionalism, 1810–2010: The Engine Room of the Constitution* (2013) 92–107.
[142] Art. 28, in Branch and Rowe (n. 140) 25.
[143] Art. 123, ibid 93.
[144] Art. 3, ibid 2.
[145] Art. 27, ibid.
[146] Grandin (n. 141) 75.
[147] E/CN.4/AC.1/3/Add.1, 11 June 1947, in Schabas (n.116) 332 at 594–665.

of the country'.[148] The self-declared 'Jacobin' wing of the Constituent Congress demanded a 'very broad system of democratic safeguards and legal backup mechanisms' which would not only 'express in the Constitution a system of workers' rights and safeguards ... which liberal constitutions never mention' but also 'gave a legal basis for the later push toward nationalization of basic industries and development of the economy through the state sector'.[149] The key message in the rejection of the traditional liberal constitution proposed by Carranza, was the *centrality of 'the social question' to the legal and political organization of the new order*.[150] Despite ominous threats of US intervention to protect its corporations' property rights in Mexico,[151] and efforts by the domestic liberal factions to limit the reach of workers' rights by legislation, the 1917 constitution 'offered a new and original version of the social compact by integrating some renewed social demands in the basis of the traditional liberal-conservative agreement'.[152] It became 'the main mirror where Latin American critical movements within the region wanted to look' but also offered a re-articulation of the social foundations of the state which led 'liberal-conservative' leaders to recognize 'that the new Constitutions had to accommodate social demands'.[153]

The *constitutionalization of the social question* was thus an important precursor and context for the presence of social rights in the Universal Declaration and beyond. The ambition of constitutionalizing social rights in the early twentieth century was to articulate and somehow entrench in politics and law the fundamental purpose of the state as a collective political *and* economic agent charged with realizing a vision not only of social provisioning, but of constructing the material, political, and legal bases of democratic egalitarian citizenship. This was a wider and deeper project than the construction of welfare states and entails the state's role in economic planning and the anti-oligarchical function of redistributing resources and taming economic monopolies.[154]

[148] A. Gilly, *The Mexican Revolution* (2005) 232.
[149] Ibid. 233.
[150] Gargarella (n. 141) 103-105. See F. Tannenbaum, *Peace by Revolution: Mexico After 1910* (1966) 166–167: 'The Constitution was written by the *soldiers* of the Revolution, not by the lawyers, who were there, but were generally in the opposition. On all critical issues the lawyers voted against the majority of the Convention. The majority was in the hands of the soldiers – generals, colonels, majors – men who had marched and counter-marched across the Republic and had fought its battles. The ideas of the Constitutional Convention, as they developed, came from scattered sources. The soldiers wanted, as General Múgica said to me, to socialize property. But they were frightened – afraid of their won courage, of their own ideas. They found all of the learned men in the Convention opposed to them. Article 27 was a compromise.'
[151] See Grandin (n. 141); Thornton (n. 141).
[152] Gargarella (n. 141) 106.
[153] Ibid. 92, 106.
[154] This is provided for in Art. 28 of the Mexican Constitution, and was also raised by Jenks, Ellingston, and the Inter American Juridical Committee in their various commentaries on draft social rights provisions.

The constitutionalization of social rights preceded any coherent concept of the welfare state, but nonetheless connoted a horizon of expectation about what the state is for and how it should be made to be this way in reality. In this grammar, the state makes social rights, but social rights also make the state by functioning as constitutive power-authorizing concepts, alongside the limitative power-constraining concepts of traditional bourgeois rights. Social rights are *structuring* political-legal concepts, bearers of the dogmatic ideal of an economic order which is firmly and consistently bounded by basic axioms of political and legal value: labour solidarity, fair shares for all, social provisioning, anti-oligarchy, and constraint on concentrations of economic power.[155] It is in this sense that we can fully understand the Inter-American Juridical Committee's terse observation that social rights rest on 'the broad principle of distributive justice' in which was embedded the idea of 'the democratic state as a cooperative commonwealth whose objective is the general welfare of its members'.[156]

6. Fair Shares and Vital Minima—*Topoi* of Social Rights in the Eighteenth and Nineteenth Centuries

We thus grasp early- to mid-twentieth century social rights *topoi* as one generative political language for a hoped-for political-economic order, which united 'the social question' with the political question of egalitarian democratic citizenship, within a language of right that is as much political-ethical as it was legal.

This understanding provides a vantage point which makes antecedent family resemblances visible. The constitutionalization of the social question ought to be understood not so much as the beginning, but simply one terminus of, an extended and iterated argument about the relationship between state and economy traversing the nineteenth century. In these polemics, rights-languages and rights-concepts (or their repudiation) were part of the innovation of powerful political languages, and crucial to the way that these languages disputed the proper, just, or true relationship between key terms such as commercial society, government, sovereign power, and legislation.[157] While Marxist social democrats in the second half of the nineteenth century turned their faces against rights language as epiphenomenal abstractions of class relations—lagging and not leading social and economic change—we can observe across that century a range of rights discourses

[155] Fishkin and Forbath have recently traced the lineages of these ideas in 19th and 20th century debates about the US Constitution: J. Fishkin and W. E. Forbath, *The Anti-Oligarchy Constitution: Reconstructing the Economic Foundations of American Democracy* (2022).

[156] See n. 113.

[157] See for example R. Walter, *Before Methods and Models: The Political Economy of Malthus and Ricardo* (2021), chapter 1. See also M. Sonenscher, *Capitalism: The Story Behind the Word* (2022).

which framed, articulated, and motivated programmatic visions for a different economic order.

It is important to note that late eighteenth and nineteenth century rights discourses did not constitute a singular tradition or lineage of political and legal thought. There were several *topoi*,[158] descending from (or reacting to) different strands of early modern and medieval natural jurisprudence thinking.[159] Christoph Menke has observed that in European rights discourses, the relationship between 'right' and 'justice' was shaped by the twin inheritances of Athens and Rome. The epoch-making medieval receptions of Aristotle's political and ethical theories, and Roman law's rediscovery and appropriation,[160] endowed European political *and* legal thought with two distinct vocabularies through which to understand what it means to give someone their due: an Aristotelian language of *fair shares*, in which citizens 'receive in exchange for their own work ... a share in another's work that is proportionately commensurate to the politically determined significance of their respective work and activity for the community.'[161] *And*, the Roman jurisprudential preoccupation with defining through legal rules the boundaries of that which is one's own and hence what is constitutive of one's rightful entitlement. The distinctively juridical quality of the relationship between self and others developed in Roman law,[162] which used the term *ius* to qualify the legal order's recognition of powers over things and persons, was key to the utterly *jurisprudential* register in which European political thought unfolded.[163] Early modern natural right discourses exemplified this jurisprudential register by mobilizing neo-Roman concepts and categories to recast the foundations of political and economic order in terms of relations grounded in *ius* that conferred power and authority over that which is one's own (*sui*). What was one's own was not only property (made in an originary sense by mixing one's will with it through labour, and then transferred and allocated by further acts of will such as contracts and gifts), but also one's liberty, in the sense of not being subjected to the will of another except by an exercise

158 See E. R. Curtius, *European Literature and the Early Middle Ages* (1973) for the notion of *topoi* of rhetorics and arguments.

159 On the complex structure of early modern natural law and natural right, see M. Scattola, *Das Naturrecht von dem Naturrecht. Zur geschichte des >ius naturae< im 16. Jahrhundert* (1999); D. Edelstein, *On the Spirit of Rights* (2018) 4–5.

160 Q. Skinner, *Foundations of Modern Political Thought*, vol. 1 (1978); vol. 2 (1979).

161 C. Menke, *Critique of Rights* (2020) 37. Menke goes on to say: 'right as one's own is what is commensurate or corresponds to each person as he is. Just as arithmetical equality of rectification presupposes that distribution disrupted by loss was rectified, so the proportional equality of exchange consists in the realization of goods and rendering of services according to their relative significance in the life of the community – in the satisfaction of needs whose regulation is the state's political responsibility' (at 29).

162 See A. Schiavone, *The Invention of Law in the West* (2012); A. Schiavone, *The Pursuit of Equality in the West* (2022).

163 See for a recent example, Skinner, 'On Neo-Roman Liberty: A Response and a Reassessment', in H. Dawson and A. de Dijn (eds), *Rethinking Liberty before Liberalism* (2022) 233.

of one's own will.[164] Selves, wills, and property were the natural-legal building blocks of artificial legal and political orders, but the question of what happened to natural rights once such orders were created became one of the fundamental problematics of rights-thinking from 1600 to 1850.[165]

The language of natural right was never categorically divorced from the Athenian register of justice as fair shares; the latter returned in the form of radical demands for a right to one's share of political authority as popular sovereignty, and as a correlative demand for a share of the economic whole made possible by pooling one's natural rights to create society and polity. It is this grammar of collective natural right that I excavate below and argue to be a critical and powerful antecedent to the constitutionalization of social rights explicated above.

A. Collective Natural Right in English Radicalism and French Jacobinism

The radical thought of the English revolution combined the natural right of self-propriety (ownership over one's self as the condition sine qua non of liberty) with a natural jurisprudence of common endowment, which challenged the justice of enclosure and concentration of agricultural lands—and the legitimacy of unconstrained private property accumulation more generally.[166] This articulation of sovereignty as an emanation of the Body of the People also brought with it a correlative supposition: that equal shares of political authority implied fair shares of material resources essential to livelihoods.[167] Political justice implied the means to not be subjected to the arbitrary will of those with vastly superior means, lest radical unfreedom return through the backdoor of the polity in the form of concentrations of land and livelihood in the hands of a select few.

This lineage of natural right was decidedly collective: individuals together exercise natural rights as a People, in order to found a non-tyrannical political order but also to restore or recover a rightful portion of the whole that may have been usurped or excessively appropriated under unjust or corrupted political arrangements. Part and parcel of this collective natural right *topos* is a problematic of distribution, especially of land, as a critical litmus test for conformity with requirements of natural justice. Spence, Price, and Paine would elaborate, in different ways, some of these themes, and the distinction between the right to live (in the sense

[164] See Skinner, 'Rethinking Liberty in the English Revolution,' in Q. Skinner, *From Humanism to Hobbes* (2018) 139, at 156–157; Edelstein (n. 159); Bourke (n. 98).

[165] Edelstein (n. 159) chapter 1.

[166] S. Marks, *A False Tree of Liberty: Human Rights in Radical Thought* (2019) 92–93.

[167] See Susan Marks' reconstruction of the Putney debates and Levellers' pamphlets on this point, highlighting the criticism of the reduction of independent farmers to wage-labour, understood as a form of servitude precisely because of the subjection to the arbitrary will of another it entailed: ibid. chapter 4.

of subsistence) and the right to a just share of the whole was not sharply drawn.[168] The last quarter of the eighteenth century saw the emergence of radicalism as a coherent political programme, and under the star of French Revolutionary ferment, radicalism 'became a vehicle of plebeian political aspirations from the 1790s'.[169] Mixing a diagnosis of economic ills with a critique of political exclusion, radicalism became 'a critique of corrupting effects of the concentration of political power and its corrosive influence upon a society deprived of proper means of political representation'.[170] The French Revolutionary terror 'led to a general retreat from the language of rights on the part of moderate Whigs and the adoption of a language of "commerce, manners and civilisation"'[171] and nineteenth century British political thought was notable for its turn from natural right to utility.[172] The 'natural rights constitutionalism' spawned by the English civil war, which had been so influential in the New England colonies over the eighteenth century,[173] would wane. But languages of collective natural rights—inspired both by English radical thought and by the Jacobin constitution in France—would re-emerge in the first part of the nineteenth century among nascent working class and popular movements associated with Chartism.[174]

On the other side of the Channel, a different but compatible idea of collective natural right was emerging from 1700, one that through the nineteenth century would deeply shape the terms through which a nascent market society would be contested. Edelstein has recently highlighted the emergence of *social naturalism* in 18th century France, which combined the jurisprudential language of natural right with arguments about their immanent realization within a well-constituted social order. He observes that 'beginning sporadically in the 1750s, then accelerating in the 1760s, French authors such as Diderot, Helvétius, d'Holbach, Raynal, Condorcet, and even future revolutionary leader Mirabeau … maintained that "society is just, good, worthy of our love, when it fulfils the physical needs of its

[168] Marks (n. 166) chapters 6–8. Paine's *Agrarian Justice* can be construed as a kind of sufficientarianism, but it seems to me this reading must be balanced with his strong insistence on originary (not historical) rights as rights held immediately of God and only overlain later by historical rights such as property, which can well be acquired unjustly due to failing to give a fair price to labour: 'All accumulation, therefore, of personal property, beyond what a man's own hands produce, is derived to him by living in society; and he owes on every principle of justice, of gratitude, and of civilization, *a part of that accumulation back again to society from whence the whole came*. This is putting the matter on a general principle, and perhaps it is best to do so; for if we examine the case minutely it will be found that the accumulation of personal property is, in many instances, the effect of paying too little for the labour that produced it.' (emphasis added). T. Paine, *Agrarian Justice Opposed to Agrarian Law and to Agrarian Monopoly; being a plan for Meliorating the Condition of Man by Creating in Every Nation a National Fund* (1796, 1819 edition) 16.

[169] Stedman Jones (n. 78) 12; E. Royle, *Chartism* (1996, 3rd ed.) 8–9.

[170] Stedman Jones (n. 78) 12.

[171] G. Stedman Jones, *An End to Poverty? A Historical Debate* (2008) 106–107.

[172] Conti, 'On the Nadir of Natural Rights Theory in Nineteenth-Century Britain', in Edelstein and Pitts (n. 98); Foucault (n. 90) 41.

[173] Edelstein (n. 159) 145–147.

[174] Stedman Jones (n. 78); Stedman Jones (n. 171) 106–107; Royle (n. 169).

members, and guarantees their safety, freedom and possession of their natural rights." '[175] On this account, the creation of society and political order did not transfer natural rights to the sovereign, but maintained them as part of an immanent *ordre naturel* that positive sovereign law should strive to realize. Society, including political and commercial society, became the 'ultimate preserve of natural rights.'[176]

This social naturalism had a curious double aspect: on the one hand, it underwrote Physiocratic arguments that, in respect of the natural laws of commercial society, positive law should govern as little as necessary (laissez faire), and natural order was epitomized by the emergence of self-organizing dynamics attributed to commerce and trade.[177] On the other hand, the notion of society as a natural order also brought with it an objective standard of justice, determined by natural laws and the realization of natural right within society. Pre-Physiocratic Jansenist theologian and Roman lawyer, Jean Domat, argued that civil laws of contract and property approximated the requirements of a natural social and legal order; but also part of this order was the duty placed on all members of society to impart 'to those who have Nothing' a 'Share of those Goods which they have a right to . . . .'[178] Leading Physiocrat, Quesnay, concluded that even within a sovereign order, 'the portion granted to every man will belong to him by natural and legitimate right [. . .].'[179] This portion was the fair share of goods guaranteed to every man by the necessarily just natural order. In Quesnay's and other Physiocratic theories, the natural right to a fair share did not imply social equality—those who make a 'bad use of our liberty' have only themselves to blame, and to eliminate inequality would thus contradict the order of society as it emerged by permitting use of natural liberty. But, the just natural order in society did entail collective duties towards members of society who are unable to work through no fault of their own.[180] Later Physiocrats, including Quesnay's pupil Pierre Paul Le Mercier de la Riviere, finance minister (*controller générale de* finance) Anne-Robert Jacques Turgot, and Pierre Samuel Dupont de Nemours, would all mention a right to assistance or public welfare for individuals incapable of working. Turgot would argue that 'the poor have unquestionable rights on the abundance of the rich'[181] while Dupont du Nemours

[175] Edelstein (n. 159) 74, footnote to quotation from Burlamaqui omitted.

[176] Edelstein (n. 159) 79.

[177] M. Foucault, *Society Must be Defended* (2003); Foucault (n. 90); A. Funkenstein, *Theology and the Scientific Imagination From The Middle Ages to the Seventeenth Century* (1986); J. Sheehan and D. Wahrman, *Invisible Hands. Self-Organization and the Eighteenth Century* (2015).

[178] J. Domat, *The Civil Law in its Natural Order: Together with the Public Law* (1722), cited in Edelstein (n. 159) 125.

[179] Cited in Edelstein (n. 159) 76.

[180] F. Quesnay, *Essai Physique sur l'oeconomie animale* (1736), cited in Edelstein (n. 159) 80.

[181] Cited in Edelstein, 'Public Welfare and the Natural Order: On the Theological and Free-Market Sources of Socio-economic Rights', in Jensen and Walton (n. 96) 47, at 55.

would argue for an article guaranteeing the right to public assistance in the 1789 Declaration of Rights of Man and Citizen.[182]

The right to a fair share required by natural law was a gloss on Ulpian's definition of justice as 'the obligation to render to each person what belongs to him' (*Iustitia est constans et perpetua voluntas ius suum cuique tribuens*)—a legal maxim that became a political dictum by which to frame the requirements of justice in a natural social order. The social naturalist theories of the Physiocrats understood the meaning of fair shares as amounting to a right to assistance to achieve a vital minimum necessary for livelihoods, not as a claim to egalitarianism. But, perhaps despite themselves and the natural order of commerce they wished to canonize, the transposition of *the social* as the bearer and guarantor of natural right and natural law, lent itself readily to a powerful transformation in the idea of what justice really demanded and who might demand it. Condorcet argued that the realization of natural rights in society was the duty of Government, and that duty was owed *to the nation* on behalf of all its members.[183] An older corporatist vernacular of 'les droit nationaux' ascribed to *each* Estate became, in anticipation of the calling of the Estates General, *les droits de la nation* that vested in a collective body which represented the people. Crucially, the task of such a body would be 'to establish the rights of the nation on a firm basis, by founding them on the natural rights of every human society.'[184] And one such natural right was the right to a fair share, the meaning of which would be subjected to a different understanding by the eruption of the democratic political egalitarianism of Jacobinism.

Proposals for the inclusion of social rights—such as education, work, and subsistence—circulated widely during the drafting of the 1789 Declaration of the Rights of Man.[185] Walton notes that the language of such model declarations 'were often coupled with duties and expressed in highly egalitarian language.'[186] Early in the Revolution, social rights declarations expressed a range of different inspirations: Physiocratic, as we have seen, but also religious and sentimental. The Physiocratic model of social provisioning, embedded as it was in the embrace of commercial society, was criticized by Jacobins as resting on a hierarchical ideal of charity by the wealthy towards the poor and thus replicating the 'insolent generosity of [the people's] former tyrants.'[187] Walton, in a recent revisiting of the 1789 and 1793 debates, concludes that social rights were not included in the first

[182] In the *Cahier de doléances* that he authored for Dupont de Nemours, he demanded that 'Anyone in a state of infancy, impotence, invalidity, or disability, has a right to free assistance from other men.' Edelstein (n. 159) 83.

[183] Edelstein (n. 159) 83.

[184] Comte d'Antraigues, *Mémoire sur les Etats Généraux* (1788), in Edelstein (n. 159) 94.

[185] Gauchet counted 13 model declarations including social rights, while Walton counts 14: M. Gauchet, *La Révolution des droits de l'homme* (1989), 96; Walton, 'Who Pays? Social Rights and the French Revolution' in Jensen and Walton (n. 96) 63, at 64 n 6.

[186] Walton (n. 185) 65.

[187] Director of the Bureau d'Esprit Public, François-Xavier Lanthenas, September 1792, cited in Walton (n. 185) 68.

Declaration because the National Assembly was bitterly divided on the possibility of financing them through taxes, and because many believed that (following Physiocratic theories, which were expounded at length in Assembly debates) economic liberalization would be the vehicle for achieving social rights. Demands to address indigency, poverty, and mendicancy grew, and numerous proposals were put to the Assembly's committees to recognize social assistance as a fundamental right, but the principle of voluntary assistance held sway until the multiple crises of 1793. With the execution of the King in January, food riots in Paris from February, and civil and foreign wars underway, Revolutionaries 'largely agreed that [social rights] should be included in the republican constitution … but remained sharply divided over financing them'.[188] Debates about the 1793 constitution reconstructed by Walton show a deeper debate about whether a liberal economy would effectively ensure the natural right to assistance, or whether the National Assembly should declare limits to property rights in order to tax wealth and set prices as a means of promoting social assistance and greater social equality.[189] The final draft of 26 April 1793 contained social rights as well as guarantees of private property and free markets, reflecting a 'concession to the sans-culottes and a pragmatic means to win public support for a regime desperately in need of soldiers'.[190] The effectiveness of Jacobin social assistance in relieving the economic crises faced by the poor in Revolutionary France was weak;[191] but what does appear to have flourished was an articulation of social right which is distinct from charity and voluntary assistance, and in which the notion of a 'fair share' as the foundation of the duty to guarantee such rights, played a more significant role: 'The 1793 Declaration of Rights is both the consecration of "bourgeois individualism," frowned on by Karl Marx but praised by Alexis de Tocqueville, and the validation of "social justice," frowned on by Tocqueville but preached by Jean Jaurés.'[192]

Confronted by war-induced scarcity and a heavy reliance on roving deputies acting as Commissioners to govern in the absence of a consolidated post-revolutionary state apparatus, Jacobin commitments to social assistance, land reform and progressive taxation were only ever very incompletely implemented. But the agenda was articulated in ways which became totemic for nineteenth century debates about the connection between social reform and a just political order.[193] An important contributor to the text of the 1793 Declaration, Gilbert

[188] Ibid. 73.
[189] Ibid. 74.
[190] Ibid. 75.
[191] Ibid. 78.
[192] J. P. Gross, *Fair Shares for All: Jacob Egalitarianism in Practice* (1996) 45.
[193] See especially the sweeping review in Moyn (n. 5), chapter 1, and the more detailed dissection of the Jacobin legacy for the language of 19th century political thought in: Chambost, 'Socialist Visions of Direct Democracy: The Mid-Century Crisis of Popular Sovereignty and the Constitutional Legacy of the Jacobins', in D. Moggach and G. Stedman Jones (eds), *The 1848 Revolutions and European Political Thought* (2018) 94.

Romme (mathematician and leading Jacobin member of the *Comité d'instruction publique*) explained the logic of social rights which expressed clearly the 'natural-rights-ist' grammar of fair shares: 'Men, in joining together in society, pool all their natural rights, in order to wage a common and successful struggle against the various obstacles which stand in the way of their well-being. Social rights are the share each man gets from the common pool.'[194] This right to a fair share reflected the first 'social law' which overrode all others, according to Robespierre, by which everything that was essential to preserve life was a 'property common to society as a whole'.[195] The distinction between subsistence and social equality remained blurry in Jacobin discourses,[196] but critical for our purposes is the rigorous logic of fair shares—a right of the whole, not of the individual—as taking priority over the individual right of property and the self-organization of the market. The ambition was not necessarily equal material conditions, but an equality of common livelihoods through the opportunity to receive the fruits of one's own labour. Nonetheless man's right to a fair share of his work entailed, on this understanding, the collective duty to ensure that work was available and even to supply the means of work where tools were in scare supply.[197] Jacobin representatives imagined, and in some cases realized, public works such as highway repairs and bridge building, financed by progressive taxes levied on the wealthy. Rejecting a comparison with the hated *corvée*, Jacobin commissioners maintained that such public works provide a wage covering basic needs and even access to a provident fund in case of illness, accident, or incapacity. Underpinning the provision of work was not only protection from immiseration, but also claim to a necessary base line for political equality. Physician Jean-Baptiste Bo explained to provincial audiences that just as no citizen could be allowed to 'buy another', no poor man could be obliged to 'sell himself': 'It is high time to erase this demarcation between the citizen who enjoys and he who labours: the Constitution endows them with the same political existence and we are bound by morality to do so.'[198] As Gross summarizes, the notion of a right to work here went beyond subsistence and,

> opened up a new vista of systematic job creation and the possibility of a labor market which would not be exclusively determined by the law of supply and demand. The affirmation of the right to work imposed on the state the ominous contractual obligation to provide it, and the notion of a contract of employment between equals generated recognition of a fair salary for services rendered ... A sense of collective responsibility was beginning to permeate economic and social relationships ...[199]

[194] Preamble to Romme's draft declaration 1793, cited in Gross (n. 192) 55.
[195] Ibid. 69–70.
[196] As stressed by Moyn (n. 5) chapter 1.
[197] Gross (n. 192) 149.
[198] Speech cited in Gross (n. 192) 152.
[199] Gross (n. 192) 153.

The Thermidorean reaction would sweep away the structures by which the Jacobin had sought to govern France,[200] ending—eventually—the Terror, and abolishing universal suffrage in its Constitution of Year III (1795). A property qualification for electoral participation was re-introduced, and an 'aristocracy of wealth' re-consecrated: 'Society in France, as elsewhere in Europe, was now set on a competitive and confrontational course, breeding further inequalities and class distinctions, and blurring the legitimacy of communal obligations.'[201]

B. Into the Nineteenth Century—The Right to Work, the Right to the Whole Produce of Labour, and Social Democracy

The *topoi* of collective natural right linked several diverse kinds of claims together around a core notion of shares in a political and economic whole. To not be at the mercy of another individual for the basic requirements of subsistence was necessary to avoid a condition similar to slavery: common livelihood required protection to avoid subjection to the arbitrary will of another who would otherwise control the conditions of such livelihood. This is an extension of the logic of self-propriety as liberty. But one's right to a fair share of the whole was also iterated as part of the idea of a right to work and receive a fair reward for the fruits of labour, where labour was the foundation of the common wealth of a society. The idea that productive uses of labour were indispensable to increasing wealth was common to both classical political economy ('the labour theory of value' accepted by Smith, Ricardo, and Marx alike) and political thought. Ideas of collective provision (of work, means of work, subsistence, and so on) rested on an implied claim and right by a collective agent *to the whole* product of this labour (Romme's 'common pool', for example) in order to guarantee its fair distribution: the duty to preserve natural right *within* the social correlates with a right *of* the social to ensure a fair share for all.

The nineteenth century Chartist movement in England, Wales, and Scotland would return to the language of natural right to make collective claims for political and social fair shares.[202] They challenged the uninterrupted exclusion of the property-less from political franchise in Britain, maintaining that the transition to political society preserved those natural rights which conduced to a cooperative and democratic society of equals.[203] A political order which did not protect those rights failed to meet the requirements of natural jurisprudence. Cardinal among them was the right to vote for all, and the right to a means of livelihood which did

[200] A. Cobban, *A History of Modern France*, vol. 1, 1715–1799 (1965) 250.
[201] Gross (n. 192) 204.
[202] Gibson, 'Natural Right and the Intellectual Context of Early Chartist Thought', 84 *History Workshop Journal* (2017) 194.
[203] Ibid. 197.

not compel members of society to subject themselves to the tyrannical power of those who controlled the means by which labour could earn a decent living. The proposal to abolish the Poor Laws in 1834 provoked a 'great popular movement'[204] engendering a unity of purpose among nascent working men's associations, factory movements, artisan guilds, journeymen, printers and newsagents, shopkeepers and tradesmen, that came together under the Chartist banner.[205]

The Chartists' 'natural rights constitutionalism'[206] appealed to a wide cross-section of working people directly affected by the adolescence of the market economy taking root in Britain and across Europe. Its message was that the litany of social and economic grievances of a generation—'overworked or unemployed, ill-paid, badly housed, de-skilled, exploited and suffering from what were seen as the effects of the Whig "class" legislation of the 1830s'[207]—was the direct result of the corrupting effects of the concentration of political power through a violation of the natural right of suffrage.[208] The unnatural monopoly of political power enabled the unnatural concentration of economic means, with the latter resulting in a deprivation of labour's natural right to the fruits of its work.[209] The political despotism of the propertied classes, on this narrative, led directly to an economic despotism that destroyed the livelihoods of working people and rendered them unable to exercise the self-propriety necessary for natural liberty. The 'combination and tyranny of capitalists'[210] could not be tamed because 'until the proletarian classes are fully and faithfully represented, justice in legislation will never be rendered unto them.'[211] The transformation of political institutions expected to be brought about by universal suffrage, would also transform the economic domination that the unenfranchised suffered at the hands of the enfranchised. Restoring the natural right of suffrage would reverse the subjection of labour to the tyranny of the 'millocrat,' 'cotton lord,' 'steam aristocracy' and others who, because of their proprietorship of land and money, had taken 'unlimited control over the productive power of the country. Under this system, the producer [worker] receives not what he earns ... not the value of his produce in money or other produce, but what the parties choose to give him.'[212]

[204] Royle (n. 169) 22. Gatherings at which Chartist leaders spoke in Hartshead Moor, Glasgow, and Birmingham attracted between 100,000 and 250,000 people in 1837–1838, and 7,000 colliers attempted, unsuccessfully, to seize the town of Newport and declare a republic in 1839.

[205] Royle (n. 169) chapter 10.

[206] Gibson (n. 202); Edelstein (n. 159) chapter 6.

[207] Royle (n. 169) 93.

[208] See Stedman Jones, 'Elusive Signifiers: 1848 and the Language of Class Struggle', in Moggach and Stedman Jones (n. 193) 452, at 435.

[209] Stedman Jones (n. 78) 17, citing Cobbett (1817): 'Whatever the pride of rank or riches or of scholarship may have induced some men to believe, or affect to believe, the real strength and all the resources of the country, have ever sprung and ever must spring from the labour of its people.'

[210] Objects of the London Democratic Association, April 1838.

[211] Ibid.

[212] *Poor Man's Guardian*, 1835, quoted in Stedman Jones (n. 78) 20.

The key demand of the People's Charter, proposed by Chartists as a draft Parliamentary Bill was what we would call a political right—the right to vote—but within the context of natural rights constitutionalism, it was inextricably linked to a demand for a fair share of the political *and social* whole: to end the possessing classes' monopoly on legislation was to turn legislation in to a means of restoring to the unenfranchised what was due to them as a matter of justice, not just fair wages but also 'abridgment of the hours of labour in factories and workshops ... the total abolition of infant labour ... [and] the destruction of inequality, and the establishment of general happiness'.[213] The editor of the *Poor Man's Guardian* (an underground paper which sold 16,000 copies a week at its peak), declared: 'Knaves will tell you, that it is because you have no property that you are unrepresented. I tell you, on the contrary, it is because you are unrepresented that you have no property.'[214] At the 1838 Kersal Moor meeting, which reportedly attracted over 100,000 people to elect a Convention that would press the Parliament to adopt the Charter, popular Northern minister J.R. Stephens declared the right to vote to be a 'knife and fork issue after all'. He articulated the right to vote as essentially *entailing* a right to a parity of decent livelihood among working people—more, certainly, than mere subsistence, and approximating a kind of common standard of living owed to all who work:

> This question of Universal Suffrage was a knife and fork question after all; this question was a bread and cheese question ...; and if any man ask him (Stephens) what he meant by Universal Suffrage, he would answer, that every working man in the land had a right to have a good coat to his back, a comfortable abode in which to shelter himself and his family, a good dinner upon his table, and no more work than was necessary for keeping him in health, and as much wages for that work as would keep him in plenty, and afford him the enjoyment of all the blessings of life which a reasonable man could desire.[215]

The political fortunes of Chartism waned after 1840, in no small part because it had been a 'hunger movement, the outcome of intolerable and widespread distress. As conditions improved with the rapid growth of British world trade, the repressiveness both of the Government and of the employers was relaxed.'[216] Rising wages, declining unemployment and piece meal legislative reform of working hours and conditions (such as the Ten Hours Act of 1947), 'seemed to give the lie to the Chartist contention that without the Charter nothing could be done to improve the condition of the people'.[217] Eclipsed by trade unionism, Fabianism, and Christian

[213] Objects of the London Democratic Association.
[214] Bornterre O'Brien, quoted in Royle (n. 169) 92–93.
[215] *Northern Star*, 29 September 1838, document 2 extracted in Royle (n. 169) 96–97.
[216] G. D. H. Cole, *British Working Class Politics 1832–1914* (1941) 22.
[217] Ibid.

ethical movements from the second half of the nineteenth century, natural rights constitutionalism as a register for articulating and demanding what we would now call social rights also declined in the British context—abetted no doubt by the Whig, Tory, and middle-class aversion to natural rights talk under the combined influence of Burke and Bentham.[218]

But for our purposes what is interesting is the framing of a critique of the social and economic consequences of capitalism within a language of natural right that can be understood as collective and constitutional, and which imperatively unites the achievement of democratic egalitarian citizenship—and the protection of natural liberty—with the taming of monopolies of political and economic power. Particular kinds of entitlements and demands (food, housing, education, a certain level of comfort, leisure) are expressions of a natural social law that must be guaranteed and reproduced through the conscious political and economic decisions of an authorized collective agent (or group of them). For the Chartists, this agent was the Parliament, an institution of political society which, for its legitimacy and continued conformity with natural legality, had to ensure the full and faithful representation of the People through Universal Suffrage, *in order to be able* to deliver justice to them in respect of the social harms flowing from the concentration of money and property in the hands of a few. The latter implied a reorganization of economic authority and a redistribution of the fruits of labour, which had accumulated unjustly to those monopolizing political power. The resulting grammar of social right is a kind of natural jurisprudence for the dispossessed and non-possessing classes, which demanded both liberty (in the sense of self-propriety) and justice (in the sense of giving each their due as part of the whole). The *suum cuique* of each political equal implies an injunction against permitting the *suum* of the proprietors of money and land from entailing a *cuique* which defied or even destroyed the nature of public power as a common, collective agent capable of representing and acting on behalf of the whole. A right to one's own becomes a right to a fair share, in order to protect against the real risk in market society that one's own becomes so disproportionately engrossed, and another's so drastically diminished, that public power ceases to be so and becomes the arbitrary private will of individuals—the classical definition of corruption itself.[219]

In France after 1799, the grammar of social rights as collective natural right would have an enduring influence in republican and proto-socialist responses to the 'social question', and to the liberal concern with limiting universal suffrage. This influence would not be in the form of the direct enumeration of rights as legal entitlements. Instead—and more powerfully—a renewed appropriation of Jacobin rhetorics of natural social right and republicanism combined with a critique of the

[218] Conti (n. 172).
[219] Pocock (n. 105) 42.

observed dynamics of market society, to outline a concept of the democratic-social state *as governor and regulator of private property and private economic right.*

In place of the protective restrictions of the corporatist structures (such as guilds) swept away by the Revolution, and after the brief Jacobin interregnum, France by the early 1800s had adopted a rigorous regime of *propriétarianisme* and liberal political economy.[220] Popular sovereignty, in the form of universal suffrage, was blamed for the excesses of Jacobinism and the Terror by ultra-royalists and liberals alike; the former declared popular sovereignty a 'juridical monster', while the latter insisted that a property-based franchise was needed to ensure that popular sovereignty's pathologies could be tamed by the superior reasoning capacities of 'French society's most accomplished and wealthy property-owning members'.[221] While the Jacobins of the 1790s 'overwhelmingly sought to legitimate the principle of private property and generally favoured moral and legal over genuine social equality',[222] the 1793 constitution continued to inspire French radicals' and socialists' visions of a 'more fully emancipated post-revolutionary society based on the restructuring of the division of labour'.[223]

Early socialism (derided later as Utopian socialism by Engels[224]) had little interest in natural rights language. It was a quasi-religious and spiritual idea, preoccupied with creating the basis for the political and economic unity of society through scientific knowledge of human psychology and physiology. It responded to the moral and spiritual disorder and crisis of 25 years of revolution, foreign and civil war, and the rapid creation of a market order.[225] The common ambition of early socialist figures such as Owen, Saint-Simon, and Fourier, despite very different theories and plans for a new world, was to 'make it possible for mankind to turn away from sterile philosophical controversy and from the destructive arena of politics and to resolve, in scientific fashion, the problem of social harmony'.[226] The social and economic upheavals attendant upon commercial and industrial revolution would come to be labelled 'the social question' for the first time, in 1831.[227]

220 Piketty (n. 19) 120–125.

221 Chambost (n. 193) 98. These were the so-called *capacitaires* to whom voting rights were limited. Stedman Jones (n. 208) 440.

222 Chambost (n. 193) 96 n.8.

223 Ibid. 96.

224 F. Engels, 'Socialism: Utopian and Scientific', *Revue Socialiste* (1880), in *Marx and Engels Selected Works*, vol. 3 (1970) 95.

225 Beecher, 'Early European Socialism', in G. Klosko (ed), *The Oxford Handbook of the History of Political Philosophy* (2011) 369, at 370: 'the first socialists ... were writing out of a broader sense of social and moral disintegration. They were looking for order and authority in a world torn apart by revolution, and their ideas were presented as a remedy for the collapse of community rather than any specific economic problem.' See also Stedman Jones, 'European Socialism from the 1790s to the 1890s', in W. Breckman and P. E. Gordon (eds), *The Cambridge History of Modern European Thought*, vol 1. The Nineteenth Century (2019) 196; Rosenblatt, 'On the Need for a Protestant Reformation: Constant, Sismondi, Guizot and Laboulaye', in R. Geenens and H. Rosenblatt (eds), *French Liberalism from Montesquieu to the Present Day* (2012) 115, at 127.

226 Beecher (n. 225) 373.

227 H. Case, 'The "Social Question," 1820–1920', 13/3 *Modern Intellectual History* (2016) 747, at 756.

The social truth of an economically liberal market order appeared to its critics and diagnosticians as the antithesis of both community and harmony. Instead, it seemed to sow only conflict, through relentless competition and by deepening the immiseration and precarity of those who, in the last instance, were considered to be the source of the production of all wealth in society—the labouring population.

Swiss political economist Jean Charles Léonard de Sismondi observed in 1824 the tendency towards overproduction and underconsumption in European markets, precipitating crises of profitability that unpredictably imperilled the manufacturing workforce.[228] Human labour, reduced increasingly to operating machines, was at the mercy of a small group of rich manufacturers, who owned the machines: 'today, a manufacturer, having summoned to himself numerous families, abandons them suddenly without employment, because he has discovered that a steam engine can perform all their work'.[229] The stark polarization between rich and poor—between those who owned the means by which labour could be employed for wages, and those who owned no property and could only sell their labour (called the proletariat by de Sismondi)—was a product not of mere bad luck or a lack of frugality, but of the new reality that 'a caprice, a rumour on the stock exchange, some distant event happening at the other end of the world can put machines out of action and with them thousands of hands.'[230] French readers of de Sismondi in the 1820s and 1830s concluded that de Sismondi had revealed that 'the battlefield is no longer on the plains, but in the workshops ... This is a true war, where the combatants employ ingenious and powerful machines which on the terrain of pauperism leave millions of workers gasping for breath, men and women, without concern for old age or infancy. It is a serious conflict between different classes of workers ... France appears to oppose England, but capital struggles far more deeply against the worker.'[231]

There were deemed to be two principal pathologies of this 'great social sore which is termed commerce'.[232] The first was its relentless and destructive competition between producers, which in turn pushed wages to starvation levels and below: 'who would be blind enough not to see that under the reign of competition the continuous decline of wages necessarily becomes a general law ...? A machine is invented ... one thousand workmen, whom the new machine displaces in the workshops, will knock at the door of the next one and will force down the wages of

[228] de Sismondi, 'De la balance des consommations et des productions', 22 *Revue Encyclopédique* (1824); de Sismondi, 'Political Economy', *Brewster's Edinburgh Encyclopedia* (1815), cited in Stedman Jones (n. 171), 147.

[229] J. C. L. de Sismondi, *Nouveax principes d'économie politique*, vol. 1 (1819), cited in Stedman Jones (n. 171) 154.

[230] E. Buret, *De la misère des classes laborieuses en Angleterre et en France* (1842), cited in Stedman Jones, (n. 171) 169.

[231] J. Blanqui, *Histoire de l'économie politique* (1842), cited in Stedman Jones (n. 171) 169.

[232] L. Blanc, *Organization of Labor* ([1840] 1848 trans.), 85 https://www.google.co.uk/books/edition/The_Organization_of_Labour_Translated_fr/pPn9ie3knDYC?hl=en&gbpv=1&pg=PP8&printsec=frontcover (last accessed 13 March 2023).

their fellow workers ... It is nothing but an industrial process by means of which the proletarians are forced to exterminate each other.'[233] The second pathology was the rapid accumulation of wealth by the owners of the machines, now called capitalists, despite the terrible consequences of competition for labour and the continuing downward pressure on wages as the apparent origin of this wealth. The latter phenomenon added a strong sense of injustice to the injury of labour's immiseration. It remained the common view among political economists and lay people that wealth produced in society was a result of human labour not inanimate objects, and that unearned income grossly disproportionate to applied labour was a pure rent, seized from those who worked by means of a legal order which expansively protected capitalists' property rights.[234] A vast imbalance in property and income was not *only* a problem of guaranteeing subsistence to those who might otherwise starve or be homeless; it was also, within this theory, a question of who or what was entitled to the value of the whole produce of labour *and in what proportion*: 'the condition of the worker has become something sacred and precious ... and henceforth, the progress of wealth will not be considered as truly useful, except to the extent that its benefits will spread out to include those who will take part. The principle has been posed, it is for systems of legislation to draw out the consequences.'[235]

This diagnosis of market society had immediate political and institutional implications. The resolution of the social question became directly tied to the emancipation of labour from the risks of immiseration through relentless competition, *and* from a legal order which enabled *too much* of the whole product of labour to be seized by those owning capital and real property. *How much* of a fair share of the whole product amounted to the just share, varied according to the relative radicalism of different visions of a new political and legal order, from reformist to revolutionary. But common to these developing democratic and social discourses was the idea that some collective agent or set of them (associations or cooperatives of workers, or, a democratic state constituted through universal suffrage), would need to act in order to claim a right over the whole product of labour, if not to confiscate it entirely, then certainly in order to temper, improve or correct its distribution. Reflecting in 1886 on almost a century of socialist thought, Austrian jurist Anton Menger concluded that 'these two conceptions of natural rights—the right to the whole produce of labour and the right to subsistence' both implied an 'organic modification of traditional forms of property'.[236]

The Society of the Rights of Man, a Parisian political club founded in 1833 to revive Jacobin political ideas, drew in Fourierists and Saint-Simonians, but also a

[233] Blanc, ibid, 15. For de Sismondi's direct influence on Blanc, see L. A. Loubère, *Louis Blanc: His Life and His Contribution to the Rise of French Jacobin-Socialism* (1961) 32–33.

[234] See the review of various theories of injustice derived from the labour theory of value in A. Menger, *The Right to the Whole Produce of Labor* ([1886] 1899), especially at 54.

[235] Blanqui (1842) 10, in Stedman Jones (n. 171) 165.

[236] Menger (n. 234) 177.

new generation of radicals for whom 'the labour question' was *the* political question of the epoch.[237] The demand to regulate and govern the destructive competition of market society, and assure to labour a just share of the value of the product of labour, was articulated by neo-Jacobin writers such as Blanc and Considérant in terms of a *right to work*. This was not a positive legal right claimed against the state. It was an idea of right which expressed an order of political, social, and economic relations that amended or replaced the ruthless dynamics of competition in a market society. In Considérant's articulation (following Fourier), the 'right to work' was a natural right preserved within society that reflected the right of man to benefit from the common pool of wealth made possible by the creation of society and produced through labour.[238] The right to work entailed *both* the right to subsistence by restraining the ruthless competition and profiteering considered responsible for the immiseration of labour, *and* the right to a just share of the whole by regulating the conditions under which labour was performed and rewarded—including by reorganizing the structure of production into labour associations and cooperatives under the supervision of the state.[239]

The neo-Jacobins went on to have a decisive influence on the political discourses surrounding the 1848 revolutions in France, and beyond. Their ideas retained the fundamental structure of what I have called 'collective natural rights' thinking, in so far as they anticipated the realization of natural rights *within* society through the creation and intervention of a unified public power. The fundamental purpose and nature of this power was reflected in its democratic constitution as a republic, through universal suffrage. The democratic constitution of the republican state within this collective natural rights grammar entailed the right, and need, to reorganize social and economic relations through legislative power, in order to end the exploitation of labour and prevent the destruction of social solidarity through excessive wealth accumulation.[240] Blanc, for example, argued that 'men could have no other goal when forming societies than to mutually protect themselves against the undertakings of the most cunning, the most audacious and the strongest. In this way, the idea of the state is born precisely from the need to protect against tyranny.'[241] Included in Blanc's typology of tyranny was 'the tyranny of property over non-proprietors ...[which is] worse than that of the ancient regime despots since it is polymorphous and invisible, holds no one to account, evolves in a framework of legal equality, and dons the mask of liberty, allowing each of society's members

[237] Loubère (n. 233) and Loubère, 'Intellectual Origins of Neo-Jacobinism', 4/3 *International Review of Social History* (1959) 415.

[238] Menger on Considérant (n. 234) 19.

[239] See Gerçek, 'The "Social Question" as a Democratic Question: Louis Blanc's *Organization of Labor*', *Modern Intellectual History* (2022) 1

[240] Loubère, 'Intellectual Origins' (n. 237) 420–423, 425; Loubère, *Louis Blanc* (n. 233) 26, 56.

[241] Louis Blanc, 'L'Etat dans la démocratie' (1849), cited in Spitz, 'The "Illiberalism" of French Liberalism: The Individual and the State in the Thought of Blanc, Dupont-White and Durkheim', in Geenens and Rosenblatt (n. 225) 252.

to enjoy what he or she has required'.[242] The democratic state must be placed above such individual tyrannies in order to constitute the real path to liberty, its social power being 'necessary for the development of an authentic individualism, one that enables each person to design and shape his or her existence without succumbing to the will of others, thus using the intellectual (knowledge) and material (social security, right to credit and to work) means that only a democratic state can guarantee for all'.[243]

The demand for a 'right to work' was framed in the vernacular of a natural constitutional right, but is better grasped as a synecdoche for the construction and authorization of a collective agent, in the form of a democratic social state, which would solve the social question through a wide range of interventions in and management of economic and social relationships.[244] In 1843, Blanc glossed 'the right to work' as a collection of correlative duties: to the healthy citizen, the state owed work; to the old and infirm, it owed aid and protection; to the young, it owed free and obligatory education.[245] In February 1848, as a member of the Provisional Government of the Second Republic, Blanc would respond to the Parisian workers' militant demand for the immediate creation of a 'right to work' by the Republic, with a proclamation which pledged 'to guarantee the existence of the worker by labour; it pledges itself to guarantee work to all citizens; it recognizes that workers should associate among themselves to enjoy the legitimate profits of their labour ... '[246] Feminist and Fourierist Jean Deroin argued in the short-lived *L'Opinion des femmes* (January to August 1849) that the basic right to life entailed the right to develop one's capacities through 'equal education for all ... the right to work; access to all social functions'.[247] Society itself was based on three principles: the right to consume, 'through the redistribution of the fruits of labour of all according to the needs of each and the necessities of her/his trade'; the right to work, 'through the distribution of the instruments of labour needed to produce, to each according to his trade, in proportion to the means of consumption'; and the

[242] Ibid. 256–257.

[243] Ibid. 257.

[244] Blanc's friend François Vidal maintained that 'the right to work, whether we know it or not, necessarily maintains the organization of work; and the organization of work implies the economic transformation of society', quoted in P. Rosanvallon, *The New Social Question* (2000) 76. Karl Marx, in his brilliant polemic, The Class Struggles in France, 1848 to 1850 (1852) declared the right to work to be 'the first clumsy formula wherein the revolutionary demands of the proletariat are summarized ... The right to work is, in the bourgeois sense, an absurdity, a miserable, pious wish. But behind the right to work stands the power over capital, the appropriation of the means of production, their subjection to the associated working class, and therefore the abolition of wage labor, of capital and of their mutual relations.'

[245] Loubère, *Louis Blanc* (n. 233) 57, citing the Jacobin-socialist daily newspaper, *Reformé*, 11, 18 September; 18, 22, 27, 28, 30 October; 1, 5 November 1843.

[246] Proclamation of 25 February 1848, quoted in Loubère, *Louis Blanc* (n. 233) 75.

[247] *L'Opinion des femmes*, 28 January 1849, cited by Bouchet, 'Socialist Vicissitudes on the Right to Work in France, 1848–1851', 33/4 *French History* (2019) 572, at 582.

right to make sovereign decisions, 'through the equal contribution of all, without sex distinctions ... regarding the means and the fruits of labour'.[248]

The actual right to work created by the Second Republic's proclamation was short-lived, although for four months over 100,000 unemployed workers were engaged in the cooperative ateliers created by the provisional government.[249] The shuttering of the national workshops at the initiative of the liberal and conservative members of the government in June 1848 provoked an uprising which was bloodily suppressed, and the final Constitution of the Second Republic would refer only in its preamble to the Republic's duty 'through brotherly help' to 'guarantee the existence of citizens in need, either by offering them a job within the limits of its resources, or distributing assistance to those who cannot work, should their family be unable to do so'.[250] But despite the dramatic political defeats suffered by the neo-Jacobin and social democratic forces in France between June 1848 and December 1851, their ideas and rhetoric had an enduring effect on democratic political culture in France and beyond, in the second half of the nineteenth century.[251] Jones notes that after the events of 1848, those 'committed to republican institutions and social reform ... took the hybrid name *democrats-socialistes*, or *démoc-socs* ... '.[252] The *démoc-socs* agenda after 1849 rehearsed many of the demands associated with the right to work and its implications:

> The *démoc-socs* sought to build a sturdy republican citizenry by alleviating immediate poverty and creating long-term conditions for workers' and peasants' independent prosperity ... Labour would be created through public works, particularly on France's railways, canals, and mines, all of which would be nationalised, and forests and common lands would be opened for grazing, fishing, and the collection of firewood. Long-term economic independence would be fostered by workers' cooperatives, state-provided cheap credit, and gratuitous primary education. State-run agricultural bazaars would guarantee equitable prices for farmers and a rational distribution of France's food supply.[253]

Démoc-socs failed to win democratic control of the Second Republic, despite attracting a large following among urban workers. But even as the French, German, Hungarian, Austrian revolutions of 1848 all ended in 'failure, marginalisation,

[248] *L'Opinion des femmes*, August 1849, cited in ibid. 582.

[249] Loubère maintains that it cost much less to run the ateliers than it did to suppress the uprising provoked by their abolition: Loubère, *Louis Blanc* (n. 233) 134–135.

[250] Preamble, article VII. Article 13 guaranteed 'the freedom of labour and of industry' and stated that society 'favors and encourages the development of labor' through, inter alia, 'the establishment by the State, the departments and the communes, of public works proper for the employment of unoccupied laborers.'

[251] Spitz (n. 241) 254.

[252] Jones, 'French Republicanism after 1848', in Moggach and Stedman Jones (n. 193) 70, at 76.

[253] Ibid. 76.

exile, imprisonment, even death' for many of their protagonists, Christopher Clark reminds us that the political and ideological consequences of these political and social revolutions were felt 'like a seismic wave [through] European administrations, changing structures and ideas, bringing new priorities into government or reorganizing old ones, reframing political debates ... Many radicals and conservatives moved inwards from the fringes to affiliate with centrist groups close to state authority, bringing with them new ideas about what the state was for.'[254]

7. From Natural Social Rights to the Social State

Perhaps one of the most powerful new ideas brought to the centre of politics by the mid-century unrest was one indebted to the radical collective natural rights idea observed, in comparable ways, in the political languages of both English Chartism and neo-Jacobin republican socialism. Both languages invoked a notion of collective right as an expression of an immanent order of justice to be imperatively realized within society, and at the same time, as a principle subtending the authority and legitimacy of the collective agent duty-bound to realize that order: the state, or Government.[255] And common to both languages was another critical implication: that democratic political equality required the rigorous restraint of economic inequality, entailing the 'suppression of the frontier between the political (as the reign of the collective will) and the economic (as the realm of the uncoordinated pursuit of individual interests)'.[256]

But who would be the bearer of this collective will? For Blanc, it was the democratic republican state; for mutualists such as Proudhon and those workers' organizations distrustful of the state's capture by other classes, it was the workers' associations themselves, who needed to extend their direct control over the means of production.[257] For another contemporary observer, German state theorist Lorenz von Stein, a strong representative state headed by a unifying monarch, would be the most plausible means through which a public power representing the

[254] Clark, 'Why Should We Think About the Revolutions of 1848 Now?', 41/5 *London Review of Books* (2019); see also Clark, 'After 1848: The European Revolution in Government', 22 *Transactions of the Royal Historical Society* (2012) 171.

[255] It is important to register that an influential discourse in mid-19th century French socialism looked to a different agent to realize this order of justice: that of workers' associations themselves: see Hayat, 'Working-Class Socialism in 1848 in France', in Moggach and Stedman Jones (n. 193) 120; and Castleton, 'The Many Revolutions of Pierre-Joseph Proudhon', in Moggach and Stedman Jones (n. 193) 39.

[256] Hayat (n. 255) 138.

[257] Proudhon initially supported the idea of organization of labour and of credit by the state in 1848, including a proposal to nationalize banks. He ultimately repudiated these positions and became a supporter of various kinds of decentralization, federalism, and communalization; faced with a choice between Bonapartist Caesarism and 'Anarchy' in 1851, he preferred the former, but in later life developed a radical anti-statism: Castleton (n. 255).

social whole could create and maintain a stable solution to the social problem. The logic of natural constitutional right disclosed the necessity and inevitability of such a public power, but in order to effectively ameliorate the conflict between labour and capital, it was now necessary to create an administrative power to organize the management of the economic and the social.

Trained in law, von Stein rose to fame in the German Confederation in his early thirties, with his first book entitled *The Socialism and Communism of Contemporary France* (1842).[258] Based on his sojourn in France between 1841 and 1842, von Stein drew on his friendships and associations with leading democratic republican and socialist figures (including Considerant, Blanc, Cabet, and Reynaud) to explain to a German audience the nature of the new concept of 'socialism'.[259] The book was a runaway success, and was 'fervently discussed' among both 'state scientists' and radical Left Hegelians.[260] Von Stein explicitly linked the growth of socialist ideas with the rise of a property-less class, the proletariat, and warned his German readership that the conflict between those who owned property and those who did not, and could not acquire it because of their immiseration, would only intensify and lead to open revolt.[261] His prognosis proved prescient in 1848, and he followed the course of the political and social revolution closely from Kiel, where he had taken up a professorship. In a three-volume analysis of France's revolutions published in 1850, von Stein argued that the 'social question' was in essence a class conflict, in which one class (the propertied, capitalist class) attained freedom at the expense of the social unfreedom of the other, unpropertied, class (the proletariat).[262] For von Stein, the reversal of this relationship would not create social freedom, but merely invert the hierarchy by replacing the dictatorship of the propertied with the dictatorship of the property-less.[263] Instead, the negative equality promised by natural rights of liberty—which legalized the domination of the propertied over the property-less—required the achievement of the positive equality demanded by the un-propertied through their agitation for universal suffrage and the right to work. The implication of the *démoc-socs* demand for positive equality, according to von Stein, was the equal possibility of 'personal independence' and 'the realization of the idea of personal fulfilment' and 'self-determination' for all.[264] For von Stein, this necessarily entailed a state constituted by universal suffrage, as the *démoc-socs* demanded, but also the *administrative capacity* on the part of that state

258 L. von Stein, *Der Sozialismus und Communismus des heutigen Frankreichs* (1842).

259 D. Siclovan, '*Lorenz von Stein and German Socialism, 1835–1872*' (2014) (PhD thesis, King's College Cambridge).

260 Ibid. 80. It is highly likely that among the Left Hegelians who read, and was influenced by, Stein's work, was a young Karl Marx: see Mengelberg, 'Lorenz von Stein, His Life and Work' in L. von Stein, *The History of the Social Movement in France, 1789–1850*, trans. and ed. Mengelberg ([1850] 1964) 25–33.

261 Siclovan (n. 259) chapter 1.

262 Von Stein, *The History of the Social Movement in France* (n. 260) 81–83, 88–90.

263 'The really successful revolution, therefore, always leads to dictatorship . . .' (ibid. 90).

264 Ibid. 90–92.

to overcome the 'the inequality among men [which] is the result of circumstances, predominantly of property and education'.[265]

> The principle of social democracy encompasses universal suffrage in the constitutional realm and the abolition of the social dependence of the working class in the realm of administration. In a social democracy the constitution is the democratic [element] and the administration is the social element ... It is the last stage in the movement of the lower class fighting against its social dependence.[266]

In Blanc's and other *démoc-socs*' demand for the right to work, von Stein saw exactly such a movement against social dependence. The realization of this demand required, *first*, the embrace of social right *through* the constitution of the state (*Verfassung*); and in its *second* necessary moment, a turn to state administration (*Verwaltung*) in order to ensure provision of social goods. The state would thus become not only 'the highest administrative power' but also the 'greatest capitalist':

> Of what use was it to preach love to the proletariat, as did the adherents of Saint-Simon, or to hold out the hope of a future harmony, as did the adherents of Fourier, or to admonish them to follow the commandments of God, as did the religious communists, or to promise them political freedom, as did the democrats? ... But now a practical solution had been presented. The state suddenly appeared in a different light. The state was no longer only the highest administrative power, but also the greatest capitalist. And since, according to the idea of liberty, each individual has equal political rights, each individual was now also entitled to share the capital owned by the state and whatever this capital procured ...
>
> This is the main influence of the theory of Louis Blanc ... [I]t taught the proletariat to think of government *not only in terms of the state constitution ... but also in terms of state administration.* From the demand that the state should use its revenues in order to provide better living conditions for the workers originated the aspiration of the proletariat to obtain control of the state in the name and in the spirit of the working class. The social element was here for the first time placed side by side with the political element in the struggle against pseudo-constitutionalism.... The theory of Louis Blanc about the organization of work marks the beginning of social democracy.[267]

Von Stein discerned a close link between the necessary and demanded role of the state in creating positive equality, and the older (German) traditions of 'state sciences' and cameralism (*Kameralwissenschaft*), leading ultimately to a prognosis of

[265] Ibid. 140.
[266] Ibid. 88.
[267] Ibid. 390–391 (emphasis added).

the active intervention of the state in the social condition of society. Adherents to a mutualist socialism, revolutionary communism and revolutionary socialism vehemently rejected von Stein's vision as failing to grasp the true nature of socialism.[268] But his basic argument that the conflict inherent in industrial society could never be resolved by the dictatorship of one class over the other, and instead required a unifying political and social power to realize the possibilities of social freedom for all,[269] found favour amongst a wide range of non- or anti-revolutionary movements after 1848. In the aftermath of Europe's revolutionary upheavals, it was increasingly accepted that:

> governance solely by a price system within a *gesellschaftliche* setting might prove insufficient to assure both enough employment and enough social assistance against deprivation. Collectivist intervention, some came to believe, was indicated in one form or another, most probably under the auspices of the state. Indeed, should this not be undertaken, increased political instability might greatly impair the capacity of the economy to provide society with goods and services.[270]

Different modalities of collective agency were candidates to be the medium and means for such intervention, from a renewed corporatism composed of representatives of different social groups (labour, capital, churches, aristocracy),[271] to the moderated statism of French solidarist theories of cooperation and association under integrative legal institutions.[272] Within this, the language of social right never disappeared; in fact, it proliferated across different visions and articulations of how to remedy the harms and injustices of capitalism and industrialization, and was salient in some streams of social Catholic and evangelical Protestant thought.[273]

[268] Siclovan (n. 259) 110–111.

[269] Stein argued that a monarchical state was best suited to stabilizing society while addressing the sources of social conflict: see ibid. 125–128.

[270] Spengler (n. 106).

[271] This vision of a reconstructed society of orders characterized an influential stream of Catholic social thought: see Behr, 'The Nineteenth Century Historical and Intellectual Context of Catholic Social Teaching', in G. V Bradley and E. C. Brugger (eds), *Catholic Social Teaching* (2019) 34. For an examination of the social rights discourses embedded within this corporatist vision—one which balanced rights and duties to repair social peace—see Walton and Schettini, 'Social Rights', in Edelstein and Pitts (n. 98).

[272] See the comprehensive account of the idea of solidarity in France in J. Hayward, 'The Idea of Solidarity in French Political and Social Thought in the Nineteenth and Early Twentieth Centuries' (1958) (PhD dissertation, University of London).

[273] For Catholic thought on rights in the 19th century, see Greenberg, 'Catholicism and Rights: Politics, Economics and Sexuality' in Edelstein and Pitts (n. 98). For the influence of Protestant social Christianity in the UK and US, especially in relation to ideas of social fellowship, social reform, and the development of personhood, see: T. Rogan, *The Moral Economists: R. H. Tawney, Karl Polanyi, E. P. Thompson, and the Critique of Capitalism* (2017) chapter 1 and 2; Fine (n. 90) chapter 6; Parry, 'Christian Socialism, Class Collaboration and British Public Life after 1848' in Moggach and Stedman Jones (n. 193) 162.

A preoccupation with 'social economy' and 'social politics' proliferated across diverse networks, institutions, and sites of activity, from universities to churches to political parties.[274] The administrative capacity and technical-infrastructural power of the state grew steadily after 1850, with states undertaking public works projects on an unprecedented scale. States also began to develop a 'more systematic approach to the formulation of economic policy ... [and an] accelerated ... "professionalization" of government through the integration into the policy-making process of groups and organisations representing various forms of technical expertise'.[275] Much as von Stein seemed to have forecast,[276] the authority and legitimacy of the state appeared increasingly tied to its capacity to shape the capitalist economy in ways that mitigated the social question—whether by stimulating growth through industrial policy and infrastructural development, nationalizing certain resources, or state-led social insurance and social provisioning. Attendant on all these activities was an expansion of the administrative capacities of the state, and the concomitant expansion of forms of technical state-knowledge, such as national statistics, as well as a specialized cadre of administrative experts.[277] A collection of German political economists and state scientists who had been careful readers and commentators on von Stein, including Karl Knies, Gustav von Schmoller, and Adolph Wagner,[278] would go on to found the *Verein für Sozialpolitik* (VfS). The VfS would become the heart of the network of political economists which would develop the German historical school of economics, and become a byword for the top-down social and economic policy nicknamed 'the Socialism of the Lectern' (*Kathedersozialisten*). It conducted a vast number of studies of social problems through the lens of state-led social reform and economic planning, realizing in many ways von Stein's hope for a union of social ideals with the state through a science of society.[279] Members of the VfS also trained an entire generation of American PhD students,[280] who would go on to argue for a positive theory of the state as regulator, economic arbitrator, and industrial and agricultural planner, in order to assure positive rights to work, fair working conditions, education, and rest.[281] These 'new' political economists in the American context

[274] Rodgers (n. 90) chapters 1 and 2.

[275] Clark, 'After 1848' (n. 254).

[276] On von Stein's idea that while history cannot predict specific events, it can forecast the approaching future through a diagnosis of conditions of possibility, see: Koselleck, 'Historical Prognosis in Lorenz von Stein's Essay on the Prussian Constitutions', in R. Koselleck, *Futures Past: On the Semantics of Historical Time*, trans. K. Tribe (2004) 58.

[277] Clark, 'After 1848' (n. 254) 183–186; Sassoon (n. 85) chapter 5.

[278] Siclovan (n. 259) 210.

[279] Ibid. 172.

[280] K. Tribe, *Constructing Economic Science: The Invention of a Discipline, 1850–1950* (2022); Rodgers (n. 90) chapter 3. Key names here are Richard T. Ely, Edward Seligson, Henry Adams, John Bates Clark, Edmund James, and Simon Patten.

[281] For the best collection of these statements, see Fine (n. 90); see (unsympathetically and noting also the strong currents of eugenics and racial nationalism professed by some of these economists, especially Ely): Miller, 'Richard T. Ely, The German Historical School of Economics, and the "Socio-Teleological" Aspiration of the New Deal Planners', 38/1 *Social Philosophy and Policy* (2021) 52. For the argument that

influenced the first generation of anti-trust laws, and their students became influential New Deal economists and policy-makers.

The socialism of the lectern buttressed the Bismarckian political project of national order and unity, and was an institutional and intellectual response by segments of the bourgeoisie and aristocracy to the precipitous rise of social democratic political parties after 1863.[282] It was opposed to the revolutionary stance of Marxist Socialism, as much as it vigorously criticized and sought to supplant the negative state idea of laissez-faire economic liberalism. Bismarck,[283] in his introduction of state-provided sickness insurance and old age pension, explained the legitimacy of such provisions by invoking them as the realization of the right to work, but with a strong emphasis on the productive, order-creating, consequences of realizing this idea:

> To sum up my position, give the labourer the right to labour as long as he is in health, give him work as long as he is in health, ensure him care when he is ill, and ensure him a provision when he is old.... Do not our moral relations demand that the man who says to his fellow citizens, 'I am healthy and willing to work but can find no work,' should have the right to say 'find me work,' and that the State should be bound to find him work? ... If such a scarcity [of work] should recur, then I hold the state still under the same obligation, and the State is engaged in undertakings of such magnitude that can well fulfil its duty of finding work for those of its citizens who cannot find it for themselves.[284]

In its Christian socialist and national socialist versions, the comprehensive order of state and economy was grasped as resting ultimately on a shared religious and national ethos, with a strong current of anti-semitism and racialism articulated through such theories.[285]

But the vision of social reform through and by the state as greatest capitalist and highest administrator nurtured a variety of state theories, economic theories, and social theories, within a range of 'thought collectives' and political movements, all of which emphasized the potential directive power of state and administration in relation to the economic. A social state ensuring social rights was in some sense

the foundational state and law theories of what would become the 'New Deal' had already been developed by the late 19th century in US political and legal thought, see W. J. Novak, *New Democracy: The Creation of the Modern American State* (2022).

[282] A. Kedar, 'National Socialism before Nazism: Friedrich Naumann and Theodor Fritsch, 1890–1914' (2010) (PhD thesis, UC Berkeley) 7, 9.

[283] Siclovan suggests that not only the VfS but also von Stein had a direct influence on Bismarck's views through his principal adviser on social issues between 1862 and 1873, Hermann Wagener: 231. It is equally likely that German Social Democratic Party founder Ferdinand Lasalle knew von Stein's work well: Siclovan (n. 259) 227–228.

[284] Bismarck, speech to Imperial Parliament, 9 May 1884, quoted in Menger (n. 234) 12–13.

[285] See Kedar (n. 282) 9–12.

the common currency of radical *and* conservative-ethical criticisms of laissez-faire capitalism at the end of the nineteenth century. The central concept which connected them to each other, was that of a strong and unified public power, authorized and legitimated by some kind of social force which enabled the state to act as an instrument for the construction of the relationship between economy and society. Who or what was the bearer of this social force? This was the decisive question which differentiated opposing political projects.[286]

The experience of 'war collectivism' in Europe and the United States during the First World War, in which large sectors of advanced capitalist economies were directly subjected to political control to ensure war production (an experience repeated 25 years later),[287] appeared to many to conclusively demonstrate the potentiality of the state as planner and organizer of the economy. For revolutionary socialists and social reformists alike—and for their liberal and reactionary opponents—the war 'had demonstrated the immense fiscal, monetary and industrial powers of the state, and accordingly how major redistributive reforms were concrete and viable—much more than conventional economic thinking had allowed.'[288] Mattei, in the British and Italian contexts she examines, rightly recovers the tension between 'enlightened social reformists' and radical workers' movements in the years immediately after the end of the First World War. The former, dubbed 'reconstructionists', believed that the war demonstrated that political agents could 'change economic conditions through inter-dependence between fiscal, monetary and industrial policy. Progressive taxes and state spending had to go hand in hand with favourable credit policy and especially with industrial harmony achieved through forms of workers' industrial control or of industrial production.'[289] The radical workers' movements argued that the path from war collectivism to state socialism would not emancipate workers, but only render them 'state serfs'.[290] War collectivism radicalized industrial workers, showing them that human collectivities *could* manage the market and that their post-war militancy had achieved substantial improvements in wages and conditions.[291] They pressed for industrial democracy as the means through which the dependence of labour on wage slavery could be brought to an end.[292] The 'social state' promised only demobilization and pacification. But common to both these modalities of confronting

[286] See Arendt's observations about state, nation, movement and class in *The Origins of Totalitarianism*, 299–303, 326–348 (n. 76).

[287] Rodgers (n. 90) chapter 7; C. Mattei, *The Capitalist Order: How Economists Invented Austerity and Paved the Way to Fascism* (2022) part I; Llanque, 'Hermann Heller and the Republicanism of the Left in the Weimar Republic', 23 Jus Politicum – Revue de droit politique (2019) 13, at 19.

[288] Mattei (n. 287) 54.

[289] Ibid. 58.

[290] Ibid. 101.

[291] Ibid. 80.

[292] Ibid. chapters 3–4.

capitalism was a language of rights as realized *through and by the new political-economic order* established by collective action:

> The working class does not ask, nor intend to ask, for mandatory social insurance for sickness, disability, and old age as a philanthropic solution to the still-unresolved social problems – *but as the expression of rights that have long matured though heretofore in vain*, in the scathing and glorious field of labour and social production.[293]

Bureaucrats working for the Italian Ministry of Military Assistance could similarly conclude that 'out of [war's] miseries and catastrophes a luminous path has been traced for the ends of the State . . . The state of law that was considered the most elevated form of state before the war . . . has suddenly been overtaken and surpassed by the highest of conceptions: the *state of law and social welfare*.'[294]

In a context where it seemed that the possibilities of reorganizing economic order through public power had been decisively demonstrated by recent experience, it is not surprising that inter-war democratic constitutions written in the aftermath of political revolution and severe social conflict (Weimar Germany, Mexico) articulated precisely the grammar of social right identified in Section 5 above. Social right was embedded in, but also authorized and expressed, a social democratic vision of an *economic constitution*.[295] This social-democratic economic constitution established liberal political rights and a sphere of free economic activity, but *encased them in* and *subjected them to* the redistributive social justice objectives of the public power.[296] While Schmitt notoriously and self-servingly declared the Weimar constitution to be a 'dilatory formal compromise'[297] between a 'bourgeois or socialist social order'[298]—paving the way in his theory for the true character of the Constitution to be resolved by a decision of its guardian, the President—his contemporary Franz Neumann saw in the Weimar constitution the logical and coherent expression of 'the idea of the social *Rechtstaat* with its material conception of equality' expressed *in nuce* by the Jacobins.[299] Citing Lorenz

[293] Society for Mutual Aid and Cooperatives, 'Il congresso regionale piemontese per le assicurazioni sociali', *L'Avanti*, 8 October 1918, cited in Mattei (n. 287) 61.

[294] Ministero per l'Assistenza Militare e le Pensioni di Guerra (ed), *L'assistenza di Guerra in Italia: assistenza militare, pensioni di Guerra* (1919), cited in Mattei (n. 287) 55.

[295] Grégoire, 'The Economic Constitution under Weimar: Doctrinal Controversies and Ideological Struggles' in G. Grégoire and X. Miny (eds), *The Idea of Economic Constitution in Europe* (2022) 53.

[296] Ibid. 62–66.

[297] *Dilatorische Formelkompromise*. C. Schmitt, *Constitutional Theory* (2008) 82–83.

[298] Ibid. 83.

[299] Neumann, 'Die soziale Bedeutung der Grundrechte in der Weimarer Verfassung', Jg.7, Heft 9 *Die Arbeit* (1930) 569. Translated by Keith Tribe and republished as Neumann, 'The Social Significance of the Basic Laws in the Weimar Constitution', 10/3 *Economy and Society* (1981) 329–347. Mommsen records that the origins of these social rights provisions lay in the contributions of Christian Socialist and former monarchist, Friedrich Naumann, labour lawyer and social democrat Hugo Sinzheimer, and socialist delegate Simon Katzenstein. H. Mommsen, *The Rise and Fall of Weimar Democracy* (1996) 58–59.

von Stein, Neumann characterized the fundamental purpose of the constitution as the realization of 'the social rights of freedom'.[300] The Constitution created the authorizing legal framework for the achievement of this purpose by expressly subordinating 'capitalist rights of freedom' (property, labour contracts, etc) to 'the principles of justice, with the objective of guaranteeing to all a humane existence. The economic freedom of the individual is to be secured within the terms of these limitations.'[301] Under this broad *chapeau*, the Constitution went on to guarantee specific rights (such as labour association, social insurance, the right to work),[302] while also creating labour councils to empower 'workers and employees ... to participate on equal terms in community with entrepreneurs in the regulation of wages and working conditions, and also in the entire economic development of the productive forces'.[303] Article 162 committed the Reich to advocate for 'the international regulation of the legal relations governing the worker, striving for a common minimum of social rights for the entire working class of mankind'.[304] It is well-known that the expectation that political democracy would realize the state-purposes encoded in the Weimar Constitution was false, and the many dimensions of Weimar's state failure do not need to be rehearsed here.[305] But writing in 1930 with the hindsight of 11 years since its ratification, Neumann lambasted the conservative judiciary for refusing to give the Constitution's social-state principles their full state-theoretical consequences.[306] The solution for him was not a rejection of social rights or constitutional provision per se. Rather, it was the urgent task of '*socialist state theory to develop and concretely present the positive social content of the second part of the Weimar Constitution* ... It is the task of socialist politics to realize these principles.'[307]

8. Coda

The story told in this chapter is not one of singular origins nor straightforward lines of descent. Rather, it is an attempt to grasp the emergence of social right as a repertoire of political and legal thought by excavating some aspects of the grammar

[300] Ibid. 339.
[301] Art. 151, Weimar Constitution, appended to Neumann, 'The Social Significance' (n. 299) 344.
[302] Arts 159, 160, 161.
[303] Art. 165.
[304] Art. 162.
[305] See generally Mommsen (n. 299).
[306] Neumann, 'The Social Significance' (n. 299) 342: 'Constitutional principles, above all those that affect the law on economic organization, have now in state theory and legal practice – especially in the High Court – been turned on their head ... the right of review given to judges must be rejected ...'. See also Mommsen (n. 299) who notes that courts developed a 'reactionary interpretation' of property rights, 'refused' to implement the constitutional commitment to the social responsibilities of ownership, and 'robbed of any real legal substance' the guaranteed social rights (59).
[307] Neumann, 'The Social Significance,' (n. 299) 342 (emphasis in the original).

of its usages, and by endeavouring to delineate at least some of the contexts of that grammar. What emerges from my account is a sequence of morphologies of what I have called 'collective natural rights' (or, 'natural social rights') claims. Collective natural rights endowed us with a claim-structure for a *fair share* of political *and* economic order. Specific rights claimed in this register included the right to work, the right to subsistence, and the right to the product of one's labour. Once braided with an analysis of capitalism and the nature of social conflict between classes, this claim-structure engendered a variety of possible answers. One such possibility, brilliantly articulated in the form of a state-theory and state-concept by Lorenz von Stein, gave us a way of *conceptualizing* a social democratic state. Stein's social-democratic state-concept rested on the concrete historical experience of French socialist movements. It explicated what he took to be the principle to be derived from this experience: that political citizenship did not create social citizens but required their creation, and the social state (as greatest capitalist and highest administrative power) was the means through which such citizens were to be created.[308] The inner determining logic of this concept and its principle produces social right: social right emerges as the manifestation of the successful management of class conflict by the political-economic order of the social state. Social freedom and positive equality are realized by and through positive rights. Notably, in Stein's account and in the language of others after him, the claim of (natural) right subtended the demand for the organization of labour and the economy through state power. The social state made social rights; but natural social right also made the social state, in the sense of being a significant register through which the demand for the positive state and social economy were framed, articulated, and motivated.

Koselleck points out that after the French Revolution, political and legal concepts served 'no longer ... merely to define given states of affairs, but [to] reach into the future.'[309] Concepts sometimes,

> had to be formulated linguistically before it was possible to enter or permanently occupy them. The experiential substance of many concepts was thus reduced, *while their claim to realization increased in proportion*. Actual, substantial experience and the space of expectation coincide less and less. It is here that the coining of numerous 'isms' belongs, serving as collective and motivating concepts capable of reordering and mobilizing anew the masses robbed of their place in the older order of estates.[310]

[308] Kästner, 'From the Social Question to the Social State', 10/1 *Economy and Society* (1981) 7; Pasquino, 'Introduction to Lorenz von Stein', 10/1 *Economy and Society* (1981) 1.
[309] Koselleck, 'Begriffsgeschichte and Social History', in Futures Past (n. 276) 80.
[310] Ibid.

The passage from collective natural right, to the right to work, to social democracy and social right, seems to me to be an instance of sequentially-iterated concepts characterized by a 'state of expectation [in] which … [the concepts] claimed to satisfy newly constituted needs'.[311] The 'kinetic energy'[312] of this array of interconnected concepts was considerable. They did not await the completed reality of the post-1945 welfare state. They prefigured it through a powerful state-concept and state-theory that attracted adherents from both social reformist and social revolutionary movements—and later, among decolonized states searching for a state-concept adequate to their urgent imperative to end their economic dependency on former colonial rulers through planned industrialization and state-led development. At certain moments, 'rights' concepts were largely evacuated. However, they never disappeared and instead lay partially buried beneath layers of state theory, administrative science, and economic policy. In democratic or anti-colonial moments of rupture and re-founding, rights-languages returned to the fore, as a means of capturing and articulating a fundamental theorem about what the state was for, and how it ought to be made to be that way in reality by the political and social movements of the time. Such a state was a public power representing the whole of society, which submits economic rationality and the market to a different order of values, by organizing it. Inherent in these rights claims was also a notion of what the nature of social freedom within the state amounted to: positive equality enabling the development of the human personality, in solidarity with others as political and social equals.

The challenge for our time is whether this profoundly political-ethical ideal can be renovated and resurrected as *the* animating principle of a social state which realizes social rights. If it can be, it holds out some hope of a more effective political-legal language to challenge inequality in the neoliberal state.

[311] Ibid. 84.

[312] Straumann, 'The Energy of Concepts: The Role of Concepts in Long-Term Intellectual History and Social Reality', 14/2 *Journal of the Philosophy of History* (2019) 147.

2

The Future of Social and Economic Rights

*Florian F. Hoffmann**

1. Social and Economic Rights: From Past to Present

In a recent collection on the human rights impact of the global financial crisis (as) of 2008, social and economic (henceforth SE) rights are described as being 'at a critical juncture'.[1] On the one hand, the past decade or so has seen an impressive rise in their presence both in domestic and international jurisprudence and in political discourse, so much so that they can now be considered to have drawn level with, if not passed, civil and political (CP) rights as the dominant global human rights concern.[2] On the other hand, the succession of financial and general economic crises since 2008 have afflicted countries of the global North as much as the global South and have not only resulted in a dramatic rise in the violation of economic and social rights,[3] but also in some puzzlement about their viability in

* This chapter is based on social rights-related work that spans a period of over 15 years, three countries (Brazil, the United Kingdom, and Germany), two hemispheres (global South and global North) and several professional transitions and reinventions. Along this stretch I have had the privilege of interlocution and inspiration from many colleagues and fellow human rights travellers, among them Philip Alston, Bethania Assy, Fernando Bentes, Marcia Nina Bernardes, Juan Pablo Bohoslavsky, Daniel Brinks, Leonardo Castilho, Basak Çali, Christine Chinkin, Gisele Cittadino, Philipp Dann, Mac Darrow, Sakiko Fukuda-Parr, Luis Eslava, Isabel Feichtner, Thomas Gammeltoft-Hansen, Varun Gauri, Conor Gearty, Siri Gloppen, Geoff Gordon, Françoise Hampson, Bettina Hollstein, Stephen Humphreys, Kalpana Kannabiran, Sarah Knuckey, Nico Krisch, Malcolm Langford, Fabio Carvalho Leite, Susan Marks, Frédéric Mégret, Carolina de Campos Melo, Yoriko Otomo, Antonio Ilê Pele, Michael Riegner, Julie Ringelheim, Wojciech Sadurski, Margot Salomon, Magdalena Sepúlveda Carmona, Margaret Satterthwaite, Ruth Alícia Urbano, Ralph Wilde, Roberto Vilchez Yamato, Alicia Yamin, and, of course and always, Andrea Ribeiro Hoffmann. Nehal Bhuta has been much more than this volume's editor and Academy convenor, and has enabled this whole endeavour. Anny Bremner, needless to say for those who know her, provided all the initial impetus, nudging, and encouragement, and Joyce Davies then led it to conclusion with much patience and good vibes in complicated times. I am deeply grateful to the above for their time at different moments, though remain, of course, fully and entirely responsible for what I have made of it in this text.

[1] Nolan, 'Introduction', in A. Nolan (ed.), *Economic and Social Rights after the Global Financial Crisis* (2014); see also Rodríguez-Garavito and McAdams, 'A Human Rights Crisis? Unpacking the Debate on the Future of the Human Rights Field' (2016) https://www.readcube.com/articles/10.2139%2Fssrn.2919703 (last visited 18 April 2023).

[2] See L. Minkler, *The State of Economic and Social Human Rights: A Global Overview* (2013); K. G. Young, *Constituting Economic and Social Rights* (2012).

[3] See Bhuta, Ticktin, and Fukuda-Parr, 'Human Rights and the Global Economy', 79 *Social Research* (2012) 785; and Salomon, 'Of Austerity, Human Rights and International Institutions', 21 *European Law Journal* (2015) 521; and Nolan (n. 1); O'Cinneide, 'Austerity and the Faded Dream of a "Social Europe"', in Nolan (n. 1) 169; Harrison and Stephenson, 'Assessing the Impact of the Public Spending Cuts: Taking Human Rights and Equality Seriously', in A. Nolan, R. O'Connell, and C. Harvey, *Human*

Florian F. Hoffmann, *The Future of Social and Economic Rights*. In: *Human Rights in Transition*. First Edition. Edited by Nehal Bhuta, Oxford University Press. © Florian F. Hoffmann 2024. DOI: 10.1093/oso/9780198901921.003.0002

times of crisis.[4] What is clear, however, is that SE rights are very much (back) on the agenda, with more and more people and institutions using them to frame the complex policy issues that beset (late-)modern welfare states in a globalized world. This is a far cry from as late as the mid-2000s, when prominent members of the international human rights community would still relativize references to SE rights by prefacing them with a sceptical 'so called'.[5] Since then, their legal fabric has hardened and their political salience has become more compelling, so that their erstwhile classification as merely programmatic second-generation (a.k.a. second-class) rights has largely been rendered anachronistic. The previously intractable debate about the justiciability of SE rights, premised, as it was, on a fundamental scepticism about the subordination of social and economic policy to the logic of legally enforceable rights, has now given way to a more creative reflection on ever more fine-tuned techniques for measuring and monitoring compliance.[6]

This ascendancy has been driven, arguably, by developments in what will here be termed frontier regions of the economic and social rights map. One of these lies in the realm of domestic fundamental rights jurisprudence, where, in the past two decades or so, and mostly, but by no means only, in transition countries of the global South, there has been an explosive increase in the rights-driven judicialization of social (and to a lesser extent economic) policy. The main protagonists of this transformation have been domestic judiciaries, who gradually discarded their earlier reticence to directly intervene in the policy process and, instead, began holding constitutional SE rights to be not only directly justiciable, but also as often overriding the administrative legal precepts by which such areas as

Rights and Public Finance (2013) 219; O'Connell, 'Let Them Eat Cake: Socio-Economic Rights in an Age of Austerity', in A. Nolan, R. O'Connell, and C. Harvey, *Human Rights and Public Finance* (2013) 59.

[4] See Saiz, 'Rights in Recession? Challenges for Economic and Social Rights Enforcement in Times of Crisis', 1 *Journal of Human Rights Practice* (2009) 277; and Nolan, 'Not Fit for Purpose? Human Rights in Times of Financial and Economic Crisis', 4 *European Human Rights Law Review* (2015) 358; Balakrishnan, Heintz, and Elson, 'Economic Crises and Human Rights?', in R. Balakrishnan, J. Heintz, and D. Elson, *Rethinking Economic Policy for Social Justice: The Radical Potential of Human Rights* (2016) 122.

[5] See Neier, 'Social and Economic Rights: A Critique', 13 *Human Rights Brief* (2006) 1.

[6] See the now classical debate between Kenneth Roth and Leonard Rubinstein: Roth, 'Defending Economic, Social and Cultural Rights: Practical Issues Faced by an International Human Rights Organization', 26 *Human Rights Quarterly* (2004) 63; and Rubenstein, 'How International Human Rights Organizations Can Advance Economic, Social and Cultural Rights: A Response to Kenneth Roth', 26 *Human Rights Quarterly* (2004) 845; as well as Nolan, Porter, and Langford, 'The Justiciability of Social and Economic Rights: An Updated Appraisal' (2007) *New York University School - Center for Human Rights and Global Justice Law Working Paper* http://www.socialrights.ca/Publications/porter_the_justiciabiliyt_of_social_and_economic_rights%20copy.pdf (last visited 18 April 2023); and Fukuda-Parr, Lawson-Remer, and Randolph, *Measuring the Progressive Realization of Human Rights Obligations: An Index of Economic and Social Rights Fulfilment* (2008); and Langford and Fukuda-Parr, 'The Turn to Metrics', 30 *Nordic Journal of Human Rights* (2012) 222; see also Alston and Gillespie, 'Global Human Rights Monitoring, New Technologies, and the Politics of Information', 23 *European Journal of International Law* (2012) 1089.

public health or education are regulated.[7] This judicial turn to a rights-oriented review of public policy was, in turn, triggered by a shift in civil society militancy away from constitution-making and legislative lobbying and towards the courts as the primary agents of policy and rights enforcement. Yet, as will be seen, after about two decades of this domestic rights revolution of sorts, the overall outcome is ambivalent, for it has not only generated significant undesired side-effects, but also considerable backlash from public authorities.[8]

The other main frontier region of SE rights is international and lies in the realm of multilateral development cooperation and economic policy coordination. It emerged, arguably, from two sets of developments, notably the gradual diffusion of SE rights into various international and regional human rights instruments, and the specific mainstreaming of human rights into both bi- and multilateral development cooperation. The most recent step in this process has been the much lobbied-for adoption of the Optional Protocol of the International Covenant of Economic, Social, and Cultural Rights (OP-ICESCR), the initial significance of which lies not so much in the empowerment of the UN Committee on Economic, Social, and Cultural Rights (CESCR) to adjudicate individual complaints—of which, so far, only relatively few have reached the Committee on account of the as yet small number of signatories of the Protocol[9]—but in the general recognition, at the international level, of the justiciability of SE rights. It has also provided additional weight to the Committee's role as an authoritative interpreter of international obligations in the realm of SE rights and has strengthened its part in the Universal Periodic Review (UPR) process within the charter-based Human Rights Council system.

[7] See R. Gargarella, P. Domingo, and T. Roux, *Courts and Social Transformation in New Democracies: An Institutional Voice for the Poor?* (2006); V. Gauri and D. M. Brinks, *Courting Social Justice: Judicial Enforcement of Social and Economic Rights in the Developing World* (2008); Gauri and Brinks, 'The Impact of Legal Strategies for Claiming Social and Economic Human Rights', in T. Pogge (ed.), *Freedom from Poverty as a Human Right: Who Owes What to the Very Poor* (2010); M. Langford, *Social Rights Jurisprudence: Emerging Trends in International and Comparative Law* (2008); A. E. Yamin and S. Gloppen, *Litigating Health Rights: Can Courts Bring More Justice to Health?* (2011); Gloppen, 'Public Interest Litigation, Social Rights, and Social Policy', in A. A. Dani and A. de Haan (eds), *Inclusive States: Social Policy and Structural Inequalities* (2008) 343; Yusuf, 'The Rise of Judicially Enforced Economic, Social, and Cultural Rights-Refocusing Perspectives', 10 *Seattle Journal for Social Justice* (2012) 3; L. Haglund and R. Stryker, *Closing the Rights Gap: From Human Rights to Social Transformation* (2015).

[8] See, generally, Gloppen, 'Public Interest Litigation, Social Rights and Social Policy', in A.A. Dani and A. de Haan (n. 7) 343, at 353; see also the account in Hoffmann and Bentes, 'Accountability for Social and Economic Rights in Brazil', in Gauri and Brinks, Courting Social Justice (n. 7) 100.

[9] See Optional Protocol to the International Covenant on Economic, Social and Cultural Rights, GA Res. 63/117, 10 December 2008; as of time of writing, 26 states have ratified and another 24 have signed it, the remaining 148 states have so far not taken any action, just over a dozen cases have been decided on the merits, though a significantly larger number of complaints is as yet pending decision; a large number of these concern just a few countries (most notably Spain and Italy) and deal primarily with potential violations resulting from evictions in the context of the various financial crises since 2008; see OHCHR, CESCR Table of Pending Cases, https://www.ohchr.org/en/treaty-bodies/cescr/table-pending-cases (last visited 12 May 2023); and OHCHR, Jurisprudence Database, https://juris.ohchr.org/AdvancedSearch (last visited 12 May 2023).

The second development goes back to the late 1990s when the UN launched its human rights mainstreaming agenda which, from the beginning, focused on the UN's development cooperation activities and which resulted in the emergence of the concept of the rights-based approach to development (RBD) that, in turn, has spread into virtually all multi- and bilateral development cooperation programmes. Although RBD places no a priori emphasis on SE rights, the focus, inherent in development cooperation, on issues of social and economic policy has meant that the SE rights component of RBD has always been prominent. A further step in this mainstreaming agenda has been what could be termed a turn to (domestic) policy in (international) human rights. It is apparent, for instance, in efforts to elaborate detailed manuals, such as the UN Guiding Principles on Foreign Debt and Human Rights and Extreme Poverty or the UN Guiding Principles on Foreign Debt and Human Rights,[10] which are directed at domestic policymakers and administrators and aim to inform policy design and implementation at the intra-state level. Again, it is issues of social and economic policy that are at the forefront of this type of intervention, and with it comes a natural emphasis on SE rights. Likewise, the Committee's adoption of indicator-guided monitoring by means of the Indicators, Benchmarking, Scoping, Assessment (IBSA) procedure reinforces the trend towards ever more detailed measuring and reporting requirements on the part of the duty bearers of SE rights.[11] In a parallel setting, the extensive work to mainstream human rights into the implementation of the Millennium Development Goals (MDGs) led to increased visibility of SE rights which have since become entrenched in the ambit of the Sustainable Development Goals (SDGs) and the Agenda 2030, as well as the Leave No One Behind (LNOB) associated with it.[12]

All this has led to an exponential rise in the presence and prominence of the SE rights agenda in development cooperation contexts, which, in turn, has provided a blueprint for a foray of SE rights discourse into the debate about the consequences of the financial crises that have rattled both developed and developing economies in the past 15 years. While human rights impact assessments of both the policies of the multilateral finance institutions and of free trade agreements had been used as experimental debating chips before, it was in the wake of widespread austerity

[10] See HRC Res. 20/23, 10 April 2011.

[11] See Riedel, Giacca, and Golay, 'The Development of Economic, Social, and Cultural Rights in International Law', in E. Riedel, G. Giacca, and C. Golay (eds), *Economic, Social, and Cultural Rights in International Law: Contemporary Issues and Challenges* (2014) 3, at 25.

[12] See M. Langford and A. Sumner, *The Millennium Development Goals and Human Rights. Past, Present and Future* (2013); see also Sachs, 'From Millenium Development Goals to Sustainable Development Goals', 379 *Lancet* (2012) 2206; K. Arts, 'Inclusive Sustainable Development: A Human Rights Perspective', 24 *Current Opinion in Environmental Sustainability* (2017) 58; and M. Kaltenborn, *Social Rights and International Development: Global Legal Standards for the Post-2015 Development Agenda* (2015).

policies in some of the affected countries that SE rights were turned into primary arguments against the indiscriminate curtailment of states' legal obligations.[13]

The backdrop to this present state of affairs of SE rights is, of course, formed by several paradigmatic transformations that have been changing the world of rights holders and duty bearers since SE rights were first articulated in the Universal Declaration of Human Rights (UDHR) nearly 70 years ago. Firstly, the state, which is (still) the main duty bearer of these rights, has changed significantly over time. In its present incarnation, it is often referred to as the 'regulatory state' (in the global North) or as the 'new developmental state' (in the global South) and it differs from its earlier, post-War self in that its main role is today deemed to be as a guarantor of the functionality of (increasingly global) markets and as an absorber of intermittent market failures.[14] As a consequence, it is markets, and not the state, that generate an ever larger portion of the raw materials for social welfare and economic development, with the state merely providing necessary if limited regulatory and arbitral authority. Hence, notwithstanding its constitutional and international (legal) obligations, the contemporary state operates in a much reduced policy space that structurally curtails its capacity to directly attend to the demands brought to it by its constituents, including in the area of social and economic policy.[15]

This condition is exacerbated by a second transformation that affects the state's ability to bear its (legal) obligations, notably the fact that, increasingly, the policy issues faced by the state, as well as their solutions, lie outside of its jurisdictional and fiscal remit. The reason for this lies in the series of internationalization and transnationalization processes commonly subsumed under the label of globalization, a process which has transformed individual states from the sovereign monads of Vattelian international law into nodes within overlapping normative networks.[16] As a consequence, many of the state's fundamental tasks can only be fulfilled

[13] Nolan (n. 1); and Salomon (n. 3).

[14] See, classically, Majone, 'The Regulatory State and Its Legitimacy Problems', 22 *West European Politics* (1999) 1; and Trubek, 'Developmental States and the Legal Order: Towards a New Political Economy of Development and Law', 1075 *University of Wisconsin Legal Studies Research Paper* (2008) 1; see also Levi-Faur, 'States Making & Market Building for the Global South: The Developmental vs. the Regulatory State', 44 *Jerusalem Papers in Regulation and Governance* (2012); H. Alviar García, 'Social Policy and the New Development State: The Case of Colombia', *IGLP Working Paper Series* (2011); and C. Scott, *Regulation in the Age of Governance: The Rise of the Post Regulatory State* (2004).

[15] See Hoffmann, 'Revolution or Regression: Retracing the Turn to Rights in "Law and Development"', 23 *Finnish Yearbook of International Law 2012-2013* (ed. J. Petman 2016) 45.

[16] This contention engages, of course, a large and diverse literature on the transformation of the state, state sovereignty, and the 'international' which cannot be reviewed here; in (international) law, relevant reflection has, inter alia, come from the Global Administrative Law (GAL) fold—see, for instance, Kingsbury, Krisch, and Stewart, 'The Emergence of Global Administrative Law', 68 *Law and Contemporary Problems* (2005) 15—as well as from systems theoretical reflections—see Teubner and Fischer-Lescano, 'Regime-Collisions: The Vain Search for Legal Unity in the Fragmentation of Global Law', 25 *Michigan Journal of International Law* (2004) 999; from an International Relations perspective, see, inter alia, B. Buzan, From International to World Society? English School Theory and the Social Structure of Globalisation (2004); and, from a different angle, J. Bartelson, *A Genalogy of Sovereignty* (1995).

collectively, in conjunction with other states, intermediated by international organizations or, indeed, alongside different types of non-state actors such as corporations or civil society organizations (CSOs).

Thirdly, these developments have gone hand in hand with a general ascendancy of the rule of law as the main contemporary mode of (good) governance. Hence, as ever more aspects of national and international political life have become legalized, judicial bodies have (been) turned into core instruments in the domestic and international policy process meant to enforce the principles underlying the idea of good governance—such as accountability, transparency, participation, human rights, and legal and administrative due process—against potentially recalcitrant domestic executives and legislatures. However, while this trend to legalization and judicialization has certainly increased the overall receptivity to human rights and, in particular, SE rights, it has also significantly tightened the legal constraints placed on governments, such as in relation to fiscal policy, and it has, thus, paradoxically raised, rather than decreased, the threshold for the fulfilment of constitutional or international legal obligations. Moreover, it has also produced a growing legitimacy crisis as judiciaries and legal experts often get the final say over policy while themselves being epistemically constrained by the particular legal horizon within which they operate. As will be seen, this tension has, for instance, been acutely present in those countries most affected by the financial crisis and the resulting austerity policies.

Fourthly, and lastly, this predicament does, then, indeed, open up a crossroads for SE rights. On the one hand, they are now more central than ever before to the way in which social wellbeing is conceived in domestic and international public policy. On the other hand, the material and administrative conditions for their fulfilment are much less favourable than they would need to be. What this may mean, concretely, will be explored in this chapter, which will proceed to look at each of the two frontier regions in order to then draw some tentative conclusions on the possible future(s) of SE rights.

2. A Present Beyond Justiciability: Monitoring and Measuring

A. Monitoring SE Rights: From Programme to Obligations

Before advancing upon any frontier, a brief overview of SE rights at the present moment is called for. Beginning with their presence in domestic law, the 'Toronto Initiative for Economic and Social Rights' (TIESR) has suggested that of the 195 state constitutions currently in existence, over 90 per cent contain at least one SE right and over 70 per cent contain at least one such right that, according to the study, qualifies as justiciable.[17] A closer look reveals a slightly more differentiated

[17] See Jung, Hirschl, and Rosevear, 'Economic and Social Rights in National Constitutions', 62 *American Journal of Comparative Law* (2014) 1043; see, generally, Toronto Initiative for Economic

picture, with not all members of this class of rights being equally entrenched, though given their highly contested history on the international level, it remains remarkable that around 85 per cent of national constitutions contain at least one of what the study considers core economic rights—notably the right to form or join a trade union, to strike, to leisure, to a fair wage, to a healthy work environment, and to (employment-related) social security[18]—and 80 per cent contain at least one of the so called 'standard social rights', notably to health care, to education, to child protection, and to (general) social security; and in approximately 40 to 60 per cent of jurisdictions, these two subsets of SE rights are deemed to be plainly justiciable. This selective but nonetheless strong domestic presence is, of course, the result of the coming together over a prolonged period of time of several factors, amongst them the proliferation of rights-oriented post-transition constitutions, an increased constitutional comparativism and, perhaps most importantly, the mentioned bottom-up judicialization often driven by organized civil society—a conjunction that will be examined in greater detail further on.

On the international front, SE rights are now spread across a significant number of dedicated and general instruments, with their main anchor being, of course, the International Covenant on Economic, Social, and Cultural Rights (ICESCR). It is currently ratified by 171 state parties—and an additional six non-ratified 'mere' signatories, of which, however, one is the United States—a ratification status nearly the same as the 173 of the International Covenant on Civil and Political Rights (ICCPR).[19] However, its long-in-the-making OP-ICESCR, which was adopted by the UN General Assembly in 2008 and has been in force since 2013, has currently only 26 state parties and a further 23 signatories, which, for the time being, significantly limits the ICESCR's direct justiciability vis-à-vis the Committee on Economic, Social, and Cultural Rights (CESCR).[20] Beyond the ICESCR system, all the instruments generally considered to be part of the 'international bill of rights', starting with the UDHR and including the ICESCR's alter-ego, the ICCPR, contain some provisions associated with SE rights.[21] The three evolved regional human

and Social Rights, https://www.tiesr.org (last visited 18 April 2023); see, generally, Tourkochoriti, 'Comparative Rights Jurisprudence: An Essay on Methodologies' (2017) *Law and Method* http://www.bjutijdschriften.nl/doi/10.5553/REM/.000030 (last visited 18 April 2023).

[18] Jung, Hirschl, and Rosevear (n. 17).

[19] See OHCH, Status of Ratification http://indicators.ohchr.org/ (last visited 18 April 2023).

[20] See n. 9.

[21] See the Universal Declaration of Human Rights (Arts. 22–27), GA Res. 217 A(III), 10 December 1948; the International Covenant on Civil and Political Rights (Arts 1, 8, 22, 23, 27) 1966, 999 UNTS 171; the Convention on the Elimination of All Forms of Discrimination Against Women (Arts 10–16) 1979, 1249 UNTS 13, (and its Optional Protocol 1999, 2131 UNTS 83); the Convention on the Elimination of All Forms of Racial Discrimination (Arts 1–2, 5) 1965, 660 UNTS 195; the Convention on the Protection of the Rights of All Migrant Workers and Members of Their Families (Arts 11, 14–15, 25–28, 30–32, 40, 43–45, 54–55, 64, 70), GA Res. 45/158, 18 December 1990; the Convention on the Rights of the Child (Arts 9, 16, 19, 24–36), GA Res. 44/25, 20 November 1989 (and also the Optional Protocol to the Convention on the Rights of the Child on the Involvement of Children in Armed Conflict (Arts 1–3), GA Res. 54/263, 25 May 2000, and the Optional Protocol to the Convention on

rights protection systems in Europe, Africa, and the Americas contain a number of SE rights in their respective base treaties but have also adopted optional protocols or dedicated declaratory commitments thereon.[22] Three incipient human rights frameworks, notably of the Association of South-East Asian Nations (ASEAN), of the Commonwealth of Independent States (CIS), and of Arab states also feature certain SE rights, as does the European Union via the European Social Charter and the Revised European Social Charter.[23] Lastly, a substantial number of treaties within the regime of the International Labour Organization (ILO) qualify as being concerned with the protection of SE rights.[24]

The normative density of SE rights on the international level is, hence, substantial, though justiciability and enforcement are not comparable with the domestic level. However, in aggregate, international mechanisms, including periodic reporting and complaints procedures, while not disposing of direct (domestic) effect, have continuously radiated into domestic systems by providing important interpretation aids to activists, litigants, and, not least, judiciaries, and by generally raising the consciousness of this class of rights among domestic actors.[25] In addition, the strain that domestic social policy has been put under in many countries of both the global North and South by the financial crises of the past decade has, arguably, not only bolstered their prominence in policy discourse, but also the interlinkage between domestic and international protection mechanisms.[26]

the Rights of the Child on the Sale of Children, Child Prostitution and Child Pornography, GA Res. 54/263, 25 May 2000); and the Convention Relating to the Status of Refugees (Arts 17–24 and 30) 1951, 189 UNTS 137.

[22] See the African Charter on Human and Peoples' Rights and Duties ('Banjul Charter') (Arts 2, 14–18, 20–22, 24) 1981, (1982), 21 I.L.M. 58 (see also the Protocol to the African Charter on Human and Peoples' Rights on the Rights of Women in Africa (Arts 12–19), 11 July 2003: http://www.refworld.org/docid/3f4b139d4.html (last visited 18 April 2023)); the African Charter on the Rights and Welfare of the Child (Arts 11, 14, 18) 1990, CAB/LEG/24.9/49; the Pretoria Declaration on Economic, Social and Cultural Rights (2004), https://www.ohchr.org/en/resources/educators/human-rights-education-training/13-pretoria-declaration-economic-social-and-cultural-rights-africa-2004 (last visited 18 April 2023); the American Convention on Human Rights ('Pact of San Jose, Costa Rica') (Arts 1, 6, 11, 14, 17, 21, 26), Organization of American States (OAS), 22 January 1969 (and the Additional Protocol to the American Convention on Human Rights in the Area of Economic, Social and Cultural Rights ('Protocol of San Salvador'), OAS, 16 November 1999; American Declaration on the Rights and Duties of Man (Arts V, VI, XI–XVI, XXII, XXIII), Inter-American Commission on Human Rights, 2 May 1948; and the First Protocol to the European Convention for the Protection of Human Rights and Fundamental Freedoms 1951, 9 ETS.

[23] Association of Southeast Asian Nations (ASEAN) Human Rights Declaration (Arts 13, 17, 19, 26–37), 18 November 2012; the Commonwealth of Independent States Convention on Human Rights and Fundamental Freedoms (Arts 4, 13–18, 21, 26–28), 26 May 1995; the Arab Charter on Human Rights (Art. 2), 15 September 1994; and the European Social Charter 1961, 35 ETS, and the Revised European Social Charter 1996, 163 ETS.

[24] International Labour Organization, Conventions http://www.ilo.org/dyn/normlex/en/f?p=NORMLEXPUB:12000:0::NO (last visited 18 April 2023); see also P. Alston (ed.), *Labour Rights as Human Rights* (2005).

[25] Riedel, Giacca, and Golay (n. 11) 34.

[26] Ibid. 3.

There is, hence, a thick interpretive sediment on the nature of the obligations imposed by SE rights, with the CESCR having played a leading, though by no means exclusive, role in its formation. Besides the Committee's 25 General Comments,[27] there are the Limburg Principles on the Implementation of the International Covenant on Economic, Social, and Cultural Rights of 1987 and the Maastricht Guidelines on Violations of Economic, Social, and Cultural Rights of 1997 which have provided the backdrop for an ever more fine-tuned account of the nature of SE rights obligations.[28] The core passage, of course, remains Article 2(1) of the ICESCR which states that:

> each State Party to the present Covenant undertakes to take steps, individually and through international assistance and cooperation, especially economic and technical, to the maximum of its available resources, with a view to achieving progressively the full realization of the rights recognized in the present Covenant by all appropriate means, including particularly the adoption of legislative measures.[29]

Its core terms, notably to 'undertake steps', 'maximum available resources', 'progressive realization', and 'appropriate means' have given rise to three interrelated definitional dichotomies that demarcate the current scope of SE rights obligations. The first concerns the means of implementation and, indirectly, the review timeline, and, thus, goes to the heart of the long-standing debate on the (in)divisibility of SE rights in terms of justiciability and enforcement. It came up within a year of the ICESCR's entry into force (in 1976), when the International Law Commission (ILC) used Article 2(1) as an example of what, at the time, it termed an 'obligation of result' which it considered to imply a greater degree of discretion on part of duty bearers to choose the means of implementation than the stricter so called 'obligation of conduct'.[30] A corollary of this distinction was, of course, that the degree of

[27] See General Comments of the Committee on Economic, Social, and Cultural Rights http://tbinternet.ohchr.org/_layouts/treatybodyexternal/TBSearch.aspx?Lang=en&TreatyID=9&DocTypeID=11 (last visited 18 April 2023); see also Alston, 'The General Comments of the UN Committee on Economic, Social and Cultural Rights', 104 *Proceedings of the ASIL Annual Meeting* (2010) 4.

[28] See UN Human Rights Commission, *note verbale* dated 5 December 1986 from the Permanent Mission of the Netherlands to the United Nations Office at Geneva addressed to the Centre for Human Rights ('Limburg Principles'), Annex, UN Doc. E/CN.4/1987/17, 8 January, 1987 (submitting the Limburg Principles on the Implementation of the International Covenant on Social, Economic and Cultural Rights); and Maastricht Guidelines on Violations of Economic, Social and Cultural Rights, Maastricht, 22–26 January 1997 https://www.refworld.org/docid/48abd5730.html (last visited 18 April 2023).

[29] Art. 2(1), International Covenant on Economic, Social and Cultural Rights, 1966, 993 UNTS 3.

[30] See International Law Commission, 'Report of the International Law Commission on Its Twenty Ninth Session', *Yearbook of the International Law Commission*, Vol. 2 (1977) 20–21, at para. 8; see also Langford and King, 'Committee on Economic, Social, and Cultural Rights: Past Present and Future', in M. Langford, *Social Rights Jurisprudence: Emerging Trends in International and Comparative Law* (2008) 477, at 482; Rosga and Satterthwaite, 'The Trust in Indicators: Measuring Human Rights', *Berkeley Journal of International Law (BJIL)* (2008) 253, at 254; Riedel, Giacca, and Golay (n. 11) 18.

scrutiny and also the review timeline differed between the two types of treaty obligation, a classification that would subsequently be interpreted as underscoring a differentiated approach to the obligations imposed by the two initial rights classes.[31]

However, this interpretation of treaty obligation has long encountered opposition in the literature and by the CESCR itself, first in the form of an insistence that Covenant rights contained both types of obligation,[32] then by a shift to an altogether different classificatory scheme, notably to the now prevalent 'respect, protect, fulfil' triad. Developed by the then Special Rapporteur on the Right to Food, Asbjørn Eide, in the late 1980s, it has since been adopted by a wide array of national human rights institutions and, as of General Comment 12 (1999), has become the predominant classificatory scheme of the CESCR.[33] As Malcolm Langford and Jeff King succinctly put it, the obligation to respect means to 'refrain from impeding', to protect implies to 'ensure others do not impede', and to fulfil entails to 'actually provide the conditions necessary for realizing' a particular right.[34] As such the scheme significantly expands the idea of rights as essentially negative protections against state action (as in the 'respect' obligation) by including both what has otherwise been called the horizontal effect (on third parties) of rights (the 'protect' obligation), and what used to be termed positive ('fulfil') obligations. The latter, in turn, has been subdivided into another obligations triad, namely 'to promote, to facilitate, and to provide', which serve a heuristic purpose when monitoring complex policy systems such as social security or health care.[35] The whole triadic SE rights analytic is, in any case, not meant to fragment obligations at the risk of rendering them less comprehensive, but, in practice, each of the three types will often be engaged to highlight different aspects of any particular obligation. However, what the triad does not concretize in and of itself is the degree and type of positive, including budgetary, action required.

[31] Although the CESCR itself did not make that point, considering the corresponding Art. 2(2) of the ICCPR to also imply 'merely' obligations of result; the distinction was then adopted in the Maastricht Guidelines (Art. 7), though merely as a qualification of the respect, protect, fulfil standard; it was, however, picked up—without reference to the latter standard—again in 2002 by the (then) Commission on Human Rights Independent Expert on the Draft Optional Protocol to the International Covenant on Economic, Social and Cultural Rights, whose report, in turn, ended up being used as additional argument to the much discussed rejoinder of the non-justiciability thesis set out by Michael Dennis and David Stewart, in 'Justiciability of Economic, Social, and Cultural Rights: Should There Be an International Complaints Mechanism to Adjudicate the Rights to Food, Water, Housing, and Health?', 98 *American Journal of International Law* (2004) 462; see also again Langford and King (n. 30) 483.

[32] See Alston and Quinn, 'Nature and Scope of States Parties' Obligations under the International Covenant on Economic, Social and Cultural Rights', 9 *Human Rights Quarterly* (1987) 156, at 185.

[33] See A. Eide (UN Special Rapporteur on the Right to Food), The Right to Food (Final Report) UN Doc. E/CN.4/Sub.2/1987/23 (1987), paras 66–69; 54; General Comment No. 12, Right to adequate food (Twentieth session, 1999), UN Doc. E/C.12/1999/5 (1999), para. 15.

[34] Langford and King (n. 30) 484.

[35] Riedel, Giacca, and Golay (n. 11) 19.

This is where a second constitutive dichotomy comes in, notably between the idea of 'minimum core obligations', on one hand, and their qualification by the 'maximum available resources' clause, on the other. As of General Comment No. 3, the CESCR has worked with the idea that there is a minimum core to each Covenant right which must be guaranteed at all times in order to avoid a breach of treaty obligations. There is general agreement that this necessarily implies the non-applicability of the 'progressive realization' criterion, i.e. that the minimum core of each right must be realized immediately. What is less clear is the degree to which the minimum core is entrenched and cannot be derogated from on any basis, including lack of resources. Initially, the CESCR had understood minimum core obligations to be, in principle, derogable on the basis of the 'maximum available resources' qualification, though in General Comments No. 13 (on education) and No. 14 (on health care) it referred to the core obligations of each right as non-derogable, relying, amongst others, on a non-derogability assumption expressed in the (earlier) Maastricht Guidelines.[36] Yet, from General Comment No. 15 (on the right to water) (2003) onwards, and in conjunction with its Statement on Maximum Available Resources of 2007, the CESCR has returned to its previous position on (non-) derogability.[37] Hence, the implementation of minimum core obligations must be assessed in terms of available resources on a case by case (i.e. country by country) basis, though this does not mean that the obligation to provide a basic 'survival kit' within the remit of a particular right (such as to food or safe drinking water) with immediate effect is thereby dispensed with.[38] Indeed, the Committee's practice firmly places the burden of proof on states to show that failure to provide the 'survival kit', even in times of armed conflict, has been literally impossible.[39]

Another debate that has arisen in the context of minimum core obligations involves two more (interrelated) dichotomies, namely between concreteness and comparability and between a substantive or a procedural approach. For on the one hand, there has been a consistent demand for maximum concreteness of the standards set out by monitoring bodies such as the CESCR, yet, on the other hand, there has been equally consistent critique of one-size-fits-all approaches that appear to establish an across-the-board comparability of implementation levels. As will be discussed again further below, there has, of course, been a general trend towards human rights indicators and quantification, and, thus, comparability,

[36] See CESCR, General Comment No. 13, UN Doc. E/C.12/1999/10,
8 December 1999; and CESCR General Comment No. 14, UN Doc E/C.12/2000/4, 11 August 2000; Maastricht Guidelines (n. 28); and Langford and King (n. 30) 493.

[37] CESCR, General Comment No. 15, UN Doc. E/C.12/2002/11, 20 January 2003; CESCR, Statement on an Evaluation of the Obligation to Take Steps to the 'Maximum of Available Resources' under an Optional Protocol to the Covenant, UN Doc. E/C.12/2007/1, 10 May 2007; as well as Langford and King (n. 30) 493.

[38] Riedel, Giacca, and Golay (n. 11) 8.

[39] Ibid. 14.

but the CESCR, for one, has so far endeavoured to steer a course between the administrative preference for concreteness and comparability, and the judicial preference for case-by-case differentiation. Hence, while providing fairly concrete definitions of substantive standards in relation to some rights, it has, on the whole, favoured procedural review on the basis of the reasonableness principle.[40] The latter, in particular, has been held to imply that state or administrative action (on Convention implementation) has to be deliberate, concrete, and targeted, as well as non-discriminatory and non-arbitrary.[41] This further implies that duty bearers are under an obligation to choose the policy option that least restricts Covenant rights, to take into special consideration marginalized and disadvantaged groups and those under heightened risk.[42] Hence, while the Committee has been careful not to be seen as a policymaker itself, the depth which its review of domestic public policy aspires to does approach that of domestic administrative tribunals (in jurisdictions where these exist) or correlate administrative (review) bodies—a fact that underlines the general 'turn to policy' on human rights that will be discussed further.

The dichotomy between immediate effect versus progressive realization has been interpreted by two further categories which stand not in a dichotomous relationship but which, instead, form what could be termed meta-categories of SE rights, namely non-discrimination and non-retrogression. The former has, arguably, become a sort of right of rights within general international and domestic rights jurisprudence.[43] Having a prima facie pedigree as a civil and political right, it was included as Article 2(2) in the ICESCR and forms, together with Article 3 on equal protection what Eibe Riedel has called 'cross-cutting and overarching principles that are to be applied in conjunction with [all Covenant] rights.'[44] It is thus considered a right of immediate effect for the breach of which no 'lack of resources' defence will be accepted. The Committee has additionally issued two General Comments, No. 16 (2005) on equal rights and No. 20 (2009) on non-discrimination in which it provides detailed outlines of the categories specifically protected.[45]

[40] Reasonableness is, of course, *prima facie* a common law construct though it has many close domestic siblings such as the principle of *proportionalité* in French law or of *Verhältnismäßigkeit* in German law; alongside the principle of proportionality, that, in turn, has primarily evolved in and through European Union law. It is now generally understood to be the leading standard in treaty interpretation; see Forman, 'Can Minimum Core Obligations Survive a Reasonableness Standard of Review Under the Optional Protocol to the International Covenant on Economic, Social and Cultural Rights?', 47 *Ottawa Law Review* (2016); and Langford, 'Domestic Adjudication and Economic, Social and Cultural Rights: A Socio-Legal Review', 6 *Sur - Revista Internacional de Direitos Humanos* (2009) 98 at 99.

[41] See Riedel, Giacca, and Golay (n. 11) 22, referring, inter alia, to CESCR, General Comment No. 16, UN Doc. E/C.12/2005/4, 11 Aug 2005.

[42] See Riedel, Giacca, and Golay (n. 11) 19.

[43] See, inter alia, W. Vandehole, *Non-discrimination and Equality in the View of the UN Human Rights Treaty Bodies* (2005).

[44] See Riedel, Giacca, and Golay (n. 11) 16.

[45] See General Comment No. 16 (n. 41) and CESCR, General Comment No. 20, UN Doc. E/C.12/GC/20, 2 Jul 2009.

Hence, besides the conditions expressly mentioned in Article 2(2), which correspond to the group category set recognized in all principal international human rights instruments, notably race, colour, sex, language, religion, political or other opinion, national or social origin, property, and birth, the Committee also ventured into fleshing out the up to then debated 'other status' category by specifically including in it the additional categories of disability, age, nationality, marital and family status, sexual orientation and gender identity health status, place of residence, as well as the general economic and social situation.[46]

With this wide remit of explicit discrimination grounds, the Committee has sought to systematize its own earlier disparate practice (across different General Comments) and to attend to criticism of apparent blindspots, for instance in the area of gender equality. Needless to say, this move to spell out as many of the relevant group categories as possible has, in turn, attracted criticism for, thereby, endorsing a targeting approach to discrimination that might limit any monitoring body's sensitivity to intersectional and cross-cutting discrimination, besides running the risk of entrenching a target-centric tunnel vision to the review of potentially discriminatory state action.[47] The Committee did, in any case, make sure to include in General Comment No. 20 all modes of discrimination, including direct and indirect, formal and substantive, third-party (i.e. private), and systemic discrimination. Positive discrimination (i.e. affirmative action) is explicitly permitted though subject to the usual reasonableness test by which measures have to 'objectively' serve a legitimate purpose, be compatible with the nature of Covenant rights, be necessary in a democratic society, and be proportional in terms of their aims.[48] In light of the deep entrenchment of especially indirect and systemic forms of discrimination in most domestic policy environments across the globe, General Comment No. 2 articulates a very wide-ranging and comprehensive non-discrimination vision, though it, again, remains to be seen to what extent international monitoring and the gradual mainstreaming of its standards into domestic administrative practice are viable and effective.

The second guiding principle is that of non-retrogression, which the Committee has interpreted as of General Comment No. 3 as a corollary of 'progressive realization' and which it has spelled out in detail in General Comment No. 19 with regard to no less complex a policy field as the right to social security which the Covenant recognizes in its Article 9.[49] In the General Comment, the Committee introduces strict scrutiny for derogations of the non-retrogression principle and lays down the review criteria for such cases; hence, any retrogressive policy has to be reasonably justified, all alternative options have to be considered, affected groups have to be

46 See Riedel, Giacca, and Golay (n. 11) 17.

47 See Langford and King (n. 30) 490.

48 See Riedel, Giacca, and Golay (n. 11) 16.

49 See CESCR General Comment No. 3, UN Doc. E/1991/23, annex III at 86 (1991); and CESCR General Comment No. 19, UN Doc E/C.12/GC/19, 4 February 2008.

consulted, and there has to have been some domestic review of the (retrogressive) measures; in addition, the Committee will look at whether the measures are discriminatory and at whether a particular measure will have an adverse effect on the overall enjoyment of the right, whether it infringes on acquired rights, or whether it deprives any group of the minimum core content of the right.[50] Once again, the standard of review is geared to the procedural aspects of policy-making, though, as with non-discrimination, it is aimed to afford the reviewing body a deep gaze into that process. What is less clear is the precise relationship between non-retrogression and the obligation to respect, an issue that has become crucially important in the wake of austerity policies implemented during the world financial crisis—and which will be discussed later on.

How are these standards applied? As was already mentioned, since the entry into force of the OP-ICESCR, there has been a quasi-judicial complaints mechanism comparable to the long-established ones of the other main international human rights instruments of the 'international bill of rights'. It allows for individual and collective—though not directly CSO-sponsored—complaints, has jurisdiction over all Covenant rights, and erects a relatively low-entry barrier by qualifying admissibility with the requirement that the complainant must be shown to have suffered significant disadvantage from the impugned state measure.[51] The extent to which so called 'macro-issues' to do with general economic policy—such as poverty reduction strategies—can be litigated in this way was subject to considerable controversy during the drafting stage. With its already mentioned Statement on Maximum Available Resources, the Committee addressed this issue and shifted its weight onto the reporting, rather than the, contentious, procedure while nonetheless laying down the procedural review criteria based on reasonableness which it would apply in assessing the adequacy of domestic policy. It remains to be seen if the OP-based complaints procedure will eventually generate enough jurisprudence to produce another layer of doctrinal sediment on top of that developed through general comments and periodic reviews. However, in the current economic and political climate, a significant expansion of the OP-ICESCR signatory group is unlikely, as is the CESCR's ability to meaningfully intervene in domestic policymaking on the basis of individual cases.

[50] Ibid. para. 42.

[51] See Riedel, Giacca, and Golay (n. 11) 29; and Courtis and Rossi, 'Individual Complaints Procedure', in M. Langford, B. Porter, and R. Brown (eds), *The Optional Protocol to the International Covenant on Economic, Social and Cultural Rights: A Commentary* (2016) 47.

B. Measuring SE Rights: Quantifying Implementation

Perhaps the most crucial aspect of SE rights at present, and the one, arguably, most consequential for their future, is what Malcolm Langford and Sakiko Fukuda-Parr have termed the 'turn to metrics' in human rights, connoting the proliferation of quantified measuring techniques and indicators for monitoring the domestic implementation of human rights.[52] It is so significant because it marks the emergence of a new quality of human rights monitoring aligned with a broader trend towards indicator-based governance that has, in turn, accompanied the mentioned rise of the regulatory (and now post-regulatory) state paradigm.[53] It is linked to such phenomena as the audit culture, the corporatization of the state, and the rise of 'expertocracy' and it represents a transformation of the meaning and source of organizational legitimacy as well as of the nature of knowledge production.[54] With regard to human rights it stands for what can be seen as a comprehensive 'turn to policy' that is characterized by a much more active role for (international) monitoring and advocacy agents and a consequently much deeper intervention into duty bearers' domestic policy process. Its broader implications will be examined in the concluding section of this chapter, at this stage the main trends in measuring SE rights shall briefly be summed up.

Traditionally, human rights monitoring and advocacy did not much take to quantification and indicators, not least on account of the law-centric episteme within which the human rights community has tended to operate and which has been characterized by the logic of adjudication, that is, the case-by-case assessment of specific facts in light of legal obligations.[55] The rendering of concrete conditions of human rights fulfilment into measurable units comparable across sectors or countries by and large fell outside the expertise of human rights professionals and, when initially attempted, tended to be received with well-warranted scepticism on account of oversimplification and potential bias.[56] However, it was, initially, in

[52] See Langford and Fukuda-Parr (n. 6).

[53] There is now an ample literature on this 'turn', see, for instance, the collections by K. Davis, A. Fisher, B. Kingsbury, and S. E. Merry, *Governance by Indicators: Global Power through Classification and Rankings* (2012); as well as T. Landman and E. Carvalho, *Measuring Human Rights* (2010), and the symposium issue edited by Caliari et al., 'Bringing Human Rights to Bear in Times of Crisis: A Human Rights Analysis of Government Responses to the Economic Crisis', 30 *Nordic Journal of Human Rights* (2012) 222; see also Fukuda-Parr, 'Indicators of Human Development and Human Rights—Overlaps, Differences ... And What About The Human Development Index?', 18 *Statistical Journal of the United Nations* (2001) 239; and also earlier commentary in Green, 'What We Talk About When We Talk About Indicators', 23 *Human Rights Quarterly* (2001) 1062, and the more recent one in Bhuta, 'Indexes of State Failure and Fragility', in A. Cooley and J. Snyder (eds.), *Ranking the World* (2015) 85; Merry, 'Measuring the World', 52 *Current Anthropology* (2011) S83–S95; and, again, Rosga and Satterthwaite (n. 30).

[54] See Merry (n. 53) S87; and Rosga and Satterthwaite (n. 30) 256.

[55] Merry (n. 53) S84.

[56] The case in point here is, of course, the well-known *Freedom of the World* index published since 1972 on a yearly basis by the Freedom House organization https://freedomhouse.org/report/freedom-world/freedom-world-2016 (last visited 18 April 2023); see also Merry (n. 53) S87.

response to the quandaries arising from objectively assessing the ICESCR's 'progressive realization' obligation that the CESCR, other UN bodies, and the wider advocacy community began to look for indicators that could measure implementation beyond the subjective interpretation of duty bearers.

Yet, the 'turn to metrics' in human rights only gained real momentum in the wake of the emergence of the rights-based development paradigm in the late 1990s when quantitative measures, long used in development discourse, entered into human rights practice.[57] Since then, the CESCR itself has been a leading proponent of the mainstreaming of quantitative measuring into monitoring, so much so that, as of its General Comment No. 13 of 1999 (on education) it has read into the 'take steps' obligation of Article 2(1) an obligation to establish measures and indicators as monitoring tools.[58] This significant interpretive step is, arguably, as much owed to the general trend towards the objectification of human rights standards as it is to the CESCR's desire, representative of all UN treaty bodies, to reinforce both its authority and its legitimacy vis-à-vis state parties. In fact, in the years since then, the move to indicators has allowed the CESCR to re-shape its role in the monitoring and implementation process in two complementary ways. Firstly, it has brought to bear the Office of the High Commissioner for Human Rights' (OHCHR) growing indicator expertise (and dataset) both to its own formulation of standards (such as in General Comments and Statements), and to its proactive consultation with state parties on the construction of country-specific indicators within their reporting obligations; and secondly, it has taken to what Ann Janette Rosga and Margaret Satterthwaite have called 'monitoring of monitoring', that is, it has monitored what it previously established as the state's duty to construct and apply its own indicators.[59]

While interrelated, both activities have to be seen as articulating two distinct roles for the CESCR. The first makes it into a privileged channel for expert information on substantive indicators and on indicator construction, a proactive knowledge repository-cum-policy-consultant which seeks to guide the state's reporting process and, thus, stakes out a role well beyond the traditional evaluation of qualitative reports and the (very) occasional adjudication of individual complaints. It is a role which not only the CESCR has been seeking, but which virtually all specialized monitoring bodies as well as advocacy organizations have aspired to, which is why the past decade has seen a multiplicity of efforts to construct ever more fine-tuned indicators and indicator-based monitoring frameworks. The

[57] See Merry (n. 53) S87; and Malhotra and Fasel, 'Quantitative Human Rights Indicators: A Survey of Major Initiatives', in *Expert Meeting on Human Rights Indicators, Abo Akademi University, Turku, Finland, 10-13 March 2005* (2005) https://eldis.org/document/A44592 (last visited 18 April 2023).

[58] See General Comment No. 13 and 14 (n. 36); and Riedel, Giacca, and Golay (n. 11) 23.

[59] See Rosga and Satterthwaite (n. 30) 275; they, in turn, refer to Hammarberg, 'Searching for the Truth: The Need to Monitor Human Rights with Relevant and Reliable Means', 18 *Statistical Journal of the UN Economic Commission for Europe* (2001) 131, at 134.

second role derives from a now formalized process known by its acronym as the IBSA (Indicator-Benchmarking-Scoping, Assessment) procedure in which the Committee advises (on indicators) and assesses (final reports) but, crucially, also makes proposals on benchmarking in the context of a mediated (scoping) dialogue with the state party. The IBSA process, thus, establishes *in nuce* the sort of inter-institutional cooperation procedure that is known from many domestic and international policymaking processes, except that, unlike these procedures, the CESCR is also tasked with assessing the policy plans it has previously helped to draft, a not unproblematic bundling of distinct functions—and a point that will be returned to below.

In terms of the first role, the CESCR and other monitoring bodies can now rely on a good 20 years of work on human rights indicators within the UN system, with organizations such as UNICEF, United Nations Development Fund for Women (UNIFEM), the Commission on the Status of Women, the UN Statistical Commission, and, of course, the OHCHR all having contributed to the knowledge base.[60] In addition, many of the specialized agencies, among them the United Nations Development Programme (UNDP), the Food and Agriculture Organization (FAO), the World Health Organization (WHO), the ILO and, of course, the World Bank have long been engaged in compiling socio-economic data and in developing specific indicator sets relevant to measuring human rights performance.[61] In 2008, the OHCHR published a *Report on Indicators for the Promotion and Monitoring of Human Rights* in which it set out its conceptual and methodological approach to indicators and drafted a set of illustrative indicators on 48 rights contained in either of the Covenants.[62] In 2012, it topped up this already comprehensive exercise when it issued a nearly 200-page manual on *Human Rights Indicators: a Guide to Measurement and Implementation* (HRI) which it directed, significantly, not only to those domestic and international bodies directly tasked with human rights monitoring and reporting, but to virtually all policymaking agents whose remit may have any bearing on human rights implementation.[63] It is, thus, alongside such projects as the various UN Guiding Principles,[64]

[60] See Malhotra and Fasel (n. 57) para. 29; and Merry (n. 53) S87.

[61] Malhotra and Fasel (n. 57) para. 36.

[62] OHCHR, Report on Indicators for the Promotion and Monitoring of Human Rights, UN Doc. HRI/MC/2008/3, 6 June 2008.

[63] It states that the manual is directed to 'stakeholders engaged in identifying, collecting and using indicators to promote and monitor the implementation of human rights nationally ... [that is] ... national human rights institutions, the United Nations human rights system in general and the treaty bodies in particular, the State agencies responsible for reporting on the implementation of human rights treaty obligations, as well as those responsible for policymaking across different ministries, public agencies at different levels of governance, statistical agencies, development practitioners, civil society organizations and international agencies with a mandate to further the realization of human rights ...' see OHCHR, Human Rights Indicators: A Guide to Measurement and Implementation, UN Doc. HR/PUB/12/5 (2012).

[64] See the *Guiding Principles on Extreme Poverty and Human Rights*, A/HRC/21/39, 27 September 2012; or the *Guiding Principles on Business and Human Rights*, A/HRC/RES/17/4, 6 July 2011.

an instance of the mentioned 'turn to policy' in human rights monitoring which essentially seeks to address the most concrete and technical level of policy-making with a view to mainstreaming a comprehensive human rights impact assessment into virtually all domestic policy.

To that end, HRI adopts a five-pronged approach to indicator construction on any particular right. The first step consists of disaggregating specific 'attributes' of each right from the core international human rights instruments so as to render highly concrete and transparent definitions of the involved obligations. Fulfilment of these is then measured in relation to three distinct aspects of implementation, namely, general commitment, specific effort, and overall results. These translate into three indicators which, following the then UN Special Rapporteur on the Right to Health, Paul Hunt's, 2003 classification, are termed structural, process, and outcome indicators.[65] The first include the basic elements necessary for the implementation of a right, such as the relevant international commitment (a.k.a. ratification of human rights treaties), as well as the fundamental structures, such as those associated with a functioning rule of law, required for its enforcement. Process indicators then measure the specific effort undertaken by a state in terms of the realization of a particular right, such as budgetary allocation, legislative or administrative action, or judicial processes that are related to compliance with the individual obligations attributable to the right. Lastly, outcome indicators purport to measure the objective level of realization of a right by aggregating the relevant socio-economic data. The fifth element of indicator construction is made up of what HRI terms 'cross-cutting human rights norms' through which the three indicator sets are meant to be further disaggregated. Unsurprisingly, it includes the meta-right of non-discrimination as well as the three core good governance principles of participation, accountability, and effectiveness.[66]

With this conceptual scheme in place, the HRI report goes on to provide detailed guidance on all aspects of indicator-based monitoring, from the compilation and interpretation of statistical data to the setting up of monitoring systems. The paradigm that emerges is not just one in which, aspirationally, domestic administrators would continuously self-assess policymaking by means of a comprehensive and detailed human rights indicator matrix, but one in which they would also be capable of plausibly correlating process and outcome data so as to establish clear causal relationships which can, in turn, be fed back into the policymaking process. As such, the HRI report incorporates a vision which, if fully implemented, would

[65] See ECOSOC, The Right of Everyone to Enjoy the Highest Attainable Standard of Physical and Mental Health—Interim Report of the Special Rapporteur of the Commission on Human Rights on the Right of Everyone to Enjoy the Highest Attainable Standard of Physical and Mental Health, Mr. Paul Hunt, E/CN.4/2003/58, 13 February 2003.

[66] They are part of the so-called PANTHER principles, notably (p)articipation, (a)ccountability, (n)on-discrimination, (t)ransparency, (h)uman dignity, (e)mpowerment, and (r)ule of law; see, for instance, FAO, The Right to Adequate Food in Emergency Programs (2014) http://www.fao.org/3/a-i4184e.pdf (last visited 18 April 2023).

reshape the way social policy is conceived and made, with the relevant rights being rendered as a quantified set of independent variables upon which all other variables would depend.

However, despite its ambitious scope, the HRI report, as the 2008 Report before it, abstains from the attempt to define a single set of universal, that is, cross-nationally applicable, indicators and, instead, merely provides illustrative indicators alongside an extensive methodology for (national) indicator construction by duty bearers. This reflects an (albeit uneasy) consensus among the treaty bodies that universal indicators are, for the time being, too difficult to construct objectively and, as such, lack legitimacy vis-à-vis states.[67] Instead, and as hinted above, the treaty bodies and the CESCR, in particular, have endorsed a paradigm in which they function as auditors of the indicator-based self-monitoring of states.

This narrowly participatory approach by the CESCR—narrow in that it is primarily about state party participation in indicator construction and benchmarking—has, however, not prevented organizations outside the remit of UN treaty monitoring from developing expert indices that transcend OHCHR's approach either by creating cross-country comparability of SE rights implementation or by fine-tuning its monitoring methodology. Indeed, there has been a surge in human rights indicator development since the late 2000s, with several indicator projects having entered the scene with the stated aim of addressing specific shortcomings of earlier efforts.[68]

Three of these are directly geared to SE rights, notably the Social Economic Rights Fulfilment Index (SERF) of 2008, the Toronto Initiative for Economic and Social Rights (TIESR) of 2010, as well as the OPERA developed by the Center for Economic and Social Rights (CESR) in 2012.[69] Each seeks to address a specific aspect of the quantification and, in the case of the first two, of the comparison of SE rights implementation. The first of these, the SERF project, emerged in the wake of the proliferation of the rights-based approach to development and in response to two fundamental challenges the latter had been facing, namely the inadequacy of the existing development indicators, most notably the widely used Human Development Index (HDI), for accurately measuring SE rights fulfilment, and the absence of a methodology for assessing the 'progressive realization' of SE rights. The latter implies both obligations of conduct and result, that is, government effort and de facto rights fulfilment, and, thus, a deep analysis of both social and economic background data as well as of specific public policies. This is, in turn, deeply entangled with the problem of comparing aggregated data across

67 See Riedel, Giacca, and Golay (n. 11) 21.

68 While these are well known in the specialist literature, they have not yet been systematically compared; for an overview, see Langford and Fukuda-Parr (n. 6).

69 On the SERF index see Fukuda-Parr, Lawson-Remer, and Randolph (n. 6); on the TIESR, see n. 17; and on the OPERA framework see CESR at https://www.cesr.org/opera-framework/ (last visited 18 April 2023).

countries, as the 'maximum available resource' specification tends not to be disaggregated according to state 'capacities'. Building on—and transcending—earlier efforts at addressing this predicament, notably by a version of the Cingranelli and Richards Human Rights Data Project (CIRI), and by a separate indicator developed by Magwe Kimenyi (KI),[70] the SERF index purports to overcome these challenges by compiling both conduct and result data via a set of core indicators—on food, education, health, housing, and work—and by then measuring these against country-specific performance benchmarks, termed 'achievement possibility frontiers' (APF), which measure a state's fulfilment of its obligations as a percentage of the benchmark. Importantly, the SERF index differentiates between 'core' (low- and middle-income) and 'OECD' (high-income) states and, thus, seeks to avoid the aggregation predicament that has been marring global cross-country comparison.[71] As such SERF has provided a powerful tool for both monitoring bodies and advocacy organizations and has become a standard measure for SE rights implementation.

The TIESR index, in turn, has the more specific objective of quantifying the presence and justiciability of core SE rights in domestic constitutions. It distinguishes between plainly justiciable and aspirational (a.k.a. programmatic) SE rights, and measures their incidence across several categories, such as evolution over time, world regions, and legal systems, and, thus, provides useful data for assessing the structural variables of state obligation.[72]

Lastly, the OPERA project was developed by the CESR with a similar aim as OHCHR's HRI and CESCR's IBSA process, notably to bring together all aspects of state obligation in a single framework that would enable a comprehensive yet contextual assessment of a duty bearer's performance.[73] In particular, it seeks to combine quantitative with qualitative approaches so as to tickle out all country-specific nuances that are missed out in a purely quantitative optic. To this end it adapts the structure-process-outcomes triad into a fourfold 'outcomes', 'policy efforts', 'resources', and 'assessment' matrix in which each cell contains several measurements that are then aggregated and evaluated in conjunction. Hence, outcomes, the equivalent of results, measure fulfilment of minimum core obligations, progressive realization, and non-discrimination. Policy efforts bring together legal structures and policy efficacy as measured by the widely used AAAAQ ('availability, accessibility, acceptability, adaptability, and quality') criteria and the good governance PANTHER ('participation, accountability, non-discrimination, transparency,

[70] The CIRI index is available at https://dataverse.harvard.edu/dataverse/cirihumanrightsdata (last visited 18 April 2023); Kimenyi, 'Economic Rights, Human Development Effort, and Institutions', in S. Hertel and L. Minkler (eds), *Economic Rights: Conceptual, Measurement, and Policy Issues* (2007) 182.

[71] See Randolph and Guyer, 'Tracking the Historical Evolution of States' Compliance with their Economic and Social Rights Obligations of Result: Insights from the Historical SERF Index', 30 *Nordic Journal of Human Rights* (2012) 297.

[72] See n. 17.

[73] See n. 69.

human dignity, empowerment, and rule of law') principles.[74] Resources calculate maximum and available resources, and the assessment then reviews the preceding three for comprehensiveness, evaluates state constraints, and finally determines state compliance.[75]

3. From Present to Future: The Domestic and the International Frontier

A. The Domestic Frontier: The Rights-Based Judicialization of Social Policy

Returning now to the two frontier regions that demarcate the future of SE rights, it is fair to start with the observation that it has been the domestic front that has dominated the SE rights literature for the past 20 or so years. The reason for this is, of course, what Charles Epp notoriously termed the 'rights revolution' that has unfolded in many constitutional democracies since the 1960s.[76] It is really the convergence of two distinct and partly conflicting revolutions and, despite its evocative name, it is essentially the product of a legal evolution that has neither been planned nor been predictable in its effects, which is why its impact has been the subject of controversial debate from the very beginning. The first—in a non-chronological sense—of these (r)evolutions has been on paper, namely in the form of the proliferation of entrenched rights in, broadly speaking, post-colonial constitutions in Africa and South Asia in the 1960s, post-authoritarian constitutions in Latin America in the 1980s, and post-socialist constitutions in Central and Eastern Europe, (some of) the successor states of the former Soviet Union, as well as the

[74] Corkery and Way, 'Integrating Quantitative and Qualitative Tools to Monitor the Obligation to Fulfil Economic, Social and Cultural Rights: the OPERA Framework', 30 *Nordic Journal of Human Rights* (2012) 324.

[75] Two further initiatives that are not exclusively geared to SE rights but that are widely referenced in rights monitoring and advocacy are the World Policy Analysis Center (WPCA) dataset and the Human Rights Measurement Framework (HRMF). The former focusses, in particular, on comparative policy analysis of obligations of conduct and, to that end, compiles a large dataset on policy approaches and their relation to particular outcomes; see the discussion of the framework in Langford and Fukuda-Parr (n. 6) 225; the HRMF, in turn, has become a widely-cited example for how rights measurement can be adapted for the specific needs of national human rights institutions (NHRI)—in this case the UK's Equality and Human Rights Commission; in its multi-step approach that brings together quantitative measurement with qualitative judgement, it broadly resembles OPERA's approach and has been applied to a number of domestic policy fields to assess policy efficacy from a human rights vantage point; see Vizard, 'Evaluating Compliance Using Quantitative Methods and Indicators: Lessons from the Human Rights Measurement Framework', 30 *Nordic Journal of Human Rights* (2012) 239.

[76] C. Epp, *The Rights Revolution: Lawyers, Activists, and Supreme Courts in Comparative Perspective* (1998); and Brinks and Gauri, 'The Law's Majestic Equality? The Distributive Impact of Judicializing Social and Economic Rights', 12 *Perspectives on Politics* (2014) 375.

seminal post-apartheid constitution of South Africa in the 1990s.[77] Although these new waves of constitutionalism were to a significant extent driven by a growing commitment to all fundamental (human) rights, SE rights have played a particularly prominent role in the post-transition constitution-drafting in Latin American, post-Soviet, and (some) African states. This contrasts with many earlier and especially Western constitutions, such as those of the United States but also, and surprisingly, of some traditional European welfare states, which make no or merely preambular or generalized mention of SE rights.[78]

Although the precise reasons for the SE 'rights creep' into new-wave constitutionalism are complex and country- or at least region-specific,[79] one common motive in post-transition constitution-drafting has certainly been the hope of effecting social transformation by means of entrenched constitutional commitments to core welfare standards.[80] The rise of this rights-based 'social constitutionalism'[81] has, however, and paradoxically, been as much a reaction against neoliberal public sector reform and the attendant weakening of traditional re-distributive welfare policies as it has been enabled by that very neoliberal orthodoxy's turn towards (legal) institutions, the rule of law, and, with these, a new form of (judicial) state interventionism.[82] This, in turn, has produced the preconditions for the second rights (r)evolution, notably the widespread judicialization of social policy that has taken off especially in middle-income democracies of the global South since the early 2000s.[83] It is this second revolution that has really brought SE rights out into the open during the past two decades and it has redirected much SE rights advocacy and academic interest onto the domestic front. Concretely, it has consisted of an exponential rise in individual and class-action type litigation on basic public goods such as health, education, housing, food, or water and sanitation in emerging

[77] See, inter alia, Ackerman, 'The Rise of World Constitutionalism', 83 *Virginia Law Review* (1997) 771; and D. Bellamy and D. Castiglione (eds) *Constitutionalism Transformation; European and Theoretical Perspectives* (1996).

[78] The German constitution, for instance, contains no explicit—and, thus, justiciable—social right but merely recognizes, in its Art. 20(1), that the Federal Republic is a 'social federal state' (the so called *Sozialstaatsprinzip* ('principle of the social [a.k.a. welfare] state'); most of its welfare state provisions are contained in ordinary legislation, such as the *Sozialgesetzbuch* (the 'social code'); see, specifically, D. Kommers and R. Miller, *The Constitutional Jurisprudence of the Federal Republic of Germany* (2012); and, from a broader perspective, Glendon, 'Rights in Twentieth-Century Constitutions', 59 *University of Chicago Law Review* (1992) 519; as well as, again, Jung, Hirschl, and Rosevear (n. 17).

[79] See, inter alia, Law and Versteeg, 'The Evolution and Ideology of Global Constitutionalism', 99 *California Law Review* (2011)163; and Brinks and Gauri (n. 74) 376.

[80] See, inter alia, Brinks and Forbath, 'The Role of Courts and Constitutions in the New Politics of Welfare in Latin America', *Law and Development of Middle-Income Countries* (2014) 221; Gargarella, Domingo, and Roux (n. 7); and Haglund and Stryker (n. 7).

[81] See Angel-Cabo and Parma, 'Latin American Social Constitutionalism: Courts and Popular Participation', in H. Alviar García, K. Klare, and L. Williams, *Social and Economic Rights in Theory and Practice: Critical Inquiries* (2015); and Brinks and Gauri (n. 74) 377.

[82] Kennedy, 'Law and Development Economics: Toward a New Alliance', in D. Kennedy and J. Stiglitz (eds), *Law and Economics with Chinese Characteristics: Institutions for Promoting Development in the Twenty-First Century* (2013) 19.

[83] See Brinks and Gauri (n. 74).

constitutional democracies such as Argentina, Colombia, Costa Rica, Brazil, India, and South Africa.[84] As a socio-legal phenomenon it has by now been documented in a number of cross-country studies and is reasonably well-understood, even if differences in legal systems and forms of judicial review still pose an inherent challenge to straightforward comparison.[85] However, there is still a vibrant and on-going debate about why this judicialization wave has built up when and where it did, about what impact on the distribution of basic goods it has had and how that impact should be assessed, and, related to this, about the overall legitimacy and efficacy of judicial interventionism in social policy.

In terms of the root causes of judicialization, several explanations have been offered at different zoom levels. On the most general level are the structural factors mentioned above, notably, the current phase in the global political economy and its turn to law and courts as a way to constrain traditional government (a.k.a. politics) in favour of (market) functional governance, and the (arguably) unintended side-effect of a greatly expanded legal opportunity structure usable and used by SE rights activists.[86] The constrained policy space of the regulatory and post-regulatory state implies, of course, a shift in the forms and locations of political conflict, with the demand for and targeted use of (SE) rights becoming a primary strategy for a progressive politics advocating social transformation.[87] Where this configuration meets the 'new developmentalism' of many governments in today's global South, domestic courts are able and increasingly willing to assume the considerable political responsibility of wide-ranging intervention into social policy.[88] Under such circumstances, judicialization is seen as a pro-majoritarian instrument against backward social structures, policy deadlocks, and ineffective bureaucracies. Together with international pressure and feedback cycles, a general climate for a 'rights revolution' is, thus, generated.[89]

At a higher resolution, this picture becomes more differentiated, with the interplay of various distinct factors being suggested in the literature. On an intermediate zoom level, it is such elements as the level of social organization,[90] the de facto level of achievement of SE rights in a given locality, the legal support structure,[91]

84 See, again, Epp (n. 76), and these empirical studies: Gauri and Brinks (n. 7); Yamin and Gloppen (n. 7); and O. Vilhena, U. Baxi, and F. Viljoen (eds), *Transformative Constitutionalism: Comparing the Apex Courts of Brazil, India and South Africa* (2003).

85 See Jung, Hirschl, and Rosevear (n. 17) 11.

86 For the concept of 'legal opportunity structure', see Gloppen, 'Studying Courts in Context: The Role of Nonjudicial Institutional and Socio-Political Realities', in Haglund and Stryker (n. 7) 291.

87 See, classically, C. Sunstein, *After the Rights Revolution: Reconceiving the Regulatory State* (1993); and Gargarella, 'Theories of Democracy, the Judiciary and Social Rights', in Gargarella, Domingo, and Roux (n. 7) 13.

88 See Brinks and Forbath (n. 80), as well as N. Dubash and B. Morgan, *The Rise of the Regulatory State of the South* (2013); and, again, Trubek (n. 14) 22.

89 For such a 'spiral' model, see T. Risse, S. Ropp, and K. Sikking, *The Power of Human Rights: International Norms and Domestic Change* (1999); see also B. A. Simmons, *Mobilizing for Human Rights: International Law in Domestic Politics* (2009).

90 Langford, 'The Justiciability of Social Rights: From Practice to Theory', in Langford (n. 7) 9.

91 Epp (n. 76) 11.

as well as the judicial and the wider (rights) culture that are deemed to impact on the likelihood and success of the legalization of social policy.[92] The most detailed model has, arguably, been elaborated by Siri Gloppen, who, building, inter alia, on Varun Gauri and Daniel Brinks' pathbreaking earlier work, distinguishes between three aspects of analysis, namely what she terms the 'anatomy of the litigation process', the 'legal opportunity structure', and the 'assessment of impact'.[93] The first of these involves constructing a detailed map of the litigation process and its consecutive elements of 'claims formation', 'adjudication', 'administrative and political response', and 'effects' and the involved actors, namely litigants, judges, politicians, and bureaucrats.[94]

This anatomical structure is brought to life by the 'legal opportunity structure' which, according to Gloppen, is determined by three elements, namely motivation (of the actors involved), barriers faced, and resources required. Motivation is actor-specific—hence, distinct for litigants as demand-side actors and judges, politicians, and bureaucrats as supply-side actors[95]—and consists of 'goals, values, norms, interests, and preferences', the realization of which, however, depend on the external factors of the 'legal opportunity structures', resources, and barriers. These include core factors such as, on the resource side, the formal basis for SE rights claims, the courts' legacy in SE rights litigation, the legal support structure, legal competence, or rights consciousness, and, on the barrier side, lack of SE rights protection, lack of standing, a formalistic legal culture, litigation costs, or the lack of amenability for 'rights talk' within the general culture, as well as penumbral factors such as the broader social, political, and cultural landscape.[96]

With this detailed map it is, in principle, possible to reconstruct a specific legalization process taking into consideration all relevant local factors and to, thus, derive non-trivial conclusions that, as a self-reflective heuristic scheme, may help improve litigation strategies and outcomes. This complex—perhaps overly complex, as Gloppen herself concedes—but highly accurate mapping exercise is complemented by other, more limited frameworks, such as one developed by (Daniel) Brinks and William Forbath, who focus on the courts' decision-making styles and construct a two-dimensional matrix with one axis ranging from activist to restrictive courts and the other from 'syllogistic'—i.e. formalist deduction from the constitutional text or judicial precedent—and 'pragmatic'—i.e. policy-oriented cost-benefit analyses—forms of judicial reasoning.[97]

[92] See Gloppen (n. 86) 293; and Langford (n. 90) 10; and Brinks and Gauri (n. 74) 378.
[93] See Gloppen (n. 86) 295; and Gauri and Brinks (n. 7); as well as Brinks and Gauri (n. 74).
[94] See, in particular, the graphic process diagrams in Gloppen (n. 86) 295.
[95] This is an earlier distinction made (amongst others) by Gauri and Brinks, 'The Impact of Legal Strategies for Claiming Economic and Social Rights', in Haglund and Stryker (n. 7) 98.
[96] Gloppen (n. 86) 295.
[97] Brinks and Forbath (n. 80) 239.

However, while these models are able to base themselves on a limited, if growing, number of comparative empirical studies, there is, as yet, neither sufficient empirical material at hand to construct a comprehensive global map, nor does the analysis, even on a limited empirical basis, of what Gloppen calls the 'micro-foundations of court-enforced human rights accountability and policy legalization' render a uniform-enough picture for a generalizable explanation of why and how legalization and judicialization occurs.[98] Indeed, as Gloppen and others in the as yet small field of empirical human rights studies readily acknowledge, more empirical data and a wider scholarly community is needed to fully understand the 'rights (r)evolution'. One particular difficulty is the latter's apparent limitation to constitutional democracies with a reasonably well-functioning rule of law—without which, of course, there is no judicial enforcement of SE rights—which leaves many 'new developmental states', such as China or, arguably, Russia, off the radar even though there are appreciable social policy deficits and a concomitant demand for the type of social accountability that rights-based litigation would provide.[99]

Yet, perhaps more important than the question of why the 'rights (r)evolution' has happened and how it works is the question of what it does to those it is, primarily, intended to help—although exactly who that is, is already part of the debate. That the judicialization of social policy does have a profound impact, be it on either party of the litigation process, on the way public authorities structure social policy, on public budgets, or, indeed, on those constituencies of social policies that are not directly parties to 'rights (r)evolutionary' action, is generally not disputed. Yet, whether that impact is to be seen as positive and, hence, judicialization as progressive from a human rights perspective, or whether it generates more negatives and would, thus, have to be seen as retrogressive, is still keenly debated. Initially, this debate was structured by broader normative positions, such as on whether courts can and should occupy a central role in social policy, or not;[100] or on whether (SE) rights-based strategies complement and reinforce welfare policies or whether, instead, they either hinder a more comprehensive approach to (re-)distribution and welfare policies or are, in fact, (ab)used to cover up the very dismantling of the latter.[101] While earlier analyses where often confined to extrapolating from the patterns identified in the well-documented public interest litigation in the United

[98] Gloppen (n. 86) 293.

[99] See, for instance, Peerenboom, 'Human Rights in China', in R. Peerenboom, C. Petersen, and A. Chen, *Human Rights in Asia: A Comparative Legal Study of Twelve Asian Jurisdictions, France and the USA* (2006) 413; see also Maru, 'Allies Unknown: Social Accountability and Legal Empowerment', 12 *Health and Human Rights Journal* (2010).

[100] For a general critique of judicialization see Hirschl, 'The New Constitutionalism and the Judicialization of Pure Politics Worldwide', 75 *Fordham Law Review* (2006) 721.

[101] See, for instance, Alviar García, 'Social Policy and the New Development State: The Case of Colombia', *Institute for Global Law and Policy, Harvard Law School, Cambridge: IGLP Working Paper Series* (2011).

States,[102] more recent arguments have sought to incorporate data from a much broader empirical sample.[103]

Nonetheless, measuring and assessing impact remains a protracted effort even beyond the availability of data, as the meaning of social transformation and the terms by which it is framed tend to be contested. The starting point is often the idea of social justice which, with regard to social policy (and SE rights), is commonly approached in terms of the fair and equitable distribution of income and basic goods across a society.[104] The impact of SE rights litigation, which is sometimes also termed its social outcome,[105] is, thus, generally assessed by the efficiency and fairness with which a particular basic good, such as health care, education, housing etc., is (re-)distributed by means of this type of intervention. While efficiency and fairness are diffuse and highly sector-specific criteria, the overwhelming focus in the SE rights literature has been on the effect on poverty and 'the poor', as defined either by income (more narrowly) or capabilities (more broadly).[106] This corresponds to a general shift in development discourse away from state-centric macroeconomic growth and towards individual and collective well-being. It, accordingly, identifies 'the poor' as the main constituency of development and refocusses development policy on poverty-reduction through pro-poor growth and good governance. The rights-based approach is the main implementation format for the latter agenda, with strategic domestic (SE) rights litigation being essentially a sub-category thereof. Most impact studies have, thus, a pro-poor focus and ultimately seek to assess the effectiveness of litigation strategies as instruments of poverty-reduction.[107]

Arguments on either side of the debate have, therefore, largely hinged on how and when impact is measured. A further caveat is that litigation has occurred—and, thus, been studied—in a highly disparate fashion across different (social) policy fields, with public health being by far the most observed staging ground for the 'rights (r)evolution'. While the most recent studies deliberately adopt a cross-sectoral optic,[108] the current impact debate is still strongly influenced by

[102] Classically in Galanter, 'Why the "Haves" Come out Ahead: Speculations on the Limits of Legal Change', 9 *Law and Society Review* (1974) 95.

[103] See, again, the range of studies in Gauri and Brinks (n. 7), Yamin and Gloppen (n. 7), and Haglund and Stryker (n. 7).

[104] See, in a UN context, DESA, Social Justice in an Open World: The Role of the United Nations, UN Doc. ST/ESA/305 (2006); see also Balakrishnan, Heintz, and Elson (n. 4).

[105] See Norheim and Gloppen, 'Litigating for Medicines: How Can We Assess Impact on Health Outcomes?', in Yamin and Gloppen (n. 7) 304 at 306.

[106] See Fukuda-Parr, Lawson-Remer, and Randolph (n. 6) 8 and Fukuda-Parr, Yamin, and Greenstein, 'The Power of Numbers: A Critical Review of MDG Targets for Human Development and Human Rights', 15 *Journal of Human Development and Capabilities* (2014) 105.

[107] Beitz, 'Protections Against Poverty in the Practice of Human Rights', in T. Pogge (ed.), *Freedom from Poverty as a Human Right Theory and Politics* (2010) 3.

[108] For example, Haglund and Stryker (n. 7).

the patterns observed in public health (litigation).[109] Yet, even with this narrower and more clearly defined focus it has been difficult to interpret the empirical evidence unequivocally, for not only is poverty, itself, a complex and highly contextual phenomenon, but (litigation) impact is also multi-faceted and time-dependent. Gloppen, for one, has suggested that impact studies should distinguish between what she terms material, symbolic, and political transformations;[110] the first are the tangible material benefits a judicial intervention generates, the second refer to changes in attitude and behaviour that result from such intervention, the third denotes shifts in the policy-making process. Each of these transformations has different time scales and the pro-poor impact of symbolic and political transformations, in particular, are often mid- or long term.

Brinks and Gauri have complemented this analytical scheme by distinguishing between individual and collective, and direct and indirect effects. They argue that a narrow focus on direct individual effects, that is, on individual litigants' success in securing a particular benefit, tends to distort litigation impact assessment as it often seems to simply confirm the distributionally negative outcome found in many of the earlier US public interest law studies.[111] These notoriously concluded that the 'haves' tended to disproportionally benefit from litigation compared to the 'have-nots'. Indeed, it is evident from many contemporary studies that better off middle-class litigants are able to appropriate a larger piece of the pie.[112] The reason is, of course, this group's better access to justice and its resulting capacity to twist the legal process to its advantage.

However, if aggregated, even individual direct effects may generate systemic ripples that produce indirect collective effects which may be less regressive—from a pro-poor perspective—than might be expected. Even more important than these ripples are, however, what Brinks and Gauri term direct collective effects, that is, class-action type litigation aimed to impact a whole category of stakeholders, such as carriers of particular diseases. Hence, in their five (middle-income) country study on litigation impact in public health and education, they find that direct collective litigation tends to produce disproportionately higher effects for 'the poor' as measured by their share of the overall population.[113] Indirect systemic effects may further compound this de facto pro-poor targeting by, for instance, producing policy change that 'positivizes' these litigation impacts.

[109] See, for instance, the prominence of public health-related case studies in all the larger collections on the theme, from Gargarella, Domingo, and Roux (2006), Gauri and Brinks (2008), and Langford (2008) to Yamin and Gloppen (2011) and Haglund and Stryker (2015); all in n. 7.

[110] See Gloppen (n. 86) 294.

[111] See Brinks and Gauri (n. 74) 380.

[112] For this 'middle class capture' thesis, see, again, Galanter (n. 102); and also Brinks and Gauri (n. 74) 387; Hoffmann and Bentes (n. 8) 142; as well as Ferraz, 'Harming the Poor through Social Rights Litigation: Lessons from Brazil', 89 *Texas Law Review* (2010) 1643, at 1667.

[113] See Brinks and Gauri (n. 74) 386.

They, thus, conclude that 'for all the seemingly commonsensical reasons to expect litigation to be an elite game, the evidence does not support a finding that only the better-off benefit'; indeed, they affirm, if somewhat cautiously, that there is 'strong evidence that human rights litigation on behalf of SE rights is not inherently anti-poor, and can actually address the needs of marginalized groups.'[114] Other studies have been much more cautious on whether the empirical evidence really tells a (litigation) success story. In a comparative health rights litigation analysis focussed not specifically on pro-poor impact but on the broader (social justice) criteria of efficiency and fairness,[115] Ole Frithjof Norheim and Siri Gloppen conclude that 'most, but not all, of the cases were classified as low priority, providing "marginal" health benefits for severe conditions at a very high cost for the health system.'[116] Octavio Ferraz, in turn, in a study based on survey data of health-rights litigation in Brazil, comes out even more strongly against the judicialization of social policy, arguing that when 'courts succumb to the pressure (or incentives) to "give teeth" to constitutional norms that recognize social rights, they end up transforming a collective and intractable issue of resource allocation among the numerous competing needs of the population into a bilateral dispute between single, needy individuals and a recalcitrant, stingy, and corrupt state.'[117] To him, the courts' (re-) distributional intervention not only reinforces the middle-class capture of public services but also, and perhaps even more problematically, diverts resources away from the systemic investments and reforms actually needed to make public services in low- and middle-income countries both efficient and equitable.[118]

What explains these starkly different interpretations of litigation impact is, of course, the complexity of the empirical scenario and the normative assumptions

[114] Ibid. 387.

[115] Which, in turn, are disaggregated to the terms by which a particular health care intervention on a particular health condition is prioritized; these are (a) the severity of the condition, (b) the effectiveness of the treatment, (c) its cost-effectiveness, and (d) the quality of evidence for all of these; the authors then use the common QALY (quality-adjusted life year) measure to classify priority-ranges for each of these items with a view to assessing the priority indicators selected health-rights cases produced; see Norheim and Gloppen (n. 105) 310.

[116] Ibid. 327.

[117] See Ferraz (n. 112) 1662; see also his contribution 'Brazil—Health Inequalities, Rights, and Courts: The Social Impact of the Judicialization of Health', in Yamin and Gloppen (n. 7) 76; and recently O. Ferraz, *Health as a Human Right: The Politics and Judicialisation of Health in Brazil* (2020).

[118] See also his further debate with the anthropologist João Biel, for instance in Ferraz, 'Where's the Evidence? Moving from Ideology to Data in Economic and Social Rights', *Open Democracy* (2015) https://www.opendemocracy.net/en/openglobalrights-openpage/wheres-evidence-moving-from-ideology-to-data-in-economic/ (last visited 18 April 2023); Ferraz, 'Inequality, Not Insufficiency: Making Social Rights Real in a World of Plenty', 12 *Equal Rights Review* (2014) 77; Ferraz, 'Letter to the Editor: Moving the Debate Forward in Right to Health Litigation', 18 *Health and Human Rights Journal* (2016) 265; and Biehl, 'Homo Economicus and Life Markets', 25 *Medical Anthropology Quarterly* (2011) 278; Biel, 'Judicialisation of the Right to Health in Brazil', 373 *The Lancet* (2009) 2182; Biehl and Petryna, 'Peopling Global Health', 23 *Saúde e Sociedade* (2014) 376; Biehl et al., 'Between the Court and the Clinic: Lawsuits for Medicines and the Right to Health in Brazil', 14 *Health and Human Rights* (2012) 17; Biehl, Socal, and Amon, 'Letter to the Editor Response: On the Heterogeneity and Politics of the Judicialization of Health in Brazil', 18 *Health and Human Rights Journal* (2016) 269.

used to convert it into evidence. For, as Alicia Yamin has argued on the basis of James March and Herbert Simon's organizational theory approach, in highly complex scenarios such as SE rights litigation which is made up of a large array of categories that act on different levels and over time, the constitution of a discrete body of evidence is almost always subject to 'uncertainty absorption'. The latter occurs at the moment of evidence selection when the facts that will count as evidence are chosen, and at the moment of evidence communication, when 'inferences are drawn from the body of evidence, and the inferences instead of the evidence itself are then communicated.'[119] Not only is the complexity of the empirical scenario thereby reduced, and, as some would have it, distorted,[120] but both moments involve normative assumptions (about the facts) that are often not transparent. Hence, most scholars who have found a positive, or at least not necessarily negative, correlation between SE rights litigation and pro-poor social transformation start from the normative premise that law in general, and rights-based judicialization, in particular, is or at least can be harnessed to be, a strategic instrument for social transformation (if only the evidence is understood 'rightly').[121] Evidence to the contrary is, in turn, often underwritten by an a priori scepticism about the power of law, and rights, in particular, to remedy structural social wrongs, such as extreme inequality, which are taken to involve a much broader political struggle.[122] Either camp interprets the evidence, hence, from an advocacy perspective, with one side endorsing progressive legalism and the other some variant of radical politics.

Yet another approach has sought to put the evidence for litigation impact into a wider (functional) perspective. Adherents of this view have argued that SE rights litigation cannot be assessed in isolation from the wider socio-political climate at any given moment. LaDawn Haglund and Robin Stryker have, for instance, argued that 'litigation conducted as part of a broad and sustained political advocacy campaign that includes institutionalized politics involving elites as well as noninstitutionalized political pressures from below will lead to greater rights-based social transformation than will litigation alone or litigation combined only with non-institutionalized pressures from below.'[123] Alicia Yamin, in turn, has stressed that litigation should be seen as a vehicle for public dialogue through

[119] See Yamin, 'Power, Suffering, and Courts: Reflections on Promoting Health Rights through Judicialization', in Yamin and Gloppen (n. 7) 333, at 363.

[120] See Rosga and Satterthwaite, 'Measuring Human Rights: UN Indicators in Critical Perspective', in Davis et al. (n. 53) 297; see also the remainder of the indicator-critical contributions in that collection.

[121] To this effect Brinks and Gauri (n. 74) 387.

[122] Most forcefully Ferraz (n. 117) 1667; as well as Mchangama, 'Legalizing economic and social rights won't help the poor', *Open Democracy* (2014) https://www.opendemocracy.net/en/openglobalrights-openpage/legalizing-economic-and-social-rights-wont-help-poor-0/ (last visited 18 April 2023); and Mchangama, 'Against a Human Rights-Based Approach to Social Justice', in D. Lettinga and L. van Troost, *Can Human Rights Bring Social Justice?* (2015) 53; more ambivalent, Norheim and Gloppen (n. 105) 328; cautiously optimistic, Yamin (n. 119).

[123] Haglund and Stryker, 'Conclusion: Emerging Possibilities for Social Transformation', in Haglund and Stryker (n. 7) 331.

which the justifiability of the conduct of public authorities in particular policy fields can be thematized.[124] Here, litigation is part of a wider turn to (bottom-up) social accountability as a component of system functionality.[125]

For even if it is difficult to interpret the evidence, there is no doubt that litigation does take place and that it does have an impact. Stakeholders on the ground are increasingly adopting a rights optic to analyse local-level situations and articulate the resulting demands in terms of rights claims; and this interaction between activists and local constituencies has in some instances crystalized into *both* sustained political pressure *and* into systematic legal mobilization 'from below'. Within this wider picture, courts enforcing (SE) rights claims can be seen to fulfil at least the following functions: firstly, they enforce 'bottom-up' accountability demands on system performance vis-à-vis public authorities; secondly, they, thereby, transmit information on system performance back to system regulators and, thus, help fill the informational gaps left by regular (top-down) accountability mechanisms; thirdly, they act as inclusion instruments by which stakeholders factually excluded from system benefits can, individually or collectively, enforce their inclusion; fourthly, they 'irritate' system governance by inserting their own logic of formal or material justice and thereby make systems (more) self-reflective of their performance; as such, and fifthly, they can, in fact, generate indirect collective effects which act on the policymaking process and may end up altering the system itself; sixthly, they also intermediate between public and private providers of basic services and can help mainstream minimum standards into mixed policy fields.

Thus, on the whole, rights-based legal intervention may be indispensable for remedying what economists have now recognized as the inevitable incidence of market failures, not least in the realm of basic services provision, and they may represent the only available path to challenge political stalemate and entrenched systemic dysfunctionalities. From this perspective, whether the final outcome is progressive, from a social justice or pro-poor perspective, or regressive will always be difficult to ascertain, as complex governance systems are highly dynamic and unpredictable. This feature renders a clear-cut determination of the efficacy and the legitimacy of judicial intervention difficult. The aggregate of successful individual actions in, say, public health, is clearly empowering for the litigants while it may represent an inefficient allocation of resources in relation to legitimate systemic priorities. It may, in other words, let some people queue-jump, though by doing so, it may also expose faulty planning or embezzlement of resources. It may indicate a major deficit in system performance—for otherwise people would not

[124] Yamin (n. 119) 366.

[125] Young and Liebenberg, 'Adjudicating Social and Economic Rights: Can Democratic Experimentalism Hel?', in Alviar García, Klare, and Williams (n. 81) 237; and Gloppen, 'Public Interest Litigation, Social Rights and Social Policy', in Dani and de Haan (n. 7) 343.

go to the considerable trouble of suing public authorities—but it may equally exaggerate the importance of 'rich people's concerns.'

It is also true that political systems may and do sometimes react badly to judicial interventionism, generating a backlash that seeks to fundamentally curtail the courts' capacity to meddle in policymaking.[126] But historical experience shows that even this is part of an ongoing and invariably dynamic story in which a backlash can end up producing further and wider, and sometimes even revolutionary change. And while a straightforward belief in the progressive effects of legal intervention is both naïve and dangerously dismissive of the centrality of politics, that politics is itself, in late-modernity, a complex field no longer confined to the traditional channels of political struggle. With the institutions of representative democracy now often deadlocked and incapable of dealing with global challenges, and with conceptions of radical democracy mostly not having yet transcended their existence as paper tigers, rights-based litigation has been one, among several, tangible means of political action, albeit a non-linear and ultimately unpredictable one.[127]

B. The International Frontier: Social Rights Accountability for Development and Against Austerity

Turning to the international frontier of SE rights and beyond the advances in monitoring and measuring discussed in Section 2, two further themes have marked the discussion around SE rights, one now reasonably established, the other still new and experimental. The former refers to the entanglement of (SE) rights with development, the latter to their recent use to frame the adverse consequences of economic austerity policies following the world financial crisis of 2008. As to 'rights in development', this concerns, of course, the emergence of the rights-based approach to development (RBD) which, over the past two decades or so, has become the dominant paradigm in development discourse and in overseas development assistance (ODA) programming, in particular. It is not exclusively about SE rights, but as development discourse itself has shifted from a focus on macroeconomic stability to one on individual well-being (a.k.a. social policy), SE rights play a leading role in RBD.

[126] Hoffmann and Bentes (n. 8) 145.

[127] See Hoffmann, 'Shooting in the Dark: Reflections Towards a Pragmatic Theory of Human Rights (Activism)', 41 *Texas International Law Journal* (2006) 403; and Hoffmann, 'International Legalism and International Politics', in A. Orford and F. Hoffmann, *Oxford Handbook of the Theory of International Law* (2016) 954; for another interesting take on why judicial intervention can be seen as legitimate, see Çalı, Koch, and Bruch, 'The Social Legitimacy of Human Rights Courts: A Grounded Interpretivist Theory of the Elite Accounts of the Legitimacy of the European Court of Human Rights', 35 *Human Rights Quarterly* (2013) 955.

This conjuncture of (SE) rights and development was by no means self-evident, as for a long time the two discourses were not seen as particularly related to one another. Indeed, they were deemed to be 'temperamentally' incompatible, with rights characterized by state-centrism, an inherently adversarial counterposing of the involved actors and a concomitant focus on violations, an orientation towards the judiciary, and an absolutist claim to trump any other concerns; in development, by contrast, states are seen, in principle, as partners, not adversaries and, in any case, are only one among several relevant stakeholders in the development process, remedies tend to come in the form of negotiated policies based on compromises, and aid is framed as a conditional grant rather than as an unconditional entitlement.[128]

The two discourses only came together after the Cold War and as a result of the tectonic shifts in the global political economy that created the conditions for the general 'rise of rights' that was alluded to above. An important precursor and conceptual companion of RBD has, however, been the idea of a 'right to development' that was initially conceived by the Senegalese jurist Keba M'baye in 1972 and first articulated in the African Charter for Human and Peoples Rights in 1981. It was brought to international prominence through the UN General Assembly's Declaration on the Right to Development of 1986,[129] and was subsequently reaffirmed in a wide range of (non-binding) instruments such as the Vienna Declaration and Program of Action (1993), the Millennium Declaration (2000), and the Durban Declaration and Program of Action (2002).[130] At the time of its inception it was closely associated with the Non-Aligned Movement (NAM) and the New International Economic Order (NIEO) programme and its objective to reframe, from a global Southern perspective, the terms on which the world economy and ODA were discussed. Within this context, the idea of a right, held by developing states, to fair and equitable development and implying, in particular, a binding commitment to international solidarity and self-determination, was a logical corollary.[131]

[128] See Vandenhole and Gready, 'Failures and Successes of Human Rights-Based Approaches to Development: Towards a Change Perspective', 32 *Nordic Journal of Human Rights* (2014) 291; and Nelson and Dorsey, 'At the Nexus of Human Rights and Development: New Methods and Strategies of Global NGOs', 31 *World Development* (2003) 2013; see also Marks, 'The Human Rights Framework for Development: Seven Approaches', in B. Mushumi, A. Negi, and A. Sengupta (eds), *Reflections on the Right to Development* (2005) 23.

[129] GA Res. 41/128, 4 December 1986.

[130] See Vienna Declaration and Program of Action, adopted by the World Conference on Human Rights in Vienna on 25 June 1993, http://www.ohchr.org/EN/ProfessionalInterest/Pages/Vienna.aspx (last visited 18 April 2023); Millennium Declaration, GA Res. 55/L.2, 18 September 2000; Durban Declaration and Plan of Action, adopted at the World Conference Against Racism, Racial Discrimination, Xenophobia and Related Violence (2002), www.un.org/en/durbanreview2009/ddpa.shtml (last visited 18 April 2023).

[131] See generally Eslava and Pahuja, 'The State and International Law: A Reading from the Global South', *Humanity: An International Journal of Human Rights, Humanitarianism, and Development* (2019) https://muse.jhu.edu/article/745684 (last visited 18 April 2023).

In fact, the language of human rights had already featured prominently in the UN theatre of the earlier decolonization struggle, where it had been employed by decolonization militants to stake an international claim both to self-determination as an entitlement and to the equality of colonial peoples. Indeed, as later revisionist historians would be adamant in pointing out, the language of human rights was then more directly linked to the interest of pre-state collectivities and post-colonial states in independence and (collective) non-discrimination than to entitlements by individuals against them.[132] As such, the right to development emerged at once as part of the trajectory of human rights within the UN and as a discourse outside of it, being, as it was, a right deemed to be held by states vis-à-vis the international community and used as a counterhegemonic bargaining chip by global Southern states. Its main aim was, thus, to reinforce the argument, put forward by the dependency theory of development prevalent in the 1960s and 1970s, that the world economy was historically unequal and, therefore, fundamentally unjust.[133] It, thus, helped anchor the language of (in)justice into development discourse and reframed development in terms of international rights and obligations, with the corollary of a common (international) responsibility for the provision of ODA.

With this pre-history, RBD emerged in the 1990s as a result of the confluence of several interrelated paradigm shifts. Firstly, human rights began to occupy a central position in the liberal triumphalist vision of a unipolar world,[134] and the previous 'rights divide' also began to be closed, with SE rights gradually gaining operational parity with their CP counterparts. Secondly, the latter process was partly brought about by a shift in development discourse towards 'human development' focussed on individual wellbeing. Rights, and SE rights, in particular, were seen as natural benchmarks for this wellbeing, an interpretation partly inspired by Amartya Sen's capabilities approach to development.[135] Based on social choice theory, the latter seeks to fuse the economic and political aspects of development by individualizing human welfare as the set of capabilities for 'achieving the kind of lives [people] have reason to value.'[136] It shifts the focus of development towards individuals, not

[132] See S. Moyn, The Last Utopia (2010) at 84; in a similar vein, see S. L. Hoffmann (ed.), *Human Rights in the Twentieth Century* (2011).

[133] See, for instance, OHCHR, Realizing the Right to Development—Essays in Commemoration of 25 Years of the United Nations Declaration on the Right to Development, HR/PUB/12/4 (2013); and Rajagopal, 'Right to Development and Global Governance: Old and New Challenges Twenty-Five Years On', 23 *Human Rights Quarterly* (2013) 893; see also S. Pahuja, *Decolonising International Law: Development, Economic Growth and the Politics of Universality* (2011) at 95.

[134] See, classically, F. Fukuyama, *The End of History and the Last Man* (1992) and S. Marks, 'The End of History—Reflections on Some International Legal Theses', 8 *European Journal of International Law* (1997) 449–477.

[135] A. Sen, *Development as Freedom* (1999); and A. Sen, 'Human Rights and Capabilities', 6 *Journal of Social Development* (2005) 151–166; see also M. Kaltenborn, *Social Rights and International Development: Global Legal Standards for the Post-2015 Development Agenda* (2015); and Pahuja (n. 133) 172.

[136] Sen (1999) (n. 135) 291.

states, and it makes these individuals' rights fulfilment a core indicator thereof.[137] This new perspective clearly informed UNDP's first Human Development Report of 1990, which used the fulfilment of human rights directly as a benchmark for development progress and set the scene for a rights-based redescription of development.[138] Thirdly, in a parallel process underwritten by the re-discovery, on the part of neoclassical economics, of the importance of institutions (and law) for development,[139] the multilateral finance institutions and other ODA donors began promoting the 'good governance' agenda with its focus on, amongst others, the rule of law and human rights.[140] While critics have argued that 'good governance' was always instrumentally related to (neo-)liberal public sector reform and the emergence of a legally disciplined 'regulatory developmental state',[141] it did co-react with the emergent 'human development' paradigm to catalyse RBD.[142] Fourthly and lastly, the constitutionalization wave of the 1990s, discussed above, further reinforced the re-focussing of rights as both justiciable claims and as performance benchmarks for domestic and international public policy.[143]

With the scene thus set, the formal inauguration of RBD came in 1997, when then UN Secretary-General, Kofi Annan's 1997 report, Renewing the United Nations: A Programme for Reform, established the official human rights mainstreaming agenda which mandated that human rights had to be part of 'everything the UN does'.[144] This represented nothing short of a re-branding of the UN

[137] Fukuda-Parr, 'The Human Development Paradigm: Operationalizing Sen's Ideas on Capabilities', 9 *Feminist Economics* (2003) 301.

[138] See UNDP, Human Development Report 1990 (1990) http://hdr.undp.org/sites/default/files/reports/219/hdr_1990_en_complete_nostats.pdf (last visited 18 April 2023); see also Alston and Robinson, 'The Challenges of Ensuring the Mutuality of Human Rights and Development Endeavours', in P. Alston and M. Robinson, *Human Rights and Development: Towards Mutual Reinforcement* (2005) 2; and Alston, 'Ships Passing in the Night: The Current State of the Human Rights and Development Debate Seen through the Lens of the Millennium Development Goals', 27 *Human Rights Quarterly* (2005) 755; as well as Gauri and Gloppen, 'Human Rights-Based Approaches to Development: Concepts, Evidence, and Policy', 44 *Polity* (2012) 485–503.

[139] Kennedy (n. 82) 43.

[140] The World Bank is often credited with inaugurating the 'good governance' terminology, see World Bank, *From crisis to sustainable growth - sub Saharan Africa: a long-term perspective study* (1989), http://documents.worldbank.org/curated/en/498241468742846138/From-crisis-to-sustainable-growth-sub-Saharan-Africa-a-long-term-perspective-study (last visited 18 April 2023); see also Thomas, 'Re-Reading Weber in Law and Development: A Critical Intellectual History of "Good Governance" Reform', 118 *Cornell Law Faculty Publications—Paper* (2008); and Gathii, 'Good Governance as a Counter Insurgency Agenda to Oppositional and Transformative Social Projects in International Law', 5 *Buffalo Human Rights Law Review* (1999) 107; and Krever, 'The Legal Turn in Late Development Theory: The Rule of Law and the World Bank's Development Model', 52 *Harvard International Law Journal* (2011) 287.

[141] See Dubash and Morgan, 'Understanding the Rise of the Regulatory State of the South', 6 *Regulation and Governance* (2012) 261.

[142] Uvin, 'On High Moral Ground: The Incorporation of Human Rights by the Development Enterprise', 17 *Praxis: The Fletcher Journal of Development Studies* (2002) 1; and Fukuda-Parr (n. 137); and Uvin, 'Final Synthesis and Questions' in P. Uvin, *Human Rights and Development* (2013), 167.

[143] See Wiener et al., 'Global Constitutionalism: Human Rights, Democracy and the Rule of Law', 1 *Global Constitutionalism* (2012) 1.

[144] Renewing the United Nations: A Programme for Reform, Report of the Secretary-General, UN Doc. A/52/L.72/Rev.1, 19 December 1997; see also Hoffmann (n. 15); and Gauri and Gloppen (n. 138).

at a moment when, just like in the aftermath of the Second World War, the world was mesmerized by recent conflict and humanitarian calamity, in this case the dual fallout over Rwanda and Bosnia, which provided an underlying impetus for an operational turn to human rights. It was to play out primarily in two of the UN's mandates, namely development and peace and security, with OHCHR and its activist (then) High Commissioner Mary Robinson, as well as some of the specialized agencies, most notably UNICEF, taking a lead role in concretizing RBD. Since then, it has become one of, if not the, dominant paradigm in contemporary development, as is evidenced by numerous programmatic statements and operational guidelines both in international and domestic ODA programming.[145] It remains, however, somewhat hazy and its ubiquity seems inversely related to any agreement on its precise legal force and content.[146]

In a welcome attempt to systematize its various meanings in different contexts, Gauri and Gloppen distinguish four 'analytic components' of RBD, notably what they term 'international legal precepts', 'donor-regulations and conditionalities', 'normative beliefs', and 'constitutional rights'.[147] The first of these is consonant with the 'deep monitoring' paradigm adopted, inter alia, in the CESCR's IBSA procedure discussed above. It (re)frames development as the process by which compliance with positivized international legal (human rights) norms is achieved, with these norms meant to fulfil a triple role as interpretation manuals for development goals, as regulatory frameworks for development processes, and as benchmarks for development outcomes.[148] Yet, even though international human rights standards occupy a nominally prominent place in RBD, international (legal) institutions have not played a significant role in it. Their continuing lack of institutional capacity and enforcement authority means that they only play a small role in the day-to-day running of RBD programmes, even though the greater visibility of the

[145] For a seminal analysis, see P. Dann, *The Law of Development Cooperation: a comparative analysis of the World Bank, the EU, and Germany* (2013); as well as Sano, 'Development and Human Rights: The Necessary, but Partial Integration of Human Rights and Development', 22 *Human Rights Quarterly* (2000) 734; and also, again, Uvin (n. 142).

[146] See, for instance, Tsikata, 'The Rights-based Approach to Development: Potential for Change or More of the Same?', 35 *IDS Bulletin* (2004) 130; Nyamu-Musembi and Cornwall, 'What Is the "Rights-Based Approach" All About? Perspectives from International Development Agencies', *IDS Working Paper* (2004) https://www.ids.ac.uk/files/dmfile/Wp234.pdf (last visited 18 April 2023); Abramovich, 'The Rights-Based Approach in Development Policies and Strategies', *CEPAL Review* (2006); and Hoffmann, 'Twin Siblings: fresh perspectives on law in development (and vice versa)' (2017) 30 *Leiden Journal of International Law* 267; as well as Hoffmann and Rached, 'Human Rights and Development' in R. Buchanan, L. Eslava, and S. Pahuja (eds), *The Oxford Handbook of International Law and Development* (2023).

[147] Gauri and Gloppen (n. 138) 4.

[148] Examples include, again, UNDP's Human Development Index and the series of Guiding Principles, see n. 64, such as the *Guiding Principles on Extreme Poverty and Human Rights*, A/HRC/21/39, 27 September 2012; or the *Guiding Principles on Business and Human Rights*, A/HRC/RES/17/4, 6 July 2011; see also Chapman, 'Rights-Based Development: The Challenge of Change and Power', 27 *Global Poverty Research Group Working Paper Series* (2005); Kindornay, Ron, and Carpenter, 'Rights-Based Approaches to Development: Implications for Human Rights', 34 *Human Rights Quarterly* 34 (2012) 472.

international SE regime has given development actors advocacy tools to politically mobilize for greater international responsibility and for domestic policy change.[149]

It is rather as 'donor regulations and conditionalities' that RBD has been most prevalent. Here rights provide substance to abstract 'good governance' principles in the context of programme design, implementation, and assessment, and are, thus, effectively converted into soft administrative guidelines for what amounts to rights-based development governance.[150] Such a procedural interpretation of 'rights in development' is primarily geared to enhancing the agency of the recipients of ODA, most notably the 'poor', and it performs a subtle semantic shift in development discourse, away from objective need and towards subjective want—often expressed as an increase in choice—the fulfilment of which is then understood as 'empowerment'. It is about increasing the control of specific constituencies over their own circumstances, and it combines greater and more equitable access to socio-economic resources such as income, education, or health, with a subjective capacity to exercise choice over their specific allocation.[151] Importantly, such rights-based empowerment also implies the ability both to enforce accountability claims vis-à-vis all development stakeholders, and particularly donor agencies and recipient governments, and to participate in development planning, a notion nominally—though not always factually—fulfilled in the shift to recipient-oriented planning procedures such as the World Bank's and the International Monetary Fund's Poverty Reduction Strategy Papers (PRSPs).[152]

To its proponents, the reconstruction of good governance principles through rights language in RBD seems, therefore, to provide an at once coherent and compelling narrative which appears to be compatible with contemporary development practice while containing the spark for a potentially revolutionary transformation of development agency.[153] Yet, this optimistic reading of RBD has not gone uncontested. The two most direct critiques have concerned its claim to have refocused development onto 'the poor' and to provide the primary toolkit for their empowerment. Here the critics have argued that RBD has merely grafted itself onto an existing pro-poor agenda developed previously by dedicated agencies such as UNDP

[149] Gauri and Gloppen (n. 138) 5.

[150] See, for instance, UNDP, *Indicators for Human Rights Based Approaches to Development in UNDP Programming: A Users' Guide* (2006) http://www.undp-aciac.org/publications/other/undp/hr/humanrights-indicators-06e.pdf (last visited 18 April 2023); or UNDP, *Lessons Learned From Rights-Based Approaches in the Asia-Pacific Region* (2005) https://www.undp.org/sites/g/files/zskgke326/files/migration/asia_pacific_rbap/RBAP-DG-2008-Undertaking-HumanRights-Based-Approach.pdf (last visited 18 April 2023); and, again, the analysis in Dann (n. 145).

[151] Pradhan, 'Measuring Empowerment: A Methodological Approach', 46 *Development* (2003) 51, at 52.

[152] See Gottschalk, 'The Effectiveness of IMF/World Bank-Funded Poverty Reduction Strategy Papers', in Y. Bangura (ed.), *Developmental Pathways to Poverty Reduction* (2015); and Weber, 'Reconstituting the "Third World"? Poverty Reduction and Territoriality in the Global Politics of Development', 25 *Third World Quarterly* (2004) 187, at 197; see also Bangura, 'Developmental Pathways to Poverty Reduction', in Y. Bangura (ed.), *Developmental Pathways to Poverty Reduction* (2015) 3.

[153] Hoffmann (n. 15).

and that it has not really added more than embellishment value to the policies and mechanisms created by the latter.[154] More cautiously, Peter Uvin, for one, has argued that 'working out the relationship between development and human rights requires more than simply stating that one automatically implies, equals, or subsumes the other'.[155]

Indeed, if that automatic subsumption was not considered to hold, then the question would arise what human rights could actually add to development beyond the existing (non-RBD) frameworks? RBD's real innovation lies, arguably, in its aspiration to radically democratize all aspects of development programming, though this is an implication hardly any of its official proponents have been prepared to advocate, not least as it would run counter to all traditional notions of needs-based planning which still prevail in development practice, the nominal turn to RBD notwithstanding.[156]

The second persistent critique has been that RBD is essentially a new type of aid conditionality which places developing states under the permanent surveillance of the various human rights monitoring mechanisms and reduces them to duty-bearers vis-à-vis individual rights claimants.[157] This argument flows, of course, from the wider contention, alluded to above, that RBD is just the latest step in the neoliberal re-framing of the state. Within this reading, the state remains fully (legally) responsible for compliance with international human rights norms, with the current interpretation of its obligations implying that virtually all acts committed by non-state actors—such as transnational corporations (TNCs)—remain, ultimately, attributable to it.[158] The ongoing transformation of the state from direct provider to regulator of public service provision within the paradigm of post-welfarist regulatory statehood changes only the nature but not the scope of this responsibility.[159] Hence, market failures, through the human rights consequences they generate, are still essentially deemed to be attributable to the state.

This continuing state-centrism on the demand side is, however, increasingly unmatchable by the state's capacity to supply public service levels in accordance with international minimum standards either through its direct financial intervention or through its (market) regulatory authority. Indeed, the current phase of global finance capitalism has significantly reduced the fiscal and, therefore, the policy space in both developed and developing states, generating a mismatch between the demand for responsibility placed on the state by the logic of sovereignty and

154 See, for instance, Tsikata (n. 146).

155 See Uvin (n. 142) 3.

156 Ibid. 7.

157 Manzo, 'Africa in the Rise of Rights-Based Development', 34 *Geoforum* (2003) 437, at 438; see also Gathii (n. 140) 158; and Pahuja (n. 133).

158 See, generally, A. Clapham, *Human Rights Obligations of Non-State Actors* (2006); and Rittich, 'The Future of Law and Development: Second Generation Reforms and the Incorporation of the Social', 26 *Michigan Journal of International Law* (2004) 199, at 217.

159 Scott (n. 14).

articulated through international (human rights) law, and its factual capacity to supply this normative demand with material substance.[160]

Yet, while the empirical state is, thus, both overburdened and overdetermined, it is, at the same time, inherently constrained by the precepts of good governance through rights. To this line of critique, then, these constraints are, in essence, devices to discipline the state and its formal institutions in relation to individuals, groups, and civil society, with empowerment and its derivatives, notably accountability, participation and (formal) equality, ultimately aiming to make 'the people' at least partially autonomous from state institutions; indeed, the increasing privileging, by donors, of (sometimes donor-organized) CSOs as primary partners in ODA projects is evidence of this. By bestowing on development the authority of a global normative framework, RBD can, thus, be seen to legitimate the bypassing of formal state institutions and, thus, to erode the very sovereignty on which international (human rights) obligations are based in the first place. The point is, thus, not that RBD fundamentally challenges the state, but, on the contrary, that it treats the state as the origin of the problem at hand, and, at the same time, relies on it as the only viable framework for a solution.

Ultimately, these critiques, as well their potential rebuttals, will have to be exposed to the light of the empirical realities RBD will have created 'on the ground'. The use of the future tense here implies that, despite the ubiquity of RBD language in development discourse, there is not yet much data to assess its impact and efficacy.[161] Partly this is because it is still relatively new and projects are only slowly beginning to reach the stage at which they, or their legacies, can be fairly assessed. Yet partly it is also because there remains considerable conceptual vagueness about whether RBD is essentially just an instrument of pro-poor development—in which case it could simply be assessed by its effectiveness in reducing poverty as compared to alternative frameworks—or whether it really aspires to representing an entirely different idea of development, one in which donors prospectively surrender control over both the objectives and the implementation of development to its stakeholders, who, in turn, are willing and able to use rights to articulate their own developmental pathways. Assessing whether stakeholders have even made tentative steps into that direction implies a very different set of criteria than the mere measurement of their socio-economic status. This uncertainty about the nature of RBD and its concomitant objectives renders it at once highly resilient to conceptual challenges and yet persistently ephemeral.

160 Hoffmann (n. 15) 60.

161 Among the few studies, see, for instance, UK Interagency Group on Human Rights Based Approaches, *The Impact of Rights-based Approaches to Development—Evaluation, Learning Process—Bangladesh, Malawi, and Peru* (2007 https://archive.crin.org/en/docs/Inter_Agency_rba.pdf (last visited 18 April 2023); and Schmitz, 'A Human Rights-Based Approach (HRBA) in Practice: Evaluating NGO Development Efforts', 44 *Polity* (2012) 523; and Kindornay, Ron, and Carpenter (n. 148).

The second topographical feature on the international frontier of SE rights is the as yet incipient application of international human rights standards, and specifically SE rights, to both the global economy, in general, and the causes and effects of economic and financial crises, in particular. As an approach it brings together several older *topoi* in international human rights research and advocacy, notably the extraterritorial application of human rights standards,[162] the human rights responsibility of both multilateral finance institutions and of multinational corporations,[163] the human rights implications of global or regional trade agreements,[164] the international labour regime,[165] and the human rights impact assessment of budgets and other macroeconomic measures.[166]

While human rights advocacy organizations have had the adverse impact of economic downturns and of the measures to counter them broadly on their radar since at least the crises in the Czech Republic, Hungary, Mexico, Thailand, Indonesia, South Korea, Argentina, and Russia in the 1990s, there has been little repercussion in the CESCR or the other treaty bodies, or, indeed, any other human rights monitoring institution.[167] It was really the burst of the housing bubble in the US in 2007/08 and the ensuing decade-long series of financial, currency, and sovereign debt crises and the consequent economic downturn in many countries in both the global North and South that has catalysed these efforts into a concerted movement.

One of its principal articulators is the Extraterritorial Obligations Consortium (ETO), a group of advocacy organizations and human rights experts that was set up in 2007 and that, in 2011, adopted the 'Maastricht Principles on the Extraterritorial Obligations of States in the Area of Economic, Social and Cultural Rights', a systematic restatement of existing international legal obligations pertaining to this

162 See, inter alia, Bhuta, 'The Frontiers of Extraterritoriality: Human Rights Law as Global Law', in N. Bhuta (ed.), *The Frontiers of Human Rights: Extraterritoriality and its Challenges* (2016), at 1; see also Balakrishnan and Heintz, 'Extraterritorial Obligations, Financial Globalisation and Macroeconomic Governance', in Nolan (n. 1) 146; as well as Wilde, 'The Extraterritorial Application of International Human Rights Law on Civil and Political Rights', in N. Rodley and S. Sheeran (eds), *Routledge Handbook on Human Rights* (2013); and, generally, M. Milanovic, *The Extraterritorial Application of Human Rights Treaties* (2011).

163 See, for instance, M. Darrow, *Between Light and Shadow. The World Bank, the International Monetary Fund and International Human Rights Law* (2003); and Bradlow, 'The World Bank, the IMF, and Human Rights', 6 *Journal of Transnational Law and Contemporary Problems* (1996) 47; and Ratner, 'Corporations and Human Rights: A Theory of Legal Responsibility', 111 *Yale Law Journal* (2001) 443; as well as from the former UN Special Rapporteur on Human Rights and Business, J. Ruggie, *Just Business: Multinational Corporations and Human Rights* (2013).

164 See T. Cottier, J. Pauwelyn, and E. Brügi (eds), *Human Rights and International Trade* (2006); and Alston, 'Resisting the Merger and Acquisition of Human Rights by Trade Law: A Reply to Petersmann', 13 *European Journal of International Law* (2002) 815.

165 Alston (n. 24).

166 A. Nolan, R. O'Connell, and C. Harvey (eds), *Human Rights and Public Finance: Budgets and the Promotion of Economic and Social Rights* (2013).

167 Nolan, Lusiani, and Courtis, 'Two Steps Forward, No Steps Back? Evolving Criteria on the Prohibition of Retrogression in Economic and Social Rights', in Nolan (n. 1) 121, at 126.

concern.[168] In 2012, members of ETO published an official Commentary of the Maastricht Principles,[169] and a continuous flow of literature has since emerged addressing the various issues that have arisen in the wake of the crisis in light of the Principles.[170] While ETO's focus has been on extraterritorial obligations as a means to promote global economic justice beyond the domestic/international dichotomy, several parallel efforts have sought to examine the human rights fallout from the crisis on the basis of existing frameworks such as the ICESCR and the CESCR.[171]

Common to these interventions is the dual aspiration to turn human rights—always understood in this context to particularly refer to SE rights—into the key markers for the human consequences of both economic crises and the policies adopted against them, as well as to turn international human rights law and its institutional infrastructure into key remedial instruments for these consequences. While previous efforts to promote these aspirations were somewhat hampered by the wide and diffuse nature of 'the globalized world economy' and the complex network of actors and, thus, lines of responsibility that characterize it, the post-2008 crises allowed for a much higher degree of focus, as many of its adverse effects on the enjoyment of human rights can be traced to specific acts or policies.

It was not, however, the root causes of these crises, such as (and primarily) market failure driven by reckless private-sector profiteering—but also by botched regulatory frameworks, negligent oversight, deceptive accounting or plain corruption on the part of governments and international organizations—that were, for the most part, singled out for human rights scrutiny. Instead, it was the reaction to these—in large measure self-inflicted—crises that were adopted by governments and international organizations, namely the notorious austerity policies, that have been at the centre of attention. The latter have mostly consisted of the notorious—and up to their revival—largely discarded-structural-adjustment programmes and their staple fare of a radical reduction of public sector spending and public service provision, deregulation, and privatization.

However, while the very significant negative impact of the compounded crises on human welfare—and, thus, on the enjoyment of SE rights—worldwide is undeniable,[172] it is less straightforward to precisely disaggregate the causality of the

[168] Maastricht Principles on Extraterritorial Obligations of States in the area of Economic, Social and Cultural Rights, adopted 28 September 2011 https://www.fidh.org/IMG/pdf/maastricht-eto-principles-uk_web.pdf (last accessed 18 April 2023).

[169] De Schutter et al., 'Commentary to the Maastricht Principles on Extraterritorial Obligations of States in the Area of Economic, Social and Cultural Rights', 34 *Human Rights Quarterly* (2012) 1084.

[170] These efforts have, in turn, been thoroughly compiled and reviewed in Wilde, 'Dilemmas in Promoting Global Economic Justice through Human Rights Law', in Bhuta (n. 162) 127.

[171] See, for instance, the evocative motto on the ETO website: 'Human rights have been locked up behind domestic bars to prevent their universal application to globalization and its much-needed regulation. Extraterritorial obligations (ETOs) unlock human rights', http://www.etoconsortium.org/ (last visited 18 April 2023); see otherwise the contributions in Nolan (n. 1).

[172] See, inter alia, CESR, *Human Rights and the Global Economic Crisis: Consequences, Causes, Responses* (2009) https://www.cesr.org/sites/default/files/CESR-Human_Rights_and_the_Global_Economic_Crisis.pdf (last visited 18 April 2023); and Sepúlveda Carmona, 'Alternatives to

retrogression in living-standards in terms of the direct effects of crisis—such as recession and the concomitant rise in unemployment—and the effects of austerity policies as reactions to these effects. Yet, even if austerity may not be the initial culprit for all of these effects, human rights advocates have argued that, contrary to the neo-classical economic rationale that underwrites these measures, they have at the very least aggravated and widened these negative consequences.

What makes austerity measures, however, really attractive as a target is, of course, the fact that they can be clearly attributed to states acting on their own or collectively through international organizations. Moreover, their direct human rights impact can be much better measured than the diffuse workings of the global economy. As a consequence, much of ETO and like efforts have concentrated on spelling out the terms of human rights accountability for austerity measures, with the focus having been on two fundamental normative challenges, namely the attributability of austerity-induced SE rights violations to state conduct under existing international human rights law, and the nature and scope of the non-retrogression obligation.

As to the former, the question arose most forcefully in the context of EU bailout measures for Member States affected by severe sovereign debt crises, such as, and most acutely, Greece. As is well-known, this bailout was organized by the European Commission (EC), the European Central Bank (ECB), and the International Monetary Fund (IMF), the so-called 'Troika,' on behalf of their respective constituencies, that is, EU Member States, (EU) member states of the Eurozone, and the member states of the IMF. This group, in turn, introduced different institutional frameworks to enable the transfer of financial assistance to Greece and other countries, most importantly the European Stability Mechanism (ESM), which was established in 2012 to act as the primary 'firewall' against financial crisis within the Eurozone.

Owing both to the political resistance of non-Eurozone EU Member States to assume financial commitments towards the common currency, and to legal restrictions imposed by the Treaty on the Functioning of the European Union (TFEU) which prohibits Member States from assuming the financial liabilities of other Member States,[173] the ESM was created not as an EU body but as a separate intergovernmental organization seated in Luxembourg. Most importantly, in this context, is the fact that by determination of the 'Troika', the ESM can only dispense funds conditionally, with the conditionalities essentially mandating the implementation of austerity policies. This is significant in two ways: it introduces

Austerity: A Human Rights Framework for Economic Recovery', in Nolan (n. 1) 23, at 23; and Salomon (n. 3).

[173] European Union, Consolidated version of the Treaty on the Functioning of the European Union, OJ 2008 C 115/01, 13 December 2007.

into the EU's political model the inherent asymmetry of donor-recipient relations framed by conditionalities as is typical in an ODA context, and these particular conditionalities can be shown to have a directly adverse effect on the enjoyment of SE rights.[174]

The question that arises in this scenario is, of course, who bears responsibility for any violations of SE rights and on what grounds. Prima facie, any breach of an international obligation is, of course, attributable to the state in whose jurisdiction it occurs, which would, in this case be the states implementing the austerity measures. This position was duly affirmed by the European Committee of Social Rights, a body under the Council of Europe, in a series of decisions against Greece in which it rejected the Greek government's defence that any potential violation of the European Social Charter—in this case of the right to social security—was exclusively due to the fulfilment of its international obligations vis-à-vis the ESM and the 'Troika'. Instead, it reaffirmed that it was the state party's responsibility to ensure that the implementation measures it adopted in fulfilment of its international obligations did not violate its obligations under the Social Charter. This position, besides leaving Greece between a rock and a hard place, also opened up the further question of whether its 'other international obligations', i.e. its ESM conditionalities, could ever be interpreted as causing a rights violation, and, thus, a breach of human rights obligations on the part of those who imposed it, or whether it was always merely the implementation by the conditionality-bound state that could do so.

This question is, arguably, at the core of ETO-type arguments, and Margot Salomon, for one, has forcefully answered it in the positive. Critically examining the European Court of Justice's (ECJ) decision in *Pringle v. Ireland* to hold the establishment of the ESM by EU Member States outside the EU's legal framework, including its Charter of Fundamental Rights, to be lawful,[175] she contends that while EU Member States may have exempted themselves from direct responsibility for Charter violations by EMS-imposed measures, their co-optation of EU institutions, notably the EC and the ECB, into the ESM effectively extends that responsibility to the latter.[176] She cites solid legal opinion that, unlike EU Member States, EU institutions are bound by the Charter even when they are not directly implementing EU law, as in the ESM's case.[177] In other words, fundamental rights obligations are inalienable by EU institutions, regardless of the particular legal framework of reference.

Salomon further complements the EU law argument with some straight ETO staple, namely the contention that all EU (and ESM) Member States are signatories

[174] Salomon (n. 3) 8.
[175] Case C-370/12, *Pringle v. Ireland* (EU:C:2012:756), Judgment (Full Court) of 27 November 2012.
[176] Ibid. 15.
[177] For instance, Salomon (n. 3) 115.

of the ICESCR and, thus, clearly bound by its obligations in whatever individual or collective context, including extraterritorially.[178] While the ETO initiative has, hence, audaciously sought to engage the neoliberal Goliath in rights-based guerrilla lawfare, Ralph Wilde, amongst others, has pointed to some of the inherent limitations of this approach. Drawing, broadly, on the analytical perspective of Third World Approaches to International Law (TWAIL), he argues that an unproblematized reliance on international human rights law 'as is' inadvertently incorporates many of the asymmetries, Eurocentrisms, and hegemonies inherent in the historical corpus of this law, besides potentially reinforcing, rather than transgressing, the very neoliberal logic ETO is staked against.[179] Wilde's argument echoes, if from a different angle, a set of contemporary 'left' critiques of human rights, in general, and SE rights, in particular, that date back to the 1990s and that, in turn, often build on the classical Marxian critique of rights as 'rights of inequality.'[180] It has been reiterated by Susan Marks where, reflecting on the London riots of 2012 and the 'right' critique of rights issued, amongst others, by then British prime minister David Cameron, she associates rights discourse with the mystification of (economic) power relations.[181] Drawing, inter alia, on Naomi Klein and Wendy Brown, Marks charges rights activism—and activists—with effectively depoliticizing the, to her, necessarily political engagement with the political economy of contemporary capitalism, which she sees as the root cause of the predicament that ETO activists then, misguidedly, try to address with 'more of the same'.[182] Samuel Moyn, the influential revisionist historian of (international) human rights, has subsequently picked up Marks' argument in order to simultaneously critique it for presuming too strong a causal relationship between the rise of international human rights and the rise of neoliberalism as of the 1970s—a claim he deems unhistorical—and endorse it for its scepticism of human rights as a tool against neoliberalism and its social consequences—which he shares. At this level of debate, the specific salience of SE rights-based anti-austerity lawfare and the role extraterritorial human rights obligations may play in it becomes, of course, a mere backdrop to a much wider inquiry about the relevance and, indeed, the future of human rights as such. It will, thus, be returned to in the concluding section.

As for the second challenge to the endeavour of 'righting' austerity, it consists of the somewhat hazy character of the non-retrogression obligation of Article 2(1)

[178] See ibid. 22.

[179] See Wilde (n. 170).

[180] For the latter, see Marx, 'Critique of the Gotha Programme' (1891) at K. Marx, *Kritik des Gothaer Programms* (2017); see also O'Byrne, 'Marxism and Human Rights: New Thoughts on an Old Debate', 23 *The International Journal of Human Rights* (2019) 638; for the 1990s critique, see, in particular, T. Evans (ed.), *Human Rights Fifty Years on* (1998).

[181] Marks, 'Four Human Rights Myths', in D. Kinley, W. Sadurski, and K. Walton (eds), *Human Rights: Old Problems, New Possibilities* (2013) 217.

[182] See also Marks, 'Human Rights and Root Causes', 74 *Modern Law Review* (2011) 57; as well as N. Klein, *The Shock Doctrine* (2007) and Brown, '"The Most We Can Hope For . . .": Human Rights and the Politics of Fatalism', 103 *South Atlantic Quarterly* (2004) 451.

of the ICESCR. This hinges on a core theme in SE rights talk at the moment, notably the empirical measurability of rights fulfilment as a basis for the attribution of legal responsibility. For while it is easy enough to identify certain normative measures, it continues to be difficult and controversial to correlate these to empirical socio-economic data in a solid enough way to ground a finding of breach of obligation. This is due both to a continuing lack of data, but also to the lack of consensus over economic models themselves.[183] As Aoife Nolan, Nicholas Lusiani, and Christian Courtis point out, a particular austerity measure, such as the curtailing of unemployment benefits, has a different connotation even in different versions of orthodox neo-classical thought, let alone in neo-Keynesian or other heterodox schools.[184] In any case, economic policy operates on an entirely different and much longer term time scale than the 'progressive fulfilment' obligation, resulting in an inherent disjuncture between what really amounts to two distinct epistemic horizons.

This naturally impacts on the ways in which responsibility can be attributed, as virtually all empirical socio-economic situations are multi-causal and require 'polycentric analysis' of both state and non-state actors.[185] Even if the 'respect' dimension of the current obligations doctrine is taken to nominally cover non-state actors, such as credit-rating institutes or hedge funds, insofar as these operate on the basis of complex transnational legal networks they partly escape national jurisdiction and, hence, responsibility. As a consequence, the CESCR and the wider ETO communities have focused on outlining negative criteria by which retrogressive measures can be linked to breaches of obligation, with the burden of proof resting on the state that undertakes such measures. In this vein, and on the basis of a thorough review of the normative material, Nolan, Lusiani, and Courtis have identified several partly overlapping 'derogation criteria' which must apply for a state to justify retrogressive (emergency) measures. These include an (a priori) time-limitation of the measures, their non-discriminatory character, the requirement of establishing an objective necessity for as well as the proportionality of the measures, their need to be manifestly reasonable, the required participatory character of their adoption, a special focus on disadvantaged and vulnerable groups, and the entrenchment of a (previously identified) minimum core content. In making this assessment, review bodies like the CESCR are then held to adopt a contextualist optic whereby such factors as the general level of development, the nature of the (economic) emergency, the existence of correlative international obligations, and the international assistance situation are considered.[186] Needless to

[183] See *Pensioners' Union of the Agricultural Bank of Greece (ATE) v. Greece*, European Committee of Social Rights, Complaint No. 80/2012, 16 January 2012, para. 75; also cited in ibid., at 12.
[184] See most recently A. Nolan and J. P. Bohoslavsky (eds), *Human Rights and Economic Policy Reform* (2021) and see Nolan, Lusiani, and Courtis (n. 167) 129.
[185] Ibid. 130.
[186] Ibid. 133.

add, the deliberateness of a measure is a crucial consideration, even though, again, the 'protect' obligation in principle mandates a very high degree of scrutiny of all socio-economic activities that a state undertakes and that may be relevant to its SE rights obligations.

Unsurprisingly, these procedural obligations bear a close doctrinal resemblance to the derogation provisions—and jurisprudence—for CP rights, though, in their sum total, they (would) impose a burden of proof that goes far beyond what the economic theories behind austerity measures are capable of justifying. Hence, this may either be a clever way of holding virtually all such measures to be *prima facie* breaches of the Covenant, or, conversely, it represents the sort of hypertrophied rights militancy that, for revisionists like Moyn, lies at the heart of what he sees as the (political) irrelevance of human rights. What, then, is the future of SE rights?

4. The Future of Social Rights: Utopia or Dystopia?

The answer depends, of course, on the time horizon to be considered, as well as on the level at which the question is asked. In terms of the former, for the short- and mid-term, many of the general future trends have been charted in the previous sections. Hence, as far as SE rights monitoring is concerned, the CESCR is likely to consolidate its combined role as a clearing house for SE rights implementation standards and, on that basis, as a pro-bono consultant to states both in relation to their ever-expanding reporting and accountability obligations, but also and increasingly to the ways in which their internal administrations design and execute relevant policies. This 'turn to policy' is, of course, a wider trend within the SE rights community and is, in itself, driven to a significant extent by the 'turn to metrics' in monitoring which has occupied the agendas of monitoring bodies and CSOs alike. It marks a significant departure from the judicial logic that heretofore had characterized human rights monitoring, with both monitoring bodies and CSOs increasingly assuming the role of expert consultants assisting governments in what amounts essentially to large-scale human rights mainstreaming exercises.

This also indicates the further rise of SE rights vis-à-vis CP rights (activism), so much so that it might not be exaggerated to claim that the future of human rights lies in SE rights. In part, this is due to the window of opportunity which the general crisis in (democratic) governance, and its articulation in form of the current string of political and economic crises, have opened both for the reception of the concerns represented by SE rights and for their inherently more dialogical, as opposed to condemnatory, modus operandi. Yet, the much-increased role which such a *de facto* partnership with overburdened and understaffed domestic administrations affords to the SE rights community has also evident drawbacks. For despite the technical—some would say technocratic—rigour with which the turn to SE rights-indicator-based governance is implemented, it still represents a subtle shift away from adjudication on the basis of formal criteria (and their inherent limitations in terms of appraising the complexities of 'real life' social policy) and towards a more political and activist role for those involved in monitoring. While this might represent a unique chance to create a new level of dialogue on the social policy issues underlying SE rights enjoyment, it will only gain relevance if the political character of the exercise is transparently acknowledged and not shrouded by a legal-technical formalism that simulates an all-encompassing objectivity.[187] Sally Engle Merry has likened indicator-based monitoring to the use of witchcraft, that is, to a political technology that guides 'supernatural forces' to a variety of purposes including 'advocacy, reform, control, and management.'[188] Rosga and Satterthwaite have added that indicators as such are, like the law itself, indeterminate and, thus, capable of being used to oppress as well as to emancipate. They accordingly admonish the global monitoring bodies to be openly self-reflective about their use of indicators and to takes sides, notably for the 'governed' with whom they should 'form strategic political alliances ... in the task of holding their governors to account'.[189] However, and ironically, where these SE advocates want to politically charge the 'turn to indicators' with an emancipatory pro-poor and pro-justice impulse, the revisionists will take their continuing focus on the obligations of states hollowed out by global capitalism as at best naïve, at worst straightforwardly pro-neoliberal.[190]

The domestic frontier faces a similar predicament in a different key, as the earlier enthusiasm about an SE-rights revolution has given way to ambivalence about the 'progressiveness' of its impact and, in some instances, open backlash from executives (and legislatures) resentful of judicial meddling.[191] Yet, at the same time, there seems to be no let-up in the advance of judiciaries who, in the wake of the global legitimacy crisis of representative (i.e. majoritarian) institutions, increasingly assume meta-executive functions and often enjoy considerable public support, especially when they target deadlock issues such as corruption or, indeed, certain types of rights violations. However, the latest judicialization wave is, arguably, driven more by the top-down (self-)empowerment of judiciaries than by the bottom-up legal mobilization that characterized the early 'rights revolutions'. In fact, in some places, the (apex) courts have now begun to curtail the effects of constitutional rights litigation on social policy, and have, at least in part, accepted the prioritization and (cost-)effectiveness rationale of public authorities. Where such attitudinal changes in domestic judiciaries are occurring, they tend to go hand in hand with

[187] For a fascinating analysis of how such legal formalism plays out on the development ground, see L. Eslava, *Local Space, Global Life* (2015).

[188] Merry (n. 53) S92.

[189] Rosga and Satterthwaite (n. 30) 315.

[190] See Hoffmann, 'Quite Enough (Still): Human Rights in (Times of) Crisis', in N. Bhuta et al. (eds), *The Struggle for Human Rights: Essays in Honour of Philip Alston* (2021).

[191] See, for instance, the study by M. C. Ingram, *Crafting Courts in New Democracies: The politics of subnational judicial reform in Brazil and Mexico* (2015).

a change in the underlying decision-making models to, in Brinks and Forbath terminology, a more pragmatic and deferential style.[192]

This naturally comes with a much higher degree of receptivity to the broader empirical implications of individual cases—that is, an increased sensitivity to their direct and indirect collective effects, and a concomitant turn to metrics-based argument. Such a trend towards quantification and indicators is, of course, part of a wider turn towards evidence-based policymaking in the domestic sphere which may come to fundamentally alter the role rights play in both adjudicatory and policy contexts. For, in essence, it shifts the normative authority of rights from (absolute) legal validity to (relative) empirical functionality, so that legal argument over rights claims would eventually hinge on which side is able to muster the better evidence. Rights would only 'win' if and when it could be shown that they provide the 'better' overall outcome, as measured by the efficiency-cum-fairness standard. This is, surely, not what SE rights advocates had in mind when they embarked on their well-intentioned mission to mainstream human rights impact assessment into all levels of policymaking. Yet, given the current economic and political climate, it may well come to pass that the judicial landscape of the future will become more functionalist while the fiscal space for social policy will further shrink. In such an environment, it will be even more important than today to understand the potential, but also the hazards, of 'rights in action' and to take the functional optic, inimical as it is to the traditional understanding of human rights, seriously enough to explore the extent to which rights, as the primary mechanisms for social (bottom-up) accountability, 'work' (better than alternative modes of governance), while resisting the epistemic traps of the 'audit culture'. The bottom line is still that despite the (likely) empirical undecidability of the (judicialization) impact debate and despite the shifting role of judiciaries, it remains an—equally empirical—fact that people 'on the ground' continue to use constitutional SE rights to claim a minimum standard of social welfare. As long as the rights-critical positions have not provided compelling argument to reduce such claims to mere false consciousness, they must be taken as serious attempts to 'shoot into the dark' and to thereby irritate the system.[193]

The same goes, in essence, for the other SE rights frontiers. Rights-based development is now so deeply entrenched in aid programming that it is likely to remain a principal component of development discourse for some time to come. Indeed, it is, arguably, even reinforced by the recent trend towards results-based (development) financing, which purports to transfer ever more ownership of the ODA process towards recipient states by shifting conditionalities from inputs to results, though at the cost of much increased good governance conditionalities, including human rights, monitoring.[194] The trends sketched above are likely to lead to more

192 Brinks and Forbath (n. 80) 239.
193 Hoffmann (2006) (n. 127).
194 See Dann (n. 145) 429; and Hoffmann (n. 15).

independent studies, outside operational imperatives, and, thus, to an ever better understanding of RBD's real impact and 'value added' in relation, primarily, to pro-poor objectives, and a similar impact debate as the one currently going on about domestic judicialization is likely to become as ubiquitous as it will be (empirically) undecidable.

As with domestic judicialization, there will be some pieces of evidence that will underscore the transformative potential of RBD, that will show that human rights have become one of very few globally understood benchmark systems by which human conditions can be described and remedies formulated, and that they are, thus, no longer just an add-on to development but its very *raison d'être*. However, other pieces of evidence will contradict this representation and, instead, find RBD to have become a self-referential process that is primarily geared to generating an input legitimacy largely abstracted from real outcomes and oriented towards the self-reproduction of the normative-institutional system at its base.[195] And again, the two narratives will stand against each other, all the while the rights within RBD will continue to live a life of their own, inherently transgressive of the (positive or negative) roles foreseen for them, usable and used by 'people on the ground', and, thus, resilient to capture by either side.

Lastly, the extension of RBD to the global North and to macroeconomic policy in the wake of the global financial crisis and the austerity reaction to it is similarly bound to stay. One reason is, of course, the gradual convergence of the predicaments of states in the global North and the global South. In this global regulatory developmental state, social policy is increasingly at the mercy of forces beyond its jurisdiction, most notably transnational (financial) markets, and its capacity to uphold those levels of welfare that lie at the basis of the conception of SE rights is likely to further erode. If anything, the global financial crisis has provided a reality check for many countries, with austerity, arguably, simply being used to mask the fact that the post-War welfare system has been rendered impossible to finance with the reduced means of the contemporary state.

For SE rights, this, again, forebodes two competing stories, notably the crossroads predicament cited in the beginning of this chapter. On the one hand, there is a clear disconnect between the optimistic foray by SE rights advocates into the deepest redoubts of (economic) policymaking and their seemingly unperturbed commitment to ever denser SE rights monitoring frameworks, while their addressees, states, and international organizations seem to be going in the opposite

[195] See Hoffmann (n. 15), where this is likened to a 'complex managerialism', as described and critiqued by Martti Koskenniemi, as in Koskenniemi, 'Constitutionalism, Managerialism and the Ethos of Legal Education', 1 *European Journal of Legal Studies* (2007) 8; Koskenniemi, 'The Politics of International Law', 1 *European Journal of International Law* (1990) 4; Koskenniemi, 'The Politics of International Law—20 Years Later', 20 *European Journal of International Law* (2009) 7; and Koskenniemi, 'Miserable Comforters: International Relations as New Natural Law', 15 *European Journal of International Relations* (2009) 395.

direction. Indeed, states' de facto commitment to SE rights protection is, arguably, as low as ever, with the main issue not being the specific minimum cores mandated by the treaties, but the very logic of SE rights, i.e. the idea that people are *entitled* to certain substantive and procedural minimum standards regardless of the overarching economic situation. This, by all accounts, many states are no longer prepared to fully support, their continuing commitment to their legal obligations notwithstanding. If, for example, one takes the Euro crisis as a case in point, then one would have to concede that not only did rights concerns play virtually no role in its management, but the relevant actors were also fundamentally unreceptive to the sort of rights-based argument advanced in ETO-type advocacy, so much so that the 'naming and shaming' logic on which rights advocacy is staked could never unfold. European publics were simply too acutely worried about their socio-economic future to massively mobilize for cross-border rights action.

This argument is reflected in two relatively recent critiques of SE rights (advocacy) which, from very different angles, converge on the conclusion that SE rights are at best irrelevant to the objectives sought by their advocates, at worst perilous diversions and (thus) fundamentally illegitimate. One, Eric Posner's *The Twilight of Human Rights Law*, is an unabashed 'right' critique of rights that essentially replicates his earlier re-reading of international law from a (political) realist and (methodological) rational choice perspective.[196] In his account, international law, and with it, international human rights law, fundamentally fails to solve what he terms global collective action problems because of both its ignorance of the true driver of state action, namely rational self-interest, and its mistaken belief that international norms can be effective in the absence of a world government.[197] SE rights, whether domestic or international, are additionally alleged to be ambiguous and inconsistent as they purport to establish clear-cut absolute claims where their implementation really always involves trade-offs and balancing acts on part of political (i.e. democratically elected) as opposed to legal decision-makers.[198] While the latter 'SE rights as programmatic' critique merely echoes earlier arguments in the justiciability debate, Posner's main point is, arguably, the international character of human rights law and its misguided premise that states and national populations can be made to incorporate the idea apparently behind human rights that there is 'a moral obligation not to harm strangers, and . . . to help them if they are in need'.[199]

[196] See E. Posner, *The Twilight of Human Rights Law* (2014) and E. Posner, *The Perils of Global Legalism* (2009).

[197] For a more detailed review of Posner's general position on international law, see Hoffmann (n. 127).

[198] Posner (2014) (n. 196) 87; see also the critical review by Hannum, 'Book Review of Eric Posner, the Twilight of Human Rights Law', *Human Rights Quarterly* (2015) 1105.

[199] Posner (2014) (n. 196) 9; as for the 'SE rights as programmatic' critique, *Twilight* is full of examples from both the domestic and international sphere of how legal human rights discourse has allegedly been dysfunctional; a recurrent illustration is Brazil, though the way it is represented is a case in point for Posner's highly tendentious, deliberately simplistic and thinly researched approach

Ironically, this last critique of international human rights is also one of the lines of attack on (conventional) SE rights discourse advanced by Samuel Moyn, even if he would likely object to being thrown in with Posner's political realist perspective. Moyn has, of course, in recent years become the *praeceptor* of a revisionist historiography of human rights with the undercurrent of his argument being that today's discourse on human rights, which are referenced to all humans and addressed, in principle, to all states, has to be sharply distinguished from the earlier discourse on the domestic-constitutional rights of citizens within nation states. Indeed, as he has exhaustively argued since his influential *The Last Utopia*, human rights have to be understood (only) as expressions of an anti-sovereigntist cosmopolitan utopia that springs from the liberal internationalist tradition.[200] This particular understanding of human rights was born, according to Moyn, in the 1970s and that period is, therefore, the (only) correct historical period in which to locate the origins of the contemporary understanding of human rights. What was termed as rights in previous periods carries, according to Moyn, the opposite connotation, notably of appeals to the protection afforded by sovereign states and, by implication, to the ideal of sovereign statehood itself. Despite their linguistic similitude, domestic and international (human) rights are, thus, entirely different ideas and spring not only from distinct but, in fact, conflicting utopias. As a consequence, to forcefully read a unified idea of human rights into what to Moyn are disparate historical episodes is not just anachronistic but misses the point of what human rights are really about.[201]

This broader historiographical point is then critically directed at contemporary SE rights (activism). Firstly, Moyn argues that the affirmation of an obligation of cross-border solidarity that underlies the idea of SE rights as international *human* rights is an (anachronistic) misreading of the intentions behind the internationalization of SE rights. The latter have to be understood in the context of the ideological capture of human rights discourse during the Cold War, with their articulation in the UDHR and the CESCR actually representing a strict (de-) limitation of their reach vis-à-vis the systemic alternative of (real-existing state) socialism.[202] Crucially, however, their implementation was, to Moyn, always closely tied to national sovereignty and it is only when several new conditions begin to be met as of

to empirical realities—especially those further away from (his) 'home'; this, alas, turns an otherwise thought-provoking argument into precisely the Eurocentric cliché his critics have come to expect.

200 Moyn (n. 132).

201 For a more detailed review of the revisionist argument advanced by Moyn and others see also Hoffmann and Assy, '(De-)Colonizing Human Rights', in J. von Bernstorff and P. Dann, *The Battle for International Law during the Decolonization Era* (2020); and J. Martinez, *The Slave Trade and the Origins of International Human Rights Law* (2011).

202 For a critical look at the rise of SE rights talk in the United States in relation to Roosevelt's 'Second Bill of Rights' programme see Moyn 'The Second Bill of Rights: A Reconsideration' in S. Voeneky and G. Neuman (eds), *Human Rights, Democracy, and Legitimacy in a World of Disorder* (2018) 111.

the 1970s that (international) rights talk transcends the confines of UN diplomacy and is transformed into a supranational normative horizon.[203] One such condition is decolonization and the achievement, by the 1970s, of national sovereignty by most former colonies. This freed human rights from their earlier association with self-determination and anti-discrimination struggles in the context of the anti-colonial struggle, while simultaneously re-launching the discourse as a device, primarily in the hands of governments in the global North, to internationally monitor and condition the newly independent states of the global South; in time, this would turn human rights into one of the primary benchmarks for (international) political legitimacy. However, the factor that is, arguably, most important for SE rights in Moyn's argument is the demise of socialism as a utopia of emancipatory politics and its replacement, again as of the 1970s, with the cosmopolitan internationalism at the core of which lie the 'new' human rights.

However, while SE rights broadly express the programme of post-War welfarism—which, in any case, starts to come under attack, both economically and ideologically, also as of the 1970s—human rights generally suffer, according to Moyn, from the crucial blindspot of (in)equality. More precisely, they neither articulate an egalitarian utopia nor do they serve as instruments against inequality—they are, to Moyn, simply silent on the question, which, in a neoliberal age in which inequality has not only grossly increased but is an essential part of the 'incentive structure', amounts to nothing less than tacit consent. Indeed, by exclusively focussing on the floor of protection rather than on any ceiling, they actually end up doing part of neoliberalism's dirty work of maintaining the lowest strata of society just about alive while removing any cap on how far upward stratification can go. Hence, insofar as human rights imply merely formal status equality and not distributive equality, they are, for Moyn, unsuitable as instruments against the neoliberal social fallout.[204]

This controversial position has since generated a vibrant and ongoing discussion on the salience not just of SE rights but of human rights in general as either drivers or impediments in the fight against growing inequality, which, in turn, has emerged, alongside poverty, as a major focal point in the debate about the neoliberal world order.[205] Indeed, while inter-state inequality is taken to have generally

[203] Seminally S. Moyn, *Not Enough: Human Rights in an Unequal World* (2018); as well as earlier iterations of the argument in Moyn, 'A Powerless Companion: Human Rights in the Age of Neoliberalism', 77 *Law and Contemporary Problems* (2014) 147, at 157; see also S. Hopgood, *The Endtimes of Human Rights* (2013); and the excellent collection in D. Lettinga and L. van Troost, *Can Human Rights Bring Social Justice?* (2015).

[204] See J. R. Pruce, 'Floors, Ceilings, and Beams: What's Missing in Samuel Moyn's Account of Inequality', *Humanity Journal* (2015) http://humanityjournal.org/blog/floors-ceilings-and-beams-whats-missing-in-moyns-account-of-inequality/ (last visited 18 April 2023); S. Fukuda-Parr, 'It's about Values: Human Rights Norms and Tolerance for Inequality', *Open Global Rights* (2015) https://www.openglobalrights.org/its-about-values-human-rights-norms-and-tolerance-for-inequality (last visited 18 April 2023).

[205] See, inter alia, P. Alston, 'Extreme Inequality as the Antithesis of Human Rights' *Open Democracy* (2015) https://www.openglobalrights.org/extreme-inequality-as-the-antithesis-of-human-rig

fallen, not least through the economic rise of China and other 'emerging economies', intra-state inequality has been on the rise in the North as much as in the South and is seen as one of the root causes for the political populist turn that has swept across many an established democracy.[206] While the detailed picture on both inter- and intra-state inequality is more differentiated and contested, its evident impact on social cohesion and political culture has placed inequality at the centre of the discussion not just about the real or potential failings of neoliberalism but also about human rights.[207] It has often been framed in the broader terms of distributive justice and the question of the relationship of rights—both as cognitive frameworks and as practical legal devices—to the latter.[208] Does a human rights optic inadvertently divert attention away from neoliberalism's underlying distributional scheme by focussing both on specific issues and on partial and minimum remedies?[209] Does human rights activism, not least in and through the courts, impede potentially more effective and macro-level collective political action, ranging from traditional party electoral politics, via collective (economic) interest representation through trade unions and similar, and to broader and often transnational social movements?[210] Are human rights, thus, mere handmaidens of neoliberalism and its production of inequality?

However, while Klein, Marks and others on the 'left' side of the debate openly endorse a Marxian response to this predicament—and with it, a Marxian critique of rights and the concomitant opposition to rights activism—[211] Moyn's overall

hts/ (last visited 18 April 2023); J. K. Galbraith, *Inequality: What Everyone Needs to Know* (2016); A. Barrera, *Distributive Justice and Economic Ethics: Distributive Justice in the Knowledge Economy* (2007); Salomon, 'Why Should It Matter That Others Have More? Poverty, Inequality, and the Potential of International Human Rights Law', 37 *Review of International Studies* (2011) 2137; Hernández-Truyol and Day, 'Property, Wealth, Inequality, and Human Rights: A Formula for Reform' 34 *Indiana Law Review* (2001) 1213; Landman and Larizza, 'Inequality and Human Rights: Who Controls What, When, and How', 53 *International Studies Quarterly* (2009) 715–736; Dehm, 'Highlighting Inequalities in the Histories of Human Rights: Contestations over Justice, Needs and Rights in the 1970s', 31 *Leiden Journal of International Law* (2018) 871.

[206] F. Bourguignon, *The Globalization of Inequality* (2015)

[207] G. MacNaughton, *Economic and Social Rights in a Neoliberal World* (2018).

[208] See, inter alia, Waldron, 'Socioeconomic Rights and Theories of Justice', 48 *San Diego Law Review* (2011) 773.; Miller, 'Justice and Global Inequality', in A. Hurrell and N. Woods (eds), *Inequality, Globalization, and World Politics* (1999) 187; Kingsbury, 'Sovereignty and Inequality' in A. Hurrell and N. Woods (eds), *Inequality, Globalization, and World Politics* (1999) 66; Aguilar and Saiz, 'Tackling Inequality as Injustice: Four Challenges for the Human Rights Agenda', *Center for Economic and Social Rights* https://www.cesr.org/tackling-inequality-injustice-four-challenges-human-rights-agenda (last visited 18 April 2023); Balakrishnan and Heintz, 'How Inequality Threatens All Human Rights' (2015) *Open Global Rights* https://www.openglobalrights.org/how-inequality-threatens-all-humans-rights (last visited 18 April 2023).

[209] See D. Kennedy, *A World of Struggle: How Power, Law, and Expertise Shape Global Political Economy* (2016).

[210] See Glasius, 'Economic and Social Rights and Social Justice Movements: Some Courtship, No Marriage, No Children Yet', in I. Lintel, A. Buyse, and B. McGonigle Leyh (eds), *Defending Human Rights: Tools for Social Justice* (2012) 127.

[211] See for a well-worked out version of this argument: W. Brown, *Undoing the Demos: Neoliberalism's Stealth Revolution* (2015).

conclusion is ironically much closer to Posner's, notably that human rights are simply irrelevant. For it is, to him, essentially civil society actors and (some) liberal elites in the global North who, starting in the 1970s, have 'spoken' the language of these new human rights, an ultimately too insignificant force either to be held co-responsible for the rise of neoliberalism or to be capable of its defeat. To Moyn, human rights have simply not been designed for the sort of use they are being put to by their activists, though he concedes that to merely state as much without offering a tangible alternative is not particularly useful either.[212]

Ultimately, the 'left' and 'right' critiques of (SE) rights—as well as Moyn's attempted 'centrist' position—converge on a surprisingly rudimentary form of political realism in which power—or rather, a fairly essentialist caricature of power—is everything. Moyn, for one, says as much when he concludes his reflection on human rights and neoliberalism with the disarmingly simplistic assertion that market fundamentalism demands 'a threatening enemy, rather than a powerless companion' (such as human rights).[213] Yet, for all their alleged powerlessness, the persistence of these critiques across the political spectrum suggests that the opposite is the case, notably that human rights (language) remain(s) a 'fact of the world' to which still very many people across the globe and in virtually all social and institutional settings turn in order to either resist oppression or to claim respect for different aspects of their personal or group identity.[214] The 'real' power of human rights is, thus, epistemic, namely as a language game by which the real-life conditions of humans can be (re-)described and brought into a simplified focus. Whatever institutional power their legalized form acquires is only a reflection of this epistemic power. And to resort to this language out of an experience of violence against oneself or out of care for (an)other is surely a political act and ought not easily be dismissed as mere false consciousness.

Both the 'left' and 'right' seem to fear this power, if for opposite reasons. The 'right' because human rights (in their legalized and internationalized variant) can and have been used to irritate the logic of capitalism (which, to Posner, is, of course, realized most purely in 'America' which he, therefore, wishes to be left alone by internationalist rights activists). The 'left' because rights can and have (also) been conceptual handmaidens for neoliberalism, though their structural indeterminacy and inherent transgressiveness—not least in and through legal process—make them at the very least unsteady bedfellows of capitalism; and, in any case, those alternative political-economic projects that seek to (re-)build the promise of (democratic) socialism beyond the authoritarian statism of its earlier namesake should not fear but welcome rights activism as a (complementary) form of political action.

[212] Ibid. 169.
[213] Ibid. 169.
[214] Rabossi, 'La Teoria de los Derechos Humanos Naturalizada', 5 *Revista del Centro de Estudios Constitucionales* (1990) 159.

As for Moyn's 'centrism', his otherwise valuable and thought-provoking dissection of human rights discourses in a variety of settings has one significant blindspot, namely the vast world beyond the West where, quite regardless of particular (mis-) readings of the meaning of human rights at different historical junctures, people continue to turn to them often as their last resort.[215] With Moyn's Western-centric view in the process of, as Philip Alston puts it, 'being swept away by the emergence of an international order no longer dominated by the West', his perspective is now itself increasingly anachronistic.[216]

It is especially in the laboratories of global capitalism, in the 'emerging markets' of the global South, but also in those countries in the global North that have found themselves on the receiving end of 'market failures', that SE rights have become one of the only remaining floodgates against the full-scale dismantling of welfare policies and a mutilation of the state into a rump permanently incapable of advancing an egalitarian politics. It is the language of SE rights that allows those exposed to the sweeping liberalization of labour markets, the privatization of education and health care, the elimination of even the most basic support for the poorest, the blanket capping of public expenditure, or, indeed, the social and economic consequences of a global pandemic, to frame their predicament in clear-cut terms beyond the muddle of economic theory and the path dependencies imposed by global (financial) markets. (SE) rights might not be a 'threatening (enough) enemy' of exploitation, injustice, and misery, but those using them surely are.[217]

[215] Although Moyn ventures outside the West when he reviews the role human rights played—or did not play—for anti-colonial activists in the run up to and during the decolonization period, his reading has largely focussed on the UN and anti-colonial politics in this context, see Moyn (n. 132) 84; for more nuanced readings see, inter alia, R. Burke, *Decolonization and the Evolution of International Human Rights* (2011); Terretta, '"We Had Been Fooled into Thinking That the UN Watches over the Entire World": Human Rights, UN Trust Territories, and Africa's Decolonization', 34 *Human Rights Quarterly* (2012) 329; and S. Jensen, *The Making of International Human Rights: The 1960s, Decolonization and the Reconstruction of Global Values* (2016).

[216] Alston, 'Does the Past Matter? On the Origins of Human Rights', 126 *Harvard Law Review* (2013) 2043.

[217] Alston, 'The Populist Challenge to Human Rights', 9 *Journal of Human Rights Practice* (2017) 1; and Alston, 'Human Rights under Siege', 14 *SUR International Journal on Human Rights* (2017) 267; see also Hoffmann, 'Facing South: On the Significance of an/other Modernity in Comparative Constitutional Law', in P. Dann, M. Riegner, and M. Bönnemann (eds), *The Global South and Comparative Constitutional Law* (2020).

3

Mutual Trust and the Future of Fundamental Rights Protection in the EU's Compound Legal Order

Christina Eckes[*]

1. Introduction

Fundamental rights protection within the EU's compound legal order always raises questions of 'who is in charge' and 'what the limits of the respective competences of the EU and the Member States are'. 'Who is in charge' is determined within the EU by a complex net of rules, consisting of the formal division of competences and organizational principles, such as the principles of conferral, sincere cooperation, and mutual trust. This complex net determines when and how public power may be exercised in practice and what Member States need to do or refrain from doing under EU law. Fundamental rights, both EU and national, act in different ways as limits to the exercise of power. They also fill, in particular, the principle of mutual trust with content. Indeed, the EU legal order is based on the mutual trust of all Member States that all of them comply with EU fundamental rights. Member States are required to demonstrate deference to each other's collective political choices and refrain from demonstrating mistrust towards the other Member States. At the same time, if enough evidence points at fundamental rights breaches in another Member State, a Member States may exceptionally deny trust and as a result refuse to cooperate.

This paper explores the reflexive relationship between fundamental rights protection and the constitutional power structures within the EU. It shows that the protection of both national and EU fundamental rights is the litmus test of legitimate but also effective cooperation within the EU. In the absence of a certain level of harmonization, i.e. certain commonly agreed basic rules, standards, monitoring, and consequences of non-compliance, the EU is not equipped with sufficiently strong mechanisms to be able to make Member States respect either EU or

[*] I would like to thank Nehal Bhuta and the members of the project 'The Architecture of Postnational Rulemaking' at the University of Amsterdam for their helpful comments on earlier drafts. All remaining errors are of course my own.

Christina Eckes, *Mutual Trust and the Future of Fundamental Rights Protection in the EU's Compound Legal Order*.
In: *Human Rights in Transition*. First Edition. Edited by Nehal Bhuta, Oxford University Press. © Christina Eckes 2024.
DOI: 10.1093/oso/9780198901921.003.0003

national fundamental rights. However, if Member States do not comply with fundamental rights this undermines the effectiveness of EU law and the functioning of the EU. The interaction between mutual trust and fundamental rights reveals an underlying tension between collective and personal autonomy. Mutual trust is an organizational principle that requires Member States to demonstrate deference to each other's collective autonomy expressed in political choices, including the determination of fundamental rights standards. Yet, if compliance with the principle of mutual trust and hence deference towards the standards of other polities results in a (perceived) violation of fundamental rights, as determined within the national context, this undermines the trust in cooperation within the compound EU legal order. Ultimately, the lack of trust by individuals may result in an exercise of personal (political) autonomy against cooperation within the EU. To put it more crudely, the principle of mutual trust in its 'state centric' interpretation by the Court of Justice of the European Union (CJEU), aimed to protect collective autonomy, finds its limit in the necessary individual trust and autonomy.

This tension is most visible within the highly politicized Area of Freedom, Security, and Justice (AFSJ), in which 'Justice' refers to the attempt to bring the different justice systems of the Member States together in a seamless network covering the whole 'Area'. Despite the fact that the Lisbon Treaty brought the AFSJ into the Treaty on the Functioning of the European Union (TFEU) and made it subject to the supranational rules of qualified majority voting, with the involvement of the Parliament and jurisdiction of the Court, the AFSJ remains in many ways characterized by intergovernmental features. EU law in the AFSJ largely requires (procedural) cooperation between the Member States rather than implementation of substantive EU rules and it is subject to multiple specific mechanisms that protect the collective autonomy of the national polities, represented by the Member States.[1] Willingness to cooperate largely depends on the compliance of Member States with EU rules, including the duty to respect national and EU fundamental rights. At the same time, if a Member State infringes fundamental rights, the principle of mutual trust may oblige other Member States to nonetheless give effect to that Member State's judicial decisions. This creates an extraterritorial ripple effect where the violation of fundamental rights by one Member States reaches persons within the jurisdiction of another Member State. This ripple effect will ultimately undermine the functioning of the AFSJ, indirectly through external pressure by the European Court of Human Rights (ECtHR), through internal pressure by a growing number of individuals who exercise their personal autonomy and vote against cooperation within the EU,[2] or through repeated or even systematic refusal

[1] E.g. the so-called emergency brake in Articles 82(3) and 83(3) TFEU, protecting fundamental aspects of its criminal justice system, Article 82(2) s.2 TFEU and the lower threshold in the AFSJ for the yellow card procedure to ensure compliance with the principle of subsidiarity in Article 7(2) of Protocol 2.

[2] See specifically the referendum in Denmark on 3 December 2015 on the country's participation in the AFSJ or more generally the UK referendum on EU membership on 23 June 2016.

to cooperate by the Member States. The paper argues that the only way forward for cooperation in the AFSJ is to move away from the rhetoric of trust to building *confidence* through transparency and introducing and monitoring basic supranational rules and standards, procedural and substantive.

Section 2 lays the groundwork of the legal analysis and argument in the rest of this paper. Sub-section A engages in particular with the political dimension of rights and identifies the understanding of human beings as persons who are owed justification as the essential reason of existence of rights. This understanding is based on and draws from Rainer Forst's work on human rights. Sub-section B sets out how and why within the EU legal order the determination of the substantive level of protection of rights is always also a procedural question of who is in charge of determining and protecting them. Sub-section C presents how and why in the politicized AFSJ, covering e.g. matters of criminal and family law, Member States and the EU institutions are particularly reluctant to harmonize procedural standards.

Section 3 introduces the principle of mutual trust and explains how it operates within the EU legal order. Sub-section A examines how the CJEU interprets the principle of mutual trust. Sub-section B explains how the Court draws limits to this principle. Amongst others, this section relies on case law of the ECtHR to demonstrate particular fundamental rights problems that flow from the principle of mutual trust and explains the interaction of mutual trust with the principle of sincere cooperation and the duty to respect national constitutional identities.

Section 4 draws conclusions about how the principle of mutual trust is influenced by the protection of fundamental rights; how in turn it influences the protection of fundamental rights in the compound legal order of the EU; and whether and how the EU can square the functioning of the AFSJ pursuant to the principle of mutual trust with ensuring respect for EU fundamental rights. Amongst other things, this section explains how the deference to collective autonomy required by the principle of mutual trust finds its limits in the personal autonomy of EU citizens, who are owed justification for departure from their collective national choices.

2. Fundamental Rights within the EU's Compound Legal Order

A. The Origin and Common Basis of Human Rights

Human rights and fundamental rights should be distinguished. Human rights have a universal vocation and fundamental rights are community specific and defined within and for a particular jurisdiction. Following from this distinction, the term 'human rights' is used in international law, e.g. the European Convention of

Human Rights (ECHR)[3] and the Universal Declaration of Human Rights (UDHR), while 'fundamental rights' is used within the EU legal order, e.g. the Charter of Fundamental Rights of the European Union. The distinction between human and fundamental rights is not this paper's particular focus but it is relevant to understanding the political dimension of human rights in the EU context, which lies at the core of this paper. The present section briefly explains the political dimension of human rights in the light of Rainer Forst's theory of human rights as originating in a right to justification. Most theoretical accounts point in one way or another to human dignity as the common underlying reason for the existence of rights that all persons enjoy because they are humans. Forst's theory does not contradict these accounts but rather further nuances how dignity should specifically be understood as a right to justification.

Forst identifies the fundamental moral right to justification as the one shared reason for the existence of all human rights.[4] He argues that the core of the human rights discourse is the understanding that being a person ('Personsein') depends on being treated as a being with a right to justification ('Rechtfertigungswesen').[5] This creates the necessity of accepting all individuals as persons to whom one owes reasons[6] and requires that all individuals be treated as persons whose rights and interests are respected both in the process of decision-making and in the substantive decision.[7] Governments have to offer their citizens legitimate reasons.[8] Human rights play in this reason-giving process the role of a language of critique ('Sprache der Kritik'), which protects citizens from unjustified societal and political oppression. Human rights are hence the fundamental and indispensable standards of the legitimacy of any societal and political order.[9] They also support a claim to determine laws that govern one's own position.[10]

Human rights, understood as ultimately based in a moral right to justification, connect the collective autonomy of a polity to personal autonomy.[11] The former is,

[3] The ECHR is more inclusive than the EU Charter but, despite the reference to human rights, obviously cannot make a universal claim.

[4] Rainer Forst, *Kritik der Rechtfertigungsverhältnisse* (2011) 54.

[5] Ibid. 67.

[6] Ibid. 66.

[7] Ibid. 77, summarizing Joshua Cohen.

[8] Ibid. 76.

[9] Ibid. Chapter 2, Menschenrechte haben 'eine politische Seite und werden als grundsatzliche Standards politischer Legitimitat angesehen'; see also 73: 'Die erste Frage der Menschenrechte ist nicht die nach der Beschränkung interner Souveränität von außen, sondern die bezüglich der wesentlichen Bedingungen der Errichtung legitimer politischer "Autorität von innen" sozusagen.'

[10] Ibid. 61.

[11] See differently but also assuming a necessary link between collective and personal autonomy: J. Rousseau, *Discourse on Political Economy and Social Contract* (1994). Rousseau understands decisions to express the collective will when they have been adopted following procedures that allow all participants to understand themselves as subject only to laws that they have given themselves. See J. Habermas, *Between Facts and Norms: Contributions to a Discourse Theory of Law and Democracy* (2015, trans. Reig) at 110: 'only those statutes may claim legitimacy that can meet with the assent of all citizens in a discursive process of legislation that in turn has been legally constituted', and at 449: 'citizens should always be able to understand themselves also as the authors of the law to which they are subject as addressees'.

in this reading, both *analogous to* and *dependent on* the latter. *In analogy* to personal autonomy, collective autonomy does not require that it is free of all legal or factual constraints but that it can form a collective will based on the assumption that it can steer its own course of action. The polity can consequently commit to legal obligations that constrain its actions without losing its autonomy; yet, it must remain in the position to form a collective will that aims to determine the political course of the polity.[12] *Depending on* personal autonomy, collective political autonomy, i.e. collective will-forming, requires that the individual participants actually possess the liberty to make decisions and determine their actions. This connects to the enabling function of human rights. It makes the protection of human rights a functional and fundamental requirement for the equal and free participation of all in the collective will-forming.[13]

As stated above, human rights make a universal claim. They are the rights that all human beings have irrespective of legal jurisdictions or power relations between different legal spheres. Fundamental rights are a specific expression of rights that are determined in the political process. This relativism of fundamental rights, as the specific expression and reading of rights within a specific jurisdiction, and the universalism of human rights, as inalienable entitlements that every person has because of their human nature, stand in apparent tension with each other.

Standards of human rights and fundamental rights differ, both in law and in practice. The relevance of these differences or variations should be determined on the basis of a distinction between the existence of rights, their interpretation, and their implementation.[14] The three categories of variations stand in a hierarchical relationship with each other: existence and wording of a right sets the limit of different interpretations, interpretation sets the limits for differences in implementation. Variation in the existence and wording of rights is limited by reason of the existence of these rights, which is here understood as ultimately being a right to justification. The core question is what the limits of these variations and deviations are. Any deviation not only from universal human rights but arguably more inclusive fundamental rights standards and practice must be justified in this light in order to be legitimate.

From a moral perspective, variations can be justified in different ways. First of all, human nature itself is not only a product of nature but also a product of culture.[15] Furthermore, moral judgments, while they must by definition be open

[12] This presupposes the distinction introduced by Rousseau between the will of all (aggregation of all individual wills) and the collective will (common will formed in a deliberative process).

[13] Cf. Habermas (n. 11). See for a detailed analysis of Habermas' stand on democracy and judicial review: Zürn, 'Deliberative Democracy and Constitutional Review', 21 *Law and Philosophy* (2002) 467–542. See also: Eckes, 'Common Foreign and Security Policy: The Consequences of the Court's Extended Jurisdiction', *European Law Journal* (2016) 492–518.

[14] This distinction is borrowed from: J. Donnelly, 'Cultural Relativism and Universal Human Rights', *Human Rights Quarterly* 400–419, 402.

[15] Similarly: ibid. 403.

to universalization, are also contingent on the historical and situational circumstances. The Universal Declaration of Human Rights expresses a 'convergence of basic cross-cultural human values'[16] and is endorsed by very different states, which protect different fundamental rights in different ways. By definition variation from universal human rights should not be possible. Moreover, certain choices are unjustifiable, such as discrimination on the basis of gender or race. Yet, even if substantive human rights are (nearly) universally agreed, their interpretation and implementation on the ground results in different outcomes.

The most problematic cases are fundamental rights standards and practices that may be, and are, justified within a particular jurisdiction pursuant to the internal standard, but are not the most defensible choice in light of an external evaluation. Ultimately, the choice between universal human rights and jurisdiction-bound fundamental rights is an expression of the choice between universalism and relativism. It imposes a hierarchy between the standard of a cosmopolitan or at least more inclusive moral community and the standard of a less inclusive cultural home community that is one's own.

Human rights are an expression of an objective moral standard. The three categories of variation: substantive rights, interpretation, and implementation start from the highest level of hierarchy and generality moving to the hierarchically inferior and more specific. The more specific any *universal* prescription is the closer it moves to a claim of moral objectivity. Moral relativism by contrast is concerned with cultural differences and sets limits to the legitimacy of imposing contingent norms across the boundaries of jurisdictions. A distinction must be made between the possibility, depending on authority, and the legitimacy, i.e. moral defensibility of imposing such standards. The discussion here is concerned with the latter. In short, a moral reason to justify departure from a more inclusive standard is self-determination. Self-determination is a human right accepted both by moral relativists and moral universalists. The reading that the very reason for the existence of human rights is justification of the exercise of power, i.e. the imposition of limits on behaviour shifts the focus to those to whom the rights are owed. This connects to Forst's theory that treating individuals as persons to whom reasons are owed is the common ground justifying the existence of human rights.

B. Fundamental Rights Within the EU: Vehicles of Power and Autonomy

Public power relations within the EU legal order are dynamic. Within a principal–agent framework, the relationships between the EU Member States and the EU

[16] Ibid. 417.

institutions start, *ex ante*, with the 28 Member States coming together and shaping the foundations of the power relationships within the EU as multiple principals. In certain domains they have agreed broad delegations of regulatory power to the supranational agent, i.e. the EU institutions. Delegations are not only made to the Commission and the Council, for example when the latter acts by qualified majority, but also to the CJEU, when the latter interprets the EU Treaties and EU secondary law. Overall, the CJEU's exercise of delegated powers, i.e. its interpretation of EU primary and secondary law has further extended the agents' powers and resulted in very broad delegations. This has—it is largely recognized—helped 'to overcome the problems of cooperation, coordination, and potential defection among the multiple principals'.[17] It has also resulted in 'what has been called "principal drift"'.[18] The original agent has taken up the position of the original principal. As a result, the relationship between national and EU actors can no longer be characterized in terms of a simple principal–agent relationship. It has grown into a multitude of different power relationships, depending on the specific issue in question, in which at times the Member States and at times the EU institutions have the determinative (principal's) position. In the AFSJ, Member States have so far been conscious of preserving their determinative position as principals by largely relying on rules of cooperation rather than harmonized EU standards. They have only reluctantly agreed to give the CJEU jurisdiction to enforce these rules of cooperation.[19]

The CJEU was the central catalyzer of the described principal drift. In the dynamic competence division of the EU, the Court's interpretation of the law often ultimately determines who is in charge in a given field, both formally, legally, and in practice. Despite the attempt to codify and hence solidify the competence division under the Lisbon Treaty, the Court's interpretation of the law remains pivotal to determining what the individual actors can or cannot do. Actual power depends centrally not only directly on competence provisions but also indirectly on the interpretation of indeterminate legal norms, such as organizational constitutional principles, but also fundamental rights. Indeed, fundamental rights protection has throughout the history of the EU played a tremendously important role in the power struggle between national constitutional courts and the CJEU.

Fundamental rights protection within the EU leads to questions of both institutional and formal legal hierarchy that affect the power relations of the EU and its Member States, as well as the relationship between EU law and national

[17] P. Lindseth, *Power and Legitimacy: Reconciling Europe and the Nation-State* (2010) 254 referring to: Menon and Weatherill, 'Legitimacy, Accountability and Delegation in the European Union', in A. Arnull and D. Wincott (eds), *Accountability and Legitimacy in the European Union* (2002) 113, at 119; Thatcher and Stone Sweet, 'Delegation to Independent Regulatory Agencies: Pressures, Functions and Contextual Mediation', 25 *West European Politics* (2002) 1, 6.

[18] Ibid.

[19] Protocol 36.

(constitutional) law. Essentially, it raises the question of who can claim the authority to control and determine the legality of actions, pursuant to which legal standard. This explains why fundamental rights have played and continue to play such an important role both as vehicles of integration and as a national defence against EU law. On the one hand, national courts have pressured the EU into protecting fundamental rights as a condition for them to accept the primacy of EU law. On the other, when EU institutions protect fundamental rights this triggers constitutionalizing processes,[20] which are largely perceived as happening at the expense of national self-determination. Indeed, fundamental rights remain the focus of the continuous tug-of-war power matches between the CJEU and the German Federal Constitutional Court (GFCC).[21] This became apparent in the *Solange* case law of the GFCC in the 1970s and 1980s and continued in the GFCC's Decision on the Treaty of Maastricht (1993) and the Treaty of Lisbon (2009). Yet the question of who may interpret and enforce fundamental rights remains relevant to the present day. Exemplary is an exchange between the GFCC and the CJEU in 2013 concerning the scope of application of the EU Charter of Fundamental Rights (CFR). In February 2013, the CJEU explained in the *Åkerberg Fransson* case that the EU Charter of Fundamental Rights is applicable to Member States' actions within the 'scope of EU law'. Arguably it interpreted the limitations in Article 51 CFR that the Charter only applies to acts of the Member States 'when they are implementing Union law' in a way that maximizes the scope of application of the Charter. In reaction the GFCC warned the CJEU that it would consider any excessively broad interpretation of the 'scope of EU law' as an *ultra vires* act.[22] The precise passage was cited by UK Supreme Court shortly after, expressing that it took a similar view.[23] However, the CJEU expressly confirmed its *Åkerberg Fransson* interpretation in a second ruling in September 2013.[24] In December 2015, the GFCC demonstrated that it remains ready and willing to fight for its interpretation of national

[20] Eckes (n. 13).

[21] Case C-617/10, *Åklagaren v. Hans Åkerberg Fransson* (EU:C:2013:105), paras 19–21.

[22] GFCC, Counter-Terrorism Database, judgment of 24 April 2013, 1 BvR 1215/07, Section C: '. . . for the questions . . . which only concern German fundamental rights, the European Court of Justice is not the lawful judge according to Art. 101 sec. 1 GG. The ECJ's decision in the case Åkerberg Fransson . . . does not change this conclusion. As part of a cooperative relationship between the Federal Constitutional Court and the European Court of Justice (cf. BVerfGE 126, 286 <307>), this decision must not be read in a way that would view it as an apparent ultra vires act or as if it endangered the protection and enforcement of the fundamental rights in the Member States (Art. 23 sec. 1 sentence 1 GG) in a way that questioned the identity of the Basic Law's constitutional order (cf. BVerfGE 89, 155 <188>; 123, 267 <353 and 354>; 125, 260 <324>; 126, 286 <302 *et seq.*>; 129, 78 <100>). The decision must thus not be understood and applied in such a way that absolutely any connection of a provision's subject-matter to the merely abstract scope of Union law, or merely incidental effects on Union law, would be sufficient for binding the Member States by the Union's fundamental rights set forth in the EUCFR. . . .'

[23] UK Supreme Court, *HS2* [2014] UKSC 3, para. 111. See more generally a list of ten national constitutional courts, which have followed in different ways the conceptualization of the GFCC of the relationship between EU law and national constitutional law: order of the Second Senate of 14 January 2014, 2 BvR 2728/13, para. 30.

[24] Case C-418/11, *Texdata Software* (EU:C:2013:588), paras 72–73.

fundamental rights. For the first time, the GFCC explicitly agreed to exercise jurisdiction in response to an alleged *individual* infringement, rather than a structural or systematic lowering of the fundamental rights protection offered by the CJEU.[25] The case will be discussed in more detail below. It is not by accident that many of these tensions flare up within the AFSJ where both fundamental rights and organizational principles governing the cooperation between Member States are of particular importance. The AFSJ deals with highly politicized and culturally different areas of law, such as criminal and family law. This explains why the AFSJ has become the prime setting of these power struggles.

The tug-of-war power matches between the CJEU and national constitutional courts in the area of fundamental rights bring the EU's dependencies on and separateness from the national to the fore and test it. Within the compound constitutional legal order of the EU, EU measures with far reaching fundamental rights implications raise questions about their compliance with national, as well as international law.[26] Article 6(3) TEU codifies the link between EU general principles on the one hand and the ECHR and national constitutional traditions on the other. The CJEU regularly relies on the more inclusive (albeit not universal) ECHR and the case law of the ECtHR to give substance to fundamental rights obligations under EU law, in particular when the case concerns compliance of Member States with EU fundamental rights.[27]

As was developed above, human rights are universal while fundamental rights have an important cultural and identity dimension that is closely interlinked with self-determination. Both the Member States and the EU are obliged under international and European law to comply with human rights. Both the Member States and the EU determine which fundamental rights are protected in which way within their own jurisdiction. This results in variations of fundamental rights protection between the Member States and the EU. The core question is to what extent may a Member State legitimately depart from European norms in the name of national culture or constitutional identity? Potential deviations from *universal human rights* by either the EU or a Member State, or both, will not be discussed as part of this chapter.

To say the least, the better, i.e. normatively more defensible, choice is not obvious between EU fundamental rights and national fundamental rights. Much seems to depend on other normative choices, including one's position between

[25] Beschluss vom 15. Dezember 2015, 2 BvR 2735/14, available at: http://www.bundesverfassungsgericht.de/SharedDocs/Entscheidungen/DE/2015/12/rs20151215_2bvr273514.html (last visited 20 April 2023). See also the refusal of the Danish Supreme Court to follow the preliminary ruling in Case C-441/14, *Ajos* (EU:C:2016:278) concerning non-discrimination on grounds of age, see an analysis at: http://eulawanalysis.blogspot.nl/2016/12/dialogue-or-disobedience-between.html?m=1 (last visited 20 April 2023).

[26] Notably the ECHR and national constitutional fundamental rights standards, see e.g. the GFCC's *Solange* line on case law.

[27] See: Joined Cases C-404/15 and C-659/15, *Aranyosi and Căldăraru* (EU:C:2016:198).

moral universalism and relativism. Universalism points to the more inclusive set of EU fundamental rights, even if by definition both EU and national fundamental rights are contingent. Moreover, cultural communities are not necessarily national communities. Yet within the EU the legal deviations in question are made by national courts or national governments and apply within the national jurisdiction. Hence in the present context the relevant communities that are expressions of (legal) culture are the European and the national ones.

EU fundamental rights are necessarily more inclusive, more widely shared, apply to and are negotiated by a larger group of people. This is formally the case for the EU Charter of Fundamental Rights as a codified rights catalogue, which is explicitly agreed and ratified by all Member States. Yet, EU fundamental rights are not universal. They are equally limited to their relevant polity, which is the EU. Their point of reference is European citizens and Member States. Moreover, while codified primary law is politically supported by the Member States and hence a legal expression of collective autonomy, i.e. self-determination and identity, the interpretations that the CJEU advances in its case law on fundamental rights are a step further removed from national democratic influence. Furthermore, the connection to personal autonomy remains less certain. It is not a priori clear in which context individuals are freer to determine their own standards and ultimately their identity: the EU or the national. Power relations may restrict the ability of individuals to fully choose the norms that apply to them. However, within the EU, the Member States are the first point of reference for the majority of the population in terms of belonging to a polity and renegotiating norms in a democratic structure that are applicable to that polity. Member States are moreover a point of reference that define and limit the possibilities for developing personal and group identity in another, i.e. European, context.

While a general convergence and integration of norms and their interpretation between different legal contexts has been observed in the field of rights,[28] the differences in interpretation and the formulation of specific fundamental rights often go to the core of what polities see as defining their identity.[29] Determining the content of a right requires making a specific choice of what is seen as important and hence protected by a particular right in a particular polity. This explains why fundamental rights are central to self-determination claims. Yet also on a more specific level of interpretation fundamental rights remain even in an interlocking compound EU legal order context bound. The interpretation of (nearly) identical rights depends on the perspective taken and the legal framework in which they are interpreted. Indeed, legal frameworks disallow or allow, or even prioritize taking

[28] De Wet and Vidmar, 'Conflicts between International Paradigms: Hierarchy versus Systemic Integration', 2 *Global Constitutionalism* (2013) 196.

[29] E.g. abortion, etc. in the public debate surrounding the Constitutional Treaty.

account of certain interests. An illustrative example is Article 52(1) CFR,[30] which *inter alia* requires a weighing exercise to reconcile rights with other 'objectives of general interest *recognised by the Union* or the need to protect the rights and freedoms of others'. This determines which interests can be weighed against fundamental rights and which cannot. Moreover, interpretation of law usually serves a host of objectives, which differ within the EU depending on whether they are interpreted and applied by a national court or by the CJEU. This is particularly true for general legal norms such as fundamental rights provisions. EU integration, the autonomy of the EU legal order, and the primacy, unity, and effectiveness of EU law are at the highest level of generality prevailing concerns of the CJEU.[31] Hence, it is relevant for the present discussion to realize that in every polity the determination, interpretation, and implementation of rights also depends on factors other than rights-inherent considerations.

From a moral perspective, the question of whether Member States should or should not be able to depart from common EU fundamental rights standards relates to the question of whether and at which level variation in the protection of rights it is justifiable both to allow and express collective autonomy and self-determination, understood as the right to determine one's own course of action and moral values. This relates to the question of to what extent expressions of certain cultural choices can be protected from legitimate criticism by outsiders either in the EU or in the national context.

C. The Area of Freedom Security and Justice: Particular Reluctance to Harmonize

The Area of Freedom, Security and Justice (AFSJ) centrally governs cooperation in criminal and civil law matters, which has its roots in the former intergovernmental third pillar. Under the Amsterdam Treaty (1999) and Lisbon Treaty (2009) Member States have reluctantly and incrementally increased supranational elements. However, Member States (and to a certain extent also the EU institutions) have also opted to protect strong intergovernmental elements by largely relying on

[30] Art. 52(1) CFR: 'Any limitation on the exercise of the rights and freedoms recognised by this Charter must be provided for by law and *respect the essence of those rights and freedoms*. Subject to the principle of *proportionality, limitations may be made only if they are necessary and genuinely meet objectives of general interest recognised by the Union* or the need to protect the rights and freedoms of others.' (emphasis added).

[31] See for integration: G. Conway, *The Limits of Legal Reasoning and the European Court of Justice* (2012). See also the CJEU's formulation in Case C-399/11, *Melloni* (EU:C:2013:107) that Art. 53 CFR allows Member States to 'apply national standards of protection of fundamental rights, provided that the level of protection provided by the Charter, as interpreted by the Court, and the primacy, unity and effectiveness of EU law are not thereby compromised' (para. 60) or Opinion 2/13 with the overarching concern for the autonomy of the European Union (Opinion 2/13, ECHR, of 18 December 2014, EU:C:2014:2454).

cooperation rather than harmonization. In particular Opinion 2/13 highlighted the difficulties of the EU to ensure actual fundamental rights protection in the intergovernmental setting of the AFSJ that is based on mutual trust, which requires Member States to act according to the presumption that all Member States protect fundamental rights at a sufficient level. The CJEU has aggravated this problem by prioritizing the effectiveness of the cooperation system, arguably without engaging with trust and justice as perceived by the individual.[32] This chapter argues that in polities that are based on personal and collective autonomy and in which fundamental rights must be justified towards the individual,[33] neglecting the individual's trust and sense of justice is not an option in the long run. It is likely to create a situation in which individuals exercise their political autonomy against European governance, with the aim to restore their trust in and sense of justice about the political structures that govern them, i.e. turn towards the national.

The case law discussed in this paper demonstrates the particular relevance of the principle of *mutual trust* within the AFSJ, in which cooperation between Member States is based on *mutual recognition*, requiring that a Member State accepts and enforces administrative and judicial decisions from all other Member State as if they originated from its own judicial system. Mutual trust is the basis of cooperation in civil and criminal matters,[34] as well as the Common European Asylum Policy.[35] At the same time, mutual trust is not restricted to the AFSJ. In its Opinion 2/13 the CJEU stated that its considerations are relevant 'particularly' with regard to the AFSJ and strongly relied on its case law in the AFSJ. Yet it also made clear that this principle reaches across the whole legal order of the EU.[36] Moreover, prompted by the opinion of AG Bot, who took a different position, the CJEU confirmed in the case of *Aranyosi* explicitly that mutual trust has the same meaning in the Common European Asylum System and in the context of the European Arrest Warrant (EAW).[37]

The EU institutions have started more actively to propose and adopt harmonized procedural standards in secondary EU law governing the cooperation in criminal matters.[38] As we will see below, this agreement on supranational procedural

[32] See also: Mitsilegas, 'The Symbiotic Relationship Between Mutual Trust and Fundamental Rights in Europe's Area of Criminal Justice', 7/4 *New Journal of European Criminal Law* (2015).

[33] See Section 2, sub-section A.

[34] See Articles 81, etc. TFEU.

[35] Joined Cases C-411/10 and C-493/10, *N. S. v. Secretary of State for the Home Department* and *M.E. and Others v. Refugee Applications Commissioner* (EU:C:2011:865).

[36] ECtHR, Opinion 2/13 of 18 December 2014 (EU:C:2014:2454) para. 191.

[37] See n. 27.

[38] Directive 2010/64/EU on the right to interpretation and translation in criminal proceedings, OJ 2010 L 280, 26 October 2010, p. 1; Directive 2012/13/EU on the right to information in criminal proceedings, OJ 2012 L 142, 1 June 2012, p. 1; Directive 2013/48/EU on the right of access to a lawyer in criminal proceedings and in European Arrest Warrant proceedings, and on the right to have a third party informed upon deprivation of liberty and to communicate with third persons and with consular authorities while deprived of liberty, OJ 2013 L 294, 6 November 2013, p. 1; see also the Commission's proposals of draft Directives on legal aid (COM (2013) 824 final, Brussels, 27.11.2013), procedural

standards has transformative harmonizing effects on national justice systems. It also has consequences for the applicable standards of fundamental rights, i.e. whether they are national or European, as well as for the automaticity of recognition of decisions of each other's justice systems.

The following Section 3 explains how the EU legal order functions based on constitutional principles of cooperation and in what way fundamental rights play an important role in filling these principles with content and determining their limits. This allows drawing conclusions on the EU's interest in ensuring fundamental rights protection both within and beyond the scope of EU law; on how the interplay of fundamental rights and the principle of mutual recognition impacts on the power division within the EU; and on the desirability of compliance with *EU* fundamental rights.

3. Mutual Trust within the EU Legal Order

A. Meaning and Consequences

> The EU legal structure is based on the fundamental premiss that each Member State shares with all the other Member States, and recognises that they share with it, a set of common values on which the EU is founded, as stated in Article 2 TEU. That premiss implies and justifies the existence of mutual trust between the Member States that those values will be recognised and, therefore, that the law of the EU that implements them will be respected.[39]

1. Origin and Meaning

The CJEU considers *mutual trust* to be part and parcel of the legal tissue of the EU, even though it is not codified in EU primary law, which only refers to the principle of mutual recognition.[40] In 2003 in the case of *Gözütok and Brügge*[41] the CJEU took the important step of introducing mutual trust as the explicit basis for the cooperation of Member States in criminal matters, now the AFSJ. It held that:

> ... there is a necessary implication that the Member States have mutual trust in their criminal justice systems and that each of them recognises the criminal law in

safeguards for children (COM (2013) 822 final, Brussels, 27.11.2013) and the presumption of innocence (COM (2013) 821 final, Brussels, 27.11.2013).

[39] ECtHR, Opinion 2/13 of 18 December 2014 (EU:C:2014:2454) at para. 168.

[40] Articles 67 ff TFEU for the AFSJ.

[41] Case C-187/01, *Gözütok and Brügge* (EU:C:2003:87).

force in the other Member States even when the outcome would be different if its own national law were applied.[42]

The Court specifically clarified that mutual trust is not based on the presumption that the other Member State provides *equal* protection, but that it provides *equivalent* protection and acts in compliance with EU fundamental rights. This entails that the outcome of the very same case might be different in two Member States and consequently also that the actual protection may be lower in the case at hand. In *Gözütok and Brügge* concerned *ne bis in idem*. In this case, and different from most of the other case law here discussed, the CJEU used mutual recognition based on mutual trust in order to *strengthen* the protection of the accused. In Opinion 2/13 in 2014, the Court further developed the relevance of trust in the EU legal order as a whole. It explicitly pointed out the 'fundamental importance' of mutual trust to the workings of the EU.[43] Indeed, mutual trust is now increasingly accepted as constituting a 'constitutional principle' of Union law.[44]

Despite the absence of any reference to 'trust' in the Treaties, it is not by chance that the CJEU refers to that concept. As has been developed by Niklas Luhmann and scholars building on his work, trust is characterized by a *relational* and a *subjective* element.[45] Its relational element derives from the fact that trust requires familiarity, i.e. previous experiences, and its function is amongst others to reduce complexity and uncertainty. Trust is an attempt to deal with uncertainty.[46] It generates risk, i.e. the risk that the trust is disappointed and the action that was taken because of this trust was not justified. In that sense, trust requires a conscious *decision* to take the risk that this trust is disappointed. This is the subjective element of trust. Relevant in the present discussion is the inherent necessity that a person can only trust if she has the autonomy to take a decision. If a person has no other option than acting in a particular way, no decision can be made. She cannot decide to trust, i.e. take a certain action with the risk of being disappointed. This decision-making element of trust hence presupposes personal autonomy. This is the case

[42] Ibid. para. 33.

[43] ECtHR, Opinion 2/13 of 18 December 2014 (EU:C:2014:2454) at para. 191.

[44] This is the explicit position both of Koen Lenaerts (President of the CJEU) and Sacha Prechal (Judge at the CJEU).

[45] See above all: N. Luhmann, *Vertrauen* (1968) and N. Luhmann, *Familiarity, Confidence, Trust. Problems and Alternatives* (1988). But also N. Luhmann, *Trust and Power* (1976) 6: 'The world is overwhelmingly complex for every kind of real system, whether it consists of physical or biological units, of rocks, plants or animals. Its possibilities exceed those to which the system has the capacity to respond. A system locates itself in a selectively constituted 'environment' and will disintegrate in the case of disjunction between environment and 'world'. Human beings, however, and they alone, are conscious of the world's complexity and therefore of the possibility of selecting their environment–something which poses fundamental questions of self-preservation. Man has the capacity to comprehend the world, can see alternatives, possibilities, can realize his own ignorance, and can perceive himself as one who must make decisions.'

[46] See also: Giddens, 'Risk, Trust, Reflexivity', in U. Beck, A. Giddens, and S. Lash (eds), *Reflexive Modernization: Politics, Tradition and Aesthetics in the Modern Social Order* (1994) 184–197.

irrespective of whether a person trusts another person in inter-human relations or whether she trusts a political structure.

The CJEU applies to the *relations between Member States*. It emphasizes the relational element that Member States as *members* of the EU shall trust each other. Furthermore, mutual recognition based on trust is a means to reduce *complexity* and *uncertainty* about the judicial systems of the other Member States and so reduce amongst others delays in judicial cooperation amongst Member States. Yet the Court ignores the subjective element of trust that presupposes a consciousness. It takes a state-centric perspective. It uses 'mutual trust' as institutional systemic trust of national authorities in each other. Whether EU citizens trust that justice is overall delivered does not play a role in the CJEU's understanding of this notion. Yet strictly speaking only persons can trust. States do not have consciousness and cannot actually trust. Moreover trust with its subjective element of having to take a decision does not lend itself to be a *normative* principle. It does not make sense to *oblige* someone to trust. You can only tell someone that they must not display signs of distrust, i.e. not check on someone. Trust requires a decision, a leap of faith, which cannot be prescribed.

Consequently, the CJEU's construction of mutual trust does not and could not require *actual trust*. It is limited to requiring Member States not to demonstrate mistrust, i.e. they may not check each other's compliance with fundamental rights, save in exceptional circumstances.[47] Hence the principle of mutual trust predominantly entails negative obligations that require Member States not to behave in such a way as to undermine the cooperation relationships within the EU. In the words of the Court:

> [W]hen implementing EU law, the Member States may, under EU law, be required to presume that fundamental rights have been observed by the other Member States, so that ... save in exceptional cases, they *may not check* whether that other Member State has *actually, in a specific case, observed the fundamental rights guaranteed by the EU*.[48]

A problem arises when the citizens, who do have a consciousness, do not feel the level of trust that the CJEU requires the Member State to display. When more than a neglectable part of the population of a Member State feels a considerable level of subjective individual mistrust, a tension arises with the actions of that Member State if it acts in compliance with the legal obligation not to display mistrust.

The Court's concept of mutual trust is essentially a good faith obligation. It has hence the same roots as the principle of sincere cooperation. In light of the above theoretical observations of Luhmann the Court should more accurately refer to

[47] ECtHR, Opinion 2/13 of 18 December 2014 (EU:C:2014:2454) at para. 192.
[48] Ibid. (emphasis added).

'confidence'. This is also in line with the prevailing wording of the codified law since a reference to mutual trust can only be found in secondary legislation on cooperation in civil matters.[49] Member States as *Herren der Verträge* have not formally enshrined either trust or confidence in the Treaties. Only mutual recognition is an organizing rule confirmed by national ratification procedures. The EAW Framework Decision, a flagship of cooperation in criminal matters, mentions only *confidence* and *recognition*, but not trust.[50] But trust remains a concept developed by the EU political institutions in secondary EU law, such as the Brussels I and II bis Regulations, and by the CJEU in its case law.

2. Lack of Trust as an Obstacle to Cooperation

A number of cases have reached the CJEU that indicate that in practice lack of mutual confidence is indeed a relevant obstacle for efficient judicial cooperation between Member States. In the case of *Lanigan*[51] the Irish authorities were requested to surrender a former member of the Irish Republican Army (IRA) to the UK authorities. The Irish authorities did not decide on the surrender within the time limits imposed by Articles 17(1)–(4) of the EAW Framework Decision due to a number of procedural incidents. The Irish High Court then made a preliminary reference to the CJEU asking for a clarification of the consequences of the fact that the time limits had been exceeded. What is most interesting in the present context is that part of the delay was due to the fact that the Irish High Court considered it necessary to request additional information from the UK authorities, 'with a view to establishing the credibility of Mr Lanigan's assertions that his surrender to the UK authorities could endanger his life'.[52] This reflects a considerable lack of confidence in the UK's compliance with common EU standards of fundamental rights, which had at least temporarily kept Ireland from executing the EAW.

Furthermore, in a case on cooperation in civil matters, the Irish Supreme Court referred several questions on the interpretation of Article 15 of the Brussels II bis Regulation (*Child and Family Agency* case[53]). A mother suffering from drug addiction gave birth to her second child in Ireland to avoid having her child taken away

[49] Council Regulation 44/2001 of 22 December 2000 on jurisdiction and the recognition and enforcement of judgments in civil and commercial matters (Brussels I Regulation), OJ 2001 L 12/1, recital 16: 'Mutual trust in the administration of justice in the Community justifies judgments given in a Member State being recognised automatically without the need for any procedure except in cases of dispute.'; see also recital 17; Council Regulation 2201/2003 of 27 November 2003 concerning jurisdiction and the recognition and enforcement of judgments in matrimonial matters and the matters of parental responsibility, repealing Regulation (EC) No 1347/2000 (Brussels IIa Regulation), OJ 2003 L 338/1, recital 21: 'The recognition and enforcement of judgments given in a Member State should be based on the principle of mutual trust and the grounds for non-recognition should be kept to the minimum required.' Interestingly, the Framework Decision on the EAW only refers to mutual recognition.

[50] Council Framework Decision 2002/584/JHA, OJ 2002 L 190/1, recital 10.

[51] Case C-237/15 PPU, *Lanigan* (EU:C:2015:474).

[52] Ibid. para. 17.

[53] Reference for a preliminary ruling from Supreme Court (Ireland) made on 4 August 2015—Case C-428/15, *Child and Family Agency (CAFA) v. J. D.* (EU:C:2016:819).

by the UK child services. The main questions referred by the Irish Supreme Court revolved around the idea of trust and what factors should be considered by national courts when determining which Member State court is best placed to rule on the merits of the case. In the light of the historical relationship between Ireland and the UK, the determination of fundamental rights matters by an English court may be considered exceptionally explosive in Ireland.[54] This is particularly relevant in the context of family law, where cultural difference may come to the fore with particular clarity. An example is the relevance of a formal legal recognition or marriage for a natural father's custody rights. And, while relying on the ECHR and the case law of the ECtHR may result in a considerable level of coherence, relevant choices resulting in different outcomes are still made by national fundamental rights and their interpretation and implementation by national authorities.[55] In situations as the one presented in the *Child and Family Agency* case the principle of mutual trust requires the judicial authorities of one Member States to accept the outcome of the considerations of the judicial authorities of another Member State. It ultimate requires them to cooperate in the implementation of ruling, which would not have been possible under their own national law.

Both cases demonstrate a lack of willingness to cooperate pursuant to the EU rules of mutual recognition. Beyond this, both cases raise questions with regard to the tension between universal human rights and fundamental rights as an expression of self-determination and collective autonomy explained in Section 2 above. If, in the case of *Lanigan* the prison conditions in the UK violate universal human rights or the inclusive minimum standard of fundamental rights expressed by the ECHR, Ireland should not execute the EAW. Legally it might violate its own obligations under the ECHR if it surrenders a person to a country where this person faces inhumane treatment.[56] Morally cooperating with a state that violates universal rights and hence making the specific rights violation possible is illegitimate. However, if e.g. in the *Child and Family Agency* case different fundamental rights and different interpretation and implementation of rights lead to different outcomes different consideration come into play. Cooperation and mutual recognition do not as such result in more inclusive standards. They do not automatically lead to agreeing or even conducting a debate on what the common EU standards should be in this area. It is also questionable to what extent the acceptance of the level of protection offered by a different community is a distinct expression of self-determination. It does however require a certain level of individual trust of considerable parts of the population to be supported and sustainable.

[54] The independent Irish Free State was only created in 1922 and remained a Dominion of the British Empire until 1931. Constitutional links with the UK were only severed completely in 1949. Catholic values, including conservative social and family policies, were part of Ireland's way of distinguishing itself from the UK.

[55] See e.g. Case C-400/10 PPU, *J. McB. v. L. E.* (EU:C:2010:582).

[56] ECtHR, *Soering v. the United Kingdom*, Appl. no. 14038/88, Judgment of 7 July 1989.

3. Presumption of Compliance but With Which Standard?

In Opinion 2/13 the Court explained that mutual trust required Member States to presume that all other Member States comply with EU law and 'particularly with the *fundamental rights recognized by EU law*'.[57] In other cases it refers to the ECHR and national constitutional traditions, rather than the common EU standards in the Charter.

To further illustrate the tension between mutual trust, understood as a presumption of compliance with an agreed standard of rights protection, and differing standards and interpretations of fundamental rights, in practice it is useful to examine the case law. The tension between the principle of mutual trust and fundamental rights as vehicles of power became most apparent in the very first preliminary reference of the French *Conseil Constitutionnel* (case of *Jeremy F*[58]), asking the CJEU to interpret the speciality clause[59] in the EAW Framework Decision. The CJEU explained the difference of fundamental rights standards that apply within the scope of EU law as compared to beyond the scope of EU law.[60] The Court emphasized that outside of EU law Member States remain bound by fundamental rights standards as they are protected by the *ECHR* and by *Member States' own national law*. It further linked the importance of compliance with these standards to the 'high level of confidence between Member States' and the 'principle of mutual recognition'. Yet, it also explained that 'the implementation of the European arrest warrant may be suspended *only* in the event of a serious and persistent breach by one of the Member States of the *principles set out in Article 6(1) EU*, determined by the Council pursuant to Article 7(1) EU with the consequences set out in Article 7(2) EU'.[61] Hence, the Court explained that mutual trust, and how it is applied in practice, justified requiring Member States to comply with fundamental rights, including *beyond* the scope of EU law. However, the CJEU also emphasized that only a breach of the *common EU fundamental rights standards* within the meaning of Article 7 TEU can justify refusal to execute an EAW. This results in a difference of standards of fundamental rights protection: within the scope of EU law, Member States need to comply with the common EU standard in Article 6 TEU and in the Charter;[62] beyond the scope of EU law they are obliged to comply with the ECHR and their own national standards. The latter are not an EU law obligation and the EU is not a relevant community in the determination of these standards. The EU possess only the limited Article 7 TEU mechanism to sanction a violation of the principles in Article 6(1) TEU, including beyond the scope of EU law. The reliance

[57] Opinion 2/13, ECHR, of 18 December 2014 (EU:C:2014:2454) at para. 191 [emphasis added].

[58] Case C-168/13, *Jeremy F. v. Premier Ministre* (EU:C:2013:358).

[59] The speciality clause ensures that a state cannot seek the surrender of a person for an extraditable offence in order to then prosecute that person for a non-extraditable offence or extradite him/her to a third state for a non-extraditable offence.

[60] Case C-168/13, *Jeremy F. v. Premier Ministre* (EU:C:2013:358), at paras 47–49.

[61] Ibid. para. 49 (emphasis added).

[62] See also Case C-617/10, *Åklagaren v. Hans Åkerberg Fransson* (EU:C:2013:105).

on external standards beyond the scope of EU law to justify mutual trust as the basis of cooperation under EU law does not result in a binding EU law obligation to meet these external standards. It may however unbind the other Member States from their obligation to cooperation with the Member State that infringes these external standards.

Besides seeking additional legitimacy through reliance on external standards that apply beyond the scope of EU law, the Court referred in Opinion 2/13 to shared *values* as they are codified in Article 2 TEU rather than fundamental *rights*. This is rather concerning. Values are notoriously indeterminate and do not offer a *legal* standard in the same way as fundamental rights do. Moreover, the CJEU cannot rely on the body of case law of the ECtHR to illustrate the content of values as it can where rights are concerned that 'correspond' to Convention rights.[63] By linking the subjective notion of trust with the set of indeterminate values in Article 2 TEU, which while they may be shared in abstract terms do not offer a legal yardstick, the Court has rendered the idea of what Member States must presume that they all comply with nebulous. This uncertainty which precise standard of protection, determined by whom, applies makes it additionally problematic to justify variation from the internal national fundamental rights standard.

B. Limits

Mutual trust:

> requires, particularly with regard to the [AFSJ], each of those States, *save in exceptional circumstances*, to consider all the other Member States to be complying with EU law and particularly with the fundamental rights recognised by EU law.[64]

To understand how the principle of mutual trust operates in practice one must understand whether and under which circumstances Member States may consider the presumption of compliance with fundamental rights as rebutted. This raises not only questions of which standard of protection, mainly EU or national, is applicable but also what the level of evidence indicating violations must reach.

Member States have in the Treaties closely linked the EU's ability to protect fundamental rights standards to its conferred competences.[65] The aim of this specific link is to avoid a competence creep through fundamental rights protection. At the

[63] See Art. 52(3) CFR.

[64] ECtHR, Opinion 2/13 of 18 December 2014 (EU:C:2014:2454) at para. 191, referring to Joined Cases C-411/10 and C-493/10, *N. S. v. Secretary of State for the Home Department* and *M.E. and Others v. Refugee Applications Commissioner* (EU:C:2011:865), at paras 78–80, and Case C-399/11, *Melloni*, judgment of 26 February 2013 (EU:C:2013:107), at paras 37 and 63 (emphasis added).

[65] See e.g. Art. 6(1) and (2) TEU.

same time, as was briefly outlined above, the very functioning of the EU depends on Member States' respect for fundamental rights; national courts only accept and apply EU law if it offers protection of fundamental rights equivalent to the national standards. This also entails that the EU cannot legitimately and legally[66] oblige Member States to enforce each other's judicial decisions in the AFSJ if these decisions are adopted in violation of *EU* fundamental rights. Any such cooperation obligation with the offending Member State would result in a situation where EU law indirectly violates its own fundamental rights standards. As a consequence, any clear violation of EU fundamental rights must be an acceptable justification for not complying with the principle of mutual trust. Yet, this observation does not answer whether Member States can rely on their own national fundamental rights standards in order to justify non-compliance with EU law.

1. Safety Valves, General Fundamental Rights Exceptions, and Harmonized Standards

Several instruments of EU secondary law contain 'safety valves' in the form of public policy clauses, which allow Member States to refrain from complying with their cooperation duties because the other Member State does not meet the *executing Member States'* fundamental rights standards. Examples are the Brussels I and II Regulations, which allow Member States to refuse the recognition of judgments of another Member State if they are 'manifestly contrary to the public policy of the Member State in which recognition is sought'.[67] 'Manifestly contrary' is a pretty high threshold. A simple difference in policy is not enough to refuse execution. The fact that Member States' fundamental rights standards are the yardstick, rather than EU standards, accommodates diversity and national choices in fundamental rights protection.

The EAW Framework Decision[68] does not provide for public policy limitations and fundamental rights are not mentioned as mandatory (Article 3) or non-mandatory (Article 4) grounds for a refusal to execute an EAW. However, the recitals of the Framework Decision[69] and Article 1(3) set out that nothing in the decision is meant to affect the protection of *the common EU fundamental rights standards*, Article 6 TEU and the Charter. In the case of *Melloni*, the CJEU was asked to address whether, despite the lack of a codified public policy clause, a Member State could refuse surrender under the EAW Framework Decision because the issuing Member State did not comply with fundamental rights as they are protected under the executing Member State's constitution. The question was whether a Member State could rely on the explicit protection of national standards in Article 53 CFR,

[66] See e.g. Art. 1(3) of the EAW Framework Decision, discussed in Section 3 sub-section B.1.

[67] Arts 22(a) and 23(a) of the Brussels II Regulation. Article 34(1) Brussels I Regulation.

[68] Council Framework Decision 2002/584/JHA, OJ 2002 L 190/1.

[69] Ibid. recital 12.

which set out that '[n]othing in this Charter shall be interpreted as restricting or adversely affecting human rights and fundamental freedoms as recognized ... by the Member States' constitutions', to make the surrender of a person convicted *in absentia* conditional upon the conviction being open to review in the requesting Member State. The CJEU concluded that this was not the case because it would allow a Member State to make the execution of an EAW subject to conditions that are not allowed under the EAW Framework Decision. The Court argued that this would ultimately 'undermine the principle of the primacy of EU law inasmuch as it would allow a Member State to disapply EU legal rules which are fully in compliance with the Charter where they infringe the fundamental rights guaranteed by that State's constitution.'[70] Hence, Member States may not protect other rights or give further going protection to the same rights when an area of EU law is fully regulated in compliance with the EU fundamental rights standards as codified in the Charter.

On the one hand, this is interpreted as depriving Article 53 CFR 'of all meaning'.[71] On the other hand, *Melloni* should be read as limited to areas that are subject to harmonized EU rules that set out the application and interpretation of fundamental rights within the specific legal context. Indeed, the EAW Framework Decision sets out three largely procedural, mandatory grounds for refusal and a number of optional grounds for refusal to execute an EAW.[72] Hence common harmonized rules for refusal exist. If a similar question of whether derogation could be justified arose in a different legal context, it would not be sufficient to simply point at the Charter as a catalogue of fundamental rights to assume harmonized standards. Hence, it is only where the EU has adopted detailed harmonized standards in a particular field of law that Member States can no longer rely on national fundamental rights standards to justify non-compliance. This is also in line with the Court's earlier internal market case law. For example, in the case of *Hedley Lomas*,[73] the UK tried to justify a quantitative restriction on exports (the refusal to issue an export licence) on animal welfare grounds in an area that was harmonized by an EU directive which however did not establish sanctions or procedures for non-compliance. Yet, the CJEU did not accept the UK's argument but held that the UK could not prohibit exporting living sheep to Spain because of animal welfare concerns. Instead, the UK should rely on the EU system of remedies and bring proceedings against Spain under what is now Article 259 TFEU or complain to the Commission that Spain did not meet harmonized EU animal welfare conditions.[74] In *Hedley Lomas*, the

[70] *Melloni*, para. 58.

[71] Besselink, 'Does EU Law Recognize Legal Limits to Integration? Accommodating Diversity and its Limits', in T. Giegerich, O. J. Gstrein, and S. Zeitzmann (eds), *The EU Between 'an Ever Closer Union' and Inalienable Policy Domains of Member States* (2014) 59.

[72] Arts 3 and 4 of Framework Decision 2002/584/JHA of 13 June 2002, [2002] OJ L 190/1.

[73] Case C-5/94, *The Queen v. Ministry of Agriculture, Fisheries and Food, ex parte: Hedley Lomas (Ireland) Ltd* (EU:C:1996:205).

[74] Directive 74/577 of 18 November 1974 on the stunning of animals before slaughter, OJ 1974 L 316/10.

Court assumed that the rules were sufficiently harmonized even though no specific reasons for non-compliance on grounds of fundamental rights were set out in the instrument of cooperation.

Melloni does not directly indicate whether non-compliance would have been possible had EU law not been harmonized in the field in question. An indicative answer to this question can be found in the cases of *N.S. and M.E.*,[75] in which the CJEU for the first time established a general fundamental rights exception. In 2011 in a preliminary ruling from a UK court, the CJEU was asked to interpret the so-called sovereignty clause in the Dublin II Regulation. The Court specifically addressed whether Member States are obliged not to transfer asylum seekers if such transfer violated EU fundamental rights.[76] No public policy limitation was included in the Dublin II Regulation; therefore, the CJEU established a general rule that a breach of EU fundamental rights could act as a limitation to the principle of mutual trust. At the same time, the CJEU restricted the reach of this general fundamental rights limitation. It required 'systemic deficiencies' and a real risk for the asylum seeker to be subjected to degrading and inhuman treatment[77] for the presumption of compliance to be rebutted so that the executing Member State is no longer obliged to act trustfully. The new Dublin III Regulation determines a change in responsibility for processing an asylum request if 'substantial grounds [exist] for believing that there are systemic flaws in the asylum procedure and in the reception conditions' in the State, which is in principle responsible.[78] In recent secondary law regulating cooperation in criminal matters, the EU institutions have equally introduced a general fundamental rights clause as a ground for refusing cooperation if such cooperation would breach the common EU standard in Article 6 TEU and the Charter.[79]

2. Rebuttability of the Compliance Presumption

Both secondary legislation and the case law of the CJEU frame the mutual trust principle as being based on a presumption that all Member States comply with harmonized EU rules and common EU standards of fundamental rights within the scope of EU law and that they comply with the ECHR outside of the scope of EU law. Even if indications of non-compliance exist, the cooperating Member State must still act within the rules of EU law, i.e. may rely on the sovereignty clause

[75] Joined Cases C-411/10 and C-493/10, *N. S. v. Secretary of State for the Home Department* and *M.E. and Others v. Refugee Applications Commissioner* (EU:C:2011:865).

[76] Ibid.

[77] Ibid. para. 89.

[78] Article 3(2) of Council Regulation 604/2013 of 26 June 2013 establishing the criteria and mechanisms for determining the Member State responsible for examining an application for international protection lodged in one of the Member States by a third-country national or a stateless person (Dublin III Regulation), OJ 2013 L 180/31.

[79] Recital 18 and 39, and Art. 1(4), but in particular the ground of refusal in Art. 11(1)(f) of Directive 2014/41/EU of 3 April 2014 regarding the European Investigation Order in criminal matters, OJ 2014 L 130/1.

under the Dublin regulation (*NS*) or may bring proceedings against the other Member State (*Hedley Lomas*). Moreover, when specific common rules and standards are agreed in a certain field, a Member State cannot justify noncompliance with EU law because national standards of the executing Member State are not met (*Melloni & Hedley Lomas*).

What constitutes sufficient evidence that the requesting Member State violates fundamental rights? What is the consequence of such evidence for the executing Member State's obligation to cooperate? The CJEU addressed these questions in the case of *Aranyosi*.[80] In this case the Court was confronted with a preliminary question concerning the duties of the executing Member State under Article 1(3) of the EAW Framework Decision. The national court asked whether 'strong indications that detention conditions in the issuing Member State infringe the fundamental rights of the person concerned and the fundamental legal principles as enshrined in Article 6 [TEU]'[81] lead to a duty of the executing Member State to request an assurance that detention conditions are compliant or whether the executing Member State may or even must lay down specific minimum requirements applicable to the detention conditions in respect of which an assurance is sought. In its reply the CJEU established a detailed framework to rebut the presumption of compliance and unbind the executing Member State from its obligation to execute the EAW, consisting of a two-tier test of rebuttal followed by a two-tier procedure ultimately allowing refusal to surrender the requested person. The test of rebuttal consists of a general element proving systematic deficiencies (first tier) and a specific element demonstrating that the person in question would likely be exposed to these deficiencies (second tier). The executing Member State must first rely on objective, reliable, accurate, and duly updated information on the detention conditions in the issuing Member State, which proves the existence of systemic or general failures concerning certain groups of prisoners or certain detention centres. The information can in particular consist of the decisions of international courts, such as the ECtHR, the decisions of the national courts of the issuing Member State or decisions, reports or other documentation of organs of the Council of Europe or the UN.[82] The CJEU emphasized the positive obligation of all Contracting Parties to the ECHR to ascertain that detention standards guarantee the respect of human dignity.[83] If such information confirms systematic deficiencies, the executing Member State needs to examine whether in the specific case the requested person would face a real risk of inhuman or degrading treatment.[84] The Court emphasized that systemic deficiencies alone are not sufficient to allow for additional action by

[80] Joined Cases C-404/15 and C-659/15, *Aranyosi and Căldăraru* (n. 27).
[81] Ibid. para. 46.
[82] Ibid. para. 89.
[83] Ibid. paras 89–90, with reference to ECtHR, *Torreggiani and Others v. Italy* (Nos 43517/09, 46882/09, 55400/09, 57875/09, 61535/09, 35315/10 and 37818/10) 8 January 2013.
[84] Ibid. para. 92 *et seq.*

the executing Member State.[85] If, however, both systemic deficiencies and a real risk that the requested person may be exposed to these deficiencies exist, the executing Member State must request additional information regarding the detention conditions of the facility to which the requested person will be transferred from the judicial authority of the issuing Member State.[86] If the executing judicial authority cannot within a reasonable time exclude the real risk for the surrendered person, it must decide whether the surrender procedure should be terminated.[87]

The CJEU hence introduced a detailed test of rebuttal consisting of a general and a specific element, in which it relied for the general element on either external authorities, including the ECtHR, or on the internal authority of the courts of the requesting Member State. The CJEU linked the general element of the test to rebut the presumption that all Member States comply with the common EU standards of fundamental rights protection very closely to the case law of the ECtHR. It stated explicitly that in *Aranyosi* the concern of the courts in the executing Member State was justified in the light of the fact that the ECtHR had found the requiring Member States, Hungary and Romania, in violation of Article 3 ECHR. The CJEU does not make a strict distinction between the ECHR interpreted by the ECtHR, national fundamental rights interpreted by national courts, and the EU fundamental rights, ultimately interpreted by the CJEU itself. The CJEU accepted both the ECtHR's and national courts' evaluation. This has a number of advantages. Firstly, it is much more likely that the ECtHR and the national courts rule on the rights violations within the requesting Member State. Secondly, it allows the CJEU to benefit from either the internal authority of the national courts or the established and widely accepted authority of the ECtHR in fundamental rights issues. However, it also blurs the three different standards, essentially presuming that not only a violation of the minimum standard of the ECHR but also a violation of national fundamental rights is necessarily a breach of common EU fundamental rights. This emphasizes the convergence and communality of rights within Europe. It does not account for existing differences which exist and may very well be justifiable in light of the above discussion of relativity of fundamental rights and the fact that they give expression to the collective autonomy of a polity.

Furthermore, once the presumption of compliance is rebutted, the executing Member State still is not generally unbound from its obligation of mutual trust. Rather than taking measures of investigation itself or even refusing surrender it must contact the issuing Member State to ask for further information. The CJEU hence effectively established a form of inquiry mechanism relying on self-assessment and guarantees amongst Member States. Hence, even if the presumption is rebutted, the principle of mutual trust continues to apply in the sense that

[85] Ibid. paras 93.
[86] Ibid. paras 95.
[87] Ibid. para. 104.

the executing Member State is required to trust the issuing Member State sufficiently to rely on their assessment of the situation and their guarantees that the surrendered person is not exposed to the identified deficiencies. The CJEU's deferential approach towards the issuing Member States also becomes apparent in the specific element. The presumption of compliance is only rebutted if the specific person is likely to be exposed to deficiencies; this excludes any general inquiries of the executing Member State into the state of affairs in the issuing Member State. It limits any conclusion that the presumption of compliance is rebutted to the individual case and does not allow 'blacklisting' Member States as generally not worthy of the state-level trust.

The key issue for the CJEU is to determine the content and limitations of the principle of mutual trust with reference to fundamental rights. From a practical perspective, an overly broad interpretation of the limits might jeopardize the functioning of the AFSJ as a whole, since Member States may structurally rely on the limitations in order not to recognize the decisions of other Member States. At the same time, alleged breaches of fundamental rights cannot simply be ignored. This would make the EU accomplice in fundamental rights violations and would justify disobedience by Member States and in particular by national courts. From a theoretical perspective, the principle of mutual recognition has been a means to protect differences between national legal orders. Differences in fundamental rights protection may also be justifiable for reasons of collective autonomy. The CJEU's determination of the content and limitations of the principle of mutual trust determines how much room for differing fundamental rights standards there is within the EU.

In the following section, the particular tension with the ECHR will be explored and further case law will be examined to investigate what the CJEU considers justified reasons for refusal to cooperate. The case law of the ECtHR is not only an indication that a Member State does not offer the required protection of fundamental rights. It also puts pressure on the CJEU to limit the principle of mutual trust and make room to rebut the presumption of compliance.

3. Mutual Trust under Pressure: Reconciling EU and ECHR Obligations

The EU principle of mutual trust stands in tension with obligations under the ECHR. It obliges Member States not to demonstrate distrust and hence refrain from checking or second guessing the other Member States' level of compliance with human rights, while the ECtHR's settled case law specifically requires the Contracting Parties to the ECHR to ensure that a person who they extradite does not become subject to inhumane treatment.[88]

[88] ECtHR, *Soering v. the United Kingdom*, Appl. no. 14038/88, Judgment of 7 July 1989.

Opinion 2/13 on the EU's accession to the ECHR gave the CJEU the opportunity to engage with the potential tension between the EU principle of mutual trust and obligations under the ECHR at an abstract level, unrestrained by the concrete facts of a particular case. However, in the three years preceding the Opinion, the ECtHR, CJEU and national courts had already entered into a judicial dialogue on the limits of the principle of mutual recognition in a series of cases concerning the Common European Asylum System. In 2011, in the *M.S.S.* case,[89] the ECtHR found Belgium in violation of Article 3 ECHR for sending an asylum seeker back to Greece where their rights under the Convention were blatantly infringed. The ECtHR made clear that the obligations under the Convention impose limits to the presumption of compliance. The ECtHR found a way to avoid a direct clash between EU and ECHR obligations. It pointed out that under the sovereignty clause of the Dublin regulation Member States could legally refrain from transferring asylum seekers back to their country of first entry. The ECtHR hence solved the apparent tension between ECHR and EU law obligations by interpreting generously the sovereignty clause in the Dublin Regulation. However, this solution does not generally resolve or even address the fundamental tension between the level of protection offered by the ECHR and the principles of mutual trust. The ECtHR's ruling further exposed the lack of any effective internal EU checks of minimum standards or EU mechanisms to ensure the national, European and international standards of human rights protection.

In the above mentioned *N.S. and M.E.* cases the CJEU followed the *M.S.S.* case.[90] It reconciled EU law with the ECtHR's ruling by declaring that the transferring Member State was obliged to examine the asylum application itself in cases such as *M.S.S.*, where numerous clear indications pointed to a violation of the ECHR.[91] In light of the wording of the Dublin-II-Regulation, this is quite a stretch,[92] but it allowed Member States to reconcile their obligations under the Convention and under EU law. However, in 2013, the CJEU introduced a higher threshold to justify departure from the Dublin II rules. In the case of *Abdullahi* a national court requested the CJEU to clarify the procedure for determining responsibility for asylum applications under the Common European Asylum System. The CJEU replied that when two Member States agreed which of them was the state that was responsible for the application under the Dublin II Regulation, the asylum seeker

[89] See ECtHR, *M.S.S. v. Belgium and Greece*, Appl. no. 30696/09, Judgment of 21 January 2011, section V International Documents Describing the Conditions of Detention and Reception of Asylum-Seekers and also the Asylum Procedure in Greece, at paras 159 *et seq.*

[90] ECtHR, *Soering v. the United Kingdom*, Appl. no. 14038/88, Judgment of 7 July 1989, para. 88 *et seq.*

[91] See ECtHR, *M.S.S. v. Belgium and Greece*, Appl. no. 30696/09, Judgment of 21 January 2011, section V International Documents Describing the Conditions of Detention and Reception of Asylum-Seekers and also the Asylum Procedure in Greece, at paras 159 *et seq.*

[92] See in particular Art. 3(2) and Recital 2 of the Dublin II Regulation (Council Regulation 343/2003 of 18 February 2003 establishing the criteria and mechanisms for determining the Member State responsible for examining an asylum application lodged in one of the Member States by a third-country national, OJ 2003 L 50/1).

could 'only' challenge that decision by 'pleading *systemic deficiencies* in the asylum procedure and in the conditions for the reception of applicants for asylum' in the responsible Member State.[93] Hence, the case concerned the *ability of the asylum seeker* to challenge the transfer decision under Dublin II rules. Yet arguably it allowed conclusions for the limits of the obligations under the principle of mutual trust under the Common European Asylum System. In this case the CJEU relied on national courts to determine the gravity of any alleged violation of fundamental rights. Hence it again accepted the national interpretation of national fundamental rights as the relevant standard.

In the EU's compound legal order, not only the CJEU but also and even primarily national courts are confronted with the task of reconciling a Member State's obligations under the ECHR with its obligations under EU law. In February 2014, two months after *Abdullahi*, the UK Supreme Court dealt in the case of *EM* with the exact question of whether and to what extent national authorities are required to check the circumstances of asylum seekers after their transfer to another Member State. The Supreme Court held that, irrespective of whether 'systemic deficiencies' existed in the reception system for asylum seekers in Italy, the Court of Appeal should examine on *a case-by-case basis* the risk that appellants would be subjected to treatment contrary to the Convention if they were returned to Italy.[94] The parties had based their arguments on the case law of the ECtHR but had not referred to the case law of the CJEU at all. The UK Supreme Court did not mention *Abdullahi* either. This case demonstrates the important role that national courts play in giving authority to the reading of either the ECtHR or the CJEU.

Shortly before the CJEU delivered its Opinion 2/13 in December 2014, the Strasbourg Court had another occasion to address the compatibility of EU Member States' obligations under the Common European Asylum System with the ECHR. In the case of *Tarakhel*, an Afghan family brought an application to the ECtHR challenging their transfer from Switzerland to Italy amongst others on the grounds that in Italy they would be treated in a way that violated Article 3 ECHR. The Strasbourg Court accepted by a majority of 14 to 3 that Switzerland had indeed breached Article 3 ECHR. The Court relied on its usual test established in *Soering*,[95] which assumes that Article 3 ECHR stands in the way of a transfer if 'substantial grounds have been shown for believing' that a 'real risk' exists of treatment contrary to that article in the state of destination. It is further noticeable in this case that the ECtHR did not give the EU the special *Bosphorus* treatment of presuming that the CJEU offers equivalent protection. The Court built its argument in *Tarakhel* centrally on an interpretation of the Dublin II Regulation that permits national authorities to 'refrain from transferring the applicants to Italy if

93 Case C-394/12, *Abdullahi* (EU:C:2013:813), at paras 60 and 62.

94 UK Supreme Court, judgment of 19 February 2014 ([2014] UKSC 12).

95 ECtHR, *Soering v. the United Kingdom*, Appl. no. 14038/88, Judgment of 7 July 1989.

they considered that the receiving country was not fulfilling its obligations under the Convention'.[96] This discretion of the Contracting Party also explains why the ECtHR did not find *Bosphorus* applicable. Instead, it found support in the UK Supreme Court's ruling in *EM*,[97] stating that:

> [i]n the case of 'Dublin' returns, the presumption that a Contracting State which is also the 'receiving' country will comply with Article 3 of the Convention can therefore validly be rebutted where 'substantial grounds have been shown for believing' that the person whose return is being ordered faces a 'real risk' of being subjected to treatment contrary to that provision in the receiving country.

The source of the risk does nothing to alter the level of protection guaranteed by the Convention or the Convention obligations of the state ordering the person's removal. It does not exempt that state from carrying out a thorough and *individualized examination* of the situation of the person concerned and from suspending enforcement of the removal order should the risk of inhuman or degrading treatment be established.[98]

Tarakhel may have come to some as a shock in the light of the *Bosphorus* doctrine, which the ECtHR had in the past applied to situations concerning the principles of mutual trust and recognition. In 2013, for example, the case of *Povse* equally concerned the scope and rebuttability of the requirement of 'mutual trust'[99] amongst Member States—this time under the Brussels IIa Regulation concerning the recognition of judgments in certain family matters.[100] In the CJEU's reading the Brussels IIa Regulation requires national courts (in the case at hand the Austrian courts) to recognize the rulings of courts of other Member States without proceeding to any review of the merits of the decision.[101] Brussels IIa, just as the European Common Asylum System, is based on the assumption that Member States 'trust' each other that they all comply with fundamental rights. Before the ECtHR, Austria consequently argued that it had merely fulfilled the obligations flowing from its membership in the EU and that hence the *Bosphorus* presumption of equivalent protection

[96] ECtHR, *Tarakhel v. Switzerland*, Appl. no. 29217/12, Judgment of 4 November 2014, para. 90; ECtHR, *Bosphorus Hava Yollari Turizm Ve Ticaret Anonim Sirketi v. Ireland*, Appl. no. 45036/98, Judgment of 30 June 2005.

[97] See reference in *Tarakhel*, paras 52 and 104.

[98] *Tarakhel*, para. 104 (emphasis added).

[99] Brussels IIa Regulation, recital 21: 'The recognition and enforcement of judgments given in a Member State should be based on the principle of mutual trust and the grounds for non-recognition should be kept to the minimum required.'

[100] ECtHR, *Povse v. Austria*, Appl. no. 3890/11, Judgment of 18 June 2013.

[101] Brussels IIa Regulation, recital 24: 'The Tampere European Council considered in its conclusions (point 34) that judgments in the field of family litigation should be 'automatically recognised throughout the Union without any intermediate proceedings or grounds for refusal of enforcement'. Despite the fact that in the particular case there were clear reasons to question that return was in the best interests of the child in question.

should apply. The Strasbourg Court accepted that the Austrian courts could not and did not exercise any discretion when giving effect to the Italian judgment.[102] It came to the conclusion that the CJEU had not been required to consider the alleged violation of the applicants' fundamental rights but that this had been for the Italian courts. It referred the applicants essentially to the Italian judicial system, with the possibility to bring another complaint to Strasbourg should the Italian courts fail to protect the applicants' rights. In short, the Strasbourg Court fully accepted the EU principle of mutual trust and recognition in the *Povse* case with the consequence that the sole responsibility for protecting human rights lies with the judicial system that is competent according to the EU rules. It is fair to conclude that both *Tarakhel* and *Povse* and the case law of the ECtHR and the CJEU in mutual trust cases stand in tension with each other.

The latter is also acknowledged by the CJEU in Opinion 2/13, where the Court concluded that the potential adverse effect of accession of the EU to the ECHR on the special characteristics of the EU and in particular the principle of mutual trust was one of the four core reasons why the draft accession agreement was incompatible with EU law.[103] The CJEU argued essentially that the EU legal order would not be able to function if Member States could check each other's compliance with fundamental rights in *specific* cases.[104] It hence reconfirmed that only *systematic deficiencies* allow departure from the principle of mutual trust. Furthermore, the Court stresses that EU law governs the relationship between the Member States to the exclusion of any other law, including the ECHR.[105] It hence linked mutual trust explicitly with autonomy and elevated it in this combination to a 'fundamental premiss',[106] a premiss for the existence of the EU legal order as the CJEU constructs it in its case law.[107] However, as we have seen above in *Aranyosi*, the CJEU has emphasized the 'real risk' test as the second step in rebutting the presumption of compliance with fundamental rights. Hence while establishing in Opinion 2/13 mutual trust in abstract as a fundamental premiss of the EU legal order the CJEU brought its position in *Aranyosi* much more in line with the ECtHR. This indicates that in practice a true clash between the courts is not likely even where they on face value initially appear to disagree.

The pressure of the ECtHR, even without accession, seems to have pushed the CJEU to at least semantically approach its position and refer to the 'real risk' test

[102] *Povse*, at paras. 79 *et seq.*, citing Article 42 of the Brussels IIa Regulation: 'shall be recognized and enforceable in another Member State without the need for a declaration of enforceability and without any possibility of opposing its recognition.'

[103] ECHR, Opinion 2/13 of 18 December 2014 (EU:C:2014:2454), para. 258.

[104] Ibid. para. 191.

[105] Ibid. para. 193.

[106] Ibid. para. 168.

[107] See: Eckes, 'International Rulings and the EU Legal Order: Autonomy as Legitimacy?', *CLEER Paper* 2016/2, available at: http://www.asser.nl/cleer/publications/cleer-papers/cleer-paper-20162-eckes/ (last visited 20 April 2023). The CJEU's vision of the EU is, as is well known, contested by national constitutional courts.

the ECtHR uses. The core difference between the approach of the CJEU and the ECtHR is the reliance on the national courts and other authorities of the Member State that allegedly breaches fundamental rights. While the CJEU in *Aranyosi* and the ECtHR in *Povse* rely on the national authorities of the suspect (requesting) Member State, the ECtHR in *Tarakhel* requires the executing Member State to carry out a thorough examination of the circumstances that the person would encounter after his or her surrender and, hence, of the situation in the suspect Member State. This difference in where the responsibility lies flows from mutual trust and the presumption of compliance with fundamental rights. It is the fundamental choice of the EU to build cooperation on mutual trust and a presumption of compliance with fundamental rights that shifts responsibility between Member States. This is also ultimately where the CJEU and the ECtHR may take different approaches and where a potential conflict might occur.

4. Other Constitutional Principles as Limits to Mutual Trust

Mutual trust is the 'horizontal' counterpart of the principle of sincere cooperation. Both principles ultimately serve the purpose of ensuring the well-functioning of the quasi-federal cooperation within the EU legal order. And both are crucial in this regard. While the principle of sincere cooperation predominantly governs the (vertical) relationship between the Member States and the EU institutions, the principle of mutual trust concerns first and foremost the (horizontal) relationships of the Member States with each other.

Article 4(3) TEU sets out that Member States shall 'facilitate the achievement of the Union's tasks and refrain from any measure which could jeopardise the attainment of the Union's objectives'. This entails a strong obligation of cooperation, which the CJEU considers as self-standing and applicable irrespective of the nature and scope of the competences of the EU and its Member States.[108] In combination with more specific rules but also with the rights set out in Article 6 TEU and in the Charter, the principle of sincere cooperation imposes obligations of conduct on the Member States. Yet sincere cooperation works two ways, it obliges not only the Member States to cooperate with the EU institutions but it also imposes obligations on the EU institutions,[109] including towards the Member States. This is how it may have meaning as a limit to the principle of mutual trust. Subject to the principle of sincere cooperation, EU law and the EU institutions, including the Commission,

[108] See e.g. Opinion 1/03, Competence of the Community to conclude the new Lugano Convention on jurisdiction and the recognition and enforcement of judgments in civil and commercial matters (EU:C:2006:81), para. 119, Case C-266/03, *Commission v. Luxembourg* (EU:C:2005:341), para. 58; Case C-433/03, *Commission v. Germany* (EU:C:2005:462), para. 64. See also comprehensively: Neframi, 'The Duty of Loyalty: Rethinking its Scope through its Application in the Field of EU External Relations', 47 *Common Market Law Review* (2010) 323.

[109] The new formulation in Art. 4(3) TEU post-Lisbon emphasizes the mutual nature, which had previously been acknowledged by the CJEU. See also Art. 13(2) TEU and Case C-409/13, *Council v. Commission* (EU:C:2015:217), at para. 83.

the Council, and also the Court, cannot require the executing Member States to act pursuant to a presumption of compliance required by the principle of mutual trust if the contrary, i.e. noncompliance of a Member State with EU fundamental rights, has been demonstrated. This would be a breach of sincere cooperation duties towards the executing Member State.

The close connection of the principles of mutual trust and sincere cooperation was an underlying theme in Opinion 2/13. While the CJEU expressed a certain level of distrust towards the Member States and towards the Commission in Opinion 2/13[110] it at the same time emphasized the relevance of the principle of mutual trust for the functioning of the AFSJ and the EU legal order as a whole. While this may seem like a contradiction at first it can be explained by the specific function of the judiciary. The judiciary reviews whether all other actors, i.e. the Member States and the 'political' institutions and bodies of the EU comply with the cooperation principles of mutual trust and sincere cooperation. As regards the executive—both the EU and the national executive, which are overlapping and interlocked—the CJEU has a review function, which precisely requires checking rather than trusting. Hence, it is not meant to trust the executive.[111] The Court, hence, rightly examined the accession agreement as to the possible ways in which the other actors might abuse it. The Court seemed to have considered that it should be as watertight as a pre-nup to avoid even the potential of abuse.[112]

The EU is equipped with limited means to hold Member States legally to their commitment to EU fundamental rights. Yet the EU institutions have a mandate to monitor Member States compliance with the values referred to in Article 2 TEU. This is specifically expressed in Article 7(1) TEU for the Council, which 'may address recommendations' to a Member State following a 'reasoned proposal' prior to determining a 'clear risk'. It also flows from the Commission's general task to ensure compliance with the treaties in Article 17 TEU and Article 258 TFEU. While both legal mechanisms (Article 7(1) TEU and Article 258 TFEU) give the institutions discretion over whether they take action against a Member State, they require the institutions to monitor Member States in order to be able to exercise this discretion in an informed manner compliant with standards of good governance. From these provisions in combination with the principle of sincere cooperation and the values in Article 2 TEU flows an active duty of the EU institutions to monitor that Member States do not 'breach' these values. This is also confirmed by recital 10 of the EAW Framework Decision as was pointed out by the CJEU in *Jeremy F*. This

[110] See Eckes (n. 107).

[111] The CJEU may however be required to 'trust' the national judiciary.

[112] Judge Sacha Prechal explained that the Court took the position of a notary warning of all the eventualities in a lasting relationship. VU talk of 6 November 2015, see also S. Gáspár-Szilágyi, *Mutual Trust before the Court of Justice—a view from CJEU Judge Sacha Prechal*, 11 November 2015, available online at https://pure.uva.nl/ws/files/2666364/174999_Mutual_Trust_before_the_Court_of_Justice.pdf (last visited 18 April 2023).

recital expresses that mutual trust finds its limit when the Council determines a breach within the meaning of Article 7(1) TEU. While the reference to the indeterminate values set out in Article 2 TEU may be criticized and it may be questioned whether values rather than rights can actually be 'breached', Article 7 TEU and the reference to the Article 7 TEU procedure in secondary law governing cooperation in criminal matters justifies monitoring of Member State compliance with fundamental rights, explicitly mentioned as one of the values in Article 2 TEU.

The reference in Article 2 TEU (and hence the monitoring obligation under Article 7 TEU) concerns noncompliance with *EU standards of fundamental rights protection*, including the rights codified in the Charter (within the scope of EU law) *and general standards* as they are codified in the ECHR (beyond the scope of EU law). The duty to respect national identities by contrast allows Member States under certain circumstances to justify derogating from EU law obligations because the other Member States do not meet *national* fundamental rights standards, in principle both in areas that are subject to harmonized EU law and in areas in which EU law has not (yet) established common standards. Article 4(2) TEU is an explicit recognition of national specificity. It hence logically protects national collective autonomy, allows for diversity within the EU and limits the harmonizing force of the exercise of EU powers, including the more inclusive EU fundamental rights standards.

Post-Lisbon, the respect of national identities has gained considerable relevance, not only in scholarly literature[113] but also before the EU Courts.[114] Parties rely on it with regularity,[115] Advocate-Generals have as a matter of principle accepted that it protects the fundamental political and constitutional structures of a Member State.[116] The CJEU found issues as broad as linguistic choices made at the national and regional level and nobility laws to fall under the national identity of a Member State.[117] The Court has so far relied on Article 4(2) TEU to interpret

[113] L. F. M. Besselink, *General Report, The Protection of Fundamental Rights Post-Lisbon: The Interaction between the Charter of Fundamental Rights of the European Union, the European Convention on Human Rights and National Constitutions* (2012), at 63 *et seq*., especially 70.

[114] The Court referred to Art. 4(2) TEU in Case C-208/09, *Sayn-Wittgenstein* (EU:C:2010:806), at para. 92; Case C-391/09, *Runevič-Vardyn and Wardyn* (EU:C:2011:291), at para. 86; and Case C-51/08, *Commission v. Luxembourg* (EU:C:2011:336), at para. 124. See, also point 59 of the Opinion delivered by Advocate General Jääskinen in Case C-202/11, *Anton Las v. PSA Antwerp NV* (EU:C:2013:239), and also para. 60 *et seq*. of the reference for a preliminary ruling in Case C-253/12, *JS v. Česká správa sociálního zabezpečení*.

[115] Art. 4(2) TEU; e.g. used as an argument by the parties: Joined Cases C-473/13 and C-514/13, *Adala Bero v. Regierungspräsidium Kassel and Ettayebi Bouzalmate v. Kreisverwaltung Kleve* (EU:C:2014:2095); Joined Cases C-58/13 and C-59/13, *Torresi* (EU:C:2014:2088), at para. 53; Reference for a preliminary ruling from the Supreme Administrative Court (Czech Republic) lodged on 24 May 2012 (Case C-253/12, *JS v. Česká správa sociálního zabezpečení*).

[116] Case C-151/12, *Commission v. Spain* (EU:C:2013:354), Opinion of AG General Kokott, at para. 34—federal constitutional structure. See also: AG Bot in Case C-399/11, *Melloni*, at paras. 138 *et seq*., stressing that 'constitutional identity certainly forms a part' of the concept of national identity, that the latter is 'inherent in their fundamental structures, political and constitutional'.

[117] Case C-202/11, *Anton Las v. PSA Antwerp NV* (note 77) and Case C-208/09, *Sayn-Wittgenstein*, (note 77). Whether 'multilingualism' as such forms part of national identity seems to be contested.

provisions of EU law and to justify national derogations from primary law.[118] However *Member States* might also attempt to challenge a provision of secondary law adopted under the TFEU that they consider adversely affecting their national identities.[119] However, the test of what is protected by national constitutional identities does not only take place before the CJEU. National courts play an important role in defining what is part of their national identity and have the means to put significant pressure on the CJEU to consider their interpretation, both in areas that have harmonized and in areas that are not subject to harmonized EU law.

In December 2015, the GFCC confirmed that it takes the protection of the German constitutional identity seriously and that it is indeed willing to exercise an identity control (*Identitätskontrolle*).[120] The facts of the case are similar to the facts in the *Melloni* case. Germany was asked to surrender a US citizen who was convicted *in absentia* by an Italian court. While the GFCC formally gave the impression that it followed the EU rules on requesting preliminary references, it agreed to review a national act that was entirely determined by EU law based on the argument that a reference was not necessary because the legal situation was clear ('*acte clair* doctrine' of the CJEU in *CILFIT*).[121] The case demonstrates that the GFCC's review extends to national acts that are determined by EU law, if this is indispensable to preserve the national constitutional identity. Review is further exercised in the individual case rather than only in cases where a structural deficit can be shown. If the GFCC comes to the conclusion that EU law conflicts with the German constitutional identity it is not applicable and hence will not be given effect within the German legal order. Further, it is interesting that the GFCC specifically refers to other national constitutions that contain safeguard clauses.[122] This could be read as a specific call on other national constitutional courts to follow the GFCC's lead and protect their national constitutional identities.

Another illustrative case in which national courts opted to protect national legal culture against cooperation obligations under the EAW framework decision is the case of Julian Assange. The Swedish *prosecutorial* authorities (rather than *judicial* authorities) issued an EAW for Assange in order to question him on allegations of sexual assault in order to decide *whether* to charge him. They relied on the EAW rather than making use of Article 9 of Second Additional Protocol on 'mutual assistance', which would allow questioning Assange via a video link and

Explicitly against: AG Jääskinen, opinion delivered on 12 July 2012 in Case C-202/11 *Anton Las v. PSA Antwerp NV*, *Anton Las v. PSA Antwerp NV*. Explicitly for: AG Kokott, Opinion delivered on 21 June 2012 in Case C-566/10 P, *Italy v. Commission* (EU:C:2012:368).

[118] See analysis of De Boer, 'Addressing rights divergences under the Charter: Melloni', 50 *Common Market Law Review* (2013) 1083.

[119] See also the Preamble to the Charter of Fundamental Rights.

[120] Beschluss vom 15. Dezember 2015, 2 BvR 2735/14, see n. 25.

[121] C-283/81, *Srl CILFIT and Lanificio di Gavardo SpA v. Ministry of Health* (ECLI:EU:C:1982:335).

[122] Beschluss vom 15. Dezember 2015, 2 BvR 2735/14, para. 44. See n. 25.

which Assange's legal representatives suggested on several occasions.[123] Assange argued that if surrendered to Sweden he might ultimately be extradited to the USA because of his role in leaking state secrets on the web platform Wikileaks. Sweden refused to grant any guarantee of non-refoulement in this regard. Assange then challenged the validity of the EAW before UK Courts and hence under UK law. The UK Supreme Court held by a majority that a 'prosecutor' rather than a 'judicial authority' could issue an EAW, even though the latter is the term used both by EU and English law.[124] However, a year later in *Lithuania v. Bucnys*, the majority of the Supreme Court took a different interpretive approach to the meaning of EU law.[125] It rejected the interpretation that a prosecutor could validly take a decision that required a judicial authority. A 2014 change to the 2003 Extradition Act[126] aimed to give legislative expression to the UK Supreme Court's ruling in *Lithuania v. Bucnys*. It specifically excluded the surrender of individuals where the warrant is not initiated by a judicial authority and determined that the requirement of a 'judicial authority' cannot be interpreted as being fulfilled by a prosecutor. It further excluded surrender of a person who has not yet been convicted. Finally, it expressly provided that the UK will no longer permit execution of an EAW without consideration of its proportionality by a court.[127] Particularly, the obligatory proportionality check conducted before executing an EAW stands in conflict with the principle of mutual trust as it is interpreted by the CJEU.[128]

From the standpoint of EU law, Article 4(2) TEU protects national identities from the harmonizing force of EU law but this does not mean that Article 4(2) TEU could be relied on by a Member State in order to justify a *lowering* of the common EU standard. By contrast, a Member State could in principle attempt to rely on the national identity clause to justify refusal to execute an EAW if such execution infringed national constitutional rights or principles that constitute the

[123] European Convention on Mutual Assistance in Criminal Matters, Strasbourg 20.IV.1959, with changes following from Additional Protocol to the European Convention on Mutual Assistance in Criminal Matters, Strasbourg, 17.111.1978 and Second Additional Protocol to the European Convention on Mutual Assistance in Criminal Matters, Strasbourg, 8.XI.2001.

[124] *Assange (Appellant) v. The Swedish Prosecution Authority (Respondent)*, judgment of 30 May 2012; Easter Term [2012] UKSC 22; appeal from: [2011] EWHC Admin 2849, available at: https://www.supremecourt.uk/cases/docs/uksc-2011-0264-judgment.pdf (last visited 20 April 2023). Two judges dissented and found this an incorrect application of English law.

[125] *Lithuania v. Bucnys* [2013] UKSC 71, available at: https://www.supremecourt.uk/cases/docs/uksc-2012-0248-judgment.pdf (last visited 20 April 2023). (Judge Mance, who dissented in the Assange case, wrote the majority opinion in this case.)

[126] Anti-social Behaviour, Crime and Policing Act 2014, see Part 12 'Extradition', available at: http://www.legislation.gov.uk/ukpga/2014/12/part/12/enacted (last visited 20 April 2023).

[127] Para. 69 of Opinion No. 54/2015 of the UNWGAD, available at: www.ohchr.org/Documents/Issues/Detention/A.HRC.WGAD.2015.docx (last visited 20 April 2023). All these changes would stand in the way of an execution of the EAW issued for Assange yet the UK Government at the same time made clear that the changes are 'not retrospective' and hence do not benefit Assange.

[128] The Lisbon Treaty has in the meantime given the UK the option to opt out of all of the pre-Lisbon EU legislation in the AFSJ and the UK Government intended to make use of this opt out while at the same time seeking to opt back into a number of legal instruments, including the EAW. The UK's opt-in into the EAW in particular became a highly politicized topic.

national constitutional identity. A possible example could be the principle of separation of powers if the executive branch rather than the judiciary issues the EAW.

The duty to respect national constitutional identities, while potentially interpreted quite restrictively by the CJEU, has not only offered national courts an EU law 'hook' to increase their pressure on the CJEU, and the EU institutions more generally, to respect national collective choices, including in terms of fundamental rights protection and not to go too far in imposing harmonized standards, particularly in the highly political and still fairly intergovernmental AFSJ. It may prove a means to limit an interpretation of mutual trust that infringes national fundamental right standards.

4. The Future of Fundamental Rights Protection in the EU: Challenges, Opportunities, and Limits

The main objective of fundamental rights is protecting individuals from the exercise of public power. Beyond this, within the EU, they provide substantive yardsticks that give meaning to the content of the duties under constitutional principles within the power relations between the Member States and the EU. They determine at the same time the content and set limits to duties under the principles of mutual trust and sincere cooperation. Hence, infringing EU fundamental rights standards may under certain circumstances unbind the other parties from their cooperation duties. The power relations within the EU further raise complex questions about which standard of right protection should apply, national, EU, or international, as determined by the ECHR.

Because of the particular way the EU is set up, it relies both on rules governing international organizations and those governing federations. This leads to particularities as regards fundamental rights protection. Both the EU and the Member States are responsible for respecting fundamental rights when they exercise public power. Additionally, the EU can hold Member States to the common EU standard of fundamental rights protection when they act within the scope of EU law. However, certain instruments of EU law, particularly within the AFSJ, require Member States to cooperate in areas, which are not governed by EU law and in which the concrete application and interpretation of fundamental rights is not determined by EU law, e.g. procedural judicial matters. Yet the EU's ability to enforce fundamental rights in areas governed by national law is very limited, essentially limited to Article 7 TEU, which kicks in only in extreme cases. As a result, cooperation may lead to an extraterritorial ripple effect where violations of fundamental rights in one Member State carry consequences beyond its borders for individuals in the cooperating Member State. It may bring even the cooperating Member State to a point where secondary EU law obliges it to breach its duty to respect and protect the fundamental rights of those within its jurisdiction under the ECHR by either surrendering the person or executing a faulty ruling of a national court.

Both the EU and its Member States are bound by the minimum standard of the ECHR and in practice by the protection standard developed by the ECtHR. Fundamental rights protection both within the EU and the Member States cannot drop below this level. Yet this leaves open where Member States should be able to deviate from the more inclusive EU standard of fundamental rights protection, in substance, in interpretation, and in implementation. Within the AFSJ this becomes relevant for example where Member States are obliged to cooperate and enforce judicial decisions that are given under circumstances that protect defence rights at different levels. In the light of the above discussion on universalism and relativism and the understanding of human rights as ultimately rooted in a right to justification, the choice between variations of rights protection in the EU and in the national context, which all comply with the more inclusive basic level of protection under the ECHR, is not obvious. Inclusivity and self-determination of a political community stand in tension. Some would argue that they stand in an inverse proportional relationship. The more inclusive a standard is, e.g. EU standards are more inclusive than national standards, the less they may be an expression of self-determination, e.g. the EU standards are arguably a more indirect expression of democratic self-determination than national standards. The powerful position of the CJEU in determining fundamental rights standards within the EU may be seen to remove them even further from political democratic influences.

Cooperation within the EU that is based on mutual recognition of each other's standards raises additional questions. By creating the uncodified constitutional principle of mutual trust as the basis of mutual recognition and connecting it intimately to the autonomy of the EU legal order, the CJEU effectively elevates a functional principle (mutual recognition), which is explicitly based on a presumption that all Member States comply with EU fundamental rights, to the same level as these fundamental rights. The Court, as was explained above, prohibited Member States from checking each other's fundamental rights compliance, either systematically or in the specific case. Even after the CJEU has brought its position closer to the position of the ECtHR, the principle of mutual trust continues to create a ripple effect where the fundamental rights violations in one Member State (the requesting Member State) have consequences for individuals in other Member States (in executing Member States). It leads effectively to an automatic extraterritoriality of a faulty decision, justified if you like by the functioning of the EU legal order in the AFSJ.

Mutual trust requires presuming compliance with fundamental rights standards as defined under EU law. At the same time, breaches of fundamental rights are an accepted limit on cooperation between Member States based on the principle of mutual trust. However, the practice of applying this limit might be less straightforward. First of all, fundamental rights must be ensured both *de jure* and *de facto*.

It is not sufficient to identify legal obligations to comply with fundamental rights. Secondly, a breach of a fundamental right as guaranteed by EU law would have to be shown. Prima facie it is not sufficient that one Member State applies a different understanding of a given fundamental right than another Member State. Cultural differences in the interpretation of fundamental rights are in principle to be accepted as part of cooperation on the basis of mutual trust and recognition. The final arbiter of whether the autonomous EU standard of protection was infringed would be the CJEU. The Court might hence be required to investigate the specific situation on a case-by-case basis. Thirdly, not every breach may permit a Member State to refuse cooperation or recognition of the other Member States legal decisions. Only a sufficiently serious breach that is documented by external authorities, such as the ECtHR, the UN, or the Council of Europe, lead to this result.

Indeed, the hurdles are very high that a Member State has to take to be legally allowed under EU law to refuse cooperation. Pursuant to the case law of the CJEU, the executing Member State has to meet three conditions to be able to legally (under EU law) take actions that may demonstrate a lack of trust. Firstly, not any rights violation is sufficient. In the examined case law on the EAW the Court referred only to degrading or inhumane treatment, which is an absolute human right from which no derogation is possible. It is hence at least questionable whether the Court would accept the violation of human rights that are subject to limitations, such as e.g. the right of access to justice. Secondly, the repeated reference to Article 7 TEU both by the Court and in secondary law emphasized the necessity to identify a serious and persistent breach and not just any breach of EU fundamental rights. Thirdly, the executing Member State is not allowed to show signs of distrust and as a consequence cannot investigate or even inquire about the situation in the issuing Member State if there are not already external reports or rulings of national courts of the issuing Member State that confirm fundamental rights breaches. This seems to exclude any independent evaluation on the part of the executing Member State. Moreover, even after meeting these conditions, the executing Member State may only take specific action, which continues to require a certain level of trust. The principle of mutual trust is not the origin of the fundamental rights violation, but the combination of the demanding conditions for rebutting it and the limited scope for action that may be interpreted as distrust lead to a ripple effect where violations of fundamental rights carry consequences beyond borders. This makes establishing clear limits of the principle of mutual trust pivotal. The principle of sincere cooperation is, on the one hand at the root of mutual trust, on the other it imposes limits on this principle. The EU institutions would breach their duty to cooperate sincerely if they required a Member State to trust another Member State against better knowledge or even judgment, i.e. where there is strong evidence that the other Member State does not comply with EU fundamental rights. The duty to respect national constitutional identities is the codified reaction of the EU to pressures exercised by national constitutional courts. It protects space for diversity and has been used by Member States to attempt to halt the EU's harmonization attempts where they affect the national understanding of fundamental rights.

In a quasi-federal system, such as the EU, that is built on cooperation between a number of different polities that continue to enjoy collective autonomy (Member States) and are constructed as systems that respect and require personal autonomy (democratic systems), the boundaries of cooperation principles, such as mutual trust (and loyalty for that matter), are defined by collective autonomy on the one hand and personal autonomy on the other.[129] Mutual trust is a principle requiring a deferential assessment of the standards of other Member States. Such a principle seems to be an essential condition of quasi-federal arrangements where they have only a very limited ability to impose a uniform standard and compel the constituent polities to follow it in practice. In other words, the principle of mutual seems the necessary by-product of respecting the collective autonomy of the Member States. At the same time, if the mutual trust obligations of the collective require action that stands in contrast to its own legal and ethical choices, this is likely to undermine the trust (and loyalty) of individuals in that collective. In societies that are in turn built on the autonomy of the individual, such as the democratic systems of the Member States, this will necessarily create tension. Normatively, the limit of mutual trust should lie where overall the highest level of human rights protection can be achieved. As long as cooperation is overall beneficial for the protection of human rights, a principle requiring deference to other fundamental rights standards, including those that are (perceived to be) lower, may not only be unavoidable but also desirable. Yet a sufficient level of individuals, who take the decision to trust the other legal system, must support any such cooperation; anything else would result in legal paternalism.

Finally, fundamental rights are problematic in another sense within the EU legal order. The EU must at all times ensure that EU actors, including the institutions, bodies, and agencies, do not violate fundamental rights.[130] The same applies when Member States give effect to EU law and arguably beyond. This latter point has become more relevant in the light of concerns whether legal changes in certain Member States, such as Poland and Hungary, meet the common EU fundamental rights standards.[131] National breaches of EU fundamental rights challenge

[129] For the link between collective and personal autonomy, see Section 2, sub-section A.

[130] The CJEU has repeatedly held that 'the acts of its institutions are subject to review of their compatibility with, in particular, the Treaties, general principles of law and fundamental rights', see e.g. Case C-583/11 P, *Inuit Tapiriit Kanatami and Others v. Parliament and Council* (EU:C:2013:625).

[131] See the 'EU framework to strengthen the rule of law', established by the Commission and activated for the first time in relation to Poland: Communication from the Commission to the Council and the European Parliament, A new EU framework to strengthen the Rule of Law, COM(2014)158 final and European Commission Speech, *Readout by First Vice-President Timmermans of the College Meeting of 13 January 2016* (13 January 2016), available at http://europa.eu/rapid/press-release_SPEECH-16-71_en.htm (last visited 18 April 2023). See also: K. Scheppele, *What Can the European Commission Do When Member States Violate Basic Principles of the European Union? The Case for Systemic Infringement Actions* (November 2013) available at https://verfassungsblog.de/wp-content/uploads/2013/11/scheppele-systemic-infringement-action-brussels-version.pdf (last visited 18 April 2023).

the whole functioning of the EU legal order. This is also why the EU possesses a mandate and (limited) legal means to bring Member States into line and why the EU institutions have an active duty to monitor fundamental rights compliance by Member States. If one or even several Member States drift into situations where they structurally no longer respect fundamental rights, the principle of mutual trust and, as a consequence, the whole functioning of the EU legal order will come under a new level of pressure.

Member States have been reluctant to agree harmonized procedural standards in the AFSJ. However, the future of fundamental rights protection in the EU may require a certain level of harmonized basic standards. The particular interdependencies of mutual trust and fundamental rights protection place the EU in a position that only a certain level of harmonized procedural standards, in combination with better monitoring and potentially even enforcement, can ensure the effective cooperation within the AFSJ. Turning a blind eye to the ripple effect of fundamental rights violations under the current system is problematic not only for fundamental rights protection but also for the functioning of the cooperation within the AFSJ. Essentially, the examined case law indicates that automatic mutual recognition ultimately requires establishing basic common EU standards not only in the form of codified fundamental rights in the Charter but also as harmonized standards for the interpretation and implementation of these common standards in a specific context, i.e. in the context of the EAW. A legal order based on mutual trust requires squaring the circle by introducing supranational elements, i.e. basic EU standards, in order to protect the collective autonomy of the Member States.

4
Human Rights Connectivity and the Future of the Treaty Body System

Sarah H. Cleveland

1. Introduction

In 2011, Amanda Mellet, a married woman who wanted her child, learned her pregnancy was fatally impaired with congenital heart defects. Because Irish law criminalized abortion except when necessary to save the woman's life, legally Mellet had to choose between continuing the pregnancy until miscarriage or stillbirth, or traveling overseas for an abortion. She chose the latter, and ultimately travelled to the UK with her husband, under great distress, at her own expense, taking 'sick leave' from work, and with no information, support, or pre- or post-abortion care from the Irish health care system.

Lacking any remedy at home, Mellet challenged her treatment before the Human Rights Committee, the UN treaty body established to monitor state compliance with the International Covenant on Civil and Political Rights (ICCPR). In 2016, the Committee found that, as applied in Mellet's case, the Irish regime violated several rights under the Covenant, particularly for women of limited economic means. Specifically, it inflicted physical and mental suffering that constituted cruel, inhuman, or degrading treatment, and it violated Mellet's right to privacy and the prohibition on non-discrimination.[1]

The Committee concluded that Ireland was obligated to provide compensation to Mellet and to amend its laws to ensure effective, timely, and accessible procedures for pregnancy termination in Ireland.[2] In response, Ireland paid 30,000 euros in compensation, provided Mellet with counseling, and established a Citizens Assembly to review and make recommendations regarding Ireland's laws on abortion.[3] The resulting Assembly report led the Joint Committee of the Irish Parliament to conclude that constitutional reform was necessary, citing as one of three critical factors warranting reform '[t]he continuing and ongoing breach of

[1] HRC, *Mellet v. Ireland*, UN Doc. CCPR/C/116/D/2324/2013 (2016), paras 7.2–9; see also HRC, *Whelan v. Ireland*, UN Doc. CCPR/C/119/D/2425/2014 (2017).

[2] *Mellet* (n. 1) para. 9.

[3] HRC, Follow-up progress report on individual communications, Ireland, UN Doc. CCPR/C/122/R.2, May 2018, 12–20.

Sarah H. Cleveland, *Human Rights Connectivity and the Future of the Treaty Body System*. In: *Human Rights in Transition*. First Edition. Edited by Nehal Bhuta, Oxford University Press. © Sarah H. Cleveland 2024.
DOI: 10.1093/oso/9780198901921.003.0004

Ireland's international human rights obligations as evidenced' in *Mellet*.[4] In a 2018 referendum, the Irish people overwhelmingly approved a constitutional amendment allowing access to abortion.

The Human Rights Committee's decision in *Mellet* built upon the Committee's own recommendations to Ireland in 2014 that Ireland should, inter alia, revise its constitutional and legislative restrictions on abortion.[5] These were accompanied by similar recommendations from numerous other treaty bodies,[6] as well as concerted engagement over a period of years by civil society organizations and individuals such as Amanda Mellet.[7]

Every day, numerous human rights situations come before the UN treaty bodies that monitor state implementation of the world's multilateral human rights instruments. Through various forms of engagement, including periodic reviews of country practices and the individual complaint mechanism used in *Mellet*, the treaty bodies provide states with authoritative interpretations of their human rights obligations, and assessments and recommendations regarding compliance. Through a constant iterative process among the treaty bodies, states, civil society, human rights survivors and other actors, the treaty bodies nudge states toward greater understanding and respect for their human rights obligations. Yet the proliferating treaty bodies face significant challenges relating to their visibility, resources, coordination, and effectiveness. This chapter considers the future of the UN treaty bodies as an integrated 'system', both among themselves and in the broader context of the international and regional human rights regime.

* * *

When the drafters of the ICCPR inserted 'the Human Rights Committee' as the oversight mechanism for the treaty in 1950,[8] they so named it because they thought the Committee would be the only such mechanism. The companion treaty to the

[4] Joint Committee on the Eighth Amendment of the Constitution (Ireland), 'Report of the Joint Committee on the Eighth Amendment of the Constitution' (2017), at para. 1.8 (citing also *Whelan v. Ireland* (see n. 1) available at: https://www.oireachtas.ie/en/committees/32/eighth-amendment-constitution/ (last visited 18 April 2023). The Joint Committee observed that 'the United Nations Human Rights Committee found Ireland to be in violation of the International Covenant on Civil and Political Rights (ICCPR). As well as directing compensation and counseling for the women concerned, the Human Rights Committee has called for Ireland to change its laws to allow for termination in cases of fatal foetal abnormality'; ibid. para. 3.6, p. 35.

[5] HRC, Concluding observations on the fourth periodic report of Ireland, UN Doc. CCPR/C/IRL/CO/4 (2014), paras 9–10.

[6] See CEDAW, Concluding observations on the combined sixth and seventh periodic reports of Ireland, UN Doc. CEDAW/C/IRL/CO/6-7, March 2017, paras 10–11, 42–43; CAT, Concluding observations on the second periodic report of Ireland, UN Doc. CAT/C/IRL/CO/2, August 2017, paras 31, 32(e); Committee on the Rights of the Child, UN Doc. CRC/C/IRL/CO/3-4, March 2016, paras 57–58; Committee on Economic, Social and Cultural Rights, Concluding observations on the third periodic report of Ireland, UN Doc. E/C.12/IRL/CO/3, July 2015, para. 30.

[7] See, e.g., L. Earner-Byrne and D. Urquhart, *The Irish Abortion Journey, 1920–2018* (2019).

[8] UN Commission on Human Rights, Report of the Sixth Session, 29 May 1950, UN Doc. E/CN.4/507, at 7, 18.

Covenant—the International Covenant on Economic, Social and Cultural Rights (ICESCR)—had no such oversight mechanism, due to perceived differences in the character and enforceability of those rights. And there was no expectation at the time for other multilateral human rights treaties, let alone other treaty bodies. The ICCPR and ICESCR were something entirely new under the sun. So was the Human Rights Committee.

The Committee was a product of compromise. It reflected the strong sentiment of certain members of the drafting UN Human Rights Commission that some type of oversight to promote ongoing state compliance with the new international human rights law obligations was required, or the treaties would be worth only the paper they were printed on. It reflected the sentiment of India and other states that there should be a means for individuals to present claims of injury under the Covenant above the national level.[9] It reflected the proposal of Australia at the 1946 Paris Conference that the UN should establish a World Court of Human Rights to judicially enforce the rights under the Covenant.[10] It further reflected the resistance of states such as the Soviet Union to a World Court of Human Rights as too intrusive into state sovereignty.[11]

The result of these various impulses was the Human Rights Committee—a quasi-judicial body, comprised of 18 independent experts from around the globe, elected by states parties to the treaty, who meet part-time on a volunteer basis to receive periodic reports from states on their implementation of rights under the Covenant and issue recommendations on areas for improvement. The Committee also issues such 'general comments as it … consider[s] appropriate'[12] regarding its interpretations of the Covenant, and reviews 'communications' from individuals regarding claimed violations of the Covenant by states parties that, like Ireland, have ratified the Covenant's Optional Protocol.

However, the Committee was not alone for long. Even before the ink was dry on the draft ICCPR—and before the two Covenants were adopted by the General Assembly—the Convention on the Elimination of all forms of Racial Discrimination (CERD) was adopted in 1965, providing for its own treaty body modelled on the Human Rights Committee. Indeed, between the establishment of the CERD Committee in 1969 and the Committee on Enforced Disappearances

[9] See UN Commission on Human Rights, India: Amendment to China-United States of America Proposal on Implementation for the Covenant on Human Rights, UN Doc. E/CN.4/151, 17 June 1948.

[10] See A. Devereux, *Australia and the Birth of the International Bill of Human Rights, 1946–1966* (2005), 180; UN Commission on Human Rights, Summary Record of 15th Meeting, U.N. Doc. E/CN.4/SR.15, 5 Feb. 1947, 2; UN Commission on Human Rights, Summary Record of the 108th Meeting, UN Doc. E/CN.4.SR.108, 7 Jun. 1949, 30 (Australia, Belgium, and Iran voting for establishment of a new court; India voting against).

[11] See UN Commission on Human Rights, Summary Record of the Thirty-Ninth Meeting, UN Doc. E/CN.4/SR.39, 15 Dec. 1947, 8.

[12] Art. 40(4), International Covenant on Civil and Political Rights 1966, 999 UNTS 171.

in 2011, ten treaty bodies came into being, with a total of 172 experts, operating under nine different treaties and an optional protocol.[13]

Each of these bodies was created by states as a free-standing institution, functioning independently within the framework of its treaty-specific powers and mandate. Each has the power to independently establish its own procedures, and has its own specific reporting and review requirements for states. Over time, these treaty bodies have evolved in the nature of their authorities and become more judicial in their procedures and practices. Most of the treaty bodies have developed substantial bodies of jurisprudence under the treaty they oversee.

The treaty bodies, in short, were not legally created to be a system. And yet nine of the ten treaty bodies exercise largely similar powers—including conducting periodic reviews of the human rights practices of states, considering individual communications for states parties that have accepted this authority, producing general comments, and for some, conducting urgent inquiries. They function according to similar but variable procedures.

The treaty bodies oversee rights that to some extent substantively overlap. For example, the CEDAW Committee, the Committee on the Rights of the Child, the Committee Against Torture, and the Human Rights Committee all may have concerns under their respective treaties regarding the treatment of children in juvenile detention facilities. The CEDAW and CRC Committees overlap as a result of their responsibility for the protection of girls and children; the CAT Committee due to its authority with respect to torture and cruel, inhuman or degrading treatment (CIDT); and the Human Rights Committee with respect to various rights under the Covenant, including the prohibitions on arbitrary detention, torture, and CIDT, protection of the right to privacy and the rights of families and children, freedom of religion, etc. These same Committees, as well as the Committee on Economic, Social and Cultural Rights, all have concerns regarding access to reproductive health care services for women and girls. Assessment of such issues by the treaty bodies in light of their respective treaties often yields substantively overlapping interpretations and recommendations.

This overlap can be a good thing. It allows for repeated consideration of a state's human rights record by multiple bodies, each bringing a somewhat different perspective to the issue. The fact that most states have ratified many of the relevant

[13] Committee on the Elimination of Racial Discrimination (1969), Human Rights Committee (1977), Committee on the Elimination of Discrimination Against Women (1981), Committee on Economic, Social and Cultural Rights (1985), Committee against Torture (1987), Committee on the Rights of the Child (1991), Committee on Migrant Workers (2004), Subcommittee on the Prevention of Torture (2007), Committee on the Rights of Persons with Disabilities (2009), Committee on Enforced Disappearances (2011). These Committees review, respectively, the Convention on the Elimination of All Forms of Racial Discrimination (CERD), the ICCPR, the Convention on the Elimination of all forms of Discrimination Against Women (CEDAW), the ICESCR, the Convention Against Torture (CAT) and its Optional Protocol, the Convention on the Rights of the Child and its Optional Protocols (CRC), the Convention on Migrant Workers (CMW), the Convention on the Rights of Persons with Disabilities (CRPD), and the Convention on Enforced Disappearances (CED).

treaties[14] means that the vast majority of states in the world are subject to periodic reviews, and potentially also to individual claims, before multiple treaty bodies. The resulting recommendations for the measures to be taken for improvement can be highly complementary. Given their differing expertise and perspectives, different treaty bodies often emphasize different aspects of rights protections.[15] Overlap in treaty body recommendations also can help to highlight the most serious human rights concerns in a country. Multiple periodic reviews create repeated opportunities for civil society engagement, media attention, and domestic and international public pressure to be brought to bear to improve a state's human rights situation.

As the *Mellet* case indicates, the treaty bodies contribute importantly to the contemporary doctrine of human rights, as well as to improving real lives on the ground for victims of human rights violations. However, the evolution of the treaty body system has lacked coherence. Multifarious reporting requirements place unnecessary and increasingly unsustainable burdens on states, civil society, and the treaty bodies themselves. The proliferation of treaty bodies, the near-complete autonomy with which they operate, and the resulting multiplication of review and reporting obligations for states, and recommendations and jurisprudence, have created increasing potential for confusion, resource duplication, reporting fatigue, substantive overlap, and potential conflict. The evolution of the treaty body system has lacked coherence, and the ten disparate part-time bodies, staffed by an under-resourced Secretariat, have experienced a trajectory of unchecked linear growth that in the long term is neither sustainable nor desirable. The treaties are, in part, the beneficiaries and victims of their own success. The treaty bodies also suffer from chronic late and non-reporting by states,[16] and low visibility in the overall human rights system. These challenges are longstanding and have grown with the increase in treaty bodies and state ratifications.[17]

[14] As of May 2020, only five states—Bhutan, Niue, Palau, Tonga, and Tuvalu—had ratified four or fewer multilateral human rights treaties. OHCHR, *Status of Ratification Interactive Dashboard*, available at: https://indicators.ohchr.org/ (last visited 18 April 2023).

[15] Jacob Blaustein Institute, *Treatment by the CAT and CERD of Issues Relevant to both Conventions: Five Case Studies* (2017), available at https://www.jbi-humanrights.org/CAT-CERD%20Study%20of%20Issues.pdf (last visited 18 April 2023). The study examined the practices of the CAT and CERD Committees in the periodic reviews of countries regarding discriminatory acts that could cause severe pain and suffering. The study found that the CAT Committee 'made significantly more detailed recommendations than [the] CERD [Committee] concerning the need for States to ensure independent investigations and accountability for perpetrators of torture and other particularly serious crimes ... and other physical integrity-related issues such as detention policies and conditions and the need to uphold the obligation of non-refoulement ... CERD was far more likely than CAT to identify broader issues affecting the situation of particularly vulnerable ethnic or minority groups and enhancing the group's susceptibility to harm, such as widely-held discriminatory attitudes against the group; profiling, and/or targeting of members of the particular group by the authorities; and/or the failure of the State party to enact or enforce legislation respecting rights of the particular group.'

[16] According to the 2020 report of the Secretary General, only 19% of periodic reports were submitted on time. UN Secretary General, Status of the human rights treaty body system, Report of the Secretary-General, UN Doc. A/74/643 (2020), para.11 (hereinafter '2020 Secretary-General Report').

[17] See generally, OHCHR, United Nations Reform: measures and proposals, UN Doc. A/66/860 (2012) (hereinafter '2012 Report').

In addition to the challenges involved in ensuring that the treaty bodies themselves function as a more coherent whole, the treaty bodies operate in parallel to the UN Charter-based mechanisms of the UN system, particularly the Human Rights Council, which has seen a corresponding expansion in human rights mechanisms. These now comprise, inter alia, the Universal Periodic Review (UPR)—a political peer review conducted every four years of the human rights record of every UN member state—and special procedures, including over 55 thematic and country special rapporteurs, as well as working groups and commissions of inquiry. Human rights issues are also addressed in the work of the UN General Assembly and the Security Council.

The UN system, in turn, is complemented by regional human rights systems—most notably in Africa, the Americas, and Europe—which are overseen by regional commissions and courts as well as supporting regional political mechanisms, such as the African Union, the Organization of American States, and the Council of Europe.[18] Human rights norms are also interpreted and enforced in other regional regimes, such as the European Union (EU), the Economic Community of West African States, the Andean Community and their accompanying courts, among others. The International Court of Justice and the ad hoc, hybrid, and international criminal courts similarly enforce overlapping norms with the international and regional human rights mechanisms. And human rights norms are also enforced directly or incorporated by domestic law into numerous national legal systems.

There is, at present, high fragmentation and lack of system-wide coordination among existing international and regional human rights mechanisms. The multifarious treaties, treaty bodies, special rapporteurs, working groups, regional commissions and courts, and other human rights mechanisms create an irregular, patchwork regime of human rights oversight. The disparate voices increase the risk that the noise in the system will prevent any particular voice from being heard and that overlap will lead to fatigue and confusion on the part of states, civil society, the media, and other actors.

I have contended elsewhere that the human rights system since its birth in the Universal Declaration of Human Rights has gone through three stages of development.[19] The first was the age of *universalization and internationalization*, when the human rights idea was introduced into the international system and codified into widely-ratified instruments. Second came the age of *institutionalization*, when

[18] Regional systems engaged in the interpretation and application of human rights standards include the African Commission on Human Rights and Court on Human and Peoples Rights, the European Court of Human Rights and the Court of Justice of the European Union, the Inter-American Commission and Court of Human Rights, the Arab Committee for Human Rights, and the Asian Human Rights Commission.

[19] S. H. Cleveland, 'Human Rights Treaty Bodies in the Age of Connectivity', in O. de Frouville (ed.), *Le Système de Protection des Droits de L'Homme des Nations Unies: Présent et Avenir* (2018), 79–81.

the major institutional architecture of our international and regional human rights mechanisms was created.

We are now in the age of *connectivity*, in which we need to better develop the substantive, communicative, and institutional relationships—or *synapses*—among these instruments, and between our human rights institutions, states, and civil society, among others.

The challenge to the future of the treaty body system then is two-fold: How to ensure connectivity among the treaty bodies so that they function as an effective, integrated system? And, how to ensure sufficient connectivity between the treaty bodies and the other mechanisms of the global human rights regime? This chapter illustrates two core aspects of this challenge: securing connectivity among the treaty bodies and with the UPR in the periodic review of states, and securing jurisprudential connectivity between the treaty bodies and the regional human rights systems.

2. Creating a Treaty Body 'System': Connectivity in the Periodic Reviews of States

The Human Rights Committee represented the dilution of an original proposal for a World Court of Human Rights. That idea has been periodically resurrected, as has the idea of a single, permanent, standing treaty body to fill the functions currently performed under the various multilateral human rights treaties—most notably in the 2006 proposal by the High Commissioner for Human Rights.[20] Although that proposal proved too ambitious for states at the time, a single, permanent treaty body may ultimately be needed to address current resource, capacity, and coordination constraints. In the current posture of the system, however, creating such a body would require amendment of the treaties themselves, and would pose significant practical and legal challenges, particularly with respect to consideration of individual communications, in light of the specificity of the individual treaties and the uneven ratifications of the treaties by states.[21] Nevertheless, in the near-to-midterm, it would be possible to achieve significant coordination of the periodic reporting and country examination function of treaty bodies with only modest

[20] OHCHR, Concept Paper on the High Commissioner's Proposal for a Unified Standing Treaty Body, UN Doc. HRI/MC/2006/2 (2006). For perspectives on a World Court of Human Rights see, e.g., O. de Frouville, *From Cosmopolitanism to Human Rights* (2021); Gaer, 'The Institutional Future of the Covenants: A World Court for Human Rights?', in D. Moeckli, H. Keller, and C. Heri (eds), *The Human Rights Covenants at 50: Their Past, Present, and Future* (2018), 334–56; Alston, 'Against a World Court for Human Rights', 28/2 *Ethics & International Affairs* (2014) 197–212; Nowak, 'It's Time for a World Court of Human Rights', in M. Cherif Bassiouni and W. A. Schabas (eds), *New Challenges for the UN Human Rights Machinery: What Future for the UN Treaty Body System and the Human Rights Council Procedures?* (2011).

[21] For an excellent explication of the current challenges posed by consideration of individual communications in a single, combined treaty body, see Gaer (n. 20) 334–356.

alteration of their current practices, through the establishment of clustered reviews and a global reporting calendar.

Under the existing periodic review system, states parties are obligated to report to each treaty body pursuant to separate timelines prescribed by the individual treaty bodies or by the constitutive instruments governing their work.[22] The resulting administrative burden imposed on states by the sheer number of periodic state reports, responses to 'lists of issues,' and follow-up reports, and the need to travel to Geneva repeatedly to engage in 'constructive dialogues' with the different Committees, is compounded by the lack of coordination between the different treaty body reporting schedules and the substantive overlap in written and oral questions and recommendations presented by the Committees to reporting states. Use of recommendations issued by one Committee to help compose a later treaty body's own list of issues promotes mutual support and consistency in the work of the treaty bodies, but also creates much repetition in state reporting, oral dialogues, and the Committees' resulting 'concluding observations,' or recommendations. It is thus perhaps not surprising that many states, especially small states, experience 'reporting fatigue,' and increasingly question the utility of having to repetitively defend before different treaty bodies—on an almost random schedule, sometimes within weeks of one another—the same policies and to face similar recommendations.

The 'simplified reporting procedure' utilized by a growing number of treaty bodies allows states to replace their periodic reports with written replies to lists of issues prepared by the respective Committee, and constitutes a partial response to the concerns of excessive reporting burdens (in part by shifting some of the burden of gathering information from the states themselves to the treaty bodies and the Office of the High Commissioner for Human Rights (OHCHR) Secretariat). The

[22] Art. 40 of the ICCPR prescribes one year from the date of entry into force of the Covenant for the initial report, and leaves it to the Human Rights Committee to designate dates for subsequent reports (in practice, the Committee currently uses a periodicity of three to six years—determining the precise period chiefly on the basis the urgency of the human rights situation in the state party and the availability of other international review mechanisms); Art. 17 of the ICESCR delegates the fixing of timelines for reporting to the UN Economic and Social Council (ECOSOC). ECOSOC Resolution 1988/4 fixed an initial two-year period for the first report, and a subsequent five-year reporting period; Art. 9 of the CERD provides for an initial reporting period of one year, followed by a two-year reporting cycle (which the Committee can change; in practice, the Committee normally asks for combined reports at four year intervals); Art. 18 of CEDAW provides for an initial reporting period of one year, followed by a reporting cycle of at least every four years (which the Committee can change); Art. 19 of the CAT provides for an initial reporting period of one year, followed by a four-year reporting cycle; Art. 73 of the Migrant Workers Convention (MWC) provides for an initial reporting period of one year, followed by a five-year reporting cycle (which the Committee can change); Art. 35 of the CRPD provides for an initial reporting period of two years, followed by a reporting cycle of at least every four years (which the Committee can change); Art. 44 of the CRC provides for an initial reporting period of two years, followed by a five-year reporting cycle; Art. 29 of the CED provides for an initial reporting period of two years; subsequent reports are requested by the Committee at intervals of three to six years. The tenth UN treaty body, the Subcommittee on Prevention of Torture (SPT) established by the Optional Protocol to the CAT, has other mechanisms for engaging with states parties.

simplified procedure does not, however, address problems of substantive repetition and coordination of the numerous periodic reviews and reporting obligations. Short of a substantial reworking of the entire system to combine the treaty bodies into a single functioning mechanism, one way to achieve substantial coherence in the periodic review process would be to create a coordinated global reporting calendar for all nine treaty bodies that conduct periodic reviews of states parties.

This proposal for a comprehensive periodic review calendar would organize reviews of states before all the treaty bodies for which the state is a party on an eight-year cycle, with the result that each treaty body would review a state once every eight years.[23] In addition, treaty body reviews would be clustered into two batches of back-to-back reviews, each four years apart. States would thus appear in Geneva twice for oral dialogues before treaty bodies during an eight-year cycle. One possibility for the clustering of treaty body reviews would be to group the reviews of a particular state by the two covenant treaty bodies together (the HRC and the CESCR), followed four years later by a clustered review before the specialized treaty bodies. This arrangement could allow for the most comprehensive review of rights in each of the clustered sessions. Another possibility might be to cluster the reviews by treaty bodies overseeing treaties focused on particular rights, on the one hand (ICCPR, CESCR, CERD, CED, CAT), and of treaties focused on particular groups (CEDAW, CRC, CRPD, CMW), on the other. The precise combination of reviews for any particular state would also depend on the state's ratification records.

Although some may feel that a four-year gap between reviews by treaty bodies is too long to provide effective continuous oversight over a state's human rights record, examination of the actual practice of the treaty bodies indicates that most treaty bodies in fact only review a particular state roughly every eight years, regardless of the periodicity indicated by their mandates or rules of procedure.[24] Moreover, in reality, the system would involve a much more constant process of treaty body engagement with states. For example, in year one, a common list of issues would be generated. In year two, the state's consolidated reply would be due. In year three, the oral dialogue would occur in Geneva. In year five, the state's follow-up report on implementation of the priority recommendations from the prior review would be due, followed by consideration of that report by the respective treaty bodies.

[23] A variant of this concept is set forth in several reports prepared for the General Assembly's 2020 review of the treaty body system, including the 2020 Secretary-General Report (n. 16) paras 60–61, and the report of the Geneva Academy; see Geneva Academy of International Humanitarian Law and Human Rights, *Optimizing the UN Treaty Body System* (2018) 21. A somewhat analogous proposal for a 'comprehensive reporting calendar' was made by High Commissioner Navi Pillay in 2012. That proposal, however, called for a predictable schedule for submission of reports of all states parties on a five-year cycle. It did not provide for coordination and clustering of the reviews themselves, with the accompanying efficiencies. See 2012 Report (n. 17) 37.

[24] Geneva Academy (n. 23) 21.

In addition, the four-year cycle of the two clustered treaty body reviews could be coordinated with the four-year Universal Periodic Review calendar of the Human Rights Council, so that the UPR for a state would follow at the two-year mark between the clustered treaty body reviews. Under this approach, a state would appear in Geneva four times in the eight-year cycle: twice for treaty body sessions and twice for UPR sessions, with each review two years apart.See an illustration of this eight-year cycle in Table 4.1.

One of the benefits of a regime in which separate treaty bodies conduct back-to-back periodic reviews of a state is that this approach allows for significant coordination of the reviews while preserving the distinct specificity of each treaty. An important ongoing concern raised regarding consolidation of the treaty bodies into a single permanent body involves the potential loss of the specific characteristics of the individual treaties. Although many of the rights in the major multilateral human rights treaties overlap in certain respects, the treaties have different operative texts; they were negotiated at different times; they have different negotiating histories; and they have somewhat distinct jurisprudence regarding their interpretation. States may also be parties to some treaties and not others, and therefore may resist a homogenized approach to treaty interpretation. In addition, the specialized treaties are designed to ensure that their particular thematic focus (whether torture or disability or children's rights, etc.) is not overlooked. Preserving the specificity of the individual treaties therefore is an important value of the current system. Another benefit of this approach is that it helps maximize coordination among the treaty bodies without requiring amendment of the treaty provisions governing their work.[25]

Clustering treaty body views in this manner would create an ongoing, continuous process of human rights oversight by the treaty bodies, with substantial opportunities for coordination and streamlining of reviews, to more sharply focus on the expertise of each treaty body. Each clustered review session could be based on a single, consolidated list of issues from the participating treaty bodies and a single written reply from the state. As a result of the clustering of reviews, states would receive more coordinated questions in the oral dialogue and more coordinated concluding recommendations from each of the treaty bodies participating in the cycle. Although such a regime would not, and should not, entirely eliminate overlap in the issues and recommendations for each treaty body, coordination or

[25] To the extent that the relevant treaties themselves establish reporting periodicity requirements (see n. 22), for example, application of those requirements appears sufficiently flexible to accommodate an eight-year calendar. Initial reports would need to be submitted according to the specific treaty-designated timelines, but subsequent treaty-mandated obligations to submit written reports could be accommodated, for example, through written replies to lists of issues and by written follow-up reports. Or for another example, although the CERD establishes a two-year reporting cycle, the CERD Committee in practice has combined two periodic reports into a single report submitted after four years. The CERD Committee likewise could consider the submission of two combined annual follow-up reports as constituting the subsequent prescribed two-year reports.

Table 4.1 Example of clustered treaty body reviews on an eight-year cycle integrated with the Universal Periodic Review (repeating every eight years)

Year	1	2	3	4	5	6	7	8
Treaty Body Cluster 1	**Clustered TB review**		State Follow-up Report / Follow-up Review				Coordinated List of Issues	State Reply to List of Issues
Treaty Body Cluster 2			Coordinated List of Issues	State Reply to List of Issues	**Clustered TB Review**		State Follow-up Report / Follow-up Review	
UPR Cycle			**UPR Review**				**UPR Review**	

consolidation of the work of the clustered treaty bodies would help to ensure that such overlap reflected an intentional effort on the part of the treaty bodies to reinforce their recommendations with respect to the most critical issues facing a state party. In other words, overlap should be intentional, to increase the effectiveness of the system, not random or accidental.

Such a clustered reporting system would significantly reduce the complexity, overlap, and redundancy of periodic reporting and oral review process, and thus facilitate states' participation in the system. It would also improve 'connectivity' among treaty body examinations: the system would encourage the treaty bodies to function more as a single coherent system, in which the treaty bodies participating in each cluster could divide topics among themselves and rely upon and reinforce each other's work in a coherent manner. It would allow streamlining of effort with respect to reporting, dialogue questions, concluding recommendations, and follow-up for states, civil society, and the treaty bodies alike.

A predictable, clustered treaty body review schedule would make each review cluster a more significant occasion, rationalize the system, and thus increase the visibility of the treaty body reviews more generally. It would thereby also increase the incentives for states to participate and report in a timely manner, as well as the visibility and access to the system for civil society, and ultimately the incentives for states to comply. Greater connectivity would thus not only rationalize the treaty body system, but enhance its overall effectiveness.

An important additional benefit of this approach would be to systematically bring egregiously late and non-reporting states into the review system. Since the beginning of the treaty body system, the workload and resources allocated to the treaty bodies have been measured according to the number of states whose reports were actually submitted and pending, rather than the number of states whose reports were due. In a system with substantial egregiously late and non-reporting by many states, this meant that only states that actually complied with their reporting obligations were subject to review, while states that failed to report evaded review altogether. In recent years, a number of treaty bodies have sought to remedy this significant loophole by scheduling reviews for very late or non-reporting states, regardless whether they had submitted a report. It has also been the experience of the Human Rights Committee that states so designated generally did ultimately submit a report and appear for the oral dialogue in Geneva. In other words, simply scheduling states for review and holding to that schedule helps bring states parties back into the review system.

In order to maintain such a calendar, states necessarily would be expected to report and participate in the oral dialogues on time (as they currently do in the UPR process). Absent a substantial justification, states that failed to report would simply be reviewed in the absence of a report. Moving to an eight-year cycle, with all states reporting, would thus result in a very significant *increase* in the overall monitoring of states by the treaty bodies over the current system. Under an eight-year cycle, the treaty bodies would be able to review all states parties in the treaty body system, without increasing the current 91 weeks of total meeting time of the treaty bodies.

Organization of treaty body reviews according to a predictable eight-year calendar would also promote greater accessibility and connectivity for the treaty body periodic reviews with the work of the Human Rights Council and its UPR and special procedures, including the work of the special rapporteurs and working groups.

The UPR, conducted for all UN member states by the Human Rights Council every 4.5 years, currently is organized entirely independently of the treaty body system. Treaty bodies themselves increasingly reference recommendations made and positions taken by states during the UPR process as part of the treaty body periodic review process, and materials submitted during the UPR process increasingly are an important source of information for treaty body reviews of states. Some information regarding treaty body reviews of a state is also compiled for the UPR process. However, the UPR and the treaty body review processes could consciously be made much more integrated and complementary.

For example, making the treaty body reviews more visible and accessible in general, and their outputs more usable by these and other entities would allow a compilation of consolidated treaty body recommendations, views, and follow-up assessments to be more readily accessed for each state reviewed in the UPR process. In addition, organizing two clustered treaty body country examinations on an eight-year calendar, punctuated by UPR examinations in the intervening years, would structurally integrate the UPR and treaty body review processes, as noted. Consolidation of treaty body reviews and coordination of their timing with the UPR would allow the UPR process to be more self-consciously employed to provide a form of political follow-up regarding state implementation of treaty body recommendations, and vice versa. The UPR is a political, peer review process, in which states are asked to 'accept' or 'note' the recommendations received from other states. This process has the advantage that states are forced to take recommendations from the UPR back to their capitols and provoke a domestic discussion. The UPR should not be used to second-guess or compete with treaty body recommendations, which are the product of an *independent, expert, detailed legal* evaluation. But with more user-friendly and accessible information from the treaty bodies and coordination of their schedules, the UPR could be used to reinforce and encourage state implementation of treaty body recommendations and individual communications.[26]

To date, the treaty bodies have not fully embraced the idea of a universal coordinated calendar. However, important progress toward this goal is being made. The Human Rights Committee has adopted a fixed predictable calendar to review the more than 170 states parties to the ICCPR over an eight-year review cycle. The Committee also adopted internal guidelines regarding the extent to which it would engage with states on issues that either had recently been examined, or would soon be examined, by other treaty bodies. The CESCR Committee is also adopting a predictable eight-year calendar. With pilot consenting states, some treaty bodies have experimented with preparing for coordinated Lists of Issues Prior to Reporting (LOIPR) and coordinated state reviews. The HRC and CESCR, for example, coordinated the LOIPR for Finland and the actual review of Senegal, while the CEDAW and CAT Committees coordinated the LOIPR for Panama. The chairpersons of the treaty bodies have also agreed to establish a predictable schedule for reviewing state reports, with an eight-year review cycle for full reviews, coupled with interim follow-up reviews, that incorporates review of all states parties.[27]

The adoption of such predictable review calendars by each treaty body would then allow the OHCHR Secretariat to publish a comprehensive predictable calendar of the reviews by all the treaty bodies. It would also allow the committees to coordinate the resulting reviews, at least to the extent that two or more treaty bodies would be reviewing the same state in close proximity in time. This would

[26] For further discussion of ways to strengthen the relationship between the treaty bodies and the UN Human Rights Council mechanisms, see generally Carraro, 'The United Nations Treaty Bodies and Universal Periodic Review: Advancing Human Rights by Preventing Politicization?', 39 *Human Rights Quarterly* (2017) 943; International Service for Human Rights et al., *The Special Procedures: Strengthening the Mechanism and Working Methods* (2016); Rodley, 'UN Treaty Bodies and the Human Rights Council', in H. Keller and G. Ulfstein (eds), *UN Human Rights Treaty Bodies: Law & Legitimacy* (2012).

[27] 34th meeting of the Chairpersons of the Human Rights Treaty Bodies (2022), https://www.ohchr.org/en/events/meetings/2022/34th-meeting-chairpersons-human-rights-treaty-bodies (last visited 12 February 2024).

be an important step towards allowing the treaty body periodic review process to function as a coordinated and mutually reinforcing system.

Returning to the opening example of Ireland, the Republic of Ireland presently is party to the two Covenants (ICCPR and ICESCR), the CAT, CEDAW, CERD, CRC, and CRPD. According to the sample eight-year calendar above, treaty body connectivity through a clustered review regime could mean, as one possible approach, that Ireland would be reviewed by the two Covenant treaty bodies on year one, with a review by the specialized treaty bodies for the treaties to which it is a party on year five. Consolidated follow-up proceedings to the relevant clustered treaty body recommendations could be conducted two years after each of the periodic reviews—in years three and seven. Ireland's UPR in the Human Rights Council could be held the same year as the treaty body follow-ups.

For the specific example of the topic in *Mellet*, such a regime would allow the treaty bodies that have engaged with the issue of Ireland's restrictions on reproductive health services (the HRC, CESCR, CAT, CEDAW, and CRC Committees)[28] to consider among themselves which treaty bodies were best positioned to address that issue for Ireland in each clustered review session. Clustering reviews on a predictable review cycle would allow the treaty bodies to coordinate on this issue from the initial point of drafting the coordinated list of issues, to decide which treaty bodies would have primary responsibility for engaging on the issue during the dialogue with the Irish delegation, and to coordinate their concluding observations on this issue. It would allow for coordinated follow-up by the clustered treaty bodies on their recommendations to Ireland. It would also create stronger synergies between the treaty body reviews and the UPR, heightening the capacity for cross-fertilization of information between the legal and political review systems, strengthening the ability of the treaty bodies to pressure states to implement UPR recommendations that the state had accepted or to accept those that they had noted, and in turn allowing states to reinforce the work of the treaty bodies through the recommendations made in the UPR process.

Greater connectivity among the treaty bodies and with the UPR process, in short, will enhance not only the profile and efficiency of the work of the treaty bodies, but also allow them to mutually leverage their efforts to enhance the overall effectiveness of the UN human rights system.

[28] See n. 6.

3. Jurisprudential Connectivity and the Regional Human Rights Systems

The treaty bodies do not exist in isolation from each other. Nor do they exist in isolation from other international and regional human rights mechanisms, including the major regional human rights systems in Europe, the Americas, and Africa. Whether consciously or not, treaty bodies and regional human rights mechanisms reinforce each other's work in a number of ways. Treaty body country examinations address issues that may also be addressed by regional human rights courts and commissions. Activities in each system also may help scrutinize and encourage implementation of recommendations and judgments made by the other system. For example, on multiple occasions in its periodic reviews of states, the Human Rights Committee has recommended that particular states take action that would implement, inter alia, decisions of the regional human rights courts and commissions.[29] The Committee has also recognized the importance of the regional human rights systems as partners in promoting human rights implementation, expressing concern when states flout or withdraw from regional human rights oversight.[30]

Nevertheless, there is a need for greater complementarity and connectivity between the UN treaty bodies and regional human rights systems, in order to preserve scarce resources, support the development of coherent jurisprudence where appropriate, and to mutually enhance the work of human rights monitoring and protection in a more self-conscious and strategic manner.[31]

[29] HRC, Concluding observations on the sixth periodic report of Hungary, UN Doc. CCPR/C/HUN/CO/6 (2018), paras 53–54 (urging revision of restrictions on foreign funding of civil society groups in light of, inter alia, 'the opinion adopted in this regard by the . . . Venice Commission'); HRC, Concluding observations on the sixth periodic report of the Dominican Republic, UN Doc. CCPR/C/DOM/CO/6, Nov. 2017, paras 5–6, 25–26 (urging restoration of recognition of the competence of the Inter-American Court and compliance with the Court's judgement in IACtHR, *Case of Expelled Dominicans and Haitians v. Dominican Republic*, Judgment (Preliminary Objection, Merits, Reparations, and Costs), 28 August 2014); HRC, Concluding observations on the third periodic report of Bosnia Herzegovina, UN Doc. CCPR/C/BIH/CO/3 (2017), paras 11–12 (expressing concern at the failure to revise elections laws to eliminate discrimination against certain ethnic groups in light of recommendations of the Committee 'and the judgments of the European Court of Human Rights'). See also HRC, Concluding observations on the fifth periodic report of the Sudan, UN Doc. CCPR/C/SDN/CO/5 (2018), paras 12–13 (expressing concern at lack of cooperation with the International Criminal Court); HRC, Concluding observations on the initial report of South Africa, UN Doc. CCPR/C/ZAF/CO/1, paras 8–9 (expressing concern over failure to comply with domestic court ruling directing cooperation with International Criminal Court).

[30] HRC, Concluding observations on the sixth periodic report of the Dominican Republic (n. 29), paras 5–6 ('The Committee supports the State party's expressed intention to once more accept the competence of the Inter-American Court of Human Rights'); HRC, Concluding observations on the seventh periodic report of the United Kingdom of Great Britain and Northern Ireland, UN Doc. CCPR/C/GBR/CO/7 (2015), paras 5–6 (expressing concern at proposal to repeal the Human Rights Act of 1998, which incorporated protections of the European Convention on Human Rights into domestic law); HRC, Concluding observations on the fourth periodic report of the Bolivarian Republic of Venezuela, UN Doc. CCPR/C/VEN/CO/4 (2015), paras 22–23 (expressing concern at denunciation of the American Convention on Human Rights).

[31] For a general discussion of connectivity within the regional human rights systems, see Cleveland (n. 19) 87–90.

One challenge in the relationship between regional and UN human rights treaty body mechanisms involves how the jurisprudence of these entities should be understood to interact. The jurisprudence of each system can be mutually reinforcing with respect to general principles of doctrine, and also with respect to specific violations in specific countries.[32]

Multiple human rights treaties at the international and regional levels protect similar rights—whether protection against torture or the right to privacy or education—but define and interpret those concepts somewhat differently. What should be the jurisprudential relationship among these systems? If states that are parties to two different treaties receive different interpretations regarding compliance with their various human rights obligations, is that a healthy dynamic for the overall system that promotes continuous examination and development of our understanding of human rights norms? Or does it result in competing obligations, disorder, and ultimately frustration and disillusionment with the system? How does the human rights system promote substantive coherence and avoid cacophony, while also preserving the distinctive legal features and the specificity of different human rights treaties? This dilemma, of course, is not unique to the human rights system. It also raises broader issues that have been considered in the fields of international law, comparative law, and international relations in terms of 'fragmentation'[33] and 'inter-judicial dialogue'.[34]

It is crucial that the various human rights norm-enunciating mechanisms not be hermetically sealed from each other. They should have robust systems for sharing information, and some jurisprudential competition among the various mechanisms is healthy for the system overall. Norms that are articulated in one forum can and should migrate and inform doctrinal developments in other jurisdictions.

The issue of jurisprudential coherence versus norm specificity also arises within the UN treaty body system. What, for example, should be the relevance of jurisprudence of the Children's Committee, the Disability Committee, or the CEDAW Committee for the Human Rights Committee's interpretation of the special

[32] For an exploration of this topic in relation to the International Court of Justice, see Rodley, 'The International Court of Justice and Human Rights Treaty Bodies', in M. Andenas and E. Bjorge (eds), *A Farewell to Fragmentation: Reassertion and Convergence in International Law* (2015) 87. Shany, 'The Interplay Between the Global and the Regional,' in N. Jain and M. Versteeq (eds), *Oxford Handbook on Comparative Human Rights Law* (Forthcoming), https://papers.ssrn.com/sol3/papers.cfm?abstract_id=4574303 (last visited 12 February 2024).

[33] Payandeh, 'Fragmentation within International Human Rights Law', in M. Andenas and E. Bjorge (eds), *A Farewell To Fragmentation: Reassertion and Convergence in International Law* (2015) 297–319; M. Koskenniemi, Fragmentation of International Law: Difficulties Arising from the Diversification and Expansion of International Law, UN Doc. A/CN.4/L.682 (2006). See also Crawford, 'Chance, Order, Change: The Course of International Law' 365 *Collected Courses of The Hague Academy of International Law* (2013) 205–229.

[34] A. Müller and H. E. Kjos, *Judicial Dialogue and Human Rights* (2017); Mac-Gregor, 'What Do We Mean When We Talk about Judicial Dialogue: Reflections of a Judge of the Inter-American Court of Human Rights', 30 *Harvard Human Rights Journal* 89 (2017); Kassoti, 'Fragmentation and inter-judicial dialogue: the CJEU and the ICJ at the interface', 8/2 *European Journal of Legal Studies* (2015) 21–49.

protection owed to children and the prohibition on discrimination on the basis of disability or sex under the ICCPR? And what, in turn, should be the relevance of the Human Rights Committee's jurisprudence on these issues to the decisions of those treaty bodies under their respective treaties?

The issue of jurisprudential coherence also arises between the treaty bodies and the regional courts of human rights, and, as a matter of practice, particularly with the European Court of Human Rights. This is true because many European countries are parties to the individual complaints mechanisms that give UN treaty bodies authority to hear individual cases, and Europe also has a human rights bar that is practised in utilizing both the European and UN human rights complaint mechanisms. All the regional systems, however, consider human rights issues that may overlap in various ways with the jurisdiction of the treaty bodies, and vice versa.

The relationship to the jurisprudence of other bodies arises particularly acutely for the Human Rights Committee because Article 5(2)(a) of the Optional Protocol to the ICCPR, which requires that 'the same matter is not *being examined* under another procedure of international investigation or settlement' (emphasis added), allows the Committee to hear cases that have already been reviewed, but are no longer pending before another international body, unless the claim was affirmatively resolved on the merits.[35] Unlike most regional and international adjudicatory bodies, this clause allows the Committee to consider the 'same matter' that was submitted by the same parties to a different regional or international mechanism, so long as the claim is no longer 'being examined' there. A number of European states have entered a reservation to this aspect of the Optional Protocol, declining to accept the Committee's competence to examine the same 'matter' that was previously considered by the Strasbourg court.

These features have produced a number of interesting dialogues between the regional human rights courts and the treaty bodies regarding interpretation and application of rights. I offer here three examples from the Human Rights Committee, involving jurisdictional conflicts, consideration of the same claim, and consideration of the same legal issue.

A. Jurisdictional Conflicts

First, with respect to *jurisdictional conflicts*, the Committee has interpreted protective reservations by European states to Article 5(2)(a) of the Optional Protocol as precluding examination when another 'procedure of international investigation or settlement' (usually the European Court) has previously based a determination

[35] HRC, *Correia De Matos v. Portugal*, UN Doc. CCPR/C/86/D/1123/2002 (2006), para. 6.2.

of inadmissibility on some consideration, even if limited, of the merits of the case.[36] Then the same matter would be deemed to have been 'examined' by the other body, even if it was rejected as manifestly ill-founded. This approach allows the Committee to consider cases that were previously rejected by another international body on purely procedural grounds (including non-exhaustion of domestic remedies, *ratione temporis*, or incompatibility *ratione materiae*), even for states that have entered a reservation to Article 5(2)(a).[37] In the view of the Committee, this is because a determination of inadmissibility on procedural grounds does not mean that the matter has been previously 'examined.'[38]

The European Court's consideration of the merits also must be clear. In *Achabal Puertas v. Spain*,[39] the Committee confronted a formulaic determination by the European Court in the form of a letter stating that a Committee of three judges had decided to declare the action inadmissible since they 'did not observe any apparent violation of the rights and freedoms guaranteed by the Convention or its Protocols.' The Committee concluded that this formulaic statement did not establish that the European Court had sufficiently considered the merits for the Committee to determine that the same matter had been previously examined by the Court.

In *Achabal*, the European Court of Human Rights had rejected the author's claim under Article 3 of the European Convention (addressing torture and cruel, inhuman or degrading treatment or punishment), and the author then brought the same claim to the Human Rights Committee under Article 7 of the ICCPR. The Committee found that Spain had violated Article 7 of the Covenant, despite the finding of inadmissibility by the European Court and Spain's reservation to Article 5(2)(a). Six members of the Committee dissented. Members Flinterman and Salvioli wrote separately to explain that the Court had sent the minimalist letter to the author three years after she had submitted her case, without the Court ever sending her application to the state party or providing any further explanation for the rejection. They further noted that in a case involving serious allegations regarding risk to the physical integrity and life of the complainant, the inadmissibility decision should make clear that the Court gave sufficient attention to the merits of the case to constitute an examination. Otherwise, the Committee could legitimately consider the communication admissible.[40]

[36] See e.g., HRC, *Wdowiak v. Poland*, UN Doc. CCPR/C/88/D/1446/2006 (2006), para. 6.2 (involving a reservation that 'excludes the procedure set out in article 5, paragraph 2(a), in cases where the matter has already been examined under another procedure of international investigation or settlement').

[37] For a critique of this practice, see O'Boyle, '*Ne bis in idem* for the Benefit of States?', in L. Caflisch et al. (eds), *Liber Amicorum Luzius Wildhaber: Human Rights—Strasbourg Views/Droits de l'homme—Regards de Strasbourg* (2007), 329.

[38] *Wdowiak*, para. 6.2.

[39] HRC, *Maria Cruz Achabal Puertas v. Spain*, UN Doc. CCPR/C/107/D/1945/2010 (2013), paras 7.2–7.3.

[40] *Achabal Puertas v. Spain* (individual opinion of members Flinterman and Salvioli) (n. 39) para. 4.

This jurisdictional dynamic was exacerbated as the European Court moved to a streamlined single-judge procedure for threshold admissibility determinations as part of the reforms adopted to address the Court's exploding caseload. When confronted with formulaic declarations from the Court that a single judge had declared an application inadmissible on the grounds that 'the conditions of admissibility laid down in articles 34 and 35 of the European Convention were not met,' the Committee declined to attempt to divine, case-by-case in light of the particular facts of each case, whether and to what extent such a declaration of inadmissibility by the Court was based on procedural grounds or involved 'a certain consideration of the merits' that would allow a reservation to bar admissibility before the Committee. The Committee instead took the position that absent any explanation by the Court that the merits of the case *had* been examined, the Committee would not consider such a communication barred by a reservation to Article 5(2)(a).[41] In short, the Committee insisted that the Court provide transparent reasoning for its inadmissibility decisions or the Committee would not defer to them.

Reasonable minds may differ regarding whether an international body such as the Committee should review human rights claims that already have been rejected by another international adjudicatory body. That decision apparently was made during the drafting of the Optional Protocol, however. There are also sound grounds for the Committee's position with respect to pro forma dismissals by the European Court. In circumstances where the Court provides no clear guidance regarding whether the grounds for inadmissibility were procedural or substantive, the parties and the Committee could expend substantial time and resources trying to divine the Court's basis for a dismissal. By contrast, it would be quite easy for the Court that made the inadmissibility decision to provide a brief explanation of the basis. Beyond that, the European Convention obligates the Court to provide reasons for its decisions, including those relating to admissibility.[42] And it is a basic principle of the rule of law, transparency, and the right to fair trial that courts should provide reasoned explanations for their decisions. Failure to explain inadmissibility decisions leaves applicants not knowing, for example, whether the grounds for rejection was one that could be repaired (such as exhaustion of domestic remedies), so that the claim might still be pursued, or whether the determination was final and on the merits.

Aspects of the Committee's position have received sharp criticism in some circles, including from the dissenting members in *Achabal*. However, this dialogue between the Committee and the European Court yielded a healthy correction

[41] HRC, *Hebbadj v. France*, UN Doc. CCPR/C/123/D/2807/2016 (2018), paras 6.2–6.4; HRC, *A.G.S. v. Spain*, UN Doc. CCPR/C/115/D/2626/2015 (2015), para. 4.2; HRC, *Mahabir v. Austria*, UN Doc. CCPR/C/82/D/944/2000 (2004), paras 8.2–8.5.

[42] Art. 45(1) ECHR ('Reasons shall be given for judgments as well as for decisions declaring applications admissible or inadmissible.').

in the practices of the Court. In 2019 the Court revised its rules of procedure to require that admissibility decisions by a single judge include a summary of the reasoning for the decision.[43] In short, the jurisdictional competition between the Committee and the European Court helped prompt an outcome that improved the transparency of the Court's inadmissibility decisions, for states, parties, and other tribunals and stakeholders alike.

B. Consideration of the Same Claim

Absent a reservation by a state party, the Human Rights Committee's Optional Protocol allows for re-examination of the same claims, brought by the same party, that have previously been considered on the merits in another body such as a regional system. This is a rare occurrence, but such a case can pose significant challenges for the Committee. One example of such a dialogue between the treaty body and a regional system is the Committee's 2017 Views in *Castillo v. Venezuela*.[44] That case involved the enforced disappearance in Venezuela in 2003 of Joe Luis Castillo, a human rights defender, and the Inter-American Commission on Human Rights' subsequent issuance of precautionary measures to protect his wife and child. The Inter-American Commission ultimately found multiple violations of the American Convention due to, inter alia, Venezuela's insufficient investigation of the disappearance, and in particular, of allegations of collusion between local authorities and paramilitaries in the disappearance.[45] On review before the Inter-American Court of Human Rights, however, the Court found no violations,[46] in a decision that was criticized in some circles as inconsistent with the Court's jurisprudence and politically motivated. Castillo's wife, Yelitze Lisbeth Moreno de Castillo, then brought the case to the Human Rights Committee on behalf of herself and her deceased husband and son.

Castillo presented a difficult situation for the Committee because, unlike many of the cases that come to that body after being summarily rejected as inadmissible by the European Court of Human Rights, here there was a detailed analysis of the facts and law on the merits from two mechanisms of a regional system—the Inter-American Commission and Court—with the two bodies reaching opposite conclusions.

In finding no violation in the case, the Human Rights Committee noted that the Inter-American Commission and Court had 'thoroughly reviewed essentially the same claims made by the author against the State party and issued fully reasoned

[43] See Rule 52A(1) ECtHR (providing that an inadmissibility decision by a single judge 'shall contain a summary reasoning').

[44] HRC, *Castillo v. Bolivarian Republic of Venezuela*, UN Doc. CCPR/C/121/D/2610/2015 (2017).

[45] IACHR, *Joe Luis Castillo González et al. v. Venezuela*, Report No. 120/10, Case No. 12.605 (22 October 2010).

[46] IACtHR, *Castillo González et al. v. Venezuela* (27 November 2012).

decisions on them.'[47] The Committee then deferred substantially to the findings of the Inter-American Court, to find no substantive or procedural violations. The Committee observed that in assessing a state party's compliance with its obligations to conduct a prompt, thorough, and effective investigation under the Covenant, 'the Committee gives considerable weight to the findings of international courts, when those have engaged in collection and analysis of evidence, including witness testimonies.' In light of the findings of the Inter-American Court, the Committee concluded that the information before the Committee did 'not contain sufficient elements to contradict those findings and thus cannot lead the Committee to the conclusion that the domestic proceedings did not meet the State party's obligations under the Covenant.'[48]

I dissented from this conclusion. I observed that the Committee never explained why it gave 'due weight' to the conclusion of the Court (admittedly the final authority in the Inter-American system) over that of the Commission, where the two had reached diametrically opposed conclusions. The Committee also did not explain why deference to the Court was warranted, where the legal standard for adequate investigations applied by the Inter-American Court appeared inconsistent with the Court's own prior and subsequent jurisprudence.[49]

More concerningly, the claim had been brought under Article 6 of the ICCPR, and the Committee never independently analysed or explained how the state's investigation satisfied the Committee's *own standards* for an adequate investigation under Article 6. These standards have long required that investigations must be independent, impartial, prompt, thorough, effective, credible, and transparent. States parties must take appropriate measures to establish the truth relating to the events leading to the deprivation of life, including revealing the reasons for targeting certain individuals.[50]

Unfortunately, because the Inter-American Court had deferred to the Venezuelan authorities regarding the appropriate scope of the investigation, and because the Committee in turn deferred to the Court's decision, neither the Committee nor the Court ever independently considered whether the investigation was adequate in light of its full potential scope.

The Committee was correct that regional human rights commissions and courts, which can receive evidence and live testimony, generally are better positioned to determine facts than UN treaty bodies. And certainly, when such an examination has been conducted, the need for stability, predictability, and coherence in the overall human rights system suggests that a treaty body should only

[47] *Castillo* (n. 44), para. 8.3.
[48] Ibid. para. 9.6.
[49] Ibid. Individual opinion of Committee member Sarah Cleveland, para. 5.
[50] Ibid. para. 11 (citing HRC, General Comment No. 36, the right to life, UN Doc. CCPR/C/GC/36 (2018), para. 28).

second-guess such a decision by a regional mechanism with great care. However, a treaty body also is not a court of appeal, engaging in deferential review of a regional court judgment. It has a horizontal relationship to the regional mechanism as it exercises jurisdiction over the same claim. If a treaty body exercises its own parallel jurisdiction in this manner, the fact that another human rights body engaged in a factual and legal analysis of the issues should not relieve the treaty body of its own responsibility to independently examine a properly-presented claim against the legal standards established by its own treaty. In other words, a treaty body may properly defer to substantiated determinations of fact by a regional human rights mechanism with the capacity to hear witnesses and receive and evaluate evidence. But its mandate obligates it to independently evaluate whether that evidence satisfies the legal requirements of the particular treaty that the treaty body oversees.

C. Consideration of the Same Legal Issue

The final example of the jurisprudential relationship between the treaty bodies and the regional systems involves the consideration by the European Court of Human Rights and the Human Rights Committee of France's 2010 law banning Muslim women from wearing the full-face veil in public.

In *Yaker v. France* and the companion case of *Hebbadj v. France*[51] before the Human Rights Committee, and in *S.A.S. v. France*[52] before the European Court of Human Rights, the Committee and Court reached inconsistent conclusions regarding the compatibility of France's ban on wearing the full-face veil (the niqab or burqa) in any public space with France's obligations under the respective treaties. The French law purported to be religiously neutral, in that it prohibited all apparel concealing the face in public.[53] However, Article 2 of the law exempted a large number of face coverings other than the full-face veil,[54] and in practice, the vast majority of the checks conducted under the Act involved Muslim women wearing the full veil. Sonia Yaker, who was twice subjected to criminal fines for wearing the niqab, and the claimant in *S.A.S.*, who wished to wear the full veil without risk of sanction, separately challenged the Act as violating, inter alia, their right to manifest their religion and as indirect discrimination on grounds of religion.

[51] HRC, *Yaker v. France*, UN Doc. CCPR/C/123/D/2747/2016 (2018); HRC, *Hebbadj v. France*, UN Doc. CCPR/C/WG/123/DR/2807/2016 (2018).

[52] ECtHR, *S.A.S. v. France*, Appl. no. 43835/11, Judgment of 1 July 2014.

[53] Art. 1, *Interdisant la dissimulation du visage dans l'espace public*, act no. 2010–1192. The French Constitutional Council also interpreted the law to exempt covering of the face in religious spaces open to the public. See Constitutional Court (France), Decision no. 2010–613 DC (7 October 2010).

[54] Art. 2(II) of the Act exempts from the prohibition clothing worn for 'health reasons,' on 'professional grounds,' that is 'part of sporting, artistic or traditional festivities or events' including 'religious processions,' or that is prescribed or legally authorized by legislative or regulatory provisions.

Both the Court and the Committee recognized that by imposing criminal penalties on the Muslim women claimants who chose to wear the full-face veil in public, the Act interfered with their ability to manifest their religion under Article 9 of the European Convention and Article 18 of the ICCPR, respectively. The two bodies diverged, however, in their application of the limitations provisions of those articles[55] and the nondiscrimination provisions under the two treaties.

Under the European Convention, the question to be addressed was whether the interference with S.A.S.'s manifestation of religion was compatible with the limitations provisions of Article 9(2). In other words, did the restriction pursue one of the legitimate aims set out in that clause and was it necessary in a democratic society to achieve that aim? Similarly, the question before the Human Rights Committee under Article 18(3) of the ICCPR was whether the law interfering with Ms Yaker's manifestation of religion pursued one of the legitimate aims set forth in that clause, and was necessary for achieving that objective as well as proportionate, and non-discriminatory.[56]

The European Court in *S.A.S.* upheld the law on the basis that France was entitled to promote the principle of 'living together.' In other words, France was entitled to require all people to show their faces in public in order to ensure 'respect for the minimum requirements of life in society.' The Court treated this purpose as part of the aim of 'protection of the rights and freedoms of others' under Article 9(2) of the European Convention. The Court reasoned that France had a 'wide margin of appreciation' in this area,[57] and that the law was proportionate to this aim, despite the fact that France was a notable outlier among Council of Europe member states in requiring such a ban, and despite acknowledging the burdens to religious freedom that the law imposed on affected women.[58] In light of these considerations, as well as the subsidiary role of the Court to national authorities in assessing local needs and conditions, the Court concluded that the law did not contravene Article 9.[59]

The Court apparently accepted France's contention that the Act was neutral with respect to religion and applied generally to all apparel that covered the face. The Court did not address the Act's numerous exceptions, including S.A.S.'s observation that the law expressly allowed for covering the face in traditional Christian festivals, but prevented a Muslim woman from covering her face even during Ramadan. The Court acknowledged that Islamophobic statements had been made during debates over the Act, and that the ban had mainly affected Muslim women who chose to wear the full veil. Nevertheless, it emphasized that 'the ban is not

[55] Both bodies concluded that the Act could not be justified on France's stated aim of promoting public safety, since the law was, inter alia, disproportionate to that aim. The European Court also rejected France's stated aim of combating gender discrimination, and France did not later advance that aim before the Committee.

[56] *Yaker* (n. 51), para. 8.5.

[57] *S.A.S.* (n. 52), para. 155.

[58] Ibid. paras 156, 146.

[59] Ibid. para. 151.

expressly based on the religious connotation of the clothing in question but solely on the fact that it conceals the face.'[60] Having concluded that the French law served a legitimate aim for purposes of restricting the right to manifest religion, the Court rejected the claim that the law was discriminatory in a paragraph.

In a powerful partial dissent, Judges Nussberger and Jäderblom critiqued the Court's reliance on the concept of 'living together' as vague and abstract and not based on the protection of Convention rights.[61] They noted that there was no right under the Convention 'not to be shocked or provoked by different models of cultural or religious identity, even those that are very distant from the traditional French and European lifestyle,' or to 'enter into contact with other people, in public places, against their will.' Nor had France explained how the impact of the veil differed from forms of face covering that were exempted from the Act. 'People can socialise without necessarily looking into each other's eyes,' the dissenters concluded.[62]

In contrast to the Court, the Human Rights Committee held that the ban on the full-face veil violated the right to freedom of religion under Article 18 and also discriminated against Muslim women based on the intersectionality of gender and religion under Article 26 of the Covenant. The Committee departed from the European Court with respect to France's stated aim of protecting the rights and freedoms of others. Under Article 18(3) of the ICCPR, this aim is framed in terms of 'the *fundamental* rights and freedoms of others'—a textual difference from the European Convention, which does not expressly require that the equivalent limitation protect rights that are 'fundamental'. The Committee emphasized that this limitation in Article 18 was to be strictly applied, and that France had not identified any specific right of other specific individuals that was infringed by wearing the full-face veil. In particular, France had failed to explain why wearing the full-face veil infringed the fundamental rights of others in a manner that other forms of covering the face allowed by the Act did not. The Committee emphasized that the ICCPR does not bestow on individuals a fundamental 'right' to see the faces of, and interact with, all other individuals in the public space. The Committee further concluded that France had not demonstrated that a criminal ban on only certain means of covering of the face in public was proportionate to that aim, or the least restrictive means to achieving it that was protective of religion or belief. The ban, and Ms Yaker's convictions thereunder, thus violated Article 18.[63]

With respect to discrimination on the basis of gender and religion, having previously rejected France's claimed purpose of 'living together' as a legitimate aim under Article 18, the Committee concluded that the Act also failed

[60] Ibid. para. 151.
[61] *S.A.S.* (Joint Partly Dissenting Opinion of Judges Nussberger and Jaderblom) (n. 52) para. 5.
[62] *S.A.S.* (n. 52) paras 7–9.
[63] *Yaker* (n. 51) paras 8.9–8.12.

to satisfy the requirements of reasonableness, objectivity, and legitimacy of aim under Article 26. Unlike the Court, the Committee here did not treat the law as a general ban on all face coverings, but focused, inter alia, on France's 'failure to explain why a blanket ban on the veil [was] reasonable or justified, in contrast to the exceptions allowable under the Act.'[64] The Committee observed that wearing the full veil could reflect a personal choice, and invoked its prior Concluding Observations to France that rather than liberating women, a comprehensive ban could result in the further exclusion and marginalization of Muslim women and girls. It also noted that the criminal penalties imposed, while low, had been imposed on some women multiple times, including Ms Yaker. The Committee concluded that the law 'disproportionately affects the author as a Muslim woman who chooses to wear the full-face veil, and introduces a distinction between her and other persons who may legally cover their face in public that is not necessary and proportionate to a legitimate interest, and is therefore unreasonable.'[65]

4. Consistency and Coherence in the Human Rights System

The overlap of the Human Rights Committee's jurisdiction under the Optional Protocol with other human rights regimes, which allows the Committee to review claims that have been reviewed under a different human rights treaty regime, reflects an acknowledgement of the distinctive features of the various human rights systems. It also reflects a presumption in favour of protection: that victims of human rights violations should not necessarily have to choose between regimes of protection. They should be able to benefit from the full protection of the overall system.

In recognition of this principle, the Committee's jurisprudence under Article 5(2)(a) of the Optional Protocol has gone so far as to allow the exercise of jurisdiction over claims that have no equivalent under the European Convention, and thus could not have been considered by the European Court. In *Mahabir v. Austria*, even where the state had entered a reservation precluding the Committee from considering the 'same matter' that was previously addressed by the European Court on the merits, the Committee took the position that the 'matter' only included substantive claims that could have been considered by the European Court. Claims based on articles of the ICCPR that had no equivalent in the European Convention

[64] Ibid. para. 8.15.
[65] Ibid. para. 8.17.

could still be examined.[66] Of course, with the elaboration of jurisprudence under the various human rights treaties and the tendency toward normative convergence within the human rights system over time, such lacunae in protection are likely to narrow and the basis for such a decision likely to become much rarer.

The decision in *Castillo*, on the other hand, underscores the normative interconnectivity of the human rights system. Part of the Committee's reason for deferring to the decision of the Inter-American Court was institutional: the Inter-American Commission and Court had the opportunity to examine witnesses and evidence, and thus were much closer to the case, in addition to being closer in time to the events. They both thus had a greater capacity to understand the nuances of the case than the Committee. An additional unstated premise undergirding the Committee's decision was that the legal obligations imposed on states to conduct an effective investigation into a disappearance under the ICCPR were substantially similar to those applied by the Inter-American system. This premise perhaps also would have been reasonable if the standard the Inter-American Court applied to the investigation in *Castillo* had been consistent with its established jurisprudence. Nevertheless, it still should have been incumbent upon the Committee to ensure itself that the scope of Venezuela's equivalent obligations under the *Covenant* had been adequately examined, something that the Committee did not do. And both of the above reasons for deferring to the Court's judgment were compromised by the fact that the Inter-American Court and Commission had reached such diametrically opposed conclusions on the facts and the law.

Nevertheless, despite the caveats regarding the particular outcome in *Castillo*, the Committee's core instinct was sound that the interests of harmony, consistency, coherence, predictability, and finality in the overall human rights system require a very good reason for diverging from the reasoned decision of a sister human rights institution in considering the same claim by the same parties.

Unlike *Castillo*, where the identical factual claim before the Committee had been considered by the Inter-American system, the Committee in *Yaker* did not exhibit an obligation to defer to the reasoning of the European Court of Human Rights. One might think that such deference would be appropriate. After all, the two bodies were reviewing the same law and the same legal grounds for its infirmity—violation of freedom of religion and discrimination against a Muslim woman wearing the full face veil. However, the Committee's care in articulating its own jurisprudence was appropriate.

[66] The Committee explained: '[T]he European Court was able to examine the same matter only insofar as the substantive rights protected under the European Convention converge with those protected under the Covenant ... The Committee observes that articles 8 and 17 [forced labour and privacy] of the Covenant largely converge with articles 4 and 8 of the European Convention. However, neither the European Convention nor its Protocols contain provisions equivalent to articles 10 and 26 of the Covenant. Accordingly, the Committee considers that the State party's reservation applies insofar as the case raises issues under articles 8 and 17 of the Covenant.' HRC, *Mahabir v. Austria*, CCPR/C/82/D/944/2000 (2004), para. 8.5.

S.A.S. and *Yaker*, of course, did not present the same claim by the same parties, but presented similar challenges to the same law under two different human rights regimes. In such a context, the justification for jurisprudential consistency may be weaker, and the considerations that warrant divergence in normative positions may, at times, be more ascendant.

Moreover, the contrasting outcomes in the two cases reflect a number of institutional and doctrinal differences between the Committee and the Court as well as the human rights instruments they are applying. From an institutional perspective, the European Court oversees an explicitly regional human rights system, premised in part on shared social, cultural, and political values and norms among the European member states. In the context of Europe, these shared values include an assumption that member states to the Convention share common commitments to democratic governance, the rule of law, and human rights. As a result, the European human rights system has developed a number of doctrines distinct to that regional system, including the principles of margin of appreciation and subsidiarity, which are premised, at least in part, on the fact that the Court is overseeing actions taken by national authorities in presumptively democratic, rights-respecting states. The Court, therefore, often emphasizes its subsidiary role with regard to the decisions of national authorities, 'who have direct democratic legitimation'[67] including through its application of a margin of appreciation, a doctrine which presumes that national authorities interpret and apply their human rights obligations democratically and in good faith.

As a doctrinal matter, the European Court has embraced a particularly deferential margin of appreciation with respect to regulation of manifestations of religion, as the Court acknowledged in *S.A.S.*[68] The Court's embrace of France's aim of promoting 'living together' itself reflected a European, or even distinctly French, conception of acceptable forms of human interaction in the public space that would be difficult to apply under a global convention. On the other hand, aspects of the Court's reasoning—such as its conclusion that there was no European consensus on the validity of a comprehensive ban on the full-face veil, despite the fact that only two European states had adopted such a ban at the time of the decision[69]—seemed more patently political than principled.

The institutional position of the Human Rights Committee is quite different. The Committee is a global mechanism, overseeing an instrument that must be applied in over 170 countries, ranging from highly democratic and rights-respecting to highly authoritarian and repressive, and spanning nearly all of the

[67] *S.A.S.* (n. 52) para. 129.

[68] Ibid.

[69] *S.A.S.* (Joint Partly Dissenting Opinion of Judges Nussberger and Jaderblom) (n. 52) para. 19 (noting that 'forty-five out of forty-seven member States of the Council of Europe, and thus an overwhelming majority, have not deemed it necessary to legislate in this area').

legal, political, social, and cultural traditions of the globe. For this reason, while the Committee necessarily defers through various doctrines to the decisions of national authorities regarding appropriate ways to implement their human rights obligations, the Committee does not apply a specific concept akin to the margin of appreciation, which is based on, inter alia, an underlying presumption regarding the bona fide democratic and human rights commitments of the relevant state.

The relevant provisions of the European Convention and the ICCPR have somewhat different texts, different negotiating histories, and different jurisprudence. As a doctrinal matter, the Committee traditionally has taken a more protective approach to restrictions on manifestations of religion under both Articles 18 and 26, demanding specific explanations from states regarding the legitimate aim being advanced and the reasonableness and proportionality of the restriction. The text of Article 18(3), with its emphasis on respect for 'fundamental' rights of others, comports with this more restrictive construction.

The Committee's more restrictive approach may also reflect the Committee's more universal institutional role. In assessing France's 'living together' contention—that it was important to require Muslim women to reveal their face in public as fundamental to promoting the ability of people to live together as a society—the Committee had to be conscious of the fact that, in a global context, the same claim could be advanced to justify precisely the opposite result. A state such as Saudi Arabia, for example (not currently a party to the ICCPR), could equally assert that requiring women to *conceal* their face, their hair, or other parts of their bodies, was necessary to promote the goal of 'living together' in that society. The Committee does not oversee a region with putative common social norms and traditions, and thus perhaps must be more sensitive to the full range of global normative diversity than its European counterpart.

Finally, facts matter. The claimants in the cases before the Committee had been criminally prosecuted and fined for violations of the Act—in the case of Ms Yaker, more than once—whereas the claimant in *S.A.S.* had not had the Act enforced against her and was challenging the Act *per se*. The claimant in *Yaker* contended that she generally wore the full-face veil in public, while the claimant in *S.A.S.* contended that she wanted to have the ability to wear the full-face veil on occasions when she chose to do so. These facts may also have influenced the respective assessments. Based on the facts before it, the European Court may have felt that the right to manifest religion of the claimant before it was less burdened by the French law than the Committee did in *Yaker*.

Ultimately, however, the decisions of the two bodies, while reaching different assessments of the validity of the law under different instruments, did not place *contradictory* obligations on France. Nothing in the *S.A.S.* decision *required* France to maintain a ban on the full-face veil. France could revise its law to comply with both of its treaty obligations. Specifically, France could act consistently with both the European Convention and the ICCPR by complying with the Human Rights Committee decision. This situation is not unusual. It is often the case that somewhat different legal obligations will arise when a state is party to different instruments imposing multiple and somewhat differing human rights obligations. The state simply must conform its laws and practices to the most protective standard. Moreover, the existence of these two decisions may help preserve a healthy debate in Europe and elsewhere over both the wisdom and legality of bans on religious dress.

From the perspective of connectivity and coherence between the treaty bodies and the regional human rights systems, and more broadly for connectivity with the human rights system, the important point is not that jurisdictions sometimes may overlap or that normative conclusions at times may differ. Consistency regarding the meaning of human rights obligations is one important value in ensuring the strength and accessibility of the human rights system. From the perspective of connectivity, however, the critical issue is not that normative assessments should never diverge. Instead, the important consideration is that each human rights system should be fully informed and aware of the positions taken by other human rights organs and the reasons therefore. The choice to conform or diverge from the position of a sister regime or mechanism should be rational, not accidental, and made based on sound reasons relevant to the institution rendering the decision.

A sophisticated understanding of the jurisprudence of other human rights mechanisms is vital to ensuring doctrinal coherence in the human rights system. It was, of course, extremely important for the Human Rights Committee to be aware of the nuance of the working methods and jurisprudence of the European Court in the *Achabal* line of cases and *Yaker*, and of the Inter-American Commission and Court in *Castillo*. Although it is generally not the practice of the Committee for its merits analysis to explicitly engage with the comparative jurisprudence of other jurisdictions, a decision such as *S.A.S. v. France* is of course given very close consideration.

As Thomas Buergenthal explained in the context of the general relationship among international and regional tribunals:

> it is important for all international tribunals ... to recognise that they are all part of the same legal system and that this fact imposes certain obligations. Of these the most basic one is the obligation to accept the methodological and doctrinal unity of the international legal system. This means, among other things, that each tribunal has an obligation to respect the general and special competence of the other judicial and quasijudicial institutions which comprise the system, to recognise that it has an obligation when rendering judgments, to take account of the case law of other judicial institutions that have pronounced on the same subject

and most importantly, to promote and be open to jurisprudential interaction and crossfertilization.[70]

This does not mean that all human rights treaty obligations can or should be interpreted alike. When a decision of one human rights body deviates from the position of another tribunal or mechanism, it should do so with knowledge, and based on considered and important reasons. Reliability of judgments is important for the credibility and legitimacy of a system. However, blindly following the jurisprudence of another jurisdiction is inconsistent with the distinct legal character of different human rights instruments, and can impede the legitimacy and overall evolution of the human rights system.

So, while there is a core of universal norms that is common to the treaty bodies and regional systems, which has been converging over the course of their evolution, the systems are not identical in all respects. Nor should they be. Indeed, the struggle to identify what is common versus particular to each human rights regime is one of the core challenges of the Age of Human Rights Connectivity.[71]

The treaty bodies and the regional human rights systems also engage in a jurisprudential dialogue at a more general level. Even when the same issue is not under consideration, connectivity between the systems ideally should foster a healthy competition and exchange of normative ideas on common issues. For this reason, in order to ensure jurisprudential coherence, the European Court of Human Rights and the Inter-American Commission and Court of Human Rights both have dedicated, full time professional registries, or secretariats, that conduct comparative research on the jurisprudence of other human rights bodies with respect to each issue that comes before the Court. Thus, for example, when the Inter-American Court of Human Rights considered Costa Rica's restrictions on access to in vitro fertilization, the Court's opinion extensively canvassed the relevant jurisprudence of the Human Rights Committee, and the CERD, CEDAW, CESCR, and CRC Committees.[72]

When Amanda Mellet brought her challenge to Ireland's criminal prohibition on access to abortion, she had the choice of a variety of fora. She could have brought her claim to the European Court of Human Rights, which had established a wide margin of appreciation for states with respect to regulation of abortion,

[70] Buergenthal, 'Proliferation of International Courts and Tribunals: Is it Good or Bad?,' 14 *Leiden Journal of International Law* (2001) 267, 274.

[71] For further discussion of regional specificity versus universality in the human rights system, see Neuman, 'Standing Alone or Together: The Human Rights Committee's Decision in AP v Russian Federation', in E. Brems and E. Desmet (eds), *Integrated Human Rights in Practice* (2017) 71; Besson, 'The Influence of the Two Covenants on States Parties Across Regions: Lessons for the Role of Comparative Law and of Regions in International Human Rights Law', in Moeckli, Keller, and Heri (n. 20) 243.

[72] IACtHR, *Case of Artavia Murillo et al. ('In Vitro Fertilization') v. Costa Rica*, Judgment (Preliminary Objection, Merits, Reparations, and Costs), 28 November 2012, paras 145–46, 148, 225–233, 286.

including in Ireland,[73] although not with respect to the particular question of fatal fetal impairment that Mellet's case presented. Alternatively, she could have brought her claim before the CAT or CEDAW treaty bodies, whose individual complaints procedure Ireland also has accepted. Each of these bodies would have brought a somewhat different perspective to the question, as each has a different treaty-based mandate and scope of authorities. To ensure appropriate connectivity within the human rights system, however, ideally any treaty body examining Mellet's case also would have access to the comparative relevant jurisprudence of its sister treaty bodies and the regional human rights courts, among other human rights mechanisms.

In contrast to the regional courts, however, the treaty bodies have no dedicated expert professional Secretariat. The human rights officers in the OHCHR Secretariat, while highly talented and deeply dedicated, are subject to UN rotation rules, and often are hired on short-term month-to-month contracts. It is therefore impossible for them to acquire the level of professional expertise in comparative human rights jurisprudence achieved by the career professionals in the regional systems. The OHCHR Secretariat also lacks the resources to provide the treaty bodies with reviews of relevant comparative human rights jurisprudence equivalent to those routinely generated by the regional secretariats. Such information, to the extent the treaty bodies receive it, is provided by the parties to a case, or by individual treaty body members or the Secretariat on an ad hoc basis. Establishment of a permanent professional registry for the treaty bodies thus would promote jurisprudential coherence. It could significantly enhance the quality of the treaty bodies' analysis and the connectivity with other human rights mechanisms, and help avoid unintentional divergences in the development of jurisprudence.

5. Conclusion

A fundamental challenge confronting the future of the UN treaty bodies is how those entities will function as a *system*, and how that system will interact in a coordinated manner with other human rights mechanisms in order to enhance the overall effectiveness of the global human rights regime. No treaty body is an island. And yet the treaty bodies were crafted as islands, and even 50 years into their life, they substantially continue to function as such. In order to improve human rights compliance in the Age of Connectivity, the work of the treaty bodies must be more visible and accessible to other international, regional and national human rights mechanisms, states, victims, civil society, and other stakeholders, and vice versa.

[73] ECtHR, *Case of A, B and C. v. Ireland*, App. no. 25579/05, Judgment of 16 December 2010.

There are numerous ways that such connectivity can and should be enhanced. But strengthening coordination of the country review function of the treaty bodies, and enhancing the normative communication among the treaty bodies and other human rights mechanisms, particularly the regional systems, would be significant steps towards strengthening and rationalizing the treaty bodies and helping a greater whole emerge from their disparate parts.

5

Feminist Futures in Human Rights

*Hilary Charlesworth**

1. Introduction

Feminism is animated by bold ambitions and hopes for the future. A common expression of the goal of feminism is equality between women and men.[1] Such a concise formulation papers over important questions such as whether equality requires identical treatment of women and men, whether it entails that both sexes end up with comparable opportunities or social goods, whether it requires recognition of a distinctive women's voice or women's qualities, or whether it means the transformation of economic and social structures, or the eradication of relationships of domination and subordination between the sexes. It assumes the value of a male comparator. The short version of the central feminist goal similarly sidesteps questions of equality *between* women, and the roles of factors such as race, disability, sexuality, and economic position in affecting women's lives. It also takes the fixed duality of sexual difference for granted. In short, the identification of feminist futures is a contentious task.

Feminism can be understood as a political ambition, but it is as much an intellectual method that challenges claims to objective and impartial knowledge in various disciplinary traditions. These roles are closely entwined. Andrea Bianchi has described feminist theories as 'overtly partisan';[2] methodologically, however, this is only accurate in the sense that they seek to uncover the partisan nature of all approaches to knowledge, especially those that assert their detachment from political perspectives. A similar charge, albeit from a queer theoretical perspective, is that feminism has 'seriously narrow[ed] intellectual inquiry, prioritizing politics over critique'.[3] Elizabeth Grosz has observed the uneasy relationship between two distinct roles of feminist theory—responding to political feminist goals and analysing the thoroughgoing masculinity of disciplinary knowledge. Feminist theories are often dismissed by the academy because of their explicitly political

* I thank Michael McArdle for helpful research assistance and Dianne Otto for valuable comments.

1 See, e.g., GA Res. 58/142, 22 December 2003, at para. 1(b); Beijing Declaration and Platform for Action, UN Doc. A/CONF.177/20/Rev.1, 27 October 1995, at para. 44.

2 A. Bianchi, *International Law Theories: An Enquiry into Different Ways of Thinking* (2016) 189.

3 Cossman et al., 'Gender, Sexuality and Power: Is Feminist Theory Enough?', 12 *Columbia Journal of Gender and Law* (2003) 601, at 624.

Hilary Charlesworth, *Feminist Futures in Human Rights*. In: *Human Rights in Transition*. First Edition. Edited by Nehal Bhuta, Oxford University Press. © Hilary Charlesworth 2024. DOI: 10.1093/oso/9780198901921.003.0005

ends; and yet they are also criticized by feminist activists for engagement with the male-dominated world of theory.[4] Feminism's tangled mix of utopian thought and critical thinking thus complicates the search for feminist futures.

In this chapter, I use the language of feminism to indicate a type of inquiry, a way of asking questions that draws attention to both particular constructions of and silences about women's lives in the field of human rights. The inquiries are animated by the goal of transformative equality: allowing women to develop their capacities fully and to exercise choices about their lives. I begin by describing some debates underlying feminist approaches and sketching feminist engagement with the international system. The second section considers how feminist inquiries have influenced the area of human rights, focussing on two projects: one institutional (gender mainstreaming) and one normative (eradicating violence against women). The argument is that, while feminist ideas and vocabulary have influenced the development of international human rights law, their adoption has also provided an alibi for the postponement of transformative feminist futures.

2. Feminist Approaches

The umbrella of feminism covers a kaleidoscope of sometimes jarring political and intellectual projects. Some accounts of feminism describe it in terms of waves, connecting it to specific historical periods. 'First wave' feminism is linked to the suffrage movement of the late nineteenth and early twentieth centuries when women's groups in the West organized around political equality through obtaining the vote and equal property rights. Campaigns for legal and social equality in the 1960s, and the identification of a global sisterhood facing universal male oppression, are elements of 'second wave' feminism; while the term 'third wave' feminism is linked to attention to the diversity of women and challenges to universal emancipatory projects, starting in the 1990s.[5]

Nancy Fraser has identified three different feminist imaginaries associated with second wave feminism.[6] One, starting in the 1960s, challenged the androcentric form of capitalist societies and located equality for women in socio-economic redistribution within states. The second, in the 1980s, emphasized the recognition of difference between women, especially those of class and race, and focussed on identity politics, sustaining a neoliberal emphasis on individual effort and achievement. This form of feminism, according to Fraser, 'harnesses the dream of women's

4 Grosz, 'A Note on Essentialism and Difference', in S. Gunew (ed.), *Feminist Knowledge: Critique and Construct* (1990) 332, at 332.

5 See Hewitt, 'Feminist Frequencies: Regenerating the Wave Metaphor', 38 *Feminist Studies* (2012) 658; N. A. McHugh, *Feminist Philosophies A–Z* (2007).

6 Fraser, 'Mapping the Feminist Imagination: From Redistribution to Recognition to Representation', 12 *Constellations* (2005) 295.

emancipation to the engine of capital accumulation.'[7] Fraser's third trajectory is designed to reinvigorate debate about the economic basis of women's inequality in capitalist societies and to use international arenas in this venture.[8]

The popular metaphor of waves suggests a linearity of feminist thought. It does not readily capture the co-existence of all these types of projects today and the intersections and frictions between them. The standard identification of the three waves of feminism also overlooks major aspects of international women's movements. For example, at the time that the women's suffrage campaigns were in full swing, other women were focussed on a broader agenda. There were a series of International Congresses of Women held from 1878 which promoted women's rights more generally. The Hague Congress of Women in 1915 was dedicated to women's contributions to peace and the centrality of women to ending the First World War.[9] A parallel tension between demands for women's equality in the public sphere on the one hand and emphasis on women as quintessential peacebuilders on the other continues today, marking, for example, the United Nations Security Council's 'Women, Peace and Security' agenda.[10]

Other categorizations distinguish varieties of feminism based on their political commitments and alliances. Thus, liberal feminism focusses on the equality of individual women, emphasizing political and legal reform as the routes to achieve this. Cultural feminism is associated with celebrations of special qualities associated with women, such as caring, empathy, and avoidance of conflict.[11] The identification of male domination as the source of women's inequality is at the heart of radical feminism,[12] while socialist feminism connects capitalist and male hierarchies.[13] Ecofeminism links the oppression of women with male control and environmental destruction.[14] Post-colonial, or Third World, feminism questions the idea that women have common interests at an international level, and the assertion of a global sisterhood. It draws attention to the significance of race and colonialism in the subjugation of women in the developing world, and Western feminism's tendency to represent Third World women as an undifferentiated set of victims of male oppression.[15]

[7] Fraser, *How Feminism Became Capitalism's Handmaiden—And How to Reclaim It*, 14 October 2013, available online at https://www.theguardian.com/commentisfree/2013/oct/14/feminism-capitalist-handmaiden-neoliberal (last visited 18 April 2023).

[8] See N. Fraser, *The Fortunes of Feminism: From State-Managed Capitalism to Neoliberal Crisis* (2013).

[9] See Baetens, 'International Congress of Women (1915)', in R. Wolfrum (ed.), *The Max Planck Encyclopaedia of Public International Law* (2012) 455; Costin, 'Feminism, Pacifism, Internationalism and the 1915 International Congress of Women', 5 *Women's Studies International Forum* (1982) 301.

[10] See Charlesworth, 'Are Women Peaceful? Reflections on the Role of Women in Peacebuilding', 16 *Feminist Legal Studies* (2008) 347.

[11] See C. Gilligan, *In a Different Voice: Psychological Theory and Women's Development* (2003).

[12] McHugh (n. 5) 111.

[13] Ibid. 32.

[14] Ibid. 134.

[15] M. J. Alexander and C. T. Mohanty (eds), *Feminist Genealogies, Colonial Legacies, Democratic Futures* (1997).

While all these taxonomies have a certain heuristic value, they streamline and simplify feminist thought and over-draw the phenomenon of intellectual competition between various strands. Dianne Otto has offered a constructive alternative to the image of a battleground of approaches by describing feminist theories as 'a shifting and contested network of ideas and allegiances that … draw on multiple and sometimes competing feminist perspectives and engage with other critical traditions in law'.[16] The idea of a feminist legal archaeology is another way to depict the eclectic methods required in the context of international law. An archaeological dig requires varied technologies and tools, depending on the terrain of inquiry.[17] In the context of feminist investigation, this might sometimes be marshalling large scale evidence of inequality and other times producing finely grained analyses of localized accounts of resistance to patriarchy.

All feminist theorizing rests on curiosity about women's lives.[18] In this vein, Marysia Zalewski has identified two questions that animate feminist scholarship. The first is: What about women? This inquiry draws attention to the presence or absence of women, what is happening to them, and the roles they are assigned. Zalewski's second question addresses the work gender is doing in that setting. She understands gender as the social and cultural constructs of masculinity and femininity.[19]

What is the relationship between the notions of sex and gender? In some contexts, the two are treated as synonyms. For example, the Rome Statute of the International Criminal Court refers to 'gender' in the description of some of the crimes within the Court's jurisdiction, defining it as 'the two sexes, male and female, within the context of society'.[20] The elision of sex and gender found in this definition, linking gender with biology, seems to imply that gender is a fixed, objective fact about a person. Valerie Oosterveld has argued however that the Rome Statute definition of gender creates a 'constructive ambiguity', leaving open the possibility of a less restricted approach.[21] We also see the merging of sex and gender in the calls for 'gender equality' found in the Millennium Development Goals (2000)[22] and the Sustainable Development Goals (2015).[23] In both these instruments, the elaboration of the notion of gender equality refers only to the comparative position

[16] Otto, 'Feminist Approaches to International Law', in A. Orford and F. Hoffman (eds), *The Oxford Handbook of the Theory of International Law* (2016) 488, at 492.

[17] See Charlesworth, 'Feminist Methods in International Law', 93 *The American Journal of International Law* (*AJIL*) (1999) 379, at 381.

[18] See C. Enloe, *The Curious Feminist: Searching for Women in a New Age of Empire* (2004).

[19] Zalewski, 'Well, What is the Feminist Perspective on Bosnia?', 71 *International Affairs* (1995) 339, at 341–342.

[20] Art. 7(3) ICCSt.

[21] Oosterveld, 'The Definition of "Gender" in the Rome Statute of the International Criminal Court: A Step Forward or Back for International Criminal Justice?', 18 *Harvard Human Rights Journal* (2005) 55.

[22] GA Res 55/2, 18 September 2002, Goal 3.

[23] GA Res 70/1, 25 September 2015, Goal 5.

of women and men, rather than challenging the ways in which gender hierarchies structure what comes to be valued.

Another account of the relationship between sex and gender makes a clear distinction between the concepts, defining sex as a matter of biology and gender as the constructed attributes of sex and the designation of social roles.[24] This approach is interested in how understandings of masculinity and femininity shape disciplinary and daily thought. As Zalweski's use of the term illustrates, gender in this sense refers not to the characteristics of particular men and women but to a set of social constructions, varying over time and place. Common features of these constructions are, first, that masculinity and femininity are defined in dualistic terms, as opposites. Second, those qualities or traits deemed masculine are assigned a greater value than those defined as feminine.[25]

While such explanations are valuable in countering the power of biological determinism and in drawing attention to the negotiability of concepts of gender, they can be taken to imply that sex differences are objective. Many scholars have however challenged the naturalness of sex as a category. For example, Judith Butler has insisted that sex is a social and political construction as much as gender is—we produce the 'naturalness' of sex discursively.[26] This is a contested issue in feminism, which typically identifies the category of women as its subject and suspends debate about the nature of the distinction between men and women. Indeed in the eighteenth century Olympe de Gouges identified the paradox that, while feminism seeks to reject sexual difference as a basis for the marginalization of women, it also relies on designating the category of 'women' as its beneficiary.[27]

Does the distinction between sex and gender inform an account of being a woman in specific contexts? Toril Moi has suggested that the distinction between sex and gender is not always productive in feminist thought, especially as a basis for understanding subjectivity. She draws on Simone de Beauvoir's observation in *The Second Sex* that 'one is not born a woman, rather we become one' to suggest that the body should be understood as a *situation*, rather than a biological entity.[28] This approach rejects the idea of biological determinism, going beyond sex to emphasize that values, norms, and social encounters are what makes us women.[29] Understanding the body as a situation means, in Moi's words, 'the concrete body

[24] See, e.g., WHO, *Gender, Equity and Human Rights* (2017), available online at https://www.who.int/teams/gender-equity-and-human-rights (last visited 18 April 2023); Council of Europe Convention on Preventing and Combating Violence against Women and Domestic Violence (Istanbul Convention) 2014, CETS No 210, Art. 3(c).

[25] See Cohn, 'Sex and Death in the Rational World of Defense Intellectuals', 12 *Signs* (1987) 687.

[26] See J. Butler, *Gender Trouble: Feminism and the Subversion of Identity* (1999); J. Butler, *Bodies that Matter: On the Discursive Limits of 'Sex'* (1993). See also D. Haraway, *Simians, Cyborgs and Women: The Reinvention of Nature* (1991) 149.

[27] See Scott, 'French Feminists and the Right of "Man": Olympe de Gouges' Declarations', 28 *History Workshop* (1989) 1.

[28] T. Moi, *Sex, Gender, and The Body* (2005) 59.

[29] Ibid. 79.

experienced as meaningful, and socially and historically situated.'[30] This account acknowledges the oppression of ideologies and practices relating to sexual difference, while nevertheless allowing for women's agency.[31] To this extent, it provides a response to Olympe de Gouges' paradox.

If we understand womanhood as a situation, the term 'gender' can operate, following Joan Scott, as 'a primary way of signifying relationships of power';[32] or as an axis of power, a 'way in which material and symbolic resources are produced and distributed in asymmetrical ways'.[33] Gender does not necessarily follow dualistic distinctions based on sex; relationships between men can be gendered, as can relationships between women, as can relationships with those who identify as trans- or third-gender.

3. The Appeal of the International Sphere

From the end of the nineteenth century, women's groups saw the international arena as a useful site for their campaigns, hoping that it might transcend the conservatism of national systems. As noted above, a series of International Congresses of Women were held from the late nineteenth century to promote women's equality. The League of Nations quickly became a repository of hope for national and international women's movements.[34] International women's organizations sent delegates to the 1919 Paris Peace Conference and advocated for the representation of women in all aspects of the League's operations. They also urged the League to address issues relating to women, such as trafficking, equal political rights, and health and education.[35] The partial success of this lobbying was reflected in provisions in the Covenant of the League stating that all positions in the League 'shall be open equally to men and women'[36] and referring to improving the conditions of women's work and eliminating trafficking in women as part of the League's work.[37]

Later, feminists believed that the League's support might counter moves to limit women's rights within states, prompted by the 1930s Depression and the spread of nationalist conservative movements.[38] One focus for feminist action was the nationality of married women: many legal systems regarded a woman who married a foreigner as automatically losing her original nationality and assuming the

30 Ibid. 74.
31 Ibid. 83.
32 J. W. Scott, *Gender and the Politics of History* (1988) 42.
33 Cossman et al. (n. 3) 618.
34 Miller, '"Geneva—The Key to Equality": Inter-War Feminists and the League of Nations', 3 *Women's History Review* (1994) 219, at 221.
35 L. J. Rupp, *Worlds of Women: The Making of an International Women's Movement* (1997) 210–217.
36 Art. 7, Covenant of the League of Nations.
37 Ibid. Art. 23.
38 See Miller (n. 34).

nationality of her husband. This could place women in a precarious position in times of conflict, or in the event of divorce. Women's groups worked, ultimately unsuccessfully, to persuade the League to adopt a treaty to redress this serious inequality.[39] Another expression of faith in the capacity of international organizations to alleviate women's inequality at the national level was a campaign for the League to adopt an equal rights treaty in the 1920s and 1930s. A draft treaty, proposed by the American feminist Alice Paul in 1926, contained a single operative clause: states parties agreed that, on ratification of the treaty, 'men and women shall have Equal Rights throughout the [ratifying state's] territory subject to their respective jurisdictions'.[40] This initiative caused dissension among international women's groups. Its proponents viewed the treaty as an antidote to the restrictive approach to the regulation of women's work taken in some national jurisdictions and by the International Labour Organization. Other women's groups supported protective treaties to support working women's social roles as mothers and wives and saw an equal rights treaty as a threat.[41]

While the equal rights treaty campaign ultimately failed, the work of the League of Nations elevated the status of women from a purely national to an international issue. Prodded by women's organizations during the 1930s, the League Secretariat began to amass information on women's social and legal situations and the Legal Committee of the League Assembly instituted an inquiry into the comparative status of women in 1937.[42] This prompted the Assembly to launch a major inquiry of its own later that year into the legal status of women throughout the world, at least in part to forestall moves to adopt some form of equal rights treaty.[43] In any event, this inquiry by a committee of experts was truncated by the start of the Second World War. The League also adopted a number of specific treaties to deal with concerns relating to women. These included slavery[44] and trafficking in women and children.[45]

At the San Francisco conference drafting the UN Charter in 1945, a few women delegates, mainly from Asia and the Americas, along with NGOs, lobbied for the inclusion of a reference to 'the equal rights of men and women' in the Preamble to the UN Charter as well as to non-discrimination on the basis of sex with respect to human rights in defining one of the purposes of the UN.[46] This group was also

[39] See Jacques, 'Tracking Feminist Interventions in International Law Issues at the League of Nations from the Nationality of Married Women to Legal Equality in the Family, 1919–1970', in S. Kimble and M. Röwekamp (eds), *New Perspectives on European Women's Legal History* (2017) 321, at 326.

[40] Quoted in Miller (n. 34), at 220–221.

[41] Ibid. at 222–224, 233–234. See also Jacques (n. 39).

[42] Ibid. at 236–237.

[43] Jacques (n. 39) 334–335.

[44] League of Nations Convention to Suppress the Slave Trade and Slavery 1926, 60 LNTS 253.

[45] International Convention for the Suppression of the Traffic of Women and Children 1921, 9 LNTS 415; International Convention for the Suppression of the Traffic in Women of Full Age 1933, 150 LNTS 431.

[46] Preamble, Art. 1.3, Charter of the United Nations, UNCIO XV, 335; amendments by General Assembly Resolution in 557 UNTS 143/638, 308/892, 119.

successful in including Article 8 in the UN Charter, which provides that the UN 'shall place no restrictions on the eligibility of men and women to participate in any capacity and under conditions of equality' in its work, echoing the spirit of Article 7 of the Covenant of the League.

The UN initially established a Commission on the Status of Women (CSW) as a subsidiary body of the Commission on Human Rights in 1946. After much lobbying by NGOs and women delegates to avoid women being relegated to a 'queue' of human rights issues, CSW became an independent body reporting directly to the United Nations Economic and Social Council (ECOSOC) in 1947.[47] It has since played an important role in promoting the drafting of treaties dealing with women's rights. These include a series of treaties addressing discrimination against women in certain areas of public life, including the Convention on the Political Rights of Women (1952),[48] the Convention on the Nationality of Married Women (1957),[49] and the Convention on Consent to Marriage, Minimum Age for Marriage and Registration of Marriages (1962).[50] The UN's most comprehensive normative instrument is the Convention on the Elimination of all Forms of Discrimination against Women (CEDAW), adopted in 1979.[51] CEDAW offers a broad account of discrimination in Article 1 as:

> any distinction, exclusion or restriction made on the basis of sex which has the effect or purpose of impairing or nullifying the recognition, enjoyment or exercise by women, irrespective of their marital status, on a basis of equality of men and women, of human rights and fundamental freedoms in the political, economic, social, cultural, civil or any other field.[52]

Notable here is the focus on discrimination affecting women, rather than discrimination on the basis of sex, which would apply to both women and men. During the drafting of CEDAW, some states advocated a treaty aimed at eliminating sex discrimination generally, but they were in a distinct minority. Most states accepted that there was a deep asymmetry in the positions of women and men and sought to address this.[53] Another feature of the definition is its coverage of direct and indirect discrimination through its attention to the 'effect or purpose' of actions. It is concerned with both procedural and substantive equality for women.

[47] H. Pietilä, *Engendering the Global Agenda: The Story of Women and the United Nations* (2002) 13–14; Jacques (n. 39) 336–337.

[48] Convention on the Political Rights of Women 1952, 193 UNTS 135.

[49] Convention on the Nationality of Married Women 1957, 309 UNTS 65.

[50] Convention on Consent to Marriage, Minimum Age for Marriage and Registration of Marriages 1962, 521 UNTS 231.

[51] Convention on the Elimination of All Forms of Discrimination against Women (CEDAW) 1979, 1249 UNTS 13.

[52] Ibid. Art. 1.

[53] Byrnes, 'Article 1', in M. A. Freeman, C. Chinkin, and B. Rudolph (eds), *The UN Convention on the Elimination of All Forms of Discrimination against Women: A Commentary* (2012) 51, at 52.

Article 1, as most of CEDAW's descriptions of specific rights, refers to 'a basis of equality of men and women' as the critical measure of non-discrimination, suggesting that male lives are the appropriate comparator for women. Scholars have argued however that Article 1 indeed supports a notion of 'transformative' equality, going beyond preventing discrimination to undertake an ambitious positive programme to achieve equality.[54] It is particularly evident in Article 3, requiring states parties to take positive measures to 'ensure the full development and advancement of women', in Article 5, which calls for the modification of social and cultural practices affecting both women and men, and in Article 11's prohibition of discrimination against women in employment on the basis of marriage and maternity.[55] CEDAW's monitoring body, the CEDAW Committee, has endorsed the notion of transformative equality,[56] which is more than simply allowing women entry into a male-defined world, requiring a transformation of social structures that rest on male domination. This entails not only institutional change, but also action to achieve a radical redistribution of resources and power in society. Sandra Fredman suggests that transformative equality involves 'a dismantling of the public–private divide and a reconstruction of the public world so that child-care and parenting are seen as valued common responsibilities of both parents and the community.' Such measures, she argues, are the basis of women being able to reach their capabilities and to fully express their choices in society.[57]

CEDAW's ambitious obligations of implementation are set out in Article 2. States parties undertake to include 'the principle of the equality of men and women' in their national legal systems and to 'ensure … the practical realisation of this principle'.[58] Article 2 also requires states to eliminate discrimination against women through legal and other 'appropriate measures', including the adoption of temporary special measures.[59] Many observers have celebrated CEDAW for its broad coverage, particularly its attention to women's civil and political rights as well as their economic, social, and cultural rights. Because of this, the treaty has been termed 'an international bill of rights for women'.[60]

Feminist campaigns on the international plane have tended to highlight common experiences women share. This is not a straightforward task. Political, social, and

[54] Ibid. at 56.

[55] Raday, 'Article 11', in M. A. Freeman, C. Chinkin, and B. Rudolph (eds), *The UN Convention on the Elimination of All Forms of Discrimination against Women: A Commentary* (2012) 279, at 304–305.

[56] See, e.g., CEDAW Committee, General Recommendation No. 25 (2004), para. 10.

[57] Fredman, 'Beyond the Dichotomy of Formal and Substantive Equality: Towards a New Definition of Human Rights', in I. Boerefijn et al. (eds), *Temporary Special Measures: Accelerating De Facto Equality of Women under Article 4(1) UN Convention on the Elimination of All Forms of Discrimination against Women* (2003) 111, at 115.

[58] CEDAW (n. 51) Art. 2(a).

[59] Ibid. Art. 4. See CEDAW Committee (n. 56) at para. 30; CEDAW Committee, General Recommendation No. 28, 16 December 2010, at paras 9, 20, 37(d).

[60] Boutros-Ghali, 'Introduction', in United Nations (ed.), *The United Nations and the Advancement of Women, 1945–1995* (1996) 5.

economic differences between women globally mean that their priorities can be far apart. At the first UN Conference on Women in 1975 in Mexico, for example, Western feminists emphasized workplace discrimination and reproductive rights as major concerns, while Third World feminists drew attention to imperial legacies and economic development.[61] More recently, as discussed below, the international feminist focus on violence against women has relied on broad brush claims about women's lives in order to generalize women's experience. Feminists have identified 'intersectional' analysis as one response to overcome essentialism.[62] This acknowledges the way that various forms of oppression, such as race, class, disability, religion, sexuality, and age, can interact and produce unique forms of discrimination that are otherwise invisible.[63] Intersectionality can easily slip into formulaic practices, however: there is an inevitable tension in tapping the international sphere as a site for action while respecting the specificities of women's lives at the local level. Feminism requires a sensitivity to context, for example through techniques such as 'world travelling'.[64] As Isabelle Gunning demonstrates in the context of human rights approaches to female genital surgeries, this means being explicit about our own historical and cultural backgrounds, trying to understand how other women might see us, and recognizing the complexities of the lives of women who are differently situated.[65]

4. Feminist Scholarship in International Law

Feminist legal scholarship began to appear in the 1980s. Denise Réaume has summarized the aim of such research on legal systems as the analysis of 'the exclusion of (some) women's needs, interests, aspirations, or attributes from the design or application of the law'.[66] It took some years for feminist voices to emerge in international law. They were inspired by a broad range of feminist scholarship, but the most immediate influences were those of feminist international relations (IR) specialists. These scholars provided perspectives that helped international lawyers unpack the gendered building blocks of international law, including conceptions of

[61] See generally, United Nations, Report of the World Conference of the International Women's Year—Mexico City, 19 June–2 July 1975, UN Doc. E/CONF.66/34 (1976), at 134.

[62] E.g. Crenshaw, 'Mapping the Margins: Intersectionality, Identity Politics, and Violence against Women of Color', 43 *Stanford Law Review* (1991) 1241; Davis, 'Intersectionality and International Law: Recognizing Complex Identities on the Global Stage', 28 *Harvard Human Rights Journal* (2015) 205.

[63] CEDAW Committee, General Recommendation No. 28 (n. 59) at para. 18.

[64] The term was introduced by Maria Lugones. See Lugones, 'Playfulness, "World"-Traveling, and Loving Perception', 2 *Hypatia* (1987) 3.

[65] Gunning, 'Arrogant Perception, World-Traveling and Multicultural Feminism: The Case of Female Genital Surgeries', 23 *Columbia Human Rights Law Review* (1991–92) 189, at 191.

[66] Réaume, 'What's Distinctive about Feminist Analysis of Law? A Conceptual Analysis of Women's Exclusion from Law', 2 *Legal Theory* (1996) 265, at 271.

the state, sovereignty, conflict, and peace.[67] Feminist IR theorists also pointed to the relationship of gender to other forms of power, such as race, nationality, and class and paid attention to the way that relations of power are constructed between diverse groups of women.[68] This scholarship encouraged international lawyers, and offered them conceptual tools, to challenge the claim that international law offers a rational, detached, and universal form of justice.

Feminist international legal writings often draw on a range of theoretical positions that can sit uneasily together; for example, the idea that women have distinctive interests and qualities may be combined with claims for equality with men. International legal scholars have pointed to apparent tensions in feminist approaches. One example is Nathaniel Berman's observation that feminist international lawyers critique the doctrines and structure of international law and yet also rely on the expansionist spirit of après-guerre internationalism to campaign for improvements in women's lives.[69]

This ambivalence about legal norms and institutions is a hallmark of feminism, and one that feminists embrace. They both challenge the masculine structures of law and yet rely on law as one means of achieving equality. Ratna Kapur and Brenda Cossman articulate this in their study of feminist engagement with the Indian legal system:

> The law has constructed women as ... passive and weak, as subordinate and in need of protection ... At the same time, law is a site where these roles and identities have been challenged ... [S]ocial reformers and feminist activists have sought ... to reconstruct women's roles and identities as more full and equal citizens.[70]

On this analysis law offers a forum for 'discursive struggle, where competing visions of the world, and of women's place therein, have been and continue to be fought out'.[71] International law then can be a site of both entrenched bias and emancipation. Other feminist scholars view international law as a safety net for women, a beacon in the face of the discrimination inherent in many national legal systems, much like the organizers of the International Congresses of Women over a century ago. Catharine MacKinnon takes this perspective in noting that 'the

[67] See, e.g., C. Enloe, *Bananas, Beaches and Bases: Making Feminist Sense of International Politics* (2000); C. Sylvester, *Feminist Theory and International Relations in a Postmodern Era* (1994); V. S. Petersen, *A Critical Rewriting of Global Political Economy: Integrating Reproductive, Productive and Virtual Economies* (2003); J. A. Tickner, *Gender in International Relations: Feminist Perspectives on Achieving International Security* (1992).

[68] See, e.g., J. J. Pettman, *Worlding Women: A Feminist International Politics* (1996).

[69] Berman, 'Power and Irony, or, International Law after the Après-Guerre', in E. Jouannet, H. Ruiz Fabri, and J. M. Sorel (eds), *Regards d'une génération de juristes sur le droit international* (2008), at 79.

[70] R. Kapur and B. Cossman, *Subversive Sites: Feminist Engagement with Law in India* (1996), at 12.

[71] Ibid.

further away from home women go, the experience has been, the more rights they get . . . making it more likely that women's violations . . . will be recognized as real'.[72] Feminist analysis has now been applied in a range of areas of international law such as international humanitarian law,[73] international criminal law,[74] the use of force,[75] and environmental law.[76]

One strand of feminist critique addresses the limited nature of the international legal understanding of equality and non-discrimination which promises equality on male-defined terms—that women be treated in the same way as a similarly situated man. This approach does not recognize the effects of structural discrimination against women or deal with a fundamental problem for women—the lack of economic, social, or political power in both the public and private worlds.

Feminists have also studied the language and imagery of the law and their dependence on gendered categories. International law lays claim to rationality, objectiveness, and abstraction, characteristics traditionally associated with Western masculinity, and it is defined in opposition to emotion, subjectivity, and contextualized thinking. Its claimed universality disguises its gendered character. An example is the development of the notion of the 'responsibility to protect' (R2P) at the turn of the twenty-first century to deal with mass atrocities. The R2P doctrine relies on gendered contrasts between action/inaction, force/passivity, order/chaos, practicality/theory, and optimism/pessimism to identify the use of force as the ultimate guarantee of stability.[77]

Feminist international legal scholarship typically presents itself as in conversation with the mainstream of international law. It challenges the mainstream to consider women's lives when applying or developing the law; it critiques the gendered assumptions of international legal principles; and it argues for an expanded referential universe. This conversation tends to be one-sided and there has been strikingly little engagement by mainstream or critical accounts of international law with feminist inquiries; indeed, feminist theories form a scholarly ghetto in international legal scholarship.[78]

The field of human rights has been a primary site for feminist scholarship in international law over the past 25 years. In his address to the 2015 EUI Summer

[72] MacKinnon, 'Creating International Law: Gender as Leading Edge', 36 *Harvard Journal of International Law* (2013) 105, at 120.

[73] See, e.g., Gardam, 'Women and the Law of Armed Conflict: Why the Silence?', 46 *The International and Comparative Law Quarterly* (1997) 55.

[74] See, e.g., L. Chappell, *The Politics of Gender at the International Criminal Court: Legacies and Legitimacy* (2015).

[75] See, e.g., G. Heathcote, *The Law on the Use of Force: A Feminist Analysis* (2011).

[76] See, e.g., Bowman, 'The Path from Feminist Legal Theory to Environmental Law and Policy', 22 *Cornell Journal of Law & Public Policy* (2013) 641.

[77] Charlesworth, 'Feminist Reflections on the Responsibility to Protect', 2 *Global Responsibility to Protect* (2010) 232.

[78] Exceptions include: Bianchi (n. 2) 183–204; B. S. Chimni, *International Law and World Order: A Critique of Contemporary Approaches* (2nd ed., 2017), at 358–439.

School, Professor Juan Mendez identified issues of 'gender' (meaning, I think, women) as an area of remarkable growth in the human rights field. Indeed, to some observers, feminist theories have now moved from the margins to the mainstream, and shape, even dominate, human rights discourse.[79] However, as we will see, while the language of feminism is regularly invoked in human rights contexts, it is a limited, even stilted, translation. Indeed, the field of 'women's human rights' largely avoids feminist terminology, perhaps to depoliticize its claims. The aim appears to be inclusion within the settled categories of human rights analysis. Mainstream human rights scholarship rarely engages with feminist critique, apart from the occasional footnote.

The most vigorous debates about feminist theorizing in human rights law have been *between* feminists, particularly between feminists who give priority to goals such as the inclusion of women in human rights institutions and those who are more interested in critique. As in other scholarly fields, the utopian instincts of political or activist feminism can be challenged by postmodern approaches, which are sceptical of grand narratives of disadvantage and advantage.[80]

One method of feminist scholarship in human rights law addresses Zalewski's first question—What about women? This work includes documenting the absence of women in the processes of defining human rights standards and in implementing them, and the silences that result.[81] Women are on the outskirts of international human rights institutions. The unequal representation of women in most of the institutions of the United Nations human rights system contravenes the obligation contained in CEDAW to ensure that women have the opportunity to participate in the work of international organizations 'on equal terms with men and without discrimination'.[82] The treaty provision appears to have little regulatory capacity. The members of the formal legal institutions are all nominated by states, a process which tends to reflect social and professional traditions in supporting men for prestigious positions as state representatives or international experts.

The composition of the UN human rights treaty bodies illustrates this well. The members of the bodies responsible for monitoring the apparently generally applicable treaties are overwhelmingly men. In August 2018, out of the nine UN human rights treaty committees with a total of 147 members, 62 were women (42%). However, 31 of the 62 women members were concentrated in two committees, the Committee on the Elimination of Discrimination against Women (22 out of 23 members) and the Committee on the Rights of the Child (9 out of 18 members). The Committee on the Rights of the Child was the only committee to have equal numbers of women and men. The Committee on Enforced Disappearances had

[79] See, e.g., J. Halley, *Split Decisions: How and Why to Take a Break from Feminism* (2006).
[80] See Benhabib, 'Feminism and Postmodernism', in S. Benhabib et al. (eds), *Feminist Contentions: A Philosophical Exchange* (1995) 17, at 29–30.
[81] See, e.g., A. Edwards, *Violence against Women under International Human Rights Law* (2010).
[82] CEDAW (n. 51) Art. 8.

three women members out of 10, and the Committee on Migrant Workers had two women members out of 14. Perhaps the most striking example is the Committee on the Rights of Persons with Disabilities, where 17 of the 18 members were men.

In normative terms women's lives are on the fringes of the traditional human rights canon, which tends to sidestep issues that have a particular significance for women, for example, the issue of illiteracy.[83] Moreover, international law focuses on states as primary violators of human rights. This obscures the significance of the activities of non-state actors, such as international monetary institutions, which can impose social and economic conditions on their loans, disproportionately affecting women's lives.[84] Posing the feminist question, 'What about women?' in the context of the international human rights system, then, highlights the absence of women's voices in its formal structures and the silences of the system with respect to many aspects of women's lives.

Feminist scholars of human rights have addressed Zalewski's second question, the role of gender, by identifying gendered hierarchies that influence human rights law. One example is the persistence of distinctions between public and private spheres of life in the liberal tradition, with human rights treaties trained on the world of public action, leaving the private, domestic world largely unregulated.[85] While there have been significant inroads into this distinction, for example through making violence against women in the domestic sphere a human rights issue, discussed further below, the distinction is regularly revived. 'Traditional values' campaigns by a coalition of states in the UN Human Rights Council to enshrine the traditional family as the basic unit of society illustrate this resurgence. The Council has adopted an annual resolution on 'the protection of the family' since 2014, which marked the twentieth anniversary of the International Year of the Family. The definition of 'the family' found in the resolutions is a limited one, apparently excluding all but families formed by heterosexual couples. It is presented as 'the fundamental group of society and the natural environment for the growth and well-being of all its members';[86] and it plays 'a crucial role in the preservation of cultural identity, tradition, morals, heritage and the values system of society.'[87] The 'protection of the family' resolutions imply that the preservation of the private sphere of the family is more significant than the protection of the human rights of

[83] See A. Robinson-Pant (ed.), *Women, Literacy and Development* (2004). In the context of the 1950 European Convention on Human Rights, see M. B. Dembour, *Who Believes in Human Rights? Reflections on the European Convention* (2006) 188–231.

[84] Detraz and Peksen, 'The Effect of IMF Programs on Women's Economic and Political Rights', 42 *International Interactions* (2016) 81.

[85] Charlesworth, 'World Apart: Public/Private Distinctions in International Law', in M. Thornton (ed.), *Public and Private: Feminist Legal Debates* (1995) 243.

[86] HRC Res. 29/22, Preamble.

[87] HRC, Draft Resolution—Protection of the Family: Role of the Family in Supporting the Protection and Promotion of Human Rights of Older Persons, UN Doc. A/HRC/35/L.21, 19 June 2017, Preamble.

individuals within the family.[88] This has repercussions for women and girls in particular, who generally have less power and status than men inside their families.

5. Feminist Projects in Human Rights Law

Two projects in the field of human rights, one institutional and one normative, illustrate the trajectories of feminist interventions on the international plane.

A. Gender Mainstreaming

The Fourth World Conference on Women, held in Beijing in 1995, endorsed 'gender mainstreaming' as a strategy to achieve women's equality in all 12 'critical areas of concern', including education, health, the economy, and human rights.[89] The notion of mainstreaming implies a contrast with a side stream, or subsidiary current. Its genesis in policy terms was the field of child education: mainstreaming meant including students with a range of learning abilities in the same classroom.[90] The idea of gender mainstreaming was to move acknowledgement of women's lives from the margins to the centre of institutional activities and regulation and thus reduce inequality.[91] During the 1990s and beyond, international institutions, from the UN, to the World Health Organization, to the World Bank, to the European Union embraced the notion of gender mainstreaming with alacrity, although the term 'gender' is untranslatable in many languages. It has been widely regarded as a story of feminist success, giving women entrée to the 'halls of power'.[92]

The price for inclusion of the transformative idea of gender in international institutions was, however, its radical simplification: the notions of biological sex and gender were effectively elided. This is clear for example in the influential description of gender mainstreaming adopted by the Economic and Social Council (ECOSOC) in 1997:

> Mainstreaming a gender perspective is the process of assessing the implications for women and men of any planned action, including legislation, policies or programmes, in all areas and at all levels. It is a strategy for making women's as well

[88] See, e.g., HRC Res. 72/145 (2017). See also Charlesworth, 'Culture and Tradition in the International Human Rights System', in G. Andreopolous (ed.), *Justice and World Order: Reassessing Richard Falk's Scholarship and Advocacy* (forthcoming).

[89] Beijing Declaration and Platform for Action (n. 1).

[90] Charlesworth, 'Not Waving but Drowning: Gender Mainstreaming and Human Rights in the United Nations', 18 *Harvard Human Rights Journal* 1, at 2.

[91] S. Kouvo, *Making Just Rights? Mainstreaming Women's Human Rights and a Gender Perspective* (2004).

[92] See, e.g., Halley (n. 79).

> as men's concerns and experiences an integral dimension of the design, implementation, monitoring and evaluation of policies and programmes in all political, economic and societal spheres so that women and men benefit equally and inequality is not perpetuated. The goal is to achieve gender equality.[93]

On this account, a 'gender perspective' appears to mean paying attention to the situations of biologically defined women and men in order to ensure equal representation of their views on public policy. Gender emerges as simply a synonym for women (and men) rather than as a way of analysing the power of social constructions of identity. The goal of 'gender equality' remains unelaborated, its vagueness allowing international institutions to adopt technocratic, procedural responses.[94] Studies of gender mainstreaming projects, often run without expertise, have observed the influence on them of conservative ideas about the roles of women and men.[95] This results in the integration of women and what are taken to be their concerns into existing policy frameworks, for example through equal opportunity programmes in the workplace, snuffing out the possibility of transformative equality.[96]

The effect of the restricted notion of gender mainstreaming in the field of human rights has in any event been mixed. It has not affected the low rates of participation of women in the international human rights system, for example in the membership of UN human rights treaty bodies noted above. The treaty bodies have a patchy record of taking up issues relating to women, much less gender. Apart from the Special Procedures of the UN Human Rights Council specifically devoted to women,[97] others have only sporadically addressed discrimination against women.[98]

The simplification of the idea of gender at the international level generally means that it now signifies a head count of women or paying attention to women's assumed vulnerability. An example is UN Security Council Resolution 1325 (UNSCR 1325) adopted on 31 October 2000, which called for an increase in women's representation in peace processes and for the incorporation of a 'gender perspective' in

[93] UNGA, Report of the Economic and Social Council for 1997, UN Doc. A/52/3, 18 September 1997, at 27.

[94] Caglar, 'Gender Mainstreaming', 9 *Politics and Gender* (2013) 336, at 338.

[95] See, e.g., Caglar, 'Gender Knowledge and Economic Knowledge in the World Bank and UNDP: Multiple Meanings of Gender Budgeting', in C. Scherrer and B. Young (eds), *Gender Knowledge and Knowledge Networks in International Political Economy* (2010) 55; Meier and Celis, 'Sowing the Seeds of Its Own Failure: Implementing the Concept of Gender Mainstreaming', 18 *Social Politics: International Studies in Gender, State, and Society* (2011) 469.

[96] Caglar (n. 94) 339.

[97] See OHCHR, *Special Rapporteur on Violence against Women, Its Causes and Consequences* (2018), available online at https://www.ohchr.org/EN/Issues/Women/SRWomen/Pages/SRWomenIndex.aspx (last visited 18 April 2023).

[98] For example, in 2017 a number of Special Procedures issued a joint statement deploring the backlash against women's rights. See OHCHR, *UN Experts Call for Resistance as Battle over Women's Rights Intensifies*, 28 June 2017, available online at https://www.ohchr.org/en/NewsEvents/Pages/DisplayNews.aspx?NewsID=21809&LangID=E (last visited 18 April 2023).

peacekeeping. Such a gender perspective is defined as giving attention to the 'special needs' of women and girls during repatriation, resettlement and reconstruction, supporting local women's peace initiatives and protecting the human rights of women and girls in any new legal order.[99]

UNSCR 1325, and the seven successor resolutions that comprise the Security Council's 'Women, Peace and Security' agenda,[100] presents gender as only about women, unconnected with masculine identities in times of conflict or violent patterns of conduct accepted because they are coded as male. The UN Secretary-General's annual report in 2017 on the implementation of UNSCR 1325 similarly calls on states to 'support measures that increase women's participation in peace processes at all levels',[101] 'address the root causes of conflict-related sexual violence',[102] and increase the number of women in national and international military forces.[103] UN peacekeeping mandates invoke the language of gender mainstreaming principally when sexual violence has been prevalent during a conflict.[104] In any event, the impact of the calls for greater engagement of women in peace and security operations has been marginal.[105]

At best, the narrow account of gender deployed in international institutions allows problems facing women to be understood as the product of particular cultures, lack of participation in public arenas, or lack of information or skills. It obscures the way that gender shapes understandings of the world. In the context of the 'Women, Peace and Security' agenda, the use of the term 'gender' has overlooked the effect of gendered thought on the way in which international conflicts are identified and resolved.[106] The international resort to the language of gender requires women to change or a change in the participation of women. In the international system, then, gender has become above all a technical issue, a head count of women and men. The relational nature of gender, the contestability of categories of femininity and masculinity, as well as the role of power relations and the ways that structures of subordination are reproduced have all but disappeared.[107]

[99] SC Res. 1325 (2000).

[100] SC Res. 1325 (2000); 1820 (2009); 1888 (2009); 1889 (2010); 1960 (2011); 2106 (2013); 2122 (2013); 2242 (2015).

[101] UNSC, Report of the Secretary-General on Women and Peace and Security, UN Doc. S/2017/861, 16 October 2017, para. 10.

[102] Ibid. para. 18.

[103] Ibid. para. 30.

[104] Kreft, 'The Gender Mainstreaming Gap: Security Council Resolution 1325 and UN Peacekeeping Mandates', 24 *International Peacekeeping* (2017) 132, 155–156.

[105] See, e.g., Bell and O'Rourke, 'Peace Agreements or Pieces of Paper: The Impact of UNSC Resolution 1325 on Peace Processes and Their Agreements', 59 *International & Comparative Law Quarterly* (2010) 941; Basini, 'Gender Mainstreaming Unravelled: The Case of DDRR in Liberia', in T. I. Gizelis and L. Olsson (eds), *Gender, Peace and Security: Implementing UN Security Council Resolution 1325* (2015) 210.

[106] See Kreft (n. 104).

[107] Baden and Goetz, 'Who Needs (Sex) When You Can Have (Gender)? Conflicting Discourses on Gender at Beijing', 56 *Feminist Review* (1997) 3, at 7; Caglar (n. 94).

B. Violence Against Women

A major focus of feminist activism and scholarship over the past three decades has been violence against women, a global phenomenon that international human rights law did not traditionally address, unless it met the narrow conditions to constitute torture. CEDAW did not refer to violence against women, reflecting the limited contemporary understandings of the prevalence or significance of such violence and the belief that it was not a matter of international concern, but one of domestic criminal regulation.[108] During the 1980s, civil society groups launched campaigns drawing attention to violence against women as an international issue[109] and the UN eventually took this up, starting with a General Assembly resolution in 1990.[110]

In 1992, the CEDAW Committee adopted General Recommendation 19 on violence against women.[111] The Recommendation presents violence against women as both a cause and a consequence of inequality between women and men and identifies such violence as a form of discrimination on the basis of sex, affecting women's enjoyment of human rights and freedoms equally with men. The Recommendation offers a broad account of violence, including both physical and mental harm and suffering and calls on states parties to prevent, investigate, punish, and make reparation for violence against women in both public and private spheres.

The Committee's inclusion of violence against women within the remit of CEDAW prompted a cascade of activity in other parts of the UN system. The following year the UN General Assembly adopted a Declaration on the Elimination of Violence against Women, taking the issue of general application beyond the treaty system.[112] The Declaration views violence against women as 'a manifestation of historically unequal power relations between men and women',[113] and, following the CEDAW Committee, presents it as a violation of women's human rights. In 1994, the UN Commission on Human Rights appointed a Special Rapporteur on the causes and consequences of violence against women, a mandate that has produced far-reaching and influential documentation and analysis.[114] The 1995 Beijing Declaration and Platform for Action designated violence against women as one of its 10 areas of critical concern, and three regional systems have adopted treaties on this issue.[115]

[108] Chinkin, 'Violence against Women', in M. A. Freeman, C. Chinkin, and B. Rudolph (eds), *The UN Convention on the Elimination of All Forms of Discrimination against Women: A Commentary* (2012) 443, at 444–445.

[109] See Bunch, 'Women's Rights as Human Rights: Towards a Re-Vision of Human rights', 12 *Human Rights Quarterly* (1990) 486.

[110] See, e.g., GA Res 45/114, 14 December 1990.

[111] CEDAW Committee, General Recommendation No. 19 (1992).

[112] UNGA Res 48/104, 20 December 1993.

[113] Ibid. Preamble.

[114] UNCHR Res 1994/45, 4 March 1994.

[115] Inter-American Convention on the Prevention, Punishment and Eradication of Violence against Women (Convention of Belém do Pará) 1994, 33 ILM 1534; Council of Europe Convention

Feminist scholars seem to have assumed that regulating violence against women would offer a platform to argue for more thoroughgoing legal change.[116] Measured in terms of the adoption of international instruments, this strategy has been productive. It has however reinforced particular images of women and the harms they face. International legal developments relating to violence against women have ended up identifying some women, especially poorer women and Third World women, as particularly susceptible to violence and in need of protection rather than as rights-holders.[117] Indeed, Otto attributes the relative success of legal campaigns to respond to violence against women, and their capacity to attract conservative support, to their reinforcement of the gendered distinction between victims and protectors.[118]

Another feature of developments in international law is a focus on sexual violence against women. This is clear in the Security Council's 'Women, Peace and Security' agenda, and in international criminal law, for example, the criminalization of rape and sexual assault during conflict.[119] The jurisprudence typically depicts women as passive victims of sexual violence perpetrated by male aggressors.[120] On this analysis, the role of international institutions is above all that of protector. Some feminist scholars have been critical of the focus on sex as the locus of women's oppression, rather than inequality, and they have urged a more complex understanding of women's lives through considering intersecting factors such as race, wealth, class, and religion.[121]

A separate critique is that the feminist activist focus on sexual violence against women has trumped other understandings of sexuality. Catherine O'Rourke has observed that '[t]he cost of feminist engagement with international law is the privileging of women's sexual "purity" that serves to reinforce, rather than to challenge, prevailing restrictive ideals of female sexuality.'[122] While some feminists

on Preventing and Combating Violence against Women and Domestic Violence 2011, CETS No 210; Protocol to the African Charter on Human and Peoples' Rights on the Rights of Women in Africa 2003, OAU Doc. CAB/LEG/66.6.

[116] Otto (n. 16), at 490.

[117] Ibid. 501; Kapur, 'The Tragedy of Victimization Rhetoric: Resurrecting the "Native" Subject in International/Post-Colonial Feminist Legal Politics', 15 *Harvard Human Rights Law Journal* (2002) 1; Kapur, 'Un-Veiling Equality: Disciplining the "Other" Woman Through Human Rights Discourse', in A. M. Emon, M. S. Ellis, and B. Glahn (eds), *Islamic Law and International Human Rights Law: Searching for Common Ground?* (2012) 265.

[118] Otto, 'The Exile of Inclusion: Reflections on Gender Issues in International Law over the Last Decade', 10 *Melbourne Journal of International Law* (2009) 11, at 15–16.

[119] Engle, 'Feminism and Its (Dis)Contents: Criminalizing Wartime Rape in Bosnia and Herzegovina', 99 *American Journal of International Law* (2005) 778.

[120] Chappell (n. 74) 90.

[121] Kapur, 'Gender, Sovereignty and the Rise of a Sexual Security Regime in International Law and Postcolonial India', 14 *Melbourne Journal of International Law* (2013) 317, at 331; Engle, 'International Human Rights and Feminisms: When Discourses Keep Meeting', in D. Buss and A. Manji (eds), *International Law: Modern Feminist Approaches* (2005) 47.

[122] O'Rourke, 'Feminist Strategy in International Law: Understanding Its Legal, Normative and Political Dimensions', 28 *European Journal of International Law* (2017) 1019, 1039.

identify sexuality as a site of violence, danger, and oppression for women, others have drawn on queer theory to emphasize that sexuality can also be a site of pleasure and liberation. In the context of the regulation of sexual relationships by UN peacekeeping troops and local populations, for example, feminist scholars have questioned the rationale for 'zero tolerance' policies, tightly controlling sexual contact. The claim is that such policies are based on a stereotype of women as passive victims rather than allowing for sexual agency.[123]

A broader account of the causes of violence against women emerges from the CEDAW Committee's updating of General Recommendation 19 in 2017.[124] General Recommendation 35 identifies the structural basis of violence against women as 'the ideology of men's entitlement and privilege over women'.[125] It acknowledges the array of contexts in which violence occurs, including actions by both state and non-state actors,[126] as well as the ways that diverse factors such as culture, tradition, and austerity economics contribute to impunity for violence against women.[127] The erosion of normative standards dealing with violence against women in the name of culture, tradition, and religion has become prevalent, however. As noted above, coalitions of states, religious groups, and conservative social movements have worked within international institutions to emphasize the family as an embattled entity in need of protection, rather than as a site of violence against women. They have associated attention to domestic violence as 'gender ideology' imposed by Western elites, a manifestation of a larger wave of illiberal populism that uses the frame of anti-colonialism.[128]

6. Conclusion

What is the relationship between feminism and the future? Although feminism is built on an imagined future of equality, its trajectory on the international plane supports Albert Einstein's observation that 'the distinction between past, present and future is only a stubbornly persistent illusion'.[129] The oppression of women is supported by an elaborate structure of male privilege, deeply resistant to change. Feminist issues have been either corralled in the margins of the international system or rendered so bland that they have no transformative bite. The apparent

[123] Otto, 'Making Sense of Zero Tolerance Policies in Peacekeeping Sexual Economies', in V. Munro and C. F. Stychin (eds), *Sexuality and the Law: Feminist Engagements* (2007) 259.

[124] CEDAW Committee, General Recommendation No. 35, 14 July 2017, updating CEDAW Committee, General Recommendation No. 19 (1992).

[125] CEDAW Committee General Recommendation No. 35, 14 July 2017, para. 19.

[126] Ibid. para. 20.

[127] Ibid. para 7.

[128] See Korulczuk and Graff, 'Gender as "Ebola from Brussels": The Anticolonial Frame and the Rise of Illiberal Populism', 43/4 *Signs: Journal of Women in Culture and Society* (2018) 797.

[129] A. Einstein (1955), quoted in Gleick, 'Time Regained', *New York Review of Books* (6 June 2013), at 48.

success of some feminist legal strategies raises new problems: feminist futurists must recognize that even modest gains may generate a backlash and that the future is not necessarily a more hospitable place for women.

The powerful emotion of hope often informs ideas about the future and feminism, like all social movements, mobilizes hope. Hope has many forms, however. Scholars have distinguished between private or individual hopes and those held by groups. A further distinction drawn in relation to group hopes is that between collective and public hope. Collective hope means that the emotion is widely experienced in a society, that the beliefs on which the hope is based are broadly shared, and that the emotions and beliefs are expressed culturally.[130] Public hope, by contrast, is articulated by political actors in a strategic way.[131] This type of hope can dull public consciousness about injustice and delay or thwart calls for change.[132] Feminist engagements with human rights law illustrate both types of hope.

The language of human rights has been central to feminist futures and the way that women's equality is imagined globally. It has underpinned collective feminist hopes. But human rights language has a double edge for feminists and can be appropriated to circumvent transformation. As we saw in the case of gender mainstreaming, international institutions have tended to deploy simplified ideas about the causes of women's inequality with men and offer public hope that change is inevitable. They have also resisted addressing the impact of economic and social systems on women's lives, focussing instead on violence against women as a standalone issue. Otto has observed that increased institutional acceptance of feminist vocabularies has been undermined by 'selective engagement' with feminist ideas, the lack of systems of accountability, and the re-emergence of stereotypes of women.[133] There has been great resistance internationally to dealing with structural discrimination against women.[134] Many imagined feminist futures in human rights law involve improving the law to include women's lives. These plans rest on an uneasy base as they require identification of special, vulnerable features of womanhood, that reinforce gendered distinctions.[135]

A regular debate in feminist international legal literature is whether feminist scholars should aim for the margins or the centre of the discipline. The margin is often understood as the place we want to leave behind as we head for the centre, the mainstream, where, it is assumed, power resides and all the action takes place. Ideas of marginality and centrality are fluid however and there are locations at which

[130] Drahos, 'Trading in Public Hope', 592 *Annals of the American Academy of Political and Social Science* (2004) 20.

[131] Ibid. Drahos points to the example of the way public hope was used in trade negotiations between the United States and the developing world on intellectual property rights over anti-retroviral drugs.

[132] Braithwaite, 'Collective Hope', 592 *The Annals of the American Academy of Political and Social Science* (2004) 6, at 8.

[133] Otto (n. 118) 12.

[134] Ibid. at 21.

[135] Otto (n. 16) 502.

they meet and even merge. The UN Security Council's adoption of Resolution 1325 in 2000 shows how a marginal international issue, women's situations in times of conflict, was given an appearance of centrality through being debated in the UN Security Council. This carapace of importance and priority has since crumbled through lack of oversight and political will.

Feminists occupy a complicated position in relation to the international human rights system: to make progress, feminist activists must work within highly politicized and patriarchal structures. Feminist theorists on the other hand are less constrained institutionally and have the capacity to question and challenge the system, articulating radical alternatives. Feminist intellectual methods may thus be more resilient and tolerant of experimentation than feminist activism on the international plane. But their momentum comes from hope, which is sustained in turn by concrete action. Without action, hope can shrivel into despair.[136] Feminists of the future will need to continue negotiating the uneasy relationship between theory and activism through a practice of critical, collective hope and constant questioning.

[136] Courville and Piper, 'Harnessing Hope through NGO Activism', 592 *The Annals of the American Academy of Political and Social Science* (2004) 39, at 56–57.

6
Climate Pathways and the Future of Human Rights

Stephen Humphreys

1. Introduction

'The future ... is characterized by two main features: first the increasing speed with which it approaches us, and second its unknown quality'—so said Reinhardt Koselleck in 1965.[1] The future is not a fact. It is not even a predicted pathway so much as a heuristic with which we organize our thoughts about the present, make sense of our current trajectories, and choose, to the extent we can, how to shape them.[2] In Koselleck's memorable expression, the future is best understood as a 'horizon of expectations', a set of more or less plausible scenarios written with present concerns and interests foremost in our minds.[3] Such scenarios need not, and in an important sense, *cannot* track any 'actual' future that comes to pass as present. That is not their job. Rather, assertions of the future re-articulate for us today how we expect the present to look retrospectively. We grasp our present, in part, by attempting to extrapolate from it. For this reason, we might expect interest in the future to spike whenever the present seems particularly nebulous or unmoored, when the horizon becomes blurry. 'Counsel' (Koselleck again) 'is henceforth to be expected not from the past, but from a future which has to be made'.[4] If this is the case today, it is no doubt partly due to the profound insecurity generated by climate change.

In a short history of futurology written in 2013, Jenny Anderson suggests that the work of future-casting has typically pitted data-driven empiricists against imaginative utopianists.[5] The contemporary art of climate science appears to

[1] R. Koselleck, *Futures Past* (2004) 22.

[2] Ibid. Chapter 7.

[3] Ibid. at 270–275, but see the discussion in contributions to 117, *The American Historical Review* (2012) 5, especially Engerman, 'Introduction: Histories of the Future and the Futures of History', 117 *American Historical Review* (2012) 1402.

[4] Koselleck (n. 1) 40. He also writes (at 22) that the experience of the 'currently unapprehendable present' tends to disappear in a policy focus on the future. Presumably, by corollary, the attempt to grasp the future renders the present more 'apprehendable', less constrained by the immediacy of the experienced moment.

[5] Anderson, 'The Great Future Debate and the Struggle for the World', 117 *American Historical Review* (2012) 1411. My thanks to Nehal Bhuta for drawing my attention to this work.

Stephen Humphreys, *Climate Pathways and the Future of Human Rights*. In: *Human Rights in Transition*.
First Edition. Edited by Nehal Bhuta, Oxford University Press. © Stephen Humphreys 2024.
DOI: 10.1093/oso/9780198901921.003.0006

embody both. In its institutionalized form, at the Intergovernmental Panel on Climate Change (IPCC)—created in 1988 with a mandate to digest science for policymakers—climate science has been an arena in which scientific 'objectivity' (in the form of consensus-seeking among teams of authors, peer reviewers, and editors) must always compete and contend with political 'reality' (in the form of the authoritative stamp of state delegates at the IPCC plenary).[6] A caucus of scientists corralled to political ends, the IPCC has navigated this founding tension remarkably smoothly.[7]

It seems apt, then, to begin with a short vignette showcasing this unusual relationship. Back in 2007 or so, the 'climate modelling community' was asked by the IPCC plenary to envisage how a *feasible* 2°C global pathway might look, since the peer-reviewed scientific literature had found little evidence that there was such a thing.[8] The conditions that might produce a result that was already, by then, international climate policy, had not seemed likely to appear of their own accord—and so the scientists were asked to imagine them.

This story may be read to show that political imperatives edge out unpalatable truths. Or it may show the reverse: that the politically necessary requires imaginative departure from the empirically evident—utopianism as the art of the possible. In practice, climate science—which started out as a branch of meteorology—has always comprised a form of forecasting.[9] But forecasting is not prediction. Indeed, beginning from the IPCC's 2000 'Special Report on Emissions Scenarios' (SRES), itself produced in response to a request from the IPCC's policymakers, climate forecasting has taken the form of a menu of scenarios. The 40 SRES scenarios were described at the time as 'alternative images of how the future might unfold', with differing emphases on various economic and social drivers, and a spectrum of assumptions about available technological and policy dynamics.[10] But 'no judgment [was] offered ... as to the preference for any of the scenarios[,] they [were] not assigned probabilities of occurrence', and 'neither must [the scenarios] be interpreted as policy recommendations'.[11] Rather '[e]ach storyline represents different demographic, social, economic, technological, and environmental developments, which may be viewed positively by some people and negatively by others'.[12]

The attempt to forecast economic and social transformation is, then, not merely a matter of identifying evolution and adaptation, but also of decision and 'preference'.

[6] For the IPCC's composition, see: https://www.ipcc.ch/about/ (last visited 18 April 2023).

[7] A good early account is Miller, 'Hybrid Management: Boundary Organizations, Science Policy, and Environmental Governance in the Climate Regime', 26/4 *Science, Technology, & Human Values* (2001) 478.

[8] Van Vuuren et al., 'RCP2.6: Exploring the Possibility to Keep Global Mean Temperature Increase Below 2°C', 109 *Climatic Change* (2011) 95, at 96.

[9] P. Edwards, *A Vast Machine* (2012).

[10] Intergovernmental Panel on Climate Change, *IPCC Special Report on Emissions Scenarios: Summary for Policymakers. A Special Report of Working Group III* (2000) 4.

[11] Ibid.

[12] Ibid.

Even today, climate empiricists lack the modelling capacity (and, fortunately, the hubris) to analyse, or even collect, the quantities of data that would be needed to foresee developments whose ordinary complexity is saturated in the perplexity of human will and choice.[13] Ultimately, climate science cannot be predictive—since one cannot predict the future of 'climate change' without predicting 'the future' *tout court*. Instead, the 40 climate scenarios of 2000 helped to set horizons of expectation. But if climate science has discovered that to set viable climate horizons requires future-casting about everything else too, it is becoming apparent that the reverse is also true. Today's 'future' scenarios in any field will be deficient if they are not also stories about climate change.

Which takes me to 'the future of human rights': any future story about human rights that neglects the scenarios and horizons of climate science will, I suggest, be deficient. But this clarifies little: both terms—'climate change' and 'human rights'—are broad and indeterminate. And given that human rights refer in principle to the material experience of concrete individuals, any statement on their 'future' in the abstract already feels vague and unanchored. (Climate science, by contrast, features numerous claims of this sort.) Even once the terms have been corralled into a kind of provisional determinacy (as I will attempt to do in this chapter), to speak of their 'future' amounts to little more than recasting present concerns along pathways of future likelihood.

Climate scenarios comprise myriad permutations of economic, social, and technological developments, subject to the variability of meteorological transformation and to political and technological action. How to relate this small universe of possibility to 'human rights'? In the following account I will draw on the climate scenarios and pathways adopted in recent IPCC reports.[14] I will indicate some likely human rights concerns raised in these scenarios, and some pathways along which we might imagine those concerns playing out.

Before I plunge in, however, another terminological caveat is needed. Chronologies are inevitably written from the perspective of one or several interests or points of view.[15] There is, perhaps, a God's eye view from which one might in principle refer to 'the future'.[16] But such a perspective is unapprehendable (to use

[13] Ibid.

[14] While the IPCC's *Special Report on Global Warming of 1.5°C* allows a nuanced comparison between 1.5°C and 2°C pathways, the probability of either actually occurring remains small. Current trends expect average global warming of at least 2.4°C above preindustrial temperatures and perhaps far higher. See V. Masson-Delmotte et al., *Global Warming of 1.5°C. An IPCC Special Report* (2018). The report website (https://www.ipcc.ch/sr15/, last visited 20 April 2023) carries an apposite moniker from Antoine de Saint Exupéry: 'Pour ce qui est de l'avenir, il ne s'agit pas de le prévoir, mais de le rendre possible'.

[15] See Humphreys, 'Against Future Generations', 33/4 *European Journal of International Law* (2022) 1061, especially 1073–1075.

[16] Konrad Leibniz had suggested that 'the whole of the coming world is present and prefigured in that of the present', a view barely modified in Stephen Hawking's notion of temporal 'light cones', which emanate from each moment or event to ultimately (at the unencompassable limit) envelope the totality of future time. See Koselleck (n. 1), at 20. S. W. Hawking, *A Brief History of Time* (1989) Ch. 2.

another term of Koselleck's) to the chronicler: in the attempt to relate a universalist history, as Theodor Adorno once put it, 'the concept of reality decays into farce'.[17] The proliferation of scenarios complicates this critique but does not escape it.

Insofar, then, as we refer to 'human rights' in the future, much depends on whose human rights we have in mind. So, if we were to describe the future of the human right not to be tortured, we would tell a different story from that relating the human right to food.[18] We would focus on a different set of likely victims, on a specific set of familiar threats, and on how we imagine these unfolding in specific places, with reference to specific historical drivers. Climate change will figure starkly in any future story about those experiencing hunger; less obviously for those at risk of torture.[19] If we start from existing themes within the languages of climate change and human rights, we will more readily converge on some topics than others.

Moreover, and more to the point, climate change is not an egalitarian catastrophe. We often speak of it affecting 'our future' if 'we' don't act (a convention I will frequently adopt here). But in practice, the future of some individuals is at much greater risk from climate change than the future of others, especially in the short to mid-term.[20] The 'some' who are at particular risk are termed 'vulnerable' in climate reports.[21] What makes certain persons vulnerable, per the climate literature, is a combination of attributes: their location, their poverty, their insecurity, their lack of voice, their existing marginalization.[22] What their vulnerability consists in may be described in various registers: sociological, political, or economic, for example. To speak, as I shall do here, of this vulnerability to climate change as predisposing individuals to possible violations of *human rights*—to food, water, shelter, health,

[17] This was Adorno's critique of Hegel. T. Adorno, *Negative Dialectics* (1973), at 330. See generally 326–334.

[18] For an excellent discussion of these various rights in juxtaposition, see S. Marks and A. Clapham, *International Human Rights Lexicon* (2005).

[19] Such an attempt might begin with Adger et al., 'Human Security' in C. B. Fields et al. (eds), *Climate Change 2014: Impacts, Adaptation, and Vulnerability. Part A: Global and Sectoral Aspects. Contribution of Working Group II to the Fifth Assessment Report of the Intergovernmental Panel on Climate Change* (2014).

[20] Grear and Gearty, 'Choosing a Future: The Social and Legal Aspects of Climate Change', in A. Grear and C. Gearty (eds), *Choosing a Future: The Social and Legal Aspects of Climate Change* (2014) 1, and Grear, 'Towards "Climate Justice"? A Critical Reflection on Legal Subjectivity and Climate Injustice: Warning Signals, Patterned Hierarchies, Directions for Future Law and Policy', in ibid. at 103.

[21] Schneider et al., '2007: Assessing Key Vulnerabilities and the Risk from Climate Change', in M. L. Parry et al. (eds), *Contribution of Working Group II to the Fourth Assessment Report of the Intergovernmental Panel on Climate Change, 2007* (2007) 779.

[22] E.g. ibid. at 784 (i.e. para. 19.1.2.4): 'Vulnerability to climate change differs considerably across socio-economic groups, thus raising important questions about equity. Most studies of impacts in the context of key vulnerabilities ... have focused on aggregate impacts, grouping developing countries or populations with special needs or situations. Examples include island nations faced with sea-level rise ... countries in semi-arid regions with a marginal agricultural base, indigenous populations facing regionalized threats, or least-developed countries ... Within developed countries, research on vulnerability has often focused on groups of people, for example those living in coastal or flood-prone regions, or socially vulnerable groups such as the elderly.'

life, and so on—is thus deliberately to institute a vocabulary of law, responsibility, and redress.[23]

Following this introduction, the chapter has four principal sections, looking first at some climate-modelled pathways (in Section 2) to inform speculative 'human rights pathways' (Section 3). I will review the 1992 United Nations Framework Convention on Climate Change (UNFCCC) and its 2015 Paris Agreement,[24] with an eye to the human rights dimensions of two key areas of climate law: global targets (Section 4) and mitigation policies (Section 5). To conclude (Section 6), I will suggest that the relative mismatch between long-standing human rights aspirations and the foreseeable climate-changed future is itself a symptom of a larger historical shift.

2. Pathways

Although climate scenarios have become refined over the decades, they remain very broadbrush.[25] The climate system is complex: to predict the physical effects of systemic meteorological change is already difficult. But since the actual trajectory of the climate system depends on policy and behavioural change, the IPCC has aimed also to factor in social, economic, and political data. Since 2011, IPCC reports have relied on 'representative pathways' to supplement their 'scenarios'. I will draw on these pathways in this section.

In its *Fifth Assessment Report*, the IPCC introduced a suite of 'Representative Concentration Pathways' (RCPs), which differ from the earlier SRES 'scenarios' in that each one is consistent with several possible scenarios. These originally included a strong 'business-as-usual' pathway (RCP8.5), a weaker one (RCP6.0), a strong mitigation pathway (RCP4.5), and a 2°C pathway (RCP2.6).[26] The numbers in each case refer to the 'radiative forcing' of greenhouse gas concentrations by 2100, measured in Watts per metre squared (W/m^2)—so radiative forcing of 2.6 W/m^2 will likely produce a global average warming of 2°C above preindustrial temperatures by 2100, and so on. Climate modellers later added three further pathways (used in the subsequent IPCC *Special Report on Global Warming of 1.5°C* and

[23] See Humphreys, 'The Covenants in the Light of Anthropogenic Climate Change', in D. Moeckli and H. Keller, *The Human Rights Covenants at 50* (2018).

[24] UN Doc. FCCC/CP/2015/L.9/Rev.1 (12 December 2015) (the 'Paris Agreement').

[25] For a succinct account of pathways, see Allen et al., 'Framing and Context' in Masson-Delmotte et al. (n. 14) 49, at 62–64 ('Cross-Chapter Box 1: Scenarios and Pathways').

[26] Collins et al., 'Long-term Climate Change: Projections, Commitments and Irreversibility', in IPCC (T. F. Stocker et al. (eds)), *Climate Change 2013: The Physical Science Basis. Contribution of Working Group I to the Fifth Assessment Report of the Intergovernmental Panel on Climate Change* (2013), especially 12.3. The IPCC adds: 'These new scenarios, Representative Concentration Pathways, are referred to as pathways in order to emphasize that they are not definitive scenarios, but rather internally consistent sets of time-dependent forcing projections that could potentially be realized with more than one underlying socioeconomic scenario.'

Sixth Assessment Report), including one likely to produce 1.5°C global warming (RCP1.9) above preindustrial temperatures, on average. The original business-as-usual scenarios assumed that then-current rates of greenhouse gas (GHG) emission increase only marginally through the twenty-first century but result in temperature increases of 4-5°C above industrial levels.[27] The RCP2.6 scenario, providing the possibility of remaining within 2°C, requires that global emissions fall by about 70% of current rates by 2050 and to 'near zero ... or below' by 2070.[28] Some emission of Methane (CH_4) will always be necessary, to food production in particular. This means that to achieve an emissions level 'near zero', or near 'net zero', consistent with a 2°C pathway, CO_2 emissions must effectively be brought *below zero* by 2070 at the latest.[29] This may be possible—in theory, at least—if the natural capacity of sinks is enhanced through Carbon Dioxide Removal (CDR) technologies.[30]

The work of modelling continues independently of IPCC reporting, feeding into each new report, undertaken at a set of well-established research centres.[31] Drawing on a set of five narrative 'shared socioeconomic pathways' (SSPs), large computing models ('integrated assessment models' or IAMs) crunch vast amounts of data to determine the conditions under which each of the RCPs is produced. Repeated iterations combining different IAMs, SSPs, and RCPs have produced thousands of climate scenarios, each one embedding different assumptions about energy use, economic growth, population size, global trade patterns, and so on.[32] The scenarios most likely to produce what the modellers refer to as an 'equitable'

[27] World Bank, *Turn Down the Heat: Confronting the New Climate Normal*, Vol. 3 (2014) 6. 'On average, the RCP8.5 is illustrative of a range of business-as-usual scenarios, reaching a global-mean warming level of about 4°C above pre-industrial levels by the 2080s, and gives a median warming of about 5°C by 2100'.

[28] O. Edenhofer et al. (eds), *Climate Change 2014: Mitigation of Climate Change. Contribution of Working Group III to the Fifth Assessment Report of the Intergovernmental Panel on Climate Change* (2014) 52. See generally, 50–56, especially the chart at 54. The RCP scenarios express concentrations of GHGs in 'parts per million of Carbon Dioxide equivalent' (ppm CO_2eq). Concentrations increase in line with cumulative emissions, and likely temperature increase estimates correspond to specific concentrations. In order to have a 'likely' (i.e. 66%) chance of meeting 2°C, cumulative emissions should remain stable at 450ppm CO_2eq. According to the European Environment Agency, this level was passed in 2020, reaching 465ppm CO_2eq (https://www.eea.europa.eu/ims/atmospheric-greenhouse-gas-concentrations, last visited 23 May 2023). Concentrations of CO_2 alone passed 424ppm in May 2023 (https://www.co2.earth/daily-co2, last visited 23 May 2023). At 500ppm CO_2eq (480–530) the 2°C target is still 'more likely than not' (>50% chance), unless there is an overshoot to 530ppm, in which case it is 'as likely as not' (50% chance). By 550ppm CO_2eq (530-580), the 2°C target is 'more unlikely than likely' (<50% chance).

[29] Van Vuuren et al. (n. 8) graph at 104.

[30] Edenhofer et al. (n. 28) 52.

[31] Six institutions are formally involved in scenario building of this sort (although there are very many more working on climate modelling): the National Institute for Environmental Studies (Japan); the Pacific Northwest National Laboratory (USA); the Netherlands Environmental Assessment Agency; the International Institute for Applied Systems Analysis (Austria); the Potsdam Institute for Climate Impact Research (Germany); and the Fondazione Eni Enrico Mattei (Italy).

[32] See the SSP Public Database, available at https://tntcat.iiasa.ac.at/SspDb/dsd (last visited 23 May 2023). For more information on SSPs and IAMs, see Humphreys (n. 15), 1075–1080.

outcome by 2100—that is, not marked by vast and quasi-permanent disparities of wealth and opportunity—combine high economic with low population growth.[33] While such a notion of climate 'equity' may capture the sorts of concerns generally associated with human rights,[34] the scenarios deal in aggregates: individuals appear neither as agents or victims, but massed as drivers and effects.

3. Common but Differentiated Rights?

An early (2008) report on the human rights dimensions of climate change included in an annex a set of 25 areas for future research and action.[35] Many of these avenues have, in the intervening years, been explored—notably, as then foreseen, the relative dearth of effective policy and the resulting experience of climate harm has led to a significant body of litigation raising human rights claims in connection with climate change.[36] As I write, it is clear there will be much more litigation in future, with as yet unpredictable results.[37] While some of the strategies outlined in the 2008 report—such as mainstreaming climate advocacy into the work of human rights groups—are now at an advanced stage, others—such as attempts to build human rights safeguards into the 'post-Kyoto regime' (i.e. the 2015 Paris Agreement) or other related regimes such as REDD+ and carbon markets—have been so far less successful.[38]

In effect, we already have, then, various nascent human rights 'pathways', which we might envisage as commencing in the recent past and continuing through an imaginable future. Laid out in more detail, these would presumably factor in, among many variables: actual human rights harms due to climate impacts; the trajectory of climate policies globally and locally; the institution of procedural human rights safeguards, or their lack, within national and international climate law and

[33] See contributions to the Special Issue of *Global Environmental Change*, vol. 42 (2017), especially Riahi et al., 'The Shared Socioeconomic Pathways and Their Energy, Land Use, and Greenhouse Gas Emissions Implications: An Overview', 42 *Global Environmental Change* (2017) 153; van Vuuren et al., 'Energy, Land-use and Greenhouse Gas Emissions Trajectories under a Green Growth Paradigm', 42 *Global Environmental Change* (2017) 237.

[34] See Allen et al. (n. 25), at 55.

[35] International Council on Human Rights Policy [ICHRP], *Climate Change and Human Rights: A Rough Guide* (2008), at 85–90. Available at https://papers.ssrn.com/sol3/papers.cfm?abstract_id=1551201 (last visited 23 May 2023).

[36] Ibid. 88 and 89–90. At the time of writing, human rights have been raised before courts in Pakistan, the United States, the Netherlands, Germany, Portugal and Switzerland, inter alia, with two cases now pending before the European Court of Human Rights, and requests for advisory opinions regarding the human rights dimensions of climate change before the Inter-American Court of Human Rights and the International Court of Justice.

[37] See, for example, C. Hodgson, 'The money behind the coming wave of climate litigation', *Financial Times* (5 June 2023).

[38] J. Dehm, *Reconsidering REDD+* (2021); La Viña et al., 'History and Future of REDD+ in the UNFCCC: Issues and Challenges', in C. Voigt (ed.), *Research Handbook on REDD+ and International Law* (2016) 11.

policy; the ratio, provenance, and scope of judicial pronouncements and their reception; corporate climate responses, themselves functioning within their own horizons of expectation; the likely (seismic) movements of capital and persons over time, from zones of climate vulnerability to spaces of relative robustness; and so on. In this section, I will not attempt to trace these imaginable human rights pathways, but will aim merely to sketch the relevance of two of the many considerations necessarily imbricated within any such pathways: global targets, on one hand; mitigation policies, on the other.

Turning to international climate law, a first step might be to notice the human rights relevance of the well-known principle of 'common but differentiated responsibilities and respective capabilities' in Article 3(1) of the UNFCCC. CBDR, as it is sometimes known, is not an invention of the UNFCCC—its roots stretch back at least to the 1972 Stockholm Declaration on the Human Environment and arguably earlier.[39] CBDR acknowledges (implicitly) the greater historical responsibility for GHG emissions of wealthier countries as well as (explicitly) their greater capacity to address the problem. The principle also, to make an obvious point, endorses the UN's division of the world into 'developed' and 'developing' countries—and presumes the latter require the developmental space to aspire to lifestyles prevalent within the former.[40] But CBDR goes beyond mere developmental*ism*: it incorporates the post-1960s attempt by newly postcolonial states to reorient the global economy by seeking guarantees within the UNFCCC framework for financial and technological transfers between wealthier and poorer countries.[41] The global effort to mitigate and adapt to climate change thus appears in the climate regime as an extension of a long-running international law contest over the appropriate distribution of wealth, cognizant of historical injustice and seasoned with the vague, perennially unfulfilled promise of compensation for colonialism.[42] (As is well known, this contest, the struggle for a 'new international economic order' (NIEO), did not succeed.[43])

The CBDR principle is not alien to human rights. Formally, as Lavanya Rajamani noticed some time ago, a version of CBDR appears in the International Covenant on Social, Economic and Cultural Rights, Article 2(1), which expects different states to 'progressively realize' their rights at varying speeds, according to their 'available resources'.[44] With this differentiation, the treaty text itself apparently assumes future human rights pathways into its purview. That same article, in a more explicit reference to the NIEO, also presupposes the importance of 'international

[39] L. Rajamani, *Differential Treatment in International Environmental Law* (2006).

[40] Mickelson, 'South, North, International Environmental Law, and International Environmental Lawyers', 11 *Yearbook of International Environmental Law* (2000) 52–81.

[41] Notably in Arts 4(5) and 4(7) UNFCCC.

[42] Mickelson (n. 40).

[43] See the special issue of *Humanity*, issue 6.1 (2015).

[44] Ibid. at 20–24. The reference depends on the explicit reference, in Art. 2(3), to differential obligations between developed and developing states.

assistance' in meeting these obligations, although the mechanics are unclear. All of this appears consonant with the UNFCCC, which likewise presupposes that 'economic and social development and poverty eradication are the first and overriding priorities of the developing country Parties' and assumes international transfers of some sort in meeting its treaty objectives.[45] However, the mechanics of CBDR are again mysterious in the UNFCCC, as in the ICESCR. Whereas the UNFCCC appears to distinguish between the different obligations of 'developed' as against 'developing' countries, it also blurs the notion of who is obliged to whom through the adoption of a spectrum of varying and overlapping terms referring to different groups of states.[46] On a close reading of the UNFCCC text, several of its putative obligations do not appear easily assignable to specific relationships between specific states.[47] Nevertheless, for what it's worth, the UNFCCC and ICESCR converge in their explicit recognition of the importance of economic development for human wellbeing and the relevance of international coordination (assistance, co-operation, but also trade and the extraterritorial effects of domestic activities) to address entrenched imbalances.[48]

In climate change too, the (incurably vague) CBDR principle is consistent with a multiplicity of possible pathways, although it may equally remain unmet. The principle appeared in the 1997 Kyoto Protocol to the UNFCCC, which capped future emissions for 'developed' countries alone—thereby giving rise to the problem of 'carbon leakage'.[49] The principle is reiterated throughout the 2015 Paris Agreement, under which all parties are to submit 'nationally determined contributions', to include limitations on GHG emissions.[50] Under Paris's version of CBDR, as applied at least, wealthier countries commit to reducing emissions below a *past* baseline,[51]

[45] UNFCCC, Art. 4(7). See Humphreys, 'Conceiving Justice: Articulating Common Causes in Parallel Regimes', in S. Humphreys (ed.) *Human Rights and Climate Change* (2009) 299–319.

[46] Annex I countries comprise the old West (Australia, Canada, Europe, New Zealand, and the United States) plus the then recently post-communist countries and Japan. Annex II is a shorter list featuring the same countries with the exception of the former Eastern bloc countries. Art. 4(2) UNFCCC, further refers to 'developed country Parties and other Parties included in Annex I'; Arts 4(3) and 4(5) refer to 'developed country Parties and other developed Parties included in Annex II'. See also Arts 4(2)(g), 4(7), 9, and 12(3).

[47] This fudge appears to have been deliberate. See Voigt, 'State Responsibility for Climate Change Damages', 77 *Nordic Journal of International Law* (2008) 1.

[48] Humphreys, 'Competing Claims: Human Rights and Climate Harms', in Humphreys (n. 45) 37–68, at 50–51.

[49] Carbon leakage refers to the inability of national-level caps to effectively restrain global emissions, since it is possible to shift emission-producing activities from countries with caps to countries without (indeed, this was actively encouraged by the Kyoto Protocol's Clean Development Mechanism). See De Schutter, 'Trade in the Service of Climate Change Mitigation: The Question of Linkage', in Grear and Gearty (n. 20); Pauwelyn, 'Carbon Leakage Measures and Border Tax Adjustments Under WTO Law', in D. Prevost and G. van Calster (eds), *Research Handbook on Environment, Health and the WTO* (2012).

[50] Paris Agreement, Art. 2.2: 'This Agreement will be implemented to reflect equity and the principle of common but differentiated responsibilities and respective capabilities, in the light of different national circumstances.' See also the preamble and Arts 3, 4, 7, 8, 9, 10, 11, 13(9) and 13(10), and 15.

[51] See, for example, the Federation of Russia's NDC (online at the UNFCCC website: http://www4.unfccc.int/submissions/INDC/Submission%20Pages/submissions.aspx (last visited 18 April 2023)).

whereas poorer countries commit to reducing *future* rates, or intensities, of emission.[52] Both past and future baseline years vary—as a result, a (necessarily partial) 'God's eye view' is graspable only across time, as a sinuous set of interweaving pathways.

4. Targets

The determination of a level of emissions amounting to 'dangerous anthropogenic interference with the climate system', as Article 2 of the UNFCCC expects, has human rights implications. The 'danger' in question extends to economic hardship, food insecurity, political instability, the precarity of migration. Conversely, if human rights are imported into an analysis of 'dangerous anthropogenic interference', this may presumably sharpen the focus onto questions of human life, health, food security, and so on.

In 2007, the Alliance of Small Island States (AOSIS), led by the Maldives, adopted just such a position to some effect, including it in the intergovernmental Malé Declaration on the Human Dimension of Global Climate Change.[53] The 'target' question is not abstract for small island states, some of which are already at risk of disappearance at current temperature levels.[54] Their persistent efforts appear to have borne fruit in the final text of the Paris Agreement, which famously 'aims to strengthen the global response to the threat of climate change . . . including by . . . [h]olding the increase in the global average temperature to well below 2°C above pre-industrial levels and to pursue efforts to limit the temperature increase to 1.5°C above pre-industrial levels'.[55] Whereas the explicit, if relatively anodyne, reference to human rights in the Agreement's preamble resulted from significant negotiation in the long run up to the Paris COP, the words 'well below 2°C' could have been taken directly from the Malé Declaration.[56] In any case, concerns for

[52] See, for example, Costa Rica's 'intended nationally determined contribution' (INDC), online at the UNFCCC website: http://www4.unfccc.int/submissions/INDC/Submission%20Pages/submissions.aspx (last visited 18 April 2023), and see discussion on the Climate Action Tracker website: http://climateactiontracker.org/countries/costarica.html (last visited 18 April 2023).

[53] Malé Declaration on the Human Dimension of Global Climate Change, Preamble and para. 1, stating that 'climate change has clear and immediate implications for the full enjoyment of human rights including inter alia the right to life, the right to take part in cultural life, the right to use and enjoy property, the right to an adequate standard of living, the right to food, and the right to the highest attainable standard of physical and mental health' and seeking to 'ensure that temperature rises fall well below 2°C above pre-industrial averages, and that greenhouse gas concentrations are less than 450ppm [CO_2eq]'. (At time of writing, this level has been surpassed: see n. 28.)

[54] IPCC, 'Summary for Policymakers', in R. Pachauri et al. (eds), *Climate Change 2014: Synthesis Report. Contribution of Working Groups I, II and III to the Fifth Assessment Report of the Intergovernmental Panel on Climate* (2014) 55–56 at 74.

[55] Art. 2.1 Paris Agreement. 'Pre-industrial' in practice has come to refer to the period prior to 1861, before which temperature measurements are not believed reliable.

[56] Preamble Paris Agreement: 'Parties should, when taking action to address climate change, respect, promote and consider their respective obligations on human rights . . .'.

human rights seem to have been relevant to the inclusion of the 1.5°C aspiration in Paris.

And yet, the very notion of a temperature target is fraught with difficulty from a human rights perspective. Mortality due to hurricanes, floods, droughts, and heatwaves has already increased beyond what would have been the case absent climate change.[57] A human rights 'based' assessment might therefore conclude that current levels of greenhouse gases—the concentration of 420+ 'parts per million' of CO_2 in the atmosphere—are already 'dangerous' given their impact on the right to life.[58] At the same time, rapid mitigation efforts, of the sort that might have put the Paris 1.5°C target within reach, carry their own human rights concerns. Absent significant transfers of resources—which have not been forthcoming—many states will be plunged into economic hardship were they to move swiftly to decarbonize.[59]

Two speculative human rights 'pathways' might flow from this observation. Along one, we can imagine the right to life (say) becoming incorporated into climate policy to provide a 'test' to aid in deciding a global policy target. Here, we would expect an evolving practice to revisit and interpret climate terms of art—'excess mortality' and so on—in the language of human rights, side by side with a refining of the Paris target ('well below' 2°C). Second, we might conceive of a human rights jurisprudence evolving in such a way as to recognize specific climate-related 'violations' due to climate impacts on rights to—to choose obvious examples—life, food, health, or shelter, were local policies inadequate to an agreed global target.

The first of these two pathways involves a problem familiar from the history of 'operationalizing' human rights in development policy.[60] Climate science offers a sliding scale of relativity: current temperatures involve more deaths than past temperatures; future temperatures more again.[61] The numbers are greater or lesser, but remain imprecise, hedged within broad 'ranges' and varying degrees of probability, and of course they do not concern specific 'victims' but rather a broad mass of abstract 'vulnerable' persons. On a sliding scale of this sort, it is difficult to locate an entry point for human rights analysis. Any position is either unhelpfully absolutist (no increase in temperature at all is permissible) or unhelpfully relativist (any degree of increase is more permissible than any next degree of increase). The challenge in either case is to justify a threshold point, beyond which the number of deaths would be meaningfully 'excessive', in a context in which the current baseline

[57] Pachauri et al. (n. 54) 55–56.

[58] See https://www.co2.earth/daily-co2 (last visited 25 June 2023). On 24 June 2023, the figure was 423.35 ppm of CO_2. This is distinct from the figure for all greenhouse gases, currently estimated at 465 ppm CO_2eq (see n. 28).

[59] Humphreys (n. 15), at 1087–1089. See too Wolf, 'The green transition won't happen without financing for developing countries', *Financial Times* (20 June 2023).

[60] For a good account: Koskenniemi, 'Human Rights Mainstreaming as a Strategy for Institutional Power', 1/1 *Humanity* (2010) 47.

[61] Pachauri et al. (n. 54).

in fact already entails mounting excess.[62] A reasonable threshold might be the point where we 'knew or should have known' about the harmful consequences of GHGs. That is: a temporal rather than a numerical threshold—although this too is problematic insofar as any such threshold was long ago passed. We would need to factor in the amount of warming already 'locked in' at the time the harmful effect was known and, additional to that, the harmful effect of steps taken to stay *within* the target—a sudden end to fossil fuels, for example, would itself trigger much harm, entering us into familiar and uncomfortable cost-benefit analyses. Putting all these factors together, what is the appropriate target beyond which temperatures ought not rise?

A question of this sort prompts rallying behind disciplinary boundaries: in law, as in politics, we might prefer to look to science for answers.[63] However, as we have seen, climate scientists avoid explicitly recommending specific scenarios—and in any case, the policy detail that would underpin any particular scenario remains black-boxed in climate models.[64] The choice of any specific global target (1.5°C or 2°C, for example) therefore cannot escape the subjective views and political calculations of the various interested actors. Indeed, the function of the IPCC is precisely to allow states in plenary to make calls of this kind by political fiat, since they cannot be derived from the science alone.[65] An explicit appeal to human rights might have, in principle, removed (or appeared to) the whiff of political *voluntas* that permeates the Paris objective, replacing it, for example with international *ethical* consensus—but in the event, no such appeal was made.[66] In practice, the target ensconced in Article 2 of the Paris Agreement reflects neither an 'objective' scientific consensus nor even the implicit claim—that a human rights analysis might have carried—to provide a less arbitrary yardstick than sheer political will (or its lack).[67] Moreover, even had it been adopted, a human rights analysis could hardly have escaped either the arbitrariness inherent in choosing a global target nor the expediency of political decision, and nor even could it have provided the legitimacy of moral authority, given the invidious trade-offs entailed even by a lower-end target.[68]

At time of writing, in mid-2023, we appear to be embarked upon the second pathway outlined above—an evolving human rights jurisprudence, sensitive to the

[62] Caney, 'Human Rights as Moral Thresholds', in S. Humphreys, *Human Rights and Climate Change* (2010).

[63] See in this regard, Humphreys, 'How to Define Unjust Planetary Change', *Nature* (31 May 2023).

[64] See the discussion in Humphreys (n. 15) 1075–1080.

[65] Miller (n. 7).

[66] The Paris negotiations involved discussion on the explicit inclusion of 'human rights language' in Art. 2, but this was ultimately rejected.

[67] This point is made explicitly by the Dutch Supreme Court in the *Urgenda* case. See Judgment of the Dutch Supreme Court [Hoge Raad], Case no. 19/00135, 20 December 2019, para. 6.2.

[68] In practice the 1.5°C target entered the Paris Agreement because it was both ambitious (championed by a 'high ambition coalition') and arbitrary (that is, its proponents appealed rather to goodwill than reasoned exposition); but also because its status, as worded, is profoundly ambiguous.

differential local impacts of various policy attempts to align with a broad global target.[69] Indeed, the global target provides an indispensible backdrop to recent climate cases. For example, the first instance ruling in the now-iconic *Urgenda* case, on 24 June 2015, predated the Paris Agreement's 1.5°C aspiration by some months, and required the state to align with the lower end of the IPCC's 2007 recommended reductions of 25–40% by 2020—based on an assumed 2°C global target. When the Supreme Court ruled on the same case on 20 December 2019, the original IPCC recommendation had been surpassed both by the lower Paris target and the proximity of the 2020 deadline.[70] The Court thus found itself in the bizarre situation of upholding a policy, partially on human rights grounds, that had already been abandoned in the scientific literature, and that, on its own analysis, appeared inadequate both to global climate policy and to the Netherlands' international obligations.[71]

Viewed in terms of future-casting, the *Urgenda* rulings highlight the profound potential slippage between the sedate temporality (let's call it) of the court process-cycle—the seven-odd years from Urgenda's original petition in 2012, through first instance, appeal, and the final Supreme Court ruling—and the accelerating temporality of actual climate change, as well as the rapidly-adjusting scientific and political responses. The time, we might conclude with Hamlet, is 'out of joint'.[72] However, post-Paris cases are not inoculated from the potential absurdism of moving targets and shifting timelines: the Paris language of 'well below' 2°C itself provides little clarity given, as the German Federal Constitutional Court put it in the 2021 *Neubauer* ruling, 'the considerable uncertainty which the IPCC itself has documented by stating ranges and levels of confidence'.[73] For the German court this uncertainty precludes a court from assessing the levels of national reductions appropriate to any given global target.

Human rights were explicitly at issue in both the *Urgenda* and *Neubauer* cases. Perhaps, then, these rulings provide some insight into the broader direction of human rights jurisprudence in this domain? A principal concern raised back in

[69] At time of writing, two climate change-centred cases are pending before the European Court of Human Rights: ECtHR, *Duarte Agostinho and Others v. Portugal and Others*, Appl. no. 39371/20 and *Verein KlimaSeniorinnen Schweiz and Others v. Switzerland*, Appl. no. 53600/20, with seven others adjourned pending rulings on these two. See Registrar, European Court of Human Rights, 'Status of climate applications before the European Court', Press release (2 February 2023).

[70] The various rulings in the the case are available on the Urgenda website: https://www.urgenda.nl/en/themas/climate-case/ (last visited 21 June 2023). See Hoge Raad (n. 67) para. 7.5.1.

[71] Ibid. paras 7.2.8–7.2.10. At para. 7.2.11, there appears to be a judicial fudge, endorsing—in the context of the Paris objective—a continuing 'international consensus' on the IPCC's earlier (2007) recommended emissions reduction target for developed countries (of 25% by 2020) even though this latter target was no longer mentioned *at all* in the wake of the Paris Agreement, something the judgment itself noted (at para. 7.2.5).

[72] The much-awaited German case of *Luciano Lliuya v. RWE AG* has taken eight years to date, with no conclusion at time of writing. Available online: http://climatecasechart.com/non-us-case/lliuya-v-rwe-ag/, last visited 26 June 2023.

[73] *Neubauer v. Germany*, Bundesverfassungsgericht [BVerfG] [Federal Constitutional Court], Order of the First Senate, Case no. BvR 2656/18/1, BvR 78/20/1, BvR 96/20/1, BvR 288/20, 24 March 2021, para. 162.

2008 seems, thus far at least, ominously borne out: that the factual responsibility of high-emitting countries for extensive human rights harms in lower-emitting counties may elude human rights courts.[74] Germany and the Netherlands are both comparatively high emitting countries in per capita terms, and thus relatively higher contributors to global climate harms. The worst of these harms—the human rights impacts of climate change—are not, however, experienced in these countries but in much more vulnerable states: Pakistan, for example, experienced devastating floods in 2022, partly attributable, on most accounts, to climate change. The matter arose explicitly in the *Neubauer* ruling, given that petitioners from Bangladesh and Nepal were joined to the petition, claiming their fundamental rights too (alongside German residents), had been violated under Germany's Basic Law, due to the German failure to reduce emissions.[75] The Court gave short shrift to this claim: 'no violation of a duty of protection arising from fundamental rights is ascertainable vis-à-vis the complainants who live in Bangladesh and Nepal.'[76] In the case of *Urgenda*, similar claims—if more abstractly formulated—involving the rights and interests of 'current and future generations in other countries' were dismissed at first instance and did not return.[77]

The courts in both *Urgenda* and *Neubauer* note that measures taken in the Netherlands and Germany to reduce emissions can benefit individuals in other countries in the world by helping rein in global emissions. But both Courts also interpret the human rights impacts of specific levels of national emission reduction solely in terms of their home territorial populations. In *Neubauer*, notably, the German state's capacity to adapt in future is further taken into account as possibly justifying a less stringent mitigation policy in the present—even though such a choice might potentially have devastating human rights consequences abroad.[78] Both courts, in other words, appear relatively unconcerned about a future human rights pathway that is potentially much more harmful abroad than at home.

5. Curbs

A grim irony of evolving global climate policy is that, as things stand at least, we appear to be headed for the worst of both worlds. Steps to curtail emissions sharply

[74] ICHRP (n. 35), at 4: 'Under human rights law, a person's government ordinarily has the primary duty to act when rights are violated. In the context of climate change, however, responsibility for impacts in the most vulnerable countries often lies not with the government nearest to hand, but with diffuse actors, both public and private, many of whom are located far away. Human rights law does not easily reach across international borders to impose obligations in matters such as these.'

[75] *Neubauer* (n. 73) paras 78–79.

[76] Ibid. para. 173 (*et seq.*). See the further discussion in Humphreys (n. 15).

[77] *Verdict of Rechtbank Den Haag*, Case no. C/09/456689/HA ZA 13-1396, 24 June 2015, para. 4.92. The Court declined to decide the matter.

[78] *Neubauer* (n. 73) paras 167, 173–179. See also para. 163.

look likely to materialize, with all the hardship they entail—but may be neither quick enough nor deep enough to head off serious human harms. This poses a conundrum for future-casting. Climate scenarios must, in a sense, assume a veil of ignorance concerning the present, imagining and articulating a set of viable futures, no matter how unlikely, in an attempt to redirect policy. The inclusion of the 1.5°C target in Article 2 of the Paris Agreement arguably marks just such a moment of wilful ignorance, recasting an aspiration that was never likely in practice as a desirable policy goal, in order to bend policy towards a 'horizon of expectation' better calibrated to various stated goals, even if these are highly unlikely to be met.[79]

Swift global reduction of greenhouse gases, especially CO_2, is and will continue to be hugely costly in numerous respects.[80] Costs are compounded in countries already struggling with human rights concerns—human rights are themselves costly (the 'highest attainable standard of healthcare' and so on). This signals a likely trade-off for many states, between the imperatives of human rights (notably 'efforts to eradicate poverty', per Article 2.1 of the Paris Agreement) and climate change mitigation. The possibility that climate change may require such a trade-off has garnered plenty of attention across decades of climate change debate. To most, it has seemed fair (or 'equitable') that states' contributions to the mitigation effort should be contingent on their relative responsibility for having caused climate change and their relative capacity to pay for mitigation (this is to restate the CBDR principle).[81]

The UNFCCC already proclaimed in 1992 that 'economic and social development and poverty eradication are the first and overriding priorities of the developing country parties' (Art. 4.7 UNFCCC). In Paris, this notion reappears in a diluted form: 'peaking will take longer for developing country Parties' (Art. 4.1 Paris); as well as in various references to the importance of 'sustainable development and poverty eradication', and in the somewhat tautological proposition that 'enhanced support for developing country Parties will allow for higher ambition in their actions' (Art. 4.5 Paris). These articulations each acknowledge the costliness of mitigation for poorer countries, and the potential trade-off with development goals, which are in turn consonant with human rights aspirations.

A number of scholars have suggested that the importance of energy to future human rights fulfilment calls for a 'new' human right—to carbon, to emit GHGs, to energy, or to technology in some form.[82] Perhaps surprisingly—to human rights

[79] See 'The world is going to miss the totemic 1.5°C climate target', *The Economist* (5 November 2022); Masson-Delmotte et al. (n. 14).

[80] Calculating the costs is, however, notoriously difficult. See Edenhofer et al., 'Technical Summary', in Edenhofer et al. (n. 28) 56–64.

[81] See the various contributions to S. Gardiner et al., *Climate Change Ethics: Essential Readings* (2010).

[82] See the discussion in Edenhofer et al. (eds) (n. 28), ch. 3 (discussing writings by Henry Shue, Simon Caney, and Alex Gosseries). See too C. Gonzalez et al., *Energy Justice: US and International Perspectives* (2018).

lawyers at least—this debate has in fact long informed international climate change law-making.[83] Relatedly, various iterations of the notion that, over the long term, the world's states ought ideally to move towards a converging standard of per capita emissions have been touted over the years.[84] The closest thing to a 'right to emit' to have emerged from the UNFCCC process is, however, not a universal human right to a carbon quota to underpin basic standards of living, but a proprietary right to trade on emissions markets (under the 1997 Kyoto Protocol). The UNFCCC Conference of the Parties (COP), meeting in Marrakech in 2007, declared that the Protocol did not 'create or bestow' a 'right, title or entitlement to emissions of any kind'. But it clearly did. The basic trading unit in emissions markets, though often characterized negatively (as a 'certified emission reduction', for example) is undoubtedly a 'right, title or entitlement' to emit greenhouse gases. The Marrakech declaration is presumably best read to mean that Kyoto did not create a universal 'human' (and certainly not 'inalienable') right to emit. What was created was a property right of sorts.

So neither Article 4.7 UNFCCC, nor the CBDR principle, nor the Kyoto Protocol created a positive human 'right to emit' carbon under international law in the interests of development or related human rights (for either states or individuals). However, they do appear to conserve existing rights to emit among developing countries, by not imposing a *requirement* to limit emissions. This would also be in line with the human right to self-determination, provided in common Article 1 of both international covenants on human rights, and of course it also accords with the conception of sovereignty reiterated in the UNFCCC's preamble.[85] The subtlety of the Paris Agreement has apparently been to persuade poorer states to give up this right voluntarily—not through any explicit cap or limitation in the Agreement itself but through the steps outlined in their 'nationally determined contributions' (NDCs). Developing countries are not explicitly required in the Paris Agreement to limit GHG emissions, and yet, almost universally, they have done so. Insofar as NDCs are binding, this is due to their status in domestic rather than international law. Nevertheless, the non-retrogression ratchet clause in the Paris Agreement (Art. 4.3) tends to extend this domestic obligation into an international law obligation.[86] This ratchet is explicitly tempered by the CBDR principle. In practice, Paris assumes away the binary notion of a 'right' to emit that one

[83] ICHRP (n. 35) 9–11.

[84] These initially went by the moniker 'contraction and convergence' (ibid. at 10). A sophisticated take on this idea is provided in Stockholm Environmental Institute/Ecoequity, Greenhouse Development Rights (2009).

[85] Preamble UNFCCC: 'States have, in accordance with the Charter of the United Nations and the principles of international law, the sovereign right to exploit their own resources pursuant to their own environmental and developmental policies.'

[86] Art. 4.3, Paris Agreement: 'Each Party's successive nationally determined contribution will represent a progression beyond the Party's then current nationally determined contribution and reflect its highest possible ambition, reflecting its common but differentiated responsibilities and respective capabilities, in the light of different national circumstances'.

has or not, in favour of a set of sunsets, horizons, and baselines. The proprietary rights that remain will almost certainly accrue to companies rather than states or individuals, but they are destined to become ever more restricted and expensive and difficult to retain, until at last—at least in principle—they disappear. That appears to be the Paris horizon of expectation of the right to emit.

From the perspective of 'future' human rights pathways, three relatively straightforward points might be added.

First, as I have already indicated, the exigency of carbon reduction places poorer countries in something of a bind: the imperative to reduce or limit carbon dependency makes the achievement of basic human rights more difficult. There are several reasons for this, essentially related to the costs of mitigation: fossil fuels remain significantly cheaper than the alternatives—and even should this change, it is costly to shift an economic infrastructure from one energy base to another, as even the wealthiest countries are discovering.[87] The IPCC is clear on the latter point: rapid mitigation (of a kind needed to stabilize global temperature rise 'well below' 2°C), would be hugely costly, and the costs would disproportionately burden developing countries.[88] At the same time, however, rapid *global* decarbonization is vital to these same countries, given that they are, in most cases, profoundly vulnerable to climate change impacts. The UNFCCC flags a way out of this conundrum—through some form of transnational 'technology transfer' (in Art. 4.5 and 4.7): subsidized access to international technologies, of a kind consistently entrenched within climate change law, but not forthcoming to date. The studies examined by the IPCC suggest that the 'effort-sharing' needed 'to ameliorate' the 'asymmetry' of the cost-burden on developing countries could be 'on the order of hundreds of billions of USD per year before mid-century'.[89]

Failing this, there is neither an obvious legal nor economic incentive for poorer countries to contribute extensively to global mitigation—and human rights considerations would tend to pull both directions. Nevertheless, as I noted a moment ago, most developing countries have in fact, in their initial NDCs, accepted limitations on future emissions (even if these limitations are, in several cases, set so loosely—that is, based on such optimistic assumptions about future economic growth—as to have little practical consequence).[90] If the major emitters do not take the lead—as advised, but famously not required, in Article 4.4 of the Paris

[87] See, for example, Wolf (n. 59).

[88] Clarke et al., 'Assessing Transformation Pathways', in Edenhofer et al. (n. 28) at 419: 'reaching about 450 ppm CO_2eq by 2100 would entail global consumption losses of 1–4 % in 2030 (median of 1.7 %), 2–6 % in 2050 (median of 3.4 %), and 3–11 % in 2100 (median of 4.8 %) relative to what would happen without mitigation.' It is difficult to know how to interpret the clause 'relative to what would happen without mitigation': it is hard to imagine that taking *no* action would not be much *more* costly (this was the key point made in the influential 2006 Stern Review).

[89] Ibid.

[90] The NDCs are available on the website of the UNFCCC secretariat (unfccc.int). Analyses are provided on the website of the Carbon Tracker Project.

Agreement[91]—the individual efforts of poorer countries are likely to be costly, ineffective, and deleterious to human rights. That is, of course, one sort of human rights pathway: cumulative deterioration. Recent floods, hurricanes, heatwaves, and wildfires indicate it is already well underway.

The second point is related: while the familiar registers of human rights law and climate law speak in terms of states 'fulfilling' human rights or 'meeting' emission reduction commitments, neither of these objectives are, properly speaking, in the gift of many developing countries (indeed it is not clear they are in the power of any states). We do not live in a command and control world in which states can easily prioritize fulfilment of, say, the 'right to housing' or the 'right to water' through budgetary and policy measures alone.[92] In practice, each of these rights—and many other 'social and economic rights' at issue in climate change—have long acted as channels for contesting the organization of the economy. For example: should the state build social housing? Or further the private market through mortgage incentives? Should it ensure free water provision to deprived populations or privatize water and rely on the market for efficient distribution? Or should it devise hybrid policies? Likewise with emission reduction: old-style command-and-control—such as outright banning of fossil fuel extraction or consumption—even now, with so much at stake, remains largely off limits. Moreover, states are tied into international trade and investment obligations that tend to preclude or at least complicate such moves.

This is as true for 'developed' as 'developing' countries. But the latter are even more constrained: there has been little appetite among development funders or major international lenders—on whom many countries depend for stable revenues—for the kinds of economic policies that would simply aim to 'fulfil' the human rights to food, water, housing, or health to those 'in need'. Rather, international development policy has long preferred to further economic structures that incentivize innovation in order to 'grow' economies that can 'lift' people out of poverty.[93] This preference for private-ordering has also extended to emission regulation. There are few signs that states' *de jure* obligations under international human rights law are about to translate into expectations for strong state action, even where these dovetail with climate goals. Nevertheless, let us flag two possible pathways here—on the first, the discourse of human rights gradually crumbles as states refuse to arrogate unto themselves the powers necessary to assure their

[91] Art. 4.4 Paris Agreement: 'Developed country Parties should continue taking the lead by undertaking economy-wide absolute emission reduction targets.' On the day the Paris Agreement was signed, 12 December 2015, the final text was held up for several hours while the term 'should' was successfully substituted in place of 'shall'.

[92] See, for an example of this dilemma with regard to housing, J. Hohmann, *The Right to Housing: Law, Concepts, Possibilities* (2013).

[93] Humphreys, 'The Rule of Law as Morality Play', 23 *Finnish Yearbook of International Law* (2016) 3–44.

credibility; on the second, human rights achievement is frankly associated with a stronger more interventionist state than is presently the liberal norm.

This takes me to a third relevant point regarding human rights pathways in the context of steep mitigation: even to acknowledge the dependence of human rights fulfilment on the capacity to grow an economy discloses an uncomfortable truth about the contemporary framing of human rights. That is, their apparent indifference to wealth inequality.[94] On most readings, nothing in the world's human rights treaties assumes there need be any limit on economic expansion, and so achievement of 'basic' human rights is implicitly compatible with wealth inequality—even extreme inequality. But this assumption is difficult to sustain in the light of climate science. Successive IPCC reports have pointed out that mitigation is best achieved by reducing energy demand, and that this is most easily managed through changing living standards and expectations: less production, slimmer diets, less waste.[95] RCP2.6, for example, expects a dramatic reduction in global energy usage on 'business-as-usual' by 2100—by approximately 25%—only achievable by reining in economic growth per se.[96] And yet—still future-casting—there is little sign at present of any legitimation of 'degrowth' in economic or development policy.[97]

RCP2.6—the 2°C world—sets a horizon of expectation in which energy use is gradually curbed, carbon emissions are buried underground, and regions converge slowly towards economic parity. In the world we still live in, by contrast, vast wealth inequality has accompanied boundless energy increase.[98] A basic question is whether the introduction of sharply bounded global energy use can in fact 'lift' a global population of billions to a basic level of subsistence *while sustaining* inequality at this level? Once there are limits to expansion, can everyone get enough to get by, even in theory, while some continue to have so much more?

Thus, climate change poses in a new light some familiar questions about wealth distribution and human rights. Is the notion of universal basic human rights realistic within the limits imposed by climate change? That is, can 'growth' continue at a rate adequate to lifting living standards for the several billions for whom they

[94] Moyn, 'A Powerless Companion: Human Rights in the Age of Neoliberalism', 77 *Law and Contemporary Problems* (2014) 147–169.

[95] Edenhofer et al. (n. 28) 'Technical Summary' at 66: 'Emissions can be substantially lowered through: changes in consumption patterns (e.g., mobility demand and mode, energy use in households, choice of longer-lasting products); dietary change and reduction in food wastes; and change of lifestyle (e.g., stabilizing/lowering consumption in some of the most developed countries, sharing economy and other behavioural changes affecting activity).' See ibid. 68 (table TS.3).

[96] Van Vuuren et al. (n. 8) graph at 102.

[97] There are, on the other hand, an increasing number of new models and ideas to draw on. See, for example, the New Economics Foundation website: http://www.neweconomics.org (last visited 18 April 2023). See J. Hickel, *Less is More: How Degrowth will Save the World* (2020).

[98] According to the World Bank, 2.1 billion people survive on less than $3.10 per day, almost a third of the world's total population. See: http://www.worldbank.org/en/topic/poverty/overview (last visited 18 April 2023).

remain inadequate? If so, can this be done while also sustaining current levels of inequality? If not, what is the human cost of sustaining current levels of inequality?

6. Conclusion

A respected international lawyer, speaking in 2008 at one of the earliest meetings at the UN's Palais des Nations in Geneva on the relationship between human rights and climate change, commented that the human rights treaties were drafted and signed before climate change was recognized or understood, and were, for that reason, not equipped to address it.[99] Human rights law, the claim goes, belongs to a past in which climate change did not yet belong to the future.

There is more than a grain of wisdom in this observation. But one might also ask whether the inadequacy of international human rights law in the face of climate change might not have to do with something more basic than ignorance of climate change. The great human rights treaties envisage a certain kind of future: a future leading into a 'social and economic order in which the rights set forth ... can be fully realized'.[100] It is unclear whether, in the 75 odd years since the Universal Declaration of Human Rights, there ever was a future pathway that would 'fully realize' all human rights for 'everyone'. But the point was at least debatable—indeed, it has been the principal stake of countless debates on 'globalization' and development and 'neoliberalism' and 'austerity' over the last decades.

The phenomenon of climate change, I suggest, radically complicates those debates, and that vision, by placing a question mark over the actual nature of the putative pathway itself—the future upon which 'we' believed we were embarked all along. An article of economic faith—the developmental presumption behind the ICESCR in particular—that had seemed, for decades, to have been an engine of progress turns out to have also been a destroyer of value. What had been considered a source of universal wealth is beginning to look like a source merely of partial wealth and *also* a source of broad-based immiseration. This story is still in the process of being told and, through its retelling, being understood—and the efforts to do so have not so far featured human rights as a principal element.[101]

[99] With thanks to Françoise Hampson for permission to quote.

[100] Art. 28, Universal Declaration of Human Rights.

[101] Dehm, 'International law, temporalities and narratives of the climate crisis', 4/1 *London Review of International Law* (2016) 167.

As yet we don't have 'representative' human rights pathways. But what if human rights scholars were to adopt this climate science technique? Might it temper the unavoidably doleful 'empirical' future of human rights, faced with climate realities, with some wilful utopianism, the pathway as map, perhaps a reboot of the original postwar motif of hope for a better world?[102] Which sort of human rights pathways are likely in conditions of climate change? Which are possible? Which are desirable?

[102] Recall, for example, the US representative at the opening of the San Francisco conference to negotiate the UN Charter on 25 April 1945: 'We are united not only for survival, not only for military victory. We are united above all in the necessity to assure a just and an enduring peace in which the peoples of the world can work together to achieve at last freedom from fear and from want.' United Nations Law Collection, *Documents of the United Nations Conference on International Organization* (1945) vol. 1, at 123.

Index

For the benefit of digital users, indexed terms that span two pages (e.g., 52–53) may, on occasion, appear on only one of those pages.